MW01611489

PRINTING THE
WRITTEN WORD

PRINTING THE WRITTEN WORD

The Social History of Books,
circa 1450–1520

EDITED BY

Sandra Hindman

Cornell University Press

ITHACA AND LONDON

Copyright © 1991 by Cornell University

All rights reserved. Except for brief quotations in a review, this book, or parts thereof, must not be reproduced in any form without permission in writing from the publisher. For information, address Cornell University Press, 124 Roberts Place, Ithaca, New York 14850.

First published 1991 by Cornell University Press.

International Standard Book Number 0-8014-2578-6 (cloth)
International Standard Book Number 0-8014-9902-x (paper)
Library of Congress Catalog Card Number 91-55236
Printed in the United States of America
Librarians: Library of Congress cataloging information
appears on the last page of the book.

⊗ The paper in this book meets the minimum requirements
of the American National Standard for Information Sciences—
Permanence of Paper for Printed Library Materials, ANSI Z39.48-1984.

For my parents

Contents

Contents

Preface

The majority of the essays in this volume originated in an interdisciplinary conference titled "From Scribal Culture to Print Culture," which I organized at Northwestern University in April 1987. The purpose of the conference was to reconsider, after more than a decade of stimulating new research by scholars in a variety of disciplines, the history of books—encompassing manuscripts and printed works—during approximately the first fifty years of printing. The decision to attempt to publish the papers, reached at the conference, was based on the interest they generated as well as on my sense that the individual importance of each essay would be better understood in the context of the broader issues. The ultimate organization of this volume into three sections—Printers, Authors and Artists, and Readers—emerged after the conference, when it became clear to me that the papers fit into subgroups that addressed larger themes.

So as to cover aspects of these larger themes not otherwise treated, two essays (those by Lilian Armstrong on Venetian illuminators and Tobin Nellhaus on blockbooks) were added to the original group.

My thanks are due to several individuals for their help in preparing the book for publication: Michael Heinlen, who thought up the title; Steven Williams, who checked some of the Latin translations; Dominique Coq, who made suggestions about the presentation of the Parisian material; Jeremy Griffiths, who offered advice on practical and conceptual details; and Lori Winters, who oversaw the preparation and submission of the manuscript. I am grateful to Bernhard

Kendler of Cornell University Press for his interest in and support of the project. I also thank the staff of the Newberry Library, Chicago, which facilitated requests for access to and photography of material in their collection that appears throughout these essays.

SANDRA HINDMAN

Chicago, Illinois

Abbreviations

B42 Bible in Latin, Mainz, Printer of the 42-line Bible [Johann Gutenberg and Peter Schoeffer], 1454–55, not after August 1456.

B48 Bible in Latin, Mainz, Johann Fust and Peter Schoeffer, August 14, 1462.

BL British Library, London.

BMC British Museum, Department of Printed Books, *Catalogue of Books Printed in the XVth Century Now in the British Museum*, 10 vols. in 12 (London, 1908–1971).

BN Bibliothèque Nationale, Paris.

Briquet C. M. Briquet, *Les filigranes: Dictionnaire historique des marques du papier des leur apparition vers 1282 jusqu'en 1600*, 2d ed. (Paris, 1923; reprinted, New York, 1966; and with additional material, Amsterdam, 1968).

De Ricci Seymour de Ricci, *A Census of Caxtons*, Illustrated Monographs, no. 15 (Oxford, 1909).

Goff Frederick R. Goff, ed., *Incunabula in American Libraries: A Third Census of Fifteenth-Century Books Recorded in North American Collections*. Reproduced from the annotated copy maintained by Frederick R. Goff (Millwood, N.Y., 1973); *Supplement* (New York, 1972).

GW *Gesamtkatalog der Wiegendrucke*, 7 vols. (Leipzig, 1925–1938); *Supplement* (Stuttgart, 1968–).

Hain   Ludwig F. T. Hain, *Repertorium bibliographicum, in quo libri omnes ab arte typographica inventa usque ad annum MD. typis expressi, ordine alphabetico vel simpliciter enumerantur vel adcuratius recensentur*, 2 vols. in 4 (Stuttgart, 1826–1838).

ONB   Österreichische Nationalbibliothek, Vienna.

Pen to Press   Sandra Hindman and James Douglas Farquhar, *Pen to Press: Illustrated Manuscripts and Printed Books in the First Century of Printing* (Baltimore, 1977).

PML   Pierpont Morgan Library, New York.

Proctor   Robert G. C. Proctor, *An Index to the Early Printed Books in the British Museum*, pt. 1, *From the Invention of Printing to the Year MD with Notes of Those in the Bodleian Library*, 4 vols. (London, 1898–1899); *Supplements* (London, 1900–1903: 4 vols., pt. 2, sec. 1 (1903), pt. 2, secs. 2, 3 (London, 1938).

Schramm   Albert Schramm, *Der Bilderschmuck der Frühdrucke*, 23 vols. (Leipzig, 1920–1943).

PRINTING THE
WRITTEN WORD

Introduction

Sandra Hindman

This volume presents a methodologically coherent point of view: namely, that we can best study the phenomenon of the impact of print from a close scrutiny of the primary sources, which are the books themselves. At the same time, evidence gathered from the books is placed in its larger social, economic, political, and intellectual context. This collection of essays, including contributions in the fields of art history, history, literature, theater, and analytical bibliography, thus combines the methods of analytical bibliography with those of the *histoire du livre* to offer an enhanced perspective of the history of the early book.

In the scholarly literature on printing, it is impossible to overlook Elizabeth Eisenstein's monumental work *The Printing Press as an Agent of Change,* which argues along the lines of Marshall McLuhan's *Gutenberg Galaxy* that print culture represents a radical break with scribal culture.[1] For Eisenstein, print culture had widespread implications for the development of "modern" society: it brought about the Italian Renaissance, the Protestant Reformation, and the scientific revolution.

Counter to Eisenstein's claim runs an argument, first carefully constructed by Curt Bühler, that sees many of the presumed innovations

---

[1]Elizabeth Eisenstein, *The Printing Press as an Agent of Change: Communications and Cultural Transformations in Early Modern Europe,* 2 vols. (Cambridge, 1979); idem., *The Printing Revolution in Early Modern Europe* (Cambridge, 1983) (an abridgement of the two-volume version); and Marshall McLuhan, *The Gutenberg Galaxy: The Making of Typographic Man* (Toronto, 1962).

[1]

of print culture as already present in scribal culture.[2] Specifically, the fifteenth-century printed book—its methods of production and its patterns of reception—is understood as owing much to the manu-script book, which continued to be made and used alongside its printed counterpart. Together with James Douglas Farquhar, I devel-oped this thesis in *Pen to Press*. Since that time, several important conferences, particularly in Wolfenbüttel, London, and Odense, whose proceedings were subsequently published, further explored the continuity between scribal culture and print culture, thus rein-forcing the counter-Eisenstein thesis.[3] These counterarguments tem-per the idea of the immediate impact of print through a more refined characterization of the early years of print culture.

Although this is not the forum for a detailed critique of Eisenstein's book, which has been eloquently and frequently reviewed else-where,[4] it is nevertheless useful to underscore some of the book's methodological drawbacks in order to bring into focus certain aims of the present collection of essays. Reviewers have been unanimous in lamenting the absence of primary rather than secondary evidence in Eisenstein's book. Eisenstein herself claims that her work is "based on monographic literature not archival research."[5] But why? With An-thony Grafton, I believe that an investigation of primary sources remains paramount to the construction of any future synthesis about the "impact of print."

Two other objections to Eisenstein's approach can also briefly be

[2]Curt Bühler, *The Fifteenth-Century Book: The Scribes, the Printers, the Decorators* (Philadelphia, 1960).

[3]Lotte Hellinga and Helmar Hartel, eds., *Buch und Text im 15. Jahrhundert / Book and Text in the Fifteenth Century: Arbeitsgesprach in der Herzog August Bibliothek Wolfenbüttel vom 1. bis 3. Marz 1978 / Proceedings of a Conference held in the Herzog August Bibliothek, Wolfenbüttel March 1–3, 1978* (Hamburg, 1981); J. B. Trapp, eds., *Manuscripts in the Fifty Years after the Invention of Printing: Some Papers Read at a Colloquium at the Warburg Institute on 12–13 March 1982* (London, 1983): and Hans Bekker-Nielsen, Marianne Borch, and Bengt Algot Sorensen, eds., *From Script to Book: A Symposium: Proceedings of the Seventh International Symposium Organized by the Centre for the Study of Vernacular Literature in the Middle Ages, Held at Odense University on 15–16 November 1982* (Odense, 1986).

[4]Michael Hunter, "The Impact of Print," *The Book Collector* 28 (1979): 335–52; Anthony Grafton, "The Importance of Being Printed," *Journal of Interdisciplinary History* 11, 2 (1980): 265–86; and Roger Chartier, "L'Ancien Régime typographique: Reflexions sur quelques travaux récents," *Annales: Économies, sociétés, civilizations* 36 (1981): 191–209.

[5]Eisenstein, *Printing Press*, I, xvi.

raised. The first is that the argument she constructs centers on the literate elites. Humanist printers, such as Aldus Manutius and Christopher Plantin, take precedence over the many second- and third-string printers whose fortunes rose and fell, especially during the uncertain early years of printing. Contemporary authors, such as Erasmus and Luther, are highlighted instead of the many medieval authors whose works, long available in manuscripts, found a new medium in print. The emphasis on highbrow printers and authors thus leads inevitably to a focus on a certain select group of readers instead of on the monastic and university circles that provided the broad-based clientele for most successful early printers, or the upwardly mobile government officials who began to construct libraries in emulation of the aristocracy, or even the urban merchants and country peasants who constitute "the people." The second objection is that her argument is limited to the history of ideas instead of being broadly situated within the social, economic, and political history of the time.

The present collection of essays self-consciously turns away from both the method and the approach of the Eisenstein thesis without denying the validity of some of Eisenstein's conclusions about the ultimate impact of print, which undeniably constitute an enormous contribution. A primary assumption underlying this volume is that to emphasize a sharp distinction between scribal culture and print culture implies that there was from one to the other a break with the past, which leads to a positivistic reading of the history of the fifteenth century as an evolutionary narrative. This focus on either the uneasy continuity or the fundamental discontinuity between scribal culture and print culture characteristic of much of the literature on the history of printing, including even those studies that present the counter-Eisenstein thesis, tends to foreclose on other issues such as the function of the book—the manuscript or the printed work—in society. I am reminded here of Natalie Davis' injunction that, in approaching the book as an artifact, we try to understand it as a carrier of relationships.[6] In pursuing Davis' point, I would argue that we pay particular attention to two sets of relationships—those between the book and its makers on the one hand and between the book and its readers on the other. Only once we have gathered and interpreted

[6]Natalie Zemon Davis, "Printing and the People," in *Society and Culture in Early Modern France* (Stanford, 1975), pp. 191–226, esp. p. 192.

concrete evidence about many books, about their makers and their users, can we begin to shape an alternative synthesis. This synthesis should retain as one of its foremost goals the integration of the book into society. With these assumptions and goals in mind, I replaced the title of the conference with the title of this volume.

Apart from Eisenstein's book, two currents in the literature on the history of printing have helped determine the shape of the present volume: analytical bibliography and the histoire du livre.[7] Analytical bibliography refers essentially to a process of physical description and analysis. Practiced largely by Anglo-American specialists (who are frequently librarians of the printed book), such an investigation leads to the construction of a narrative history, which might focus on a variety of topics, for example, on the sequence of editions of a text or on the oeuvre of a printer. In recent years analytical bibliography has been considerably enriched by the application to the study of incunables of codicological methods of description, as formulated and refined by Delaissé and his students for the study of later medieval manuscripts.[8] In a sense this new direction for incunable research results from the realization that manuscripts and printed books in the early years of print culture are a lot alike.[9] It is an approach that has opened the doors to much new evidence, as can be seen from many of the essays in this volume, such as Paul Saenger and Michael Heinlen's, which are based on codicological analyses of the books.

Potentially the most productive approach in the literature on the history of printing is represented by the second current, the histoire du livre. Histoire du livre is a term that derives ultimately from the work of the social historian Lucien Febvre, particularly as it was continued by his disciple Henri-Jean Martin and, in turn, by Martin's students. Although concerned, like Eisenstein, with the impact of

---

[7]On the relationship between these two currents, see John Feather, "Cross-Channel Currents: Historical Bibliography and *l'Histoire du Livre*," *The Library*, ser. 6, 2 (1980): 1–15; Chartier, "L'Ancien Régime"; and Roger Chartier and Daniel Roche, "New Approaches to the History of the Book," in *Constructing the Past: Essays in Historical Methodology*, ed. Jacques LeGoff and Pierre Nora (Cambridge, 1985), pp. 198–214.

[8]On Delaissé and the codicological method, see L. M. J. Delaissé, "Towards a History of the Medieval Book," in *Miscellanea Andre Combes* (Rome, 1967), II, 27–39; Albert Gruijs, "Codicology or the Archeology of the Book? A False Dilemma," *Quaerendo* 2 (1972): 87–108; Albert Derolez, "Codicologie ou archéologie du livre?" *Scriptorium* 28 (1973): 47–49.

[9]For a call to treat the incunable like a manuscript, see Dominique Coq, "L'incunable, un batard du manuscrit?" *Gazette du livre medieval* 1 (1982): 10–11.

print, which even provides the subtitle to Febvre and Martin's seminal book *L'apparition du livre,* their work studies the making and using of books from a fundamentally sociological perspective.[10] Febvre's intention runs throughout his work: already in 1930 he says, "There is not a history of printing where there are not technical notions, economic notions, historical and sociological notions."[11] The challenge of *L'apparition du livre* is being met on both sides of the Atlantic, for example, by Martin, Daniel Roche, and Roger Chartier in France, by Carlo Ginzburg in Italy, and by Robert Darnton and Natalie Davis in America, to cite just a few.

Chief among the spokespeople for the histoire du livre is Darnton, who has articulated the status and goals of what he terms the "important new discipline."[12] Struck by the large number of disciplines involved and by their sometimes competing methodologies, Darnton has proposed a general model for the study of the history of books. According to his model, analysis of books understands the book as part of a "communications circuit."[13] In this circuit all facets of the life span of the book deserve study, from the conditions of its production to the conditions of its reception. Darnton thus identifies those six persons whose roles might be more thoroughly examined, singly and in combination, in this model circuit from the beginning to the end: (1) author, (2) publisher, (3) printer, (4) shipper, (5) bookseller, and (6) reader. For Darnton, not unlike Febvre and Martin, in whose footsteps he follows, the roles of these individuals should ideally be studied in relation to all other systems in the surrounding environment, that is, intellectual history, social and economic history, and political history.

In order to construct an interdisciplinary book history for the fifteenth century, to which this volume sets out to contribute, a few refinements to Darnton's communications circuit are necessary. First,

[10]Lucien Febvre and Henri-Jean Martin, *L'apparition du livre* (Paris, 1957); and idem., *The Coming of the Book: The Impact of Printing, 1450–1800,* trans. David Gerard, ed. Geoffrey Nowell-Smith and David Wootton (London, 1976).

[11]Lucien Febvre, *Annales d'histoire économique et sociale,* quoted in Wallace Kirsop, "Literary History and Book Trade History: The Lessons of *L'apparition du livre,*" *Australian Journal of French Studies* 16 (1979): 488–535, esp. p. 498.

[12]See especially Robert Darnton, "What Is the History of Books?" in *Books and Society in History: Papers of the Association of College and Research Libraries Rare Books and Manuscripts Preconference 24–28 June 1980,* ed. Kenneth E. Carpenter (New York, 1983), pp. 3–26.

[13]See Darnton's diagram in "What Is the History of Books," p. 6.

[5]

we need to expand the field to include the manuscript book among the books studied. For Darnton, the new discipline is primarily about printed books, as he makes clear in "What Is the History of Books?" when he defines book history as the "social and cultural history of communication by print" (p. 3). In this respect, Darnton implicitly follows Febvre and Martin, for whom *L'apparition du livre* addresses the emergence of the book, *le livre*, with the invention of printing. Second, we should include rare books and fine editions among the books studied. Again, for Darnton, following the book historians of the *Annales* school, the ordinary book, from which the literary experience of the ordinary reader can be captured, offers the most promise for the new discipline. Third, we must include illustrated books.[14] For Darnton, artists are altogether absent from his communications circuit, although for Chartier, whose views are similar to Darnton's, a history of reading—the last step in the communications circuit—must include a history of reading images as well as words.[15]

The essays in this volume present new insights into the operations of printers (who were sometimes booksellers and publishers), their interactions with authors and artists, and the reception of their books by readers. Printed books are the focus of most of the essays, which also consider, when relevant, the simultaneous production and reception of manuscripts. More than half the essays are concerned with questions that arise from the study of illustrated books. The essays fall into three parts, which are not mutually exclusive, and they thus fit well into the revised model of Darnton's communications circuit. Part I is on printers; Part II is on authors and artists; and Part III is on readers. The change in order (authors after instead of before printers) reflects my belief in the autonomy of the printer-publisher-bookseller in the fifteenth century.

As case studies the essays in this volume share a perspective with certain scholars of the histoire du livre, who believe that a comprehensive sociocultural history of the book will only grow out of a

---

[14]For the proposal of a similar model for the study of the illustrated manuscript and printed book in the later Middle Ages, see Sandra Hindman, "State of Research in Northern Renaissance Art: The Illustrated Book," *Art Bulletin* 68 (1986): 535–42.

[15]See Roger Chartier, ed., *Pratiques de la lecture* (Paris, 1985), pp. 9–10; and idem., *The Culture of Print* (Princeton, 1990).

collection of microhistories.[16] The microhistories presented here are chronologically focused on the incunable period, roughly from c. 1450 to c. 1520, and they investigate a wide range of examples from different countries, including Germany, France, Italy, and England. Even though, in treating illustrated books, many of the essays deal with high-end production and reception, they interpret the data from these case studies with a view toward questions of broad implications: How did illustrated production relate to unillustrated production? What did it take to become a successful printer of illustrated books? What was the relation between authors, artists, and printers? How did readers comprehend books with woodcuts and/or miniatures differently from unillustrated books? Taken together, these essays thus help to construct a new synthesis on the history of the book in the fifteenth century.

Part I focuses on printers. Although the roles of printers, among those individuals in the communications circuit, initially seem to be best understood for the period after c. 1500, many central questions remain unanswered for the incunable period.[17] This situation exists in part because only a few fifteenth-century printers, who are for the most part exceptional, have so far been systematically studied. These include figures such as Peter Schoeffer in Mainz, Aldus Manutius in Venice, and William Caxton in England.[18] Printers who were less successful, less prolific, or less well educated have been virtually ignored. Yet the groundwork of analytical bibliographers, which supplies the oeuvres for a large number of pre-1500 printers, provides much of the basic data for such an investigation, even if archival data are often sparse and sometimes nonexistent.

Among the key questions treated in these essays is that of the still

[16]On this point, see Chartier, "L'Ancien Régime," p. 191; for an example of a microhistory with broad implications, see Carlo Ginzburg, *The Cheese and the Worms: The Cosmos of a Sixteenth-Century Miller*, trans. Anne Tedeschi and John Tedeschi (Baltimore, 1980).

[17]For the sixteenth century, the most impressive study remains Leon Voet, *The Golden Compasses: A History and Evaluation of the Printing and Publishing Activities of the Officina Plantiniana of Antwerp*, 2 vols. (Amsterdam, 1969, 1973).

[18]See the studies by Hellmut Lehmann-Haupt, *Peter Schoeffer of Gernsheim and Mainz* (Rochester, N.Y., 1950); Martin Lowry, *The World of Aldus Manutius: Business and Scholarship in Renaissance Venice* (Ithaca, 1979); Norman F. Blake, *Caxton: England's First Publisher* (London, 1976); and idem., "William Caxton: A Review," in *From Script to Book*, pp. 107–26.

obscure role of the printer in relation to the publisher and the bookseller. In the incunable period many master printers were also publishers; that is, they selected and edited the works produced in their
print shops. Most printer-publishers were also booksellers. But some
booksellers appear never to have been printers or publishers. They
seem rather to have entered into alliances with others in the print
trade for whom they marketed their imprints. The essays by Martha
Tedeschi and myself clarify the definition of these roles as they
evolved in the fifteenth century, particularly with regard to issues of
the nature of production and the calculation of a market.

Other important questions, many of them based on the relationship between manuscripts and printed works, also emerge from
this group of essays. Given that many clients still expected books to
resemble manuscripts, what was the status of the lavishly illustrated
book compared to the unadorned imprint? Did such production put a
strain on the resources of printers, for whom labor (along with paper)
represented one of the major capital expenditures? What decisions did
early printers, who used illustrations successfully, make? What about
scribes who became printers? Do certain features of their production
stand out as unique?

The complexity of what it meant to "go into printing" underlies
Sheila Edmunds' essay "From Schoeffer to Vérard: Concerning the
Scribes Who Became Printers." By taking a close look at the actual
roles of scribes-turned-printers, Edmunds first overturns the my-
thology that "countless" scribes became printers. She weeds out a
master list of seventeen scribes, arriving at a smaller number that,
when considered with other data, represents no more than 4 to 6
percent of the printers active before 1500. Then Edmunds shows that
many of these former scribes were not really printers at all. They
assumed ancillary roles in the printing industry; some became type
designers, woodcutters, or publishers.

After briefly surveying the careers of the remaining scribes-turned-
printers, some of whom (such as Felice Feliciano of Verona and Damiano Moille of Parma) are little known, Edmunds is finally able to
discern among this group a number of common characteristics related
to intellectual, social, and aesthetic considerations. These individuals
displayed a keen awareness of potential copy, with the result that the
choice of their imprints bears a greater relationship to manuscripts
than that of many other printers. They were much the same age.

Born around 1420 or 1430, these were men already trained in one technology when printing became a fact of life, but they were still young enough to retrain. Here Edmunds reminds us that many scribes continued to find work in the age of print culture, since secretary, municipal clerk, and notary were all occupations that demanded skilled penmanship. The quality of the products produced by this group of scribes-turned-printers is high. They used red printing, well-designed typefaces, and calligraphic ornament. In short, their products catered to the manuscript clientele to which they were originally accustomed.

Following this overview of a certain type of early printer are two essays on printers in Germany and France, respectively. These case studies permit us to examine the roles of individual printers and the business decisions they made in relation to the success of their operations. Martha Tedeschi's piece, "Publish and Perish: The Career of Lienhart Holle in Ulm," looks at a printer who seems to have operated independently, without alliances with publishers or booksellers, and who went bankrupt. Holle attempted to capture the deluxe manuscript market for printed books. Tedeschi shows that he never recovered from miscalculating his clientele and from poor business practices, in particular regarding his first book, Ptolemy's *Cosmographia*. A deluxe pseudomanuscript version of the *Cosmographia* with new maps hand-colored in the shop, Holle's edition found no ready market among those interested in modern cartography for scientific or scholarly purposes. He was therefore unable to recover from the debts he incurred for materials in undertaking the project, which he did without financial backing.

In considering Holle's second ambitious project, fables by Bidpai known as the *Buch der Weisheit,* Tedeschi goes on to suggest that, plagued by debts, Holle tried unsuccessfully to change his strategy. He chose a vernacular text that had already been printed locally and thus had an established market. But Holle then made the same mistake he made with the *Cosmographia*. He had 132 full-page woodcuts newly designed and cut. His press lasted less than a year after a second edition of the *Buch der Weisheit*. In the early, uncertain market for printing, the simulation of the manuscript book, including the design and execution of a full cycle of woodcut illustrations, such as Holle had done for the *Cosmographia* and for the *Buch der Weisheit,* was apparently not wise business practice.

Eberhard König's essay in Part II helps put Holle in perspective. Examining the question of why the Bible was so frequently chosen for printing by the earliest printers, such as Gutenberg, Fust and Schoeffer, and Eggestein, König points to the early provenance of many copies in Benedictine monasteries. He suggests that the Benedictine reform in Germany led foundations to reevaluate their libraries and stimulated an interest in providing new and accurate texts of the Bible. The first successful printers thus calculated their market well, responding to a broadly based institutional need. In earmarking this preexisting market, they fit the pattern for commercial success as outlined by Miriam Chrisman for Strasbourg.[19]

My essay, "The Career of Guy Marchant (1483–1504): High Culture and Low Culture in Paris," presents a revisionist assessment of the Parisian printer Guy Marchant, who also stands in marked contrast to Holle. Marchant published approximately 150 volumes, mostly before 1500, and his sons carried on his flourishing business after his death. Marchant should more accurately be viewed as a specialist in the short, inexpensive tract volume than as a printer of "popular" works. Other business decisions he made that account for his commercial success include the production of works for the university market, the restriction of press runs, and the use of multiple title pages to facilitate simultaneous distribution to several booksellers at once. At the same time that Marchant printed Latin theological and humanist tracts for a university clientele, he also kept an eye on the vernacular market, for which he printed books mostly sold through other booksellers. The pattern of Marchant's production and distribution suggests, in fact, that there existed already a highly specialized book trade in Paris.

Unlike Holle, Marchant was a printer who managed to use illustrations with considerable commercial success. He often reused utilitarian woodcuts that had little relation to the text but that enhanced the appearance of his volumes. Since he repeated the cuts frequently (and may have purchased or had recut designs from other printers), there was virtually no expense involved. For his lavishly illustrated imprints of the *Danse macabre* and the *Calendrier der bergers,* which were reedited and reissued many times, he also reused woodcuts. Probably the initial expense was met by royal clients' purchasing

[19]Miriam Usher Chrisman, *Lay Culture, Learned Culture: Books and Social Change in Strasbourg, 1480–1599* (New Haven, 1982).

handcolored copies on parchment. Furthermore, it would seem that the printing of frequent editions was a strategy that enabled Marchant to test his expected market.

Although Marchant himself was a publisher and a bookseller, as well as a printer, he consistently collaborated with other printers and booksellers to ensure a wide circulation of his works, and he sought a broad-based university market for his more ordinary books. This and other essays gathered here thus suggest that in the early years of printing there was not a clear-cut separation between the roles of printer, publisher, and bookseller, and that in general, early printers who took on multiple responsibilities and who frequently collaborated were most successful.

Essays in Part II, which is on authors and artists, assess the ways in which printers interacted with those individuals who supplied the textual and pictorial content of their books. This category should ideally be expanded to differentiate editors, translators, commentators, and authors on the one hand from illuminators, woodcutters, decorators, and rubricators on the other. We are far from being able to construct a history of the conditions under which these different individuals worked, but the case studies offered here help throw some light on a few crucial questions: When did the author begin to demand some sort of legal control over his work? When did illuminators collaborate with printers or act as free agents? Although these essays do not supply enough evidence to allow us to build up a convincing picture of the independent author or artist, they offer glimpses of the origins of this condition. It would appear that the fifteenth century was a critical period for the emergence of authorial and artistic identities in a modern sense.

Cynthia J. Brown's essay, "Text, Image, and Authorial Self-Consciousness in Late Medieval Paris," explores the changing nature of authorship in the early sixteenth century. Focusing on two case studies, works by the French rhetoricians André de la Vigne and Pierre Gringore, she convincingly builds up a picture of increased authorial self-consciousness, which surfaced in part because of tensions between printers and authors. She reviews a lawsuit filed in 1504, in which La Vigne successfully sued the printer Michel Le Noir over the rights to print one of his texts. The lawsuit reflects a wider phenomenon, however, evident from an analysis of the books themselves. By 1505 Gringore had usurped the role of bookseller. In his works he published a statement forbidding anyone to sell, distribute, or have the work printed for one year without his permission. Brown finds corroborating evidence for emerging authorial autonomy in the frequent intrusion of the author's identity on title pages and in colophons. In the end, she suggests, these transformations of authorial self-consciousness are even inscribed in changes in the concept of literature itself. From the work of La Vigne to that of Gringore, she observes a shift in the use of the first-person narrator, not unlike the fictional dreamer in much medieval literature, beginning with the *Roman de la Rose,* to the persona of the nonfictionalized "I." These changes in the nature of authorship are also reflected, Brown argues, in the imagery accompanying manuscript and printed copies of La Vigne's and Gringore's writings.

Eberhard König's essay, "New Perspectives on the History of Mainz Printing: A Fresh Look at Illuminated Imprints," examines the roles of artists responsible for the decoration in illuminated Mainz imprints. He finds that most illuminators and many rubricators, perhaps with the exception of the Fust Master, did not work for printers. Many early printed books from Mainz appear to have left the print shop unadorned, with spaces left for illustration that were filled in only when the books reached their destination. Copies of the Gutenberg Bible and the 1462 Bible decorated in local styles are found not only in various parts of Germany but also in Italy, England, and the Netherlands. Operating in this manner, German printers probably kept down costs of labor. They also helped create a situation in which artists, who were autonomous from print shops, could forge independent identities.

Italy, particularly Venice, presents a situation entirely different from that outlined by König for Germany, as Lilian Armstrong demonstrates in "The Impact of Printing on Miniaturists in Venice after 1469." Armstrong identifies at least twenty artists to whom Venetian printers such as Nicolas Jensen and Vendelinus de Spira turned for decoration of their books in the 1470s and 1480s. She notes that certain distinguished miniaturists must have taken on individual commissions. But she stresses that many lesser artists, seeking regular employment, probably allied themselves with printers, publishers, or booksellers through contracts or informal agreements. Along these lines, she reviews the evidence of a contract between the miniaturist Master Antonio of Bergamo, who promised to work exclusively for the bookseller Antonio d'Avignone. In addition to illuminating books, Antonio of Bergamo agreed to help with binding and with selling. What emerges from Armstrong's essay is a clearer picture of the relative roles of the artist and the printer in the Venetian book trade during the era just before Aldus Manutius.

Steps toward a history of reading are taken in the essays in Part III, which is on readers. A comprehensive sociology of reading would address certain broad questions: Who read books? What books did they read? How did they read them?[20] As my essay shows, we can begin to answer these questions by using the *inventaires après décès,* notarial records of books in the estates of the deceased.[21] Ownership records are another source for identifying readership, as Lotte Hellinga's essay demonstrates for books imported into England and Scotland. Library catalogues are also useful, especially for monasteries and universities. The most trivial kinds of observations can sometimes provide information on what people read, or did not read. For example, Paul Saenger and Michael Heinlen suggest that pastedowns and binders' waste can tell us what people were not reading.

How and why people read are among the most complex and intriguing questions concerning readership. For early modern Europe, historians of the book have begun to probe this issue in ways that should eventually enable us to understand better the "how" and the "why," as Darnton has put it.[22] For example, they have formulated new questions about where people read, whether standing up or sitting down, in public or in private, using what kind of furniture, and wearing what kind of clothing. They have pointed out that there are different kinds of reading, not just oral or silent but intensive (one

---

[20]For a summary of the state of research for early modern Europe, see Robert Darnton, "First Steps toward a History of Reading," *Australian Journal of French Studies* 23 (1986): 5–30; reprinted in idem., *The Kiss of Lamourette: Reflections in Cultural History* (New York, 1989).

[21]For French inventories of the fifteenth and sixteenth centuries, which could profitably be consulted for the ownership of manuscripts as well as of printed books, see Alexander H. Schutz, *Vernacular Books in Parisian Private Libraries of the Sixteenth Century According to the Notarial Inventories,* University of North Carolina Studies in the Romance Languages and Literatures, no. 25 (Chapel Hill, 1955); and A. Labarre, *Le livre dans la vie amienoise du seizième siècle: l'enseignement des inventaires après décès, 1503–1576,* Publications de la Faculté des Lettres et Sciences humaines de Paris-Sorbonne, research ser. no. 66 (Paris, 1971).

[22]Darnton, "First Steps," pp. 15ff.

book over and over) or extensive (many books once each). They have reminded us that some books were not meant to be read at all but functioned as symbolic objects. They have offered new ideas about literacy through a study of the teaching of reading and writing.

Darnton has proposed a model for the further study of the history of reading, which is useful here.[23] He suggests five approaches: (1) a study of the literary and artistic depictions of reading to learn about the ideals and assumptions underlying reading in the past; (2) a study of the teaching of reading and writing; (3) a study of accounts of reading by actual readers either in their autobiographies or their marginal notes and glosses; (4) a close integration of literary theory with empirical research in order to understand better how readers construe meaning; and (5) a study of books as physical objects using advances in analytical bibliography. The essays presented in this volume make significant advances in the third, fourth, and fifth areas, bringing us closer to an idea of how books, including illustrated books, were read in the fifteenth century.

Instead of considering the topic of the importation of books from the point of view of the production of printers and their marketing strategies, which is the more typical approach, Lotte Hellinga uses a study of importation to examine the identities of readers and the sources of their books in her essay "Importation of Books Printed on the Continent into England and Scotland before c. 1520." Her sample includes about one thousand imported books with early English and Scottish ownership.

Hellinga follows two lines of inquiry. First, she considers the geographical origin of the imported books beginning in the 1470s. She finds that the largest proportion came from Italy (especially from Venice), followed by books from Germany, then France, then the Low Countries. Second, she considers the identities of the readers of imported books, which helps to explain the origins of their reading material. Individuals in university circles were among the largest group of readers of imported books; most of their books came from Italy, particularly from Venice, which specialized in books for scholars. Next was an ecclesiastical clientele, the secular clergy and monastic houses, who bought books from German-speaking centers. The

---

[23]Darnton, "First Steps"; and see also Roger Chartier, "Du livre au lire," in *Pratiques de la lecture,* pp. 62–88.

last group of readers includes professional men such as lawyers, doctors, and schoolmasters. Hellinga presents interesting data comparing readers of indigenously produced vernacular works. For example, whereas many women owners can be found for English books, not a single female owner emerges in the entire thousand-book sample. Hellinga's study is made possible only through consultation of copy-specific data in incunables, not just the names of early owners but the language and paleography of their marginal notes.

In their essay "Incunable Description and Its Implications for the Analysis of Fifteenth-Century Reading Habits," Paul Saenger and Michael Heinlen show how the recording and interpretation of copy-specific data, according to a model they devised for incunables in the Newberry Library, also provides evidence for reading habits at the end of the Middle Ages. They discuss the addition to incunables of manuscript texts of works not in print in order to personalize the imprint, and show how readers of incunables (like those of manuscripts) shaped their own reading experience, as well as the experience of subsequent communities of readers, through reader's notes, rubrication, editing, and even punctuation. During the incunable period the desire "to render each page into a memorable image, easily retainable and accessible to subsequent readers" is distinct from the modern reader's personal reaction to the text.

Many of Saenger and Heinlen's preliminary conclusions are provocative, easily justifying their call for the increased application of codicology to the early printed book. They cite the preponderance of mnemonic devices used from the eleventh century onward, including pointing hands, *nota* marks, redundant numbers, encoded signs, biblical references, authorial identification, and schematic diagrams. They also suggest that the use of color, so characteristic of manuscripts as well as incunables, functioned mnemonically. At the same time, they suggest that printing gradually effected a return to a blacker, cleaner page, and they wonder whether an important mnemonic quality was thus lost. Noting that the roles played by the medieval reader-emendator came to be assumed by the printer by the end of the fifteenth century, they conclude that "reading became increasingly an activity of the passive reception of a text that was inherently clear and unambiguous."

The idea that printing brought with it a different aesthetic of the page, what Chartier calls the *mise en texte,* which affected how reading occurred, as Saenger and Heinlen suggest, is advanced also by Michael Camille in discussing illustrated books. In "Reading the Printed Image: Illuminations and Woodcuts of the *Pèlerinage de la vie humaine* in the Fifteenth Century," Camille compares woodcuts and miniatures in Guillaume de Deguileville's popular work. Analyzing the woodcuts and miniatures in terms of cognitive psychology and reception aesthetics, he concludes that in the miniatures the use of extraneous details, the application of color, and the presence of rubrics all encourage a discursive reading of image and text. In the woodcuts, by contrast, the elimination of extraneous detail, the use of a black and white aesthetic, and the absence of rubrics encourage a more integrative reading of image and text. Camille further suggests that even features such as the reuse of woodcuts, usually considered to be a labor-saving device for early printers, can be understood as having functioned to prompt an integrative reading through the simple repetition of familiar visual patterns or figures. For Camille, the woodcuts thus become "a sophisticated rethinking of the pace and flow of the pictorial narrative." Print finally encodes a kind of literacy that, unlike spoken language, involves more mental experience as the reader perceives fast-written signs.[24]

Tobin Nellhaus' essay "Mementos of Things to Come: Orality, Literacy, and Typology in the *Biblia pauperum*" continues the discussion of the influence of oral and literate strategies of thought on reading in early print culture. Nellhaus argues that the relationship between speaking and writing in manuscript culture fostered the development of typology and similitudes as conceptual devices. After reviewing how the structure of the *Biblia pauperum* encourages the reader's use of typology, he proposes that typology itself is a kind of ritual that "helps to sustain the memory of special deeds and consecrate their meaning." He then explores the dynamics of oral and written communication and the place of the *Biblia pauperum* within the social contexts of orality and literacy. In the end, he offers new evidence not only in support of the *Biblia pauperum* as an aid to personal meditation, a view that has been previously advanced in the literature on the blockbooks, but also on how the *Biblia pauperum* was read and used for devotion.

---

[24]This is the view of Walter J. Ong, *Orality and Literacy: The Technologizing of the Word* (New York, 1982).

Nellhaus' essay has far-reaching implications. It provides a context for understanding the entire group of blockbooks as strategies for memory in a society where writing (in contrast to hearing) was acquiring a privileged place. He suggests how other books of this much discussed but little understood genre—the *Speculum humanae salvationis*, the *Apocalypse*, the *Ars moriendi*, and the *Ars memorandi*—reinforce devotion through memory. For Nellhaus, the blockbooks are thus a final, complex elaboration of strategies of medieval conceptualization. His thesis ultimately reinforces the hypotheses of Saenger and Heinlen and Camille concerning changes in patterns of reading in the fifteenth century. As the printing press undercut the need for the memory arts, it irreversibly transformed the relationship between orality and literacy.

Essays in the three parts of this volume do not directly offer proof to support the idea of a communications revolution with the advent of the printing press. But they do suggest that there were, from the onset of print culture, repercussions beyond those previously imagined. What emerges clearly in many of these essays is a sense of the ongoing tension resulting from the confrontation between two forms of communication, written and printed, in the fifteenth century.

The tension is apparent on many different fronts. We see printers hustling to capture new markets in changed conditions. Some made wise decisions, others did not. It appears that the business of printing commercially successful illustrated books was one of the most difficult tasks faced by early printers. We see authors and artists scrambling to respond to the possibilities offered by print. Both eventually won an increased autonomy through their separation from the print shop. It may be that even the nature of literature and illustration changed. We see readers grappling with the new form of the book. Some treated it like a manuscript, a surface on which to record individual responses for future readers, whereas others gradually realized the potential of the uniformly black but otherwise bare printed page. It may be that the reading of pictures changed simultaneously, from disjunctive to integrative.

Drawing from a wide range of intellectual perspectives and relying on evidence from the books themselves, these studies thus present a detailed and complex picture of the production and reception of the early printed book. Their conclusions, however tentative, suggest that we are only just beginning to learn what was entailed, broadly speaking, in printing the written word.

PART I

PRINTERS

[1]

From Schoeffer to Vérard: Concerning The Scribes Who Became Printers

Sheila Edmunds

Popular views to the contrary, in the late Middle Ages scribes were not simply monks writing glamorous parchment manuscripts. To be sure, monastic scribes were still at work, but laymen too had long been engaged in writing codices, not all "glamorous" or on parchment. Since the fourteenth century, manuscripts could be either written in a formal book hand on the familiar parchment, sometimes with decorations in gold leaf and opaque paint, or written in an informal cursive script on paper, decorated, if at all, with pen-and-wash illustrations. Often these paper manuscripts, which are usually in a vernacular language, look somewhat amateurish (particularly the illustrations), but many were undoubtedly professional.[1] Scribes might even specialize in one category or the other; for example, the Augsburg scribe Heinrich Molitor, a layman, made nothing but traditional parchment manuscripts of an ecclesiastical or scholarly nature, while his kinsman Conrad concentrated on paper.[2]

---

[1]For an "amateurish" manuscript, see a German copy of *The Travels of Sir John Mandeville*, New York Public Library, Spencer Collection, MS 37, in *The Secular Spirit: Life and Art at the End of the Middle Ages*, exhibition catalogue (New York, 1975), p. 152, no. 173. For "professional" productions, see a German *Speculum humanae salvationis*, PML, MS M. 782, in Meta Harrsen, *Central European Manuscripts in the Pierpont Morgan Library* (New York, 1958), pp. 70–71, no. 59, and a Flemish *Histoire de Jason*, PML, MS M. 119, in *The Secular Spirit*, pp. 163–64, no. 181.

[2]See Berthold Riehl, "Studien zur Geschichte der bayerischen Malerei des 15. Jahrhunderts," *Oberbayerisches Archiv für Vaterländische Geschichte* 49 (1895–96): 86–105; Hellmut Lehmann-Haupt, *Schwäbische Federzeichnungen: Studien zur Buchillustration*

Art historians tend to treat the word *scribe* as though it were applicable solely to these professional, book-occupied classes. Yet many other men—secretaries, municipal clerks, notaries, public letter writers—were also employed as scribes for contracts, wills, deeds, decrees, and the like, and some, such as the Ferrarese notary Iacobus Antonius Severinus, the Nuremberg notary Selbaldus von Plaben, and Jean de Dudens, notary of Annecy, were perfectly capable of making books.[3] Then there were the clerics, academics, students, and occasional physicians who copied texts for their various professional needs. In studies of early printers this group is usually distinguished as a separate class whose *intellectual* occupation attracted them to the new art of printing; the fact that such men were obliged to *write* from time to time is rarely mentioned. Still another group, generally disregarded, can be typified by the Augsburg brothers Hector and George Mülich, who separately and together produced seven extant paper manuscripts.[4] Wealthy merchants, the Mülichs could have hired professionals had they wished. Their manuscripts, copied for their own pleasure, were an avocation, not a livelihood.

Augsburgs im 15. Jahrhundert (Berlin, 1929), chap. 2; Carl Wehmer, "Augsburger Schreiber aus der Frühzeit des Buchdrucks," *Beiträge zur Inkunabelkunde*, N.F., 2 (1938): 108–20.

[3]For Severinus' copy of Thomas de Ferraria, *Trattato del ben governare*, Milan, Biblioteca Trivulziana, MS 86, see Caterina Santoro, *I codici miniati della Biblioteca Trivulziana* (Milan, 1958), pl. LV (mislabeled Taddeo Crivelli); for Selbaldus von Plaben's manuscript, a *Vocabularius* in Latin and German, New York, Union Theological Seminary Library, MS 24, see *The Secular Spirit*, p. 170, no. 188; for Jehan's manuscript, a transcription of Chiquart Amiczo, *Du fait de cuisine*, Sion, Archives de la Valais, MS S. 103, see Terence Scully, ed. and trans., *Chiquart's "On Cookery,"* American University Studies, ser. 9 (History), no. 22 (New York, 1986). On relationships between scribes and the law, see Hans Liermann, *Richter, Schreiber, Advokaten*, Bibliothek des Germanischen National-Museum Nürnberg, no. 9 (Munich, 1957).

[4]See Ernst Wilhelm Bredt, *Der Handschriftenschmuck Augsburgs im XV. Jahrhundert*, Studien zur deutsche Kunstgeschichte, no. 25 (Strasbourg, 1900), pp. 26–30, 40–50; Lehmann-Haupt, *Schwäbische Federzeichnungen*, pp. 53–58, 198–99; D. J. A. Ross, *Illustrated Medieval Alexander-Books in Germany and the Netherlands* (Cambridge, 1971), chap. 6; Dieter Weber, *Geschichtsschreibung in Augsburg: Hektor Mülich und die reichsstädtische Chronistik des Spätmittelalters* (Augsburg, 1984), pp. 55–58, 274–81; and Sheila Edmunds, "Questions of Transmission: Text, Image, and Technique in Early Copies of Hartlieb's *Alexanderbuch*," in *Text and Image*, ed. David W. Burchmore, *Acta* 10 (1986): 117–33. A booklet that Georg Mülich wrote about his pilgrimage to the Holy Land in 1449, which Weber describes as "nicht mehr auffindbar" (p. 57 n. 65), is located in the Harvard College Library, MS Riant 55; see Seymour de Ricci and W. J. Wilson, *A Census of Medieval and Renaissance Manuscripts in the United States and Canada*, 3 vols. (New York, 1935–1940), I, 1006.

Another amateur scribe, a less well-to-do merchant, is of special interest because he has left a rare account of the circumstances in which he wrote a book. Burkhard Zink was born at the end of the fourteenth century and settled in Augsburg, a major textile center, as a factor for a wool merchant. Eventually he established himself in business and later also became a minor municipal officer. In the 1460s he composed a chronicle of the city of Augsburg known through sixteenth-century copies, in which, about halfway through, he suddenly breaks from convention to deliver a captivating autobiography.[5]

The part of concern to us has to do with Zink's early married life, in 1420. His wife was the daughter of a pious poor widow who could offer as dowry only "a little bed and some thingamajigs like saucepans worth about £10." He worried about money. Finally he went to his wife, who was reassuring. (All discourse exchanged hereafter is my translation of the chronicle.) "My Burkhard," Elisabeth said, "don't worry. Let us help each other, and everything will be all right. I will spin four pounds of wool each week, and will earn 32 pence." Burkhard was so heartened by her enterprise that he thought to himself: "I can write a little; I will see whether I can find a priest who will give me something to write." He went to one of his former teachers, by now a member of the Augsburg cathedral chapter, and told him, "I have just taken a wife, and I don't know what I should do. I would gladly write for pay, if I had something to write." The priest replied, "If you will write for me for a whole year, I will pay you." Then he brought Zink a large parchment book borrowed from a colleague; the book was called *Compendium sancti Thome*.[6] He let Zink take it home with him and gave him one gulden cash (over 200 pence) to buy paper and to encourage him to write fast. Zink went home and sat right down and in a week wrote four sexterns of regal-sized paper. These he took back to the priest, who was so pleased with Zink's application and script that he promised to pay 4 gross (32 pence) a sextern—an interesting comparison to Elisabeth's anticipated earnings. Zink concludes the episode with a charming domestic image: "And my wife

---

[5]*Die Chroniken der deutschen Städte,* 37 vols. (1862–1929; reprinted, Stuttgart, 1961–1968), V, 122–43; see also Weber, *Geschichtsschreibung,* pp. 37–39.

[6]I am indebted to Robert E. Lerner, Department of History, Northwestern University, for suggesting that this manuscript was probably Hugo Ripelin's *Compendium theologicae veritatis.* See Georg Steer, *Hugo Ripelin von Strassburg* (Tübingen, 1981).

and I sat together, and I wrote and she spun, and [we] often earned £3 a week, and everything turned out all right."

I have not succeeded in tracing Zink's six hundred-page paper copy of the "Compendium sancti Thome," but I was agreeably surprised to discover in Munich an unnoticed paper manuscript which Zink compiled, evidently for himself, between 1436 and 1437.[7] It is not a work of calligraphic beauty, but it throws an interesting light on medieval literacy. He copied one text, he says, seeking to excuse possible errors, "from a very shadowy and obscure exemplar."[8] Here was a humble, though obviously gifted merchant, literate in German as was necessary for business, but also interested in copying Latin exemplars—a rare occurrence in paper manuscripts outside Italy. Zink had once entertained hopes of attending the University of Vienna, and although that dream had long since been abandoned, he still retained enough of his youthful education to seek out Latin texts, apparently for pleasure, and to compose a reasonably grammatical Latin sentence.

This introduction to the multiplicity of fifteenth-century scribes and their functions and motives is not a digression. The true nature of each scribe's occupation would determine whether or not he was attracted to printing. If he made books for his livelihood, Gutenberg's invention posed an economic threat. Otherwise he was under no such compulsion. Academics, clerics, and cultivated laymen like the Mülichs, perhaps even Zink, probably welcomed the new ease with which they could now acquire texts, while the documents normally inscribed by court secretaries, municipal clerks, notaries, and so on did not usually (with the exception of papal bulls and indulgences) require multiple copies. Indeed, in the sixteenth century elaborate calligraphic manuals, both printed and manuscript, were addressed to those who continued to pursue careers that demanded fine penmanship.

Nevertheless, in accounts of the development of the printed book it is almost axiomatic that scribes went into printing. According to Curt

---

[7]Bayerische Staatsbibliothek, MS clm 4146; not cited in the critical literature, but see *Catalogus codicum manu scriptorum Bibliothecae Regiae Monacensis* (1878; reprinted, Wiesbaden, 1969), III, 2, p. 46; and Bénédictins du Bouveret, *Colophons des manuscrits occidentaux des origines au XVIe siècle*, 6 vols. (Fribourg, 1965–1982), I, 301, no. 2394.

[8]MS clm 4146, fol. 116: "Librum scripsit Burckhardus Zingg ex exemplari valde tenebroso et obscuro."

Bühler, "*Countless* scribes, from Peter Schoeffer to Antoine Vérard, forsook the careers for which they had been trained in order to try their success with the new 'artium omnium magistra.'"[9] Rudolf Hirsch starts a discussion of printers' diverse backgrounds by remarking: "To begin with the most usual transfer, scribes became printers."[10] But was it so "usual"? The evidence suggests otherwise.

Many scribes who "went into printing" assumed ancillary roles. Giovan Marco "Cinico" da Parma, copyist and miniaturist for the Neapolitan court, and Pietro Molino ("valente calligrafo") became editors for Neapolitan publishers. In Florence the calligrapher Pietro Cennini proofread for his goldsmith father, as the colophon of the single book the elder Cennini produced declares. (Should Pietro really be considered, for having done this, one who "went into printing"?) Others rubricated printed pages. In the 1460s, for example, Hans Bämler in Augsburg rubricated for local Swabian clients at least four books printed at Strasbourg,[11] but some rubricators presumably worked directly for a printer at his shop. Some scribes may have provided models for type: Peter Schoeffer for Fust in Mainz, Heinrich Molitor for Günther Zainer in Augsburg, and possibly Colard Mansion for Caxton in Bruges. But Molitor, apart from this presumed effort, had no other connection with printing, and a scribe need not truly have "gone into printing" in order to supply a printer or type founder with a well-executed alphabet.

Of course, some scribes did indeed establish their own shops and actively engage in producing printed books. Bühler, after mentioning Schoeffer as the first and Vérard as the last "to try their success," names eleven more, to which I would add another four, making a preliminary total of seventeen. (The number, of course, is unlikely ever to be absolute.) Since my concern as an art historian is with the

---

[9]Curt Bühler, *The Fifteenth-Century Book* (Philadelphia, 1960), p. 48.

[10]Rudolf Hirsch, *Printing, Selling, and Reading, 1450–1550* (Wiesbaden, 1967), p.18.

[11]An Eggestein Bible (H. 3037; Wolfenbüttel, Herzog August Bibliothek, Bibel-Slg. 2^0 155); Mentelin's Aquinas, *Summa theologica* (H. 1454; Munich, Bayerische Staatsbibliothek, 2^0 Inc. s.a. 1146a); and two copies of Mentelin's Augustine, *De civitate Dei* (Manchester, John Rylands University Library, Inc. 3.A.8, and Chantilly, Musée Condé, XXX^1.D.11). See Victor von Klemper, "Der Augsburger Drucker Johann Bämler als Rubrikator," *Gutenberg Jahrbuch* (1928): 105–6. For reproductions of the first page of the Bible and two pages of the Chantilly Augustine, see S. Edmunds, "The Place of the London *Haggadah* in the Work of Joel ben Simeon," *Journal of Jewish Art* 7 (1980): 25–34, figs. 22–24; for a folio in the *Summa*, see Edmunds, "Questions of Transmission," fig. 4.

relationships between the scribes' early and later work, the preliminary list was soon reduced. Unless specimens of a scribe's early work could be identified, one could scarcely make instructive comparisons. Consequently, for lack of surviving manuscripts, nine men on the preliminary list were effectively excluded from further study: Johann Mentelin of Strasbourg; Günther Zainer, Johann Schüssler, and Jodocus Pflanzmann of Augsburg; Andreas Belfortis, a Frenchman, at Ferrara; Johann Schriber of Augsburg, at Venice and Bologna; Johann of Paderborn (or of Westphalia) at Louvain, whose device, called a self-portrait, he printed in red; Francesco del Tuppo at Naples; and Julyan Notary, another Frenchman, active in London at the very end of the century, whom I cite because of his surname but about whom practically nothing is known.

The exclusion of Günther Zainer involved a second reason. Not only does none of his scribal work survive, but it probably never existed. Although he was listed for five years as scribe in the Augsburg tax rolls, these entries occur at dates when Günther is known to have been printing. The identification is in all probability merely a tax collector's label, recording an occupation for a newcomer to the city at a time when book printing was still novel (Zainer established Augsburg's first press) and the vocabulary unsettled. (There was a further problem in Augsburg in that *trucker* already signified printers of textile patterns or of woodcuts.) At any rate, to judge from the taxes Zainer paid between 1468 and 1478,[12] he was far too wealthy to have built up his fortune simply as a scribe; scribes as a group had a low economic position. In Augsburg most scribes, including the prolific Heinrich and Conrad Molitor, belonged to the bluntly named class of "have-nots," that is, those without taxable property. Significantly, Hans Bämler and Johann Schüssler, two Augsburg scribes who did become printers, were a cut above this class. In fact Zainer's name suggests that he came from a metalworking background.

Johann Mentelin, by contrast, warrants some attention despite the lack of identifiable early work. He was born near Mainz between 1420 and 1430, and became a citizen of Strasbourg in 1447. His occupation at the time was given as *gulden-schriber,* that is, a writer of gold-leaf

---

[12]See Carl Wehmer, "Über die Augsburger Steuerbücher als Quelle für die Geschichte des Augsburger Buchgewerbes," *Gutenberg Jahrbuch* (1933): 288–94.

letters, a particularly demanding specialty. A member of the Strasbourg Maler- und Goldschmiedzunft—to which Günther Zainer later
belonged—Mentelin is sometimes dubiously credited with having
been a goldsmith, a notary, and an illuminator. One of the first to
follow in Gutenberg's footsteps, Mentelin was operating a press at
Strasbourg—the third in Europe—by at least 1460, and continued to
produce large folio volumes until about 1476.

Since Mentelin's Latin Bible of c.1460 exhibits characteristics of
Mainz presses, it is thought that he learned to print by working, first
in the role of calligrapher and illuminator, for Gutenberg, probably
during Gutenberg's Strasbourg period (that is, *before* 1450), or possibly in Mainz after 1450. For the most part Mentelin published well-
tested material such as Aquinas' *Summa,* a copy of which was rubricated by Hans Bämler; Augustine's *City of God,* two copies of which
were illuminated by Bämler; and the Epistles of Saint Jerome, a copy
of which, now in Paris, was bound in "Gyslingen" (Geislingen), near
Ulm. Mentelin ventured into a new area with his publication of the
first venacular Bible, of which Hector Mülich purchased a copy
(Munich, Staatsbibliothek, Rar. 285) in 1466.

After the eliminations and a priori exclusions, eight scribes-turned-
printers remain: two Germans, two Netherlanders (one working in
Italy), three Italians, and one Frenchman. At their head, beyond dispute, is Peter Schoeffer. Born in Gernsheim between 1420 and 1430,
which appears to be the crucial decade, he was in Paris in 1449,
perhaps as a student at the university. (In later, printed colophons he
would refer to himself as *clericus,* a person of learning.) In Paris he
completed a manuscript copy of Aristotle's *Organon,* a standard text-
book on logic, with the triumphant inscription: "Here is the end of all
books of logic both old and new, completed by me Peter of
Gernsheim otherwise of Mainz in the year one thousand four hundred
49, in Paris, most glorious of all cities." Schoeffer's manuscript was
destroyed during the Franco-Prussian War, but fortunately the bold
textura colophon had been reproduced in an eighteenth-century engraving.

Further knowledge of Schoeffer's calligraphy comes from later inscriptions and business letters. In 1474, for example, Schoeffer recorded, in *rotunda* (or *fere humanistica*) letters, the donation of one of
his books to a Franciscan monastery in Prussia; the signature below is
in *lettre bâtarde,* and his device appears at the bottom. (Generically

[27]

speaking, these three kinds of script—textura, rotunda, and batârde—are the bases of most fifteenth-century type. The formal textura, with its compressed, angular letters, leads to the so-called Gothic or pointed-letter type, which in the north became customary for liturgical books. The semiformal rotunda, also called *Gotico-antico,* is a rounded alphabet which derives from and eventually merges back into Roman; it was generally employed for serious theological or scholarly material. Of the three kinds, the cursive or bâtarde, an "everyday" or "business" script, varies the most markedly from region to region; English-speaking readers are most familiar with *italic,* which, as the name indicates, is a type based on an Italian cursive. Bâtarde type was usually reserved for vernacular literature.) In a model study of a scribe's activities as a printer, Hellmut Lehmann-Haupt reproduced all Schoeffer's inscriptions, juxtaposed his script in 1474 to his type of a decade earlier, and compared the flourished letters of 1449 to woodcut initials Schoeffer employed nearly fifty years later.[13] The claim that Schoeffer was a type designer seems fully justified.

Schoeffer's 130 surviving books, chiefly in the fields of theology, liturgy, and canon law, are mostly addressed to the learned and wealthy. Needless to say, his type is generally textura or fere humanistica. Only late in his career did Schoeffer use a bâtarde for a few books in the vernacular, such as the illustrated and widely influential *Der Gart der Gesundheit* (or German *Herbarius*) of 1485 and his undated *Küchenmeisterei,* both of which were clearly intended for popular consumption.

Color, by contrast, was an early, brief, and magnificent experiment. The Mainz Psalters of 1457 and 1459, and the missal of c. 1458, printed in partnership with Fust, Gutenberg's former "banker," were adorned with extraordinary two-color initials and printed rubrics. The Psalters' *Beatus* initial has understandably been reproduced many times; the other colored letters are equally superb. Fust and Schoeffer were well aware of the initials' significance and quality, and the Psalters' colophon proudly states that the book is "decorated by the beauty of its capital letters and distinguished by its rubrications." Schoeffer and Fust clearly equated their work with typographic fac-

[13]Hellmut Lehmann-Haupt, *Peter Schoeffer of Gernsheim and Mainz* (Rochester, N.Y., 1950).

simile, "the art of writing artificially." A taste for red printing, here and in the missal grandly displayed, is a characteristic particularly attributed to printers who were once scribes or who are thought to have been.

Compared to Schoeffer, the Neapolitan printer Arnald of Brussels is little known, perhaps because his books were few and are now exceedingly rare. Arnald was the third scribe (counting Mentelin) to become a printer. How Arnald came to be so far from home is unknown; perhaps he was drawn to the scholarly court around King Alfonso the Magnanimous.[14] In the 1460s and 1470s Arnald served the court of Alfonso's successor, King Ferdinand, making copies of state papers such as pragmatics, capitulars, and letters of patent. Even while he was a printer, between 1472 and 1477, he continued to serve as "scribe to His Majesty and his council."

About sixty specimens of Arnald's small but legible rotunda hand are preserved in six paper manuscripts.[15] The earliest, a copy in Naples of the late classical Latin lexicon by Nonius Marcellus, is signed and dated 1455. The remainder, containing dates from 1464 to 1492, are compendia of various treatises, some now bound with the work of other scribes, and some on paper with the same watermark as Arnald's printed books. They cover geography, astronomy, medicine (he made his copy of the celebrated *Tacuinum sanitatis,* he comments, "from a corrupt exemplar"), and alchemy, to which he devoted one whole volume, now in the Lehigh University library. One brief section of the Lehigh manuscript gives directions for making gold and silver letters as well as fifty recipes for making colors. For all six manuscripts, the intervals among the transcriptions suggest personal

---

[14]The assertion by Mario Emilio Cosenza, *Biographical and Bibliographical Dictionary of the Italian Printers and of Foreign Printers in Italy* (Boston, 1968), p. 41, that Arnald "arrived in Naples with the printer Sixtus Riessinger" is untenable: Arnald is documented in Naples more than a decade before Riessinger established his press.

[15]Naples, Biblioteca Nazionale, cod. V.B.32, and cod. IV.D.22bis; BN, MS lat. 10264, MS lat. 10271, and MS lat. 10252; and Lehigh University Library, Bethelem, Pa. See Mariano Fava and Giovanni Bresciano, *La stampa a Napoli nel XV secolo,* 3 vols. (Leipzig, 1911–1913), I, chap. 4; II, 67–87; Leopold Delisle, "L'imprimeur napolitain Arnaud de Bruxelles," *Bibliothèque de l'Ecole des Chartes* 58 (1987): 741–43; Lynn Thorndike, *History of Magic and Experimental Science,* 8 vols. (New York, 1923–1958), IV, 235–36; 466–49; 659; and W. J. Wilson, "An Alchemical Manuscript by Arnaldus de Bruxella," *Osiris* 2 (1936): 220–405. In the Lehigh manuscript the formulas for scribes and illuminators occur on fols. 102–5v. I am indebted to Robert E. Lerner for the Thorndike and Lehigh University citations.

compilations, while the exceptionally generous margins imply that Arnald did not need to pinch pennies.

In the five years Arnald operated a press, he published about twenty unillustrated Latin texts, appropriately printed in roman type.[16] Most of his books were scientific, such as the treatise "On the Baths of Pozzuoli," which he edited, and Macer Floridus' metrical *De virtutibus herbarum* of 1477, the first herbal ever printed; but he printed as well Cicero's *Rhetorica nova*, Augustino Dati's *Elegantiole*, and the so-called Letters of Mahomet II. This rather unusual selection of texts may be a reflection as much of Arnald's own intellectual pursuits as of those of the university or the court in Naples.

Although Arnald worked only five years as a printer, his career was lengthy and prolific compared to those of the three native Italian scribes who became printers. The Ferrarese notary Iacobus Antonius Severinus, mentioned earlier for his surviving codex,[17] has been reasonably identified with Severinus Ferrariensis, a name appearing in about nine books printed between 1475 and 1477, of which the *Statuta civitate Ferrariae* is the most notable. More intriguing, however, is a series of pamphlets printed in 1475, in which his name in the colophons is followed by the initials *F.F.* Although this was once interpreted as the conventional *fieri fecit*, indicating Severinus was not so much a "practical printer" as one who subsidized or financed a press, it now seems more probable that the initials indicate that he collaborated with Felice Feliciano of Verona.[18]

Born in 1433, Feliciano was by profession a calligrapher, by inclination an epigrapher, author, and member of a circle of humanists that included such figures as Andrea Mantegna and Giovanni Bellini. Autobiographical details abound in Felice's own writings. Although styled *scriptor* in his will (1466), he clearly preferred, and made frequent use of, the epithet *antiquarius*. Like Arnald of Brussels, with whom he otherwise had little in common, Felice displayed an interest in alchemy, which in Felice's case drove him near bankruptcy. A persistent theme in his epistles and poems (in both Italian and Latin, some being addressed to Ieber, the eighth-to-ninth-century Arab al-

---

16 See *BMC* VI, xlii, 857–58; Fava and Bresciano, *La stampa a Napoli*, III, nos. 79–101; and Frank J. Anderson, *An Illustrated History of the Herbals* (New York, 1977), chap. 4.

17 See note 3.

18 See *BMC* VI, li, 608–9, and *Editori e stampatori del quattrocento*, intro. by Raffaello Bertieri (Milan, 1929), p. 49.

chemist) is his destitution, which on the whole he seems to have regarded quite cheerfully ("I was willingly poor, happy in fact as in name"),[19] though he did express a poetic wish to throw boccie balls at Ieber's forehead.[20] Poverty, which prompted him to precede one sonnet with the plea "Felice to Cyllenio: not having writing paper I found a piece of mangy and moth-eaten skin to write on: and I beg you to send paper,"[21] may explain why some of his manuscripts are composed of both parchment and paper.

More manuscripts inscribed by Felice survive than by any other scribe-printer.[22] Among their contents are a novella attributed to Alberti, collections of ancient inscriptions, a life of Cyriacus of Ancona, copies of his own poems and letters—one of which states that he has been printing in Ferrara—and the earliest known essay on ancient Roman capitals.[23] The brief explanatory text, composed by Felice c.1460, was illustrated with large, bicolored, glyptically designed majuscules. Other manuscripts were ornamented with calligraphic devices and occasionally with figural illustrations. In addition, broad knotted or braided pen-work borders may frame a text, usually a dedicatory passage, or pictures. Generally Felice employed a rather upright humanist script, but on occasion he used elaborate conjoined cursive majuscules probably inspired by Cyriacus, as, probably, was his practice of using multicolored inks.[24]

Although printing was introduced at Verona in 1472, and a copy in the Vatican of the first book printed there, Robertus Valturius' *De re militari,* contains inscriptions and pen decorations by Felice,[25] he was directly involved with printing only some years later. A curious,

---

[19]"Sponte fui pauper, tam re quam nomine felix" (the play on his name involved is lost in translation); Venice, Biblioteca Marciana, cod. lat. X, 205 (=3310), fol. 20v, cited in *Felice Feliciano Veronese: Alphabetum Romanum,* ed. Giovanni Mardersteig (Verona, 1960), p. 136.

[20]C. Mazzi, "Sonetti de Felice Feliciano," *La bibliofilia* 3 (1901–2): 55–68, no. 40.

[21]Ibid., no. 11.

[22]See Charles Mitchell, "Felix Felicianus *Antiquarius,*" *Proceedings of the British Academy* 47 (1961): 208f., with a summary checklist (pp. 220–21) identifying over fifty manuscripts and incunabula related to Felice, most of which are autograph.

[23]Rome, Biblioteca Vaticana, cod. Vat. lat. 6852; see Mardersteig, *Felice Feliciano.* For a facsimile, see *Alphabetum Romanum: Vat. Lat. 6852 aus der Bibliotheca Apostolica Vaticana,* 2 vols. (Zurich, 1985).

[24]Mitchell, "Felix Felicianus *Antiquarius,*" p. 206; and G. Mardersteig, "Felice Feliciano," in P. Hofer et al., *Hippolito e Lionora, from a Manuscript of Felice Feliciano in the Harvard College Library* (Verona, 1970), p. 111.

[25]Vatican Library, Stamp. Rossiano 1335; see Augusto Campana, "Felice Feliciano e la prima edizione del Valturio," *Maso Finiguerra* 5 (1940): 211–22.

rather tentative step in this direction is a copy of *Prognosticum super Antichristi adventu,* or *De adventu Antichristi,* an astrological prediction composed at Padua by John of Lübeck in 1474, which Feliciano inscribed and presented to the bishop of Trent in 1475. Written on paper in pale blue ink, the text is framed throughout with a repeated printed woodcut interlace, closely related to the kind of borders he had previously executed by hand.[26] It is highly probable that he was the designer. Later in the same year, as he himself testified, he was in Ferrara, collaborating with Severinus. By 1476, however, he had returned to Pojano, outside Verona, where, acting as editor, and with the financial help of Innocenzo Zileto, he published—on the same paper used for *De adventu Antichristi*—an Italian version of Petrarch's *Libri degli uomini famosi.* The book is not distinguished for its typography, but at the beginning of each section braidwork borders serve as frames for portraits or figures of the famous men to be inserted by hand. The border blocks are of two different designs, one being that used in *De adventu Antichristi.*[27] Mardersteig has suggested that Felice also had a share in the planning and decoration of two later Veronese incunabula,[28] but he is not known to have published anything else himself. He died near Rome in 1479.

Damiano Moille of Parma turned his hand to nearly as many diverse activities as did Felice, but they were on the whole more conventionally associated with book arts. Born in 1439, and thus somewhat younger than other scribes-turned-printers, he worked from 1478 on for the Parmesan Convent of Saint John Evangelist as bookbinder, paper seller, calligrapher, miniaturist, and unexpectedly, ceramicist. For two choir books belonging to a convent at Padua he executed large calligraphically decorated initials.[29]

According to a notarial record, Damiano was printing books by 1474, but the earliest surviving is a Chorale on which he collaborated with his brother Bernard in the spring of 1477. The first printed

[26]Trent, Biblioteca Communale, cod. 1659; see Giuseppe Gerola, "Codicetto trentino del 1475 a fregi silografati," *Accademie e biblioteche d'Italia* 8 (1934): 39–42.

[27]See Arthur M. Hind, *An Introduction to a History of Woodcut,* 2 vols. (1935; reprinted, New York, 1963), II, 414–15; and Mardersteig, *Felice Feliciano,* p. 28. Two copies, one in the British Library, the other in the Vatican (Stamp. Chigi II, 679), have painted illustrations within the frames, in the latter apparently by Felice.

[28]Mardersteig, *Felice Feliciano,* p. 28.

[29]See Domenico Fava, "Le conquiste tecniche di un grande tipografo del quattrocento," *Gutenberg Jahrbuch* (1940): 147–56, figs. 1–3.

example of this kind of liturgical book, with splendid giant *fere humanistica* type and woodcut neumes, it survives in a unique copy in Lodi.[30] Despite this impressive beginning, Damiano was never more than an intermittent printer, bringing out two or three more books in the early 1480s. One remarkable project may have been inspired by Felice's treatise on Roman capitals: a small instructional manual— likewise surviving in a single copy—containing a diagrammatic alphabet of woodcut Roman capitals, accompanied by Italian explanations, in a shapely roman type, of how to construct each letter with ruler and compass, the only book of its how-to-do-it kind printed in the fifteenth century.[31]

This prolonged attention to the Italian scribe-printers may give them undue prominence and is certainly chronologically misleading. The first dated book published by Hans Bämler of Augsburg appeared in April 1472, only four months after Arnald of Brussels' first printed book and well before anything printed by Severinus, Feliciano, or Moille. Bämler was probably born between 1420 and 1430. He entered the tax rolls in 1453 as a *schreiber* (scribe); through these rolls his financial standing can be traced for the next half-century. He was named as *trucker* (printer) only in 1477, five years after he had established his press. His printing career continued until 1495, when apparently he retired; he died in 1503, one year after Schoeffer.

Bämler printed almost nothing but books in German. Apart from the vernacular content, they are notable for two features: color and illustrations. Color printing is extensive for headpieces and, in a few early books, quasi-calligraphic borders, but what sets Bämler apart from his fellow scribe-printers is that about half his publications, a very large proportion, were illustrated with woodcuts, both full-page frontispieces and smaller narrative or descriptive pictures. In 1475, for example, he published the first two botanical woodcuts ever made.[32] On one occasion he illustrated a text, the *Chronicle of All Kings, Emperors, and Popes* by Jacob Twinger von Königshofen, and also edited it—eliminating much ancient material, adding recent or con-

---

[30]Ibid., pp. 152–54, fig. 4.

[31]Parma, Biblioteca Palatina, 1229; see Stanley Morison, *A Newly Discovered Treatise on Classic Letter Design* (Paris, 1927); see also *BMC* VII, xlviii, 940–41; Bertieri, *Editori e stampatori*, p. 92; and Fava, "Le conquiste tecniche," pp. 154–56, figs. 5, 6.

[32]See Albrecht Schramm, *Die Bilderschmuck der Frühdrucke*, 23 vols. (Leipzig, 1920– 1943), III, figs. 462, 463; and Anderson, *An Illustrated History of the Herbals*, chap. 10.

temporary figures, and inserting a short autobiographical passage, a rare practice exercised more frequently and tellingly by William Caxton.

Normally Bämler's types were fine German bâtardes, forerunners of the type known as Schwabacher. In their slender proportions and variety of letter forms, his types resemble the cursive inscriptions in the Strasbourg books Bämler handled between 1466 and 1468. A decade before that, Bämler had illuminated, with opaque paint and gold leaf, two miniatures on vellum,[33] signing himself *artifex* (artist). In three of the Strasbourg volumes he called himself *illuminator*. He never employed the label "rubricator," as is sometimes said, and the distinction between rubricator and illuminator would not have been unimportant, I think, to an officer, as Bämler was, of the Guild of Painters, Glaziers, Sculptors, and Gold-Leaf Makers (Zunft der Maler, Glaser, Bildschnitzer und Goldschlager). Once, in his very last publication, he referred to himself as "citizen of Augsburg."

The commonly held view that Bämler went to Strasbourg in the mid-1460s and there acquired knowledge of the new art of printing is virtually without foundation. He did not have to go to Strasbourg to rubricate those books; we know from other examples that Strasbourg books were circulating and had reached Augsburg by the mid-1460s. During the relevant years Bämler paid the annual tax required of every Augsburg resident. Moreover, his types are completely local in character and betray not the slightest influence of Strasbourg models. So if Bämler did not learn printing in Strasbourg, as has been assumed, where did he?

The answer seems inescapable: in the shop of Augsburg's first printer, Günther Zainer of Reutlingen. Zainer arrived in Augsburg in 1467. His first publications required, as usual, the insertion of capitals and rubrics. Copies of two of Zainer's earliest books with Bämleresque rubrication have come to my attention.[34] They could, however, have been done at the behest of a Bämler client rather than at the printer's direction, so they do not prove that Bämler was then working in Zainer's shop.

[33]PML, MS M. 45; see Harrsen, *Central European Manuscripts,* pp. 68–69.
[34]J. de Aurbach, *Summa de sacramentis* (Hain 2124), March 1469 (Munich, Bayerische Staatsbibliothek, 2⁰ Inc. c.a. 18); and Balbus, *Catholicon* (H. 2252), April 1469 (Berlin, Preussischer Staatsbibliothek, 2⁰ Inc. 2,1). None of the rubrication has been published.

But in 1471 Zainer made a momentous decision: he proposed adding pictures to his next book, and with his first volume of Voragine's *Legenda aurea,* issued in the autumn of 1471, the illustrated book was irreversibly established. To print this volume Zainer adopted a clumsy procedure: the pictures were printed first, then the sheets were put through the press again for the text, and sometimes the registration did not work.[35] Obviously, the woodblocks did not fit the forms (pages of type), nor could capitals be printed—they were still added by hand. Six months later, on April 27, 1472, the second volume appeared, and its first page demonstrated that the difficulties had been resolved.[36] For the first time ever there was a woodcut initial, from which springs a foliate border in a typically "manuscript" arrangement. Also for the first time, the woodcuts—decorated initial and illustration—were printed with the text in a single impression. Obstacles to the efficient printing of illustrated books had been largely overcome, and Augsburg was launched on two decades of leadership in the field.

The decorated woodcut initial and the illustrations in the second volume of the *Legenda aurea* can be readily compared with Bämler's work as an illuminator. The similarities of such things as foliated borders, decorated "dots," squat, neckless figures, and acute perspective, as in the historiated initial opening the Chantilly *City of God,*[37] have convinced me that Bämler simply drew his accustomed figures and decorative patterns on wood. (He thus preceded Feliciano in transposing familiar motifs to a different medium.) The actual cutting of Bämler's blocks was probably turned over to a *formschneider,* a woodblock cutter, because in the early 1470s Bämler was much occupied; besides launching his own shop in 1471, he continued to supply more woodblocks for Zainer's publications, such as an initial *D* with the Christ Child offering New Year's greetings, which appeared on Zainer's German calendar for 1472.[38] Zainer, however, has received all the credit for having created this frequently imitated concept for a calendar decoration, nor has Bämler hitherto been connected to the stunning large (4 inches high) historiated initials in

---

[35]For example, see Schramm, *Die Bilderschmuck,* II, figs. 1, 2, 11, 25, 30, 47.
[36]Ibid., fig. 129.
[37]For reproduction, see Edmunds, "The Place of the London *Haggadah,*" fig. 23.
[38]See Paul Heitz and Konrad Haebler, *Hundert Kalendar-Inkunabeln* (Strasbourg, 1905), p. 16, no. 5.

Zainer's German Bible of c.1475, probably the first Bible published with illustrations.[39]

While Bämler's contribution to the illustrated book has been, I believe, underestimated, Colard Manion's reputation has suffered the reverse fate. Although now deprived of his former eminence as Caxton's teacher, he remains nonetheless a documented scribe-turned-printer. From 1450 into the early 1480s Mansion maintained a shop in Bruges for an aristocratic clientele, producing luxury manuscripts "by [his] hand or one as good," as one document put it. Unfortunately, no autograph manuscript "by his hand" is known with certainty. Some of the five frequently attributed to him[40] were owned by men known to be his patrons, and two are manuscripts of Mansion's translation of *Le dialogue des créatures,* but none is signed. About 1474 he was associated with Caxton, perhaps as junior partner, in the production of four books. After Caxton departed for England, Mansion printed two dozen mostly French texts, in which his adherence to a "manuscript aesthetic" is obvious. At first he even retained lines of uneven length. His best-known type, a heavy, much ligatured bâtarde, resembles examples of the local script, such as was used in an *Ordre de chevallerie* sometimes attributed to him.[41] It is possible, but not demonstrable, that Mansion's calligraphic expertise, like Schoeffer's, was transferred to type design. Another peculiarity of Mansion's presswork, one shared with Caxton, is the awkward method of color printing, in which the form was first completely inked in black, and then the part to

[39]For reproductions, see Schramm, *Die Bilderschmuck,* II, figs. 609–79. On the argument concerning the priority of Pflanzmann's or Zainer's Bibles, see Kenneth A. Strand, *German Bibles before Luther* (Grand Rapids, Mich., 1966). In my view the illustrations in Pflanzmann's Bible are more likely to have been derived from Zainer's initials than the reverse.

[40]Boccaccio, *De casibus virorum et foeminarum illustrium,* in French (BN, MS fr. 132), for Louis de Bruges; *Le livre de penétence d'Adam* (BN, MS fr. 183), for Louis de Bruges; *Le traittié intitulé le dialogue des créatures* (present whereabouts unknown), for Louis de Bruges; *Le traittié intitulé le dialogue des créatures* (Vienna, MS 2572), for Philippe de Crevecour; *Le livre de lordre de chevalerie* (BL, MS Reg. 14 E ii), for Edward IV. See Henri Michel, *L'imprimeur Colard Mansion et le "Boccace" de la Bibliothèque d'Amiens* (Paris, 1925), chap. 1; L. A. Sheppard, "A New Light on Caxton and Colard Mansion," *Signature,* n.s., 15 (1952): 28–39; Paul Saenger, "Colard Mansion and the Evolution of the Printed Book," *Library Quarterly* 45 (1975): 405–18; George D. Painter, *William Caxton* (New York, 1977), chap. 9; Lotte Hellinga, *Caxton in Focus: The Beginning of Printing in England* (London, 1982).

[41]BL, MS Reg. 14 E ii, reproduced in William Blades, *The Life and Typography of William Caxton* (London, 1882), pl. IV.

be printed red was wiped and reinked. His first dated printed work, *De la ruyne des nobles hommes et femmes* (a translation of Boccaccio), has a further technical interest, because its sixteen illustrations were not the usual woodcuts but were copper engravings, and thus required more special presswork. Only his last book, his own prose version of Ovid's *Metamorphoses*, was also illustrated, with thirty-four woodcuts. It was published in May 1484, shortly before he fled Bruges for financial reasons.

Finally, Antoine Vérard of Paris, generally regarded as the last scribe-turned-printer, concludes this study only with my considerable reservations. Like the idea of Bämler's sojourn in Strasbourg, certain concepts about Vérard have become so fixed as to be almost immutable. In 1868, for instance, an English historian said: "Verard, who had previously been an illuminator and possibly a block-book engraver, soon became very eminent when he adopted the new art of printing."[42] In 1982 the French writers Martin and Chartier refer flatly to the "former Tourangeau calligrapher Antoine Vérard," and then two pages later state: "Almost nothing is known of this person before 1485. *On soupçonne* he was a native of Tours and directed *un atelier de copie.*"[43] There is, in fact, no documentation of Vérard's origins, and no specimens of his writing prior to his becoming a printer are known—and possibly not after. He materializes in Paris out of nowhere in 1485 and becomes, until his death c.1514, the leading Parisian publisher of books in the vernacular, books often printed on vellum and so elaborately painted that the resemblance to manuscripts can be disconcerting.[44] Certainly Vérard's inclination toward what I have called manuscript aesthetic is very striking. But if Vérard died, let us say, in his seventies (the probable age of Schoeffer and Bämler), he must have been born between 1435 and 1445, a birthdate significantly later than those of all the previously mentioned scribes except Damiano, and I have seriously considered eliminating him from the group.

[42]H. N. Humphreys, *History of the Art of Printing* (London, 1868), p. 128.

[43]Henri-Jean Martin and Roger Chartier, *Histoire de l'édition française*, 3 vols. (Paris, 1982), I, 189, 191. The disposition of Vérard's estate suggests he may have been Tourangeau; see Jérome Pichon and Georges Vicaire, *Documents pour servir à l'histoire des libraries* (Paris, 1895), pp. 3–14.

[44]See Eleanor P. Spencer, "Antoine Vérard's Illuminated Vellum Incunables," in *Manscripts in the Fifty Years after the Invention of Printing*, ed. J. B. Trapp (London, 1983), pp. 62–65.

Vérard has remained, on probation so to speak, for two reasons, neither conclusive. The first is a group of four vellum manuscripts, none explicitly signed, destined for royal owners, among them a *Poème sur la passion*.[45] This singular manuscript, apparently made c.1503, is illustrated with impressions, on the vellum, of the Large Passion series engraved some two decades earlier by Israel van Meckenem, over-painted in grisaille, so it is a half-printed, half-manuscript book. In it is the strongest evidence we have that Vérard was a scribe. The poem begins with a rhymed prologue, expressed in the first person and written in the rounded humanist script employed for the poem as well. Indented beneath the prologue, in red and in the same hand, is the subscription: "Cest vostre treshumble et tresobeyssant serviteur. Anthoine verard libraire" (Your very humble and very obedient servant, Anthoine Vérard, bookseller). In visual effect the format overrides the occupational label, and implicitly conveys the message that Vérard was both author of the prologue and scribe of the manuscript.

Second, and much weaker proof, many of Vérard's title pages incorporate imitation calligraphy, with woodcut letters, usually exuberantly flourished *L*s containing profiles, figures, and animals, but whether these letters were modeled on his script cannot be determined. As many colophons in Vérard's publications attest, he was primarily an entrepreneur, a publisher and bookseller who hired the services of various printers. Other craftsmen could be responsible for "his" manuscripts and the flourished *L*s.

With Vérard we encounter a publisher who no longer needed to turn to manuscript sources alone. On several occasions Vérard's books were derived almost blatantly from other publications, among them Mansion's *Métamorphoses*, the model for Vérard's *Bible des poètes* (1494). Mansion may have also indirectly suggested, with his engraved illustrations for *De la ruyne*, the use of the Meckenem plates in a book format. Could Vérard have been Brugeois rather than Tourangeau, or (and here wild speculation enters in) *could he be Mansion in disguise?* I am not really serious about this hypothesis, which was prompted by the coincidence that Mansion disappears from the re-

---

[45]BN, MS fr. 1686. The previous literature is scant, but see G. Duval, "Notes sur quelques manuscrits exécutés dans l'atelier d'Antoine Vérard," *La correspondance historique et archéologique* 7 (1900): 65–72; John MacFarlane, *Antoine Vérard* (1900; reprinted, Geneva, 1971), p. xviii; Mary Beth Winn, "Antoine Vérard's Presentation Manuscripts and Printed Books," in Spencer, *Manuscripts in the Fifty Years*, p. 67; and Sheila Edmunds and Mary Beth Winn, "Vérard, Meckenem, and B. N. MS Fr. 1686," *Romania* 108 (1987); 288–344.

cords in 1484 while Vérard appears in 1485, but it is no more nor less substantiated than several so-called established facts in this field of study. That Peter Schoeffer, for example, was a professional scribe is an assumption, not a certainty.

Be that as it may, the scribes I have considered in some detail started printing with one great advantage over smiths and woodcutters, two other occupational groups attracted to printing: scribes were already aware of the kinds of books likely to appeal to their markets, and they knew the locations of manuscript sources. One-third of Mansion's printed texts, as van Praet made known long ago,[46] can be traced to manuscripts in the collection of Mansion's patron, Louis de Bruges; Zainer and Bämler each printed an illustrated text from a compendium[47] that George Mülich transcribed in 1450; and Bämler published at least eight other books based on locally produced manuscripts.[48]

Apart from this awareness of potential copy, the only features that seem to be broadly shared by the group are their respective age and the quality of their products. So far as can be determined, none was really a youth when he began printing. Schoeffer would have been around thirty-five when he and Fust began their enterprise; Damiano was in his thirties; the others were in their forties. Their age should not be particularly surprising, because, as Gutenberg's fate so sadly demonstrates, printing required capital. Men born between 1420 and 1430 were old enough, when the printing press appeared, to have established business connections or perhaps earned some capital of their own. Many scribes interested in printing may have been hindered by lack of funds or patronage. For half our group, however, it is possible to identify or suggest a source of financial support: Fust for Schoeffer, Louis de Bruges or Caxton for Mansion, and, more tentatively, the Mülichs for Bämler and the Neapolitan court for Arnald. Men born after 1440—that is, those in their teens when the printed book became a fact of life—probably consciously chose their training for one career or the other.

As for the quality of their products, on the whole these men are associated with generally well printed books, not an invariable char-

---

[46]See Joseph B. B. van Praet, *Notice sur Colard Mansion, libraire et imprimeur* (Paris, 1829), and *Recherches sur Louis de Bruges seigneur de Gruthuse: Suivies de la notice des manuscripts qui lui ont appartenu* (Paris, 1831).

[47]Giessen, Universitätsbibliothek, no. 813; Lehmann-Haupt, *Schwäbische Federzeichnungen*, pp. 187–90, no. 8.

[48]Ibid., chap. 7.

acteristic of incunabula. For Schoeffer, and possibly Bämler, the type is sufficiently close to their script to suggest that they were their own type designers. And Schoeffer, Bämler, and Mansion perpetuated the scribal practice of red lettering, while Feliciano transferred calligraphic ornament to the new context.

Now, if for statistical purposes the nine printers not considered for lack of manuscripts and the peripheral "Cinico" of Parma, Molino of Naples, and Pietro Cennini were reinstated, the number of identifiable professional scribes who were once engaged in making manuscript books and who subsequently went into printing would represent approximately 4 to 6 percent of the probable total number of printers who worked before 1500. Admittedly the lack of biographical information for many known (not to mention unknown) printers makes these calculations quite hypothetical, but it still appears excessive to speak of "countless" scribes' becoming printers, and therefore it seems equally true that it was not a "usual" practice.

The differences among the final group of eight suggest that the paramount considerations in determining their careers were opportunity and the character of each individual, most of whom apparently did not think of themselves, even before they became printers, as *scribes*. Shoeffer was active for forty-six years, and the high quality of his publications, as well as his fundamental importance in the history of printing, is beyond debate. Bämler, who operated for twenty-three years in an intensely competitive market, had moderate financial success and as a woodcut designer did much to shape the character of the early illustrated book. By comparison, the men who worked in Italy are relatively minor figures, but Arnald's presswork, combined with his passion for scientific subjects, and Damiano's *chorale* and calligraphic manual were remarkable achievements. Vérard, active in publishing for about twenty-five years, was highly successful in terms of quantity and patronage, and Mansion, whose type so vividly reproduced the local script, indirectly contributed to Vérard's success. All deserve credit for attempting—and generally succeeding in—the difficult task of "retooling" themselves. Even for the most gifted and tenacious, the personal transition can hardly have been easy: one can readily imagine the doubts and agonizing experienced by these middle-aged scribes as they familiarized themselves with the operations of that new invention, the press.

[2]

Publish and Perish:
The Career of Lienhart Holle in Ulm

Martha Tedeschi

L ienhart Holle was the third printer to establish a press in the city of Ulm.[1] His was also the shortest-lived and quantitatively least productive firm. Officially in operation for only two years—from spring 1482 to late 1483—Holle's press produced six imprints. At the end of that time he declared bankruptcy and was banished from the town for his debts. On several documented occasions after that ignominious departure he reappeared in Ulm, but he was never again recorded as an independent printer. The legend that he went on to try his fortune in Nuremberg has been revealed as a simple misreading of a document.[2] We must assume, on the basis of the last notice of Holle as a debtor in Ulm in 1499, that he died a poor man around the turn of the century.

Students of the early history of printing are familiar with such stories. For many fifteenth-century German printers, to publish was also to perish. In her book on early Strasbourg printing, entitled *Lay Culture, Learned Culture,* Miriam Chrisman lists the large number of one-man printing shops that went out of business after producing

I thank Sandra Hindman and Larry Silver, both of the Department of Art History, and Robert Lerner, Department of History, Northwestern University, for their advice and assistance in the preparation of this essay. I am also grateful to the staffs of Special Collections and The Hermon Dunlap Smith Center for the History of Cartography, Newberry Library, for their generous assistance.

[1]"Lienhart Holle" is now the form commonly used in scholarship in the English language. The correct and original form of the name, however, was "Lienhart Holl."

[2]Peter Amelung, *Der Frühdruck im deutschen Südwesten, 1473–1500: Eine Ausstellung der Württembergischen Landesbibliothek,* vol. 1, Ulm (Stuttgart, 1979), p. 270.

only a handful of books.[3] Her study is based, of necessity, on the larger and more productive Strasbourg presses, since documentation of the smaller firms is scarce and often unreliable. This has been a deterrent to scholarship on the smaller and less prolific businesses of many other German printing centers as well. As a result, we have perhaps gained a better understanding of what constituted good business practice in the early printing industry than of what circumstances and procedures drove so many individuals to hasty financial ruin.

The instability of the printing industry was certainly a fact of life in the south German city of Ulm, about one hundred miles southeast of Strasbourg. A prosperous imperial free city with a flourishing linen and fustian trade and large territorial holdings, Ulm received its first paper mill in 1469 and its first press, that of Johannes Zainer, in 1473.[4] Between that date and the end of the century, five printers established their firms there.[5] All but one of them at various times in their careers experienced financial distress. Johannes Zainer's firm suffered increasing difficulties and eventually ground to a halt following the death in 1478 of his patron, author, and financial backer, the physician Heinrich Steinhöwel. Johannes Reger and Conrad Dinckmut were both forced to close their presses and leave Ulm in the late 1490s, a time when the Swabian cities were paying heavily in manpower, goods and taxes to support the emperor.[6] The early 1480s—when Lienhart Holle's meteoric publishing career took place—seems to have been a time of growth and productivity but also of increased competition for printers operating in Ulm.

The reason for the premature demise of the Holle firm is one of the intriguing, but poorly documented, questions in the early history of Ulm printing. Fortunately for this study, Peter Amelung's 1979 exhi-

---

[3]Miriam Usher Chrisman, *Lay Culture, Learned Culture: Books and Social Change in Strasbourg, 1480–1599* (New Haven, 1982), pp. 6–7.

[4]Lucien Febvre and Henri-Jean Martin, *The Coming of the Book: The Impact of Printing, 1450–1800*, trans. David Gerard (London, 1976), p. 42 cites the appearance of the first paper mills in this area. In addition to the mill at Ulm, a paper mill was established at Augsburg in 1460 and another at Ettlingen in 1482.

By the sixteenth century, Ulm's territory embraced three towns, fifty-five villages, and twenty-two parishes, a total of about 830 km, according to Thomas A. Brady, Jr. *Turning Swiss: Cities and Empire, 1450–1550* (Cambridge, 1985), p. 13 n. 16.

[5]The five fifteenth-century firms in Ulm were those of Johannes Zainer (1473–1493) and his son (1496–1500); Conrad Dinckmut (1476–1496); Lienhart Holle (1482–1484); Johannes Reger (1486–1499); and Johannes Schäffler (1492–1502).

[6]This is discussed by Brady, *Turning Swiss*, p. 60–61.

bition catalogue for the Landesbibliothek in Stuttgart made available for the first time considerable new documentation on early Ulm printers.[7] The present study of Holle's publishing strategy in the production of illustrated books is indeed indebted to this important resource.

However fleeting, Holle's career is of significance, on the one hand, because it is typical of the countless small German presses that were unable to survive in the new market. On the other hand, Holle provides a particularly interesting contrast to these small establishments in his choice of texts, and in the degree of ambition and economic risk implied by the two lavishly illustrated books that he published. Although Holle issued six publications during his two years in business, two of these texts were modest books with little decorative work, while another three were reprintings of the same text.[8] This essay, therefore, is devoted to his two most ambitious books: the *Cosmographia* of Ptolemy, from July 1482, and the fable book called *Buch der Weisheit der alten Weisen,* issued first in May and then again in July 1483 and June 1484. An analysis of these two productions will, I hope, elucidate the nature of Holle's endeavor: his attempt to capture a very select segment of the book-buying market; the problems he experienced in producing a deluxe printed book for a still manuscript-dominated field; his lack of financial astuteness; and, finally, his shift in publishing strategies and audiences when he saw his business begin to fail. From Holle's career we learn of the limitations as well as the accomplishments of the early press.

Holle's occupation and whereabouts prior to the opening of his press in 1482 are unknown. Early scholarship perpetuated the myth that he had first been a successful merchant of playing cards; Amelung, however, has traced this supposition back to an eighteenth-century genealogy of the Holle family. This, in turn, seems to have been based on nothing more than the knowledge that Ulm had been

[7]Amelung, *Der Frühdruck im deutschen Südwesten.* See also the review of Amelung's catalogue by Bernard F. Rosenthal in *Papers of the Bibliographical Society of America* 75 (1981): 222–28.

[8]Holle's six imprints include one edition of the Ptolemy *Cosmographia,* three printings of the *Buch der Weisheit der alten Weisen,* and two works not discussed here: [Johannes von Tepl], *Der Ackermanns von Böhmen* [Ulm, Lienhart Holle, c.1482–83]; *GW* 199; and Karl IV, Romischer Kaiser, *Die Goldenen Bulle von 1356* (Ulm, Lienhart Holle), [6.9.14]84, Hain 4080.

[43]

an important center of playing card production in the fifteenth century.[9] Actually, Holle is first recorded in Ulm in 1478, when the bookseller and paper merchant Hans Harscher sponsored his admittance into the Roman Brotherhood of the Holy Spirit.[10] From his association with Harscher, we might deduce that Holle was already employed in the book trade; at that time, however, he was certainly not yet operating as an independent printer. Although Amelung presents some evidence that might link Holle to the *Lenhart buchtrucker* listed in Augsburg in 1475, three years before his first appearance in an Ulm document, his presence there remains conjectural.[11]

Our first true knowledge of Holle as a printer comes with the publication of his first book, Ptolemy's *Cosmographia*, in the summer of 1482.[12] Holle's edition was the first printed Ptolemy to be issued outside Italy, and the first anywhere to be illustrated with woodcut maps. The manuscript original that served as his model was first identified in 1902 by Joseph Fisher: it is the codex—now housed in the Schloss Wolfegg, Württemberg—written and illustrated by the Benedictine monk Donaus Nicolaus Germanus. Thought to be the product of the astronomical and mathematical interests of the Benedictine house of Reichenbach, the scribe Nicolaus was transferred to the famous house of Tegernsee in 1456.[13] An important center of humanistic learning, Tegernsee had numerous ties to the cartographic school then active in Vienna. Nicolaus went on in the 1460s to work in Italy, where he produced numerous manuscript copies of the *Cosmographia*, and where his first recension served as the model for the printed Rome edition of 1478.[14] How the copy of Nicolaus' third version—inscribed with the date 1468—came into the hands of Lienhart Holle

[9]Amelung, *Der Frühdruck im deutschen Südwesten*, p. 263.

[10]Ibid., p. 263.

[11]Ibid., p. 262.

[12]Goff P-1084; Hain 13539; Schramm VII, 14; Proctor 2556; *BMC* II, 538. The two most recent studies of the Ulm Ptolemy in addition to Amelung's are the facsimile with an introduction by R. A. Skelton (Amsterdam, 1963) and the exhibition catalogue by Karl-Heinz Meine, *Die Ulmer Geographia des Ptolemaus von 1482* (Ulm, 1982).

[13]Dana Bennett Durand, *The Vienna-Klosterneuberg Map Corpus: A Study in the Transition from Medieval to Modern Science* (Leiden, 1952), p. 65.

[14]The Rome edition of 1478 (Goff P-1083) was preceded by two earlier printed editions, that of Vicenza (1475, Goff P-1081), which had no maps, and that of Bologna (1477, Goff P-1082), with engraved maps printed from copper plates. These three editions, like the Ulm Ptolemy, were in Latin. The first edition in Italian (Goff B-342) was printed in Florence in 1482, coincidentally by a German named Nicolaus.

is a matter of conjecture. Some of Nicolaus' copies of the *Cosmographia* would certainly have come north to the south German monasteries with which he had been associated. Yet it is also possible that the manuscript was imported especially for Holle from Italy by the bookseller Hans Harscher, who, as we will see, was responsible for purchasing Italian paper for the edition.

Perhaps the most important observation regarding the manuscript is that Holle clearly set out to copy its format as precisely as possible. A point-by-point comparison of corresponding maps from the manuscript and printed versions supports this idea. That imitation of the manuscript was Holle's primary purpose is further borne out by the typeface he used: a large, rounded, almost roman type so close to the hand of the scribe that there can be little doubt that it was designed with this intention.[15] Thus his dedication to faithful reproduction of the manuscript clearly caused him to go to further expense than was absolutely necessary. With the fields of cartography and geography still completely dominated by manuscript books, Holle no doubt believed his success was dependent on giving his printed atlas a manuscript appearance. He furthermore may have intended the work for a wealthy, aristocratic clientele accustomed to investing in deluxe manuscript books.

A large folio, the book is characterized by an ambitious decorative program. It consists of a woodcut presentation scene (fig. 2.1) accompanying the dedicatory letter to Pope Paul II (fig. 2.2), a small cut representing Ptolemy at the beginning of the Ptolemaic text that follows, woodcut initials throughout the text, thirty-two woodcut maps each occupying the full inside spread of a folded page (fig. 2.3), and ornamental woodcut borders which enclose the descriptive text for each map (fig. 2.4).

It is well known that the use of woodcuts in early book production was among the least expensive means of providing a text with illustrations.[16] Not only was the preparation of a woodblock less costly than that of a copperplate engraving, but printers often repeated the same cuts within the text numerous times, as in the celebrated case of the

---

[15]Skelton makes this observation in his introduction to the 1963 facsimile, p. vi.

[16]There are numerous general studies on the application of the woodcut medium to early book illustration. See, for example, Arthur M. Hind, *An Introduction to a History of the Woodcut*, 2 vols. (New York, 1963), in which the subject is treated according to region and school.

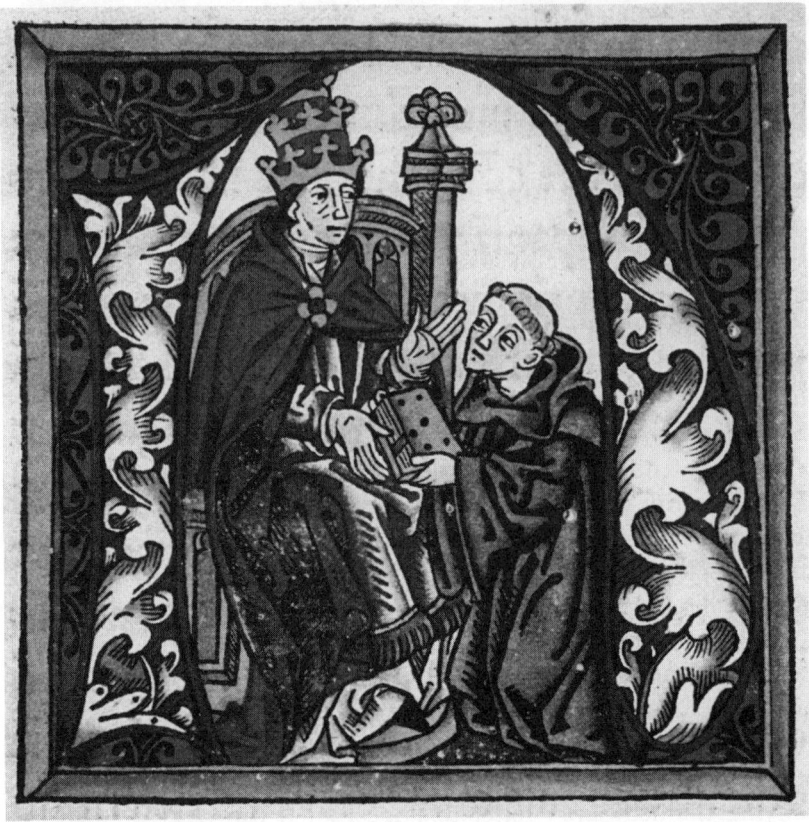

Figure 2.1. Donnus Nicolaus Germanus Presents His Book to Pope Paul II, hand-colored woodcut, from Ptolemy, *Cosmographia,* Ulm, Lienhart Holle, 1482. Courtesy of the Newberry Library, Chicago.

Nuremberg Chronicle, in which 645 blocks served as 1,809 illustrations through repetition.[17] Printers often economized as well by either acquiring or copying the blocks of other printers, or reusing blocks from their own previous publications.[18]

Holle employed none of these cost-cutting devices. Instead, he embarked on the hitherto untried endeavor of having thirty-two large

[17]Hind, *History of the Woodcut,* I, 375.

[18]Anton Koberger used all of these methods for cutting the cost of illustration. See Adrian Wilson, *The Making of the Nuremberg Chronicle* (Amsterdam, 1976). In Ulm, both Johannes Zainer and Conrad Dinckmut often reused and repeated woodcuts in their books.

BEATISSIMO PATRI PAVLO SE
CVNDO PONTIFICI MAXIMO.
DONIS NICOLAVS GERMANVS

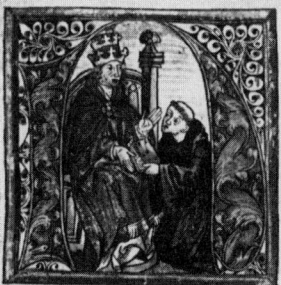

On me fugit beatiffime pater. Cuiq; fummo
ingenio exquifitaq; doctrina ptolomeus cof
mographus pinxiffe in his aliquid nouari
attemptaremus fore:ut hic nofter labor in
multorū reprehenfiones incurreret. Omnes
enim q hanc noftram picturā que his tabu
las quas ad te mittimus continetur viderit
geometrice prefertim rationis ignari.ab ea
quā ptolomeus edidit.paululum abborren
tem·certe nos·uel imperitie vel temeritatis
arguent·Nā plane nos.aut ignoraffe quid
egerimus·aut temere aufos effe·tantū opus
cōtaminare affirmabūt·cum aliq ex parte il
lud immutatū cernent·non enim fibi perfua
dere poterunt.nec fas effe exiftimabūt ut tā
tum virū quantus certe is fuit·fi quis alius
pingendi orbis terrarū melior modus ex=
titiffet·is eū fugiffet.cū is folus fuerit.q̄ tā
inter multos excelletes cofmographos q̄ an
te fe floruerūt modū videret·quo fitū terra
rum·oīm in tabulis primus pingeret·Quafi
vero aut princeps ille poetarū homerus a
pififtrato in ordine redigi.aut lucretiū dini
nū opus a cicerone emēdari.aut tolletane in
bule ab alfonfo corrigi nequiuerint· Quare
hi fane erunt q̄ nihil laudabūt nifi qd̄ fe in
telligere poffe confidāt·quenq, fperabūt ani

mo & cogitatione coplecti valere.eūde be
no pingendi orbis modū effe cenfebunt.Et
cū obryentur crebritate linearū longitudina
liū nō eq, diftantiū rarā illā & vafta ptolo=
mei picturam rectis lineis diftinctā fe malle
q̄ hanc noftrā multiplice & comodā pendē
tibus inclinatifq, lineis difcretā dicet.Neq,
vero nos hec ideo nunc dicimus vt quicq̄
ī ptolomei pictura reperiatur qd̄ corrigi vl
emēdari·aut in ordine redigi oportuerit·cū
omia ita fcienter ac prudenter vir ille pinx
erit.vt nihil qd̄ ad rationē fitus terrarū i ei
us tabulis deeffe videatur.fed vt illos fue
argueremus ignorantie qui et cū nullā taliū
terrā fcientiā.aut cognitione tineant tū inui=
dia & liuore quodā moti fi quid uiderit ab
altero editum quod ingenijs eorx impar fit
ftatim ad eius vituperatione fefe couertūt.
At fi qui erūt qui non oīno geometrie fiue
cofmographie expertes fint quiq, ipm pto
lomeū fepius legerit ac pictura deinde no
ftrā placata mente contemplauerit·hi certe
nos aliq̄ laude dignos nō reprhenfione vt
illi putabūt.Profpicient enim nos opus ita
difficile atq, arduū fufcepiffe & ita egregie
ad exitū pduxiffe vt illud mirari cogantur
pfertim cū nulla in re nos a ptolomei inten
tione licet a pictura paululū deuiciffe cōpe=
rient.Quod vt iam ita effe plane perfpicere
poffis·B·P·quefo quid ille dicat et qd̄ nos
fecerimus parūper attēde·Ptolomeus qdē
quod facile in eius intellexerim fcriptis du
plice pingēdi orbis terrarū ratione effe tra
dit. Vnā em̄ effe afferit·cū p circulis vt ei9
verbis vtar que funt in octauo circa princi
piū libro rectas lineas facimus particularibz
in tabulis meridianos ipos non inclinatos
& flexos·fed inuice eque diftantes adnota
mus.Alterā vero effe teftatur cum eius for
mā vbiq, flexis & inclinatis lineis ut ipfius
terre fitus ratio exigit & nō rectis exprimi
mus.Harū porro rationū & fi pofteriorem
magis approbat vtpote artificioforē ac fub
tiliore·fuperiorē tamē i pictura fecutus eft·

Figure 2.2. Dedicatory Letter to Pope Paul II, page of type with woodcut
illustation, Holle typeface #1, from Ptolemy, *Cosmographia,* Ulm, Lienhart
Holle, 1482. Courtesy of the Newberry Library, Chicago.

[47]

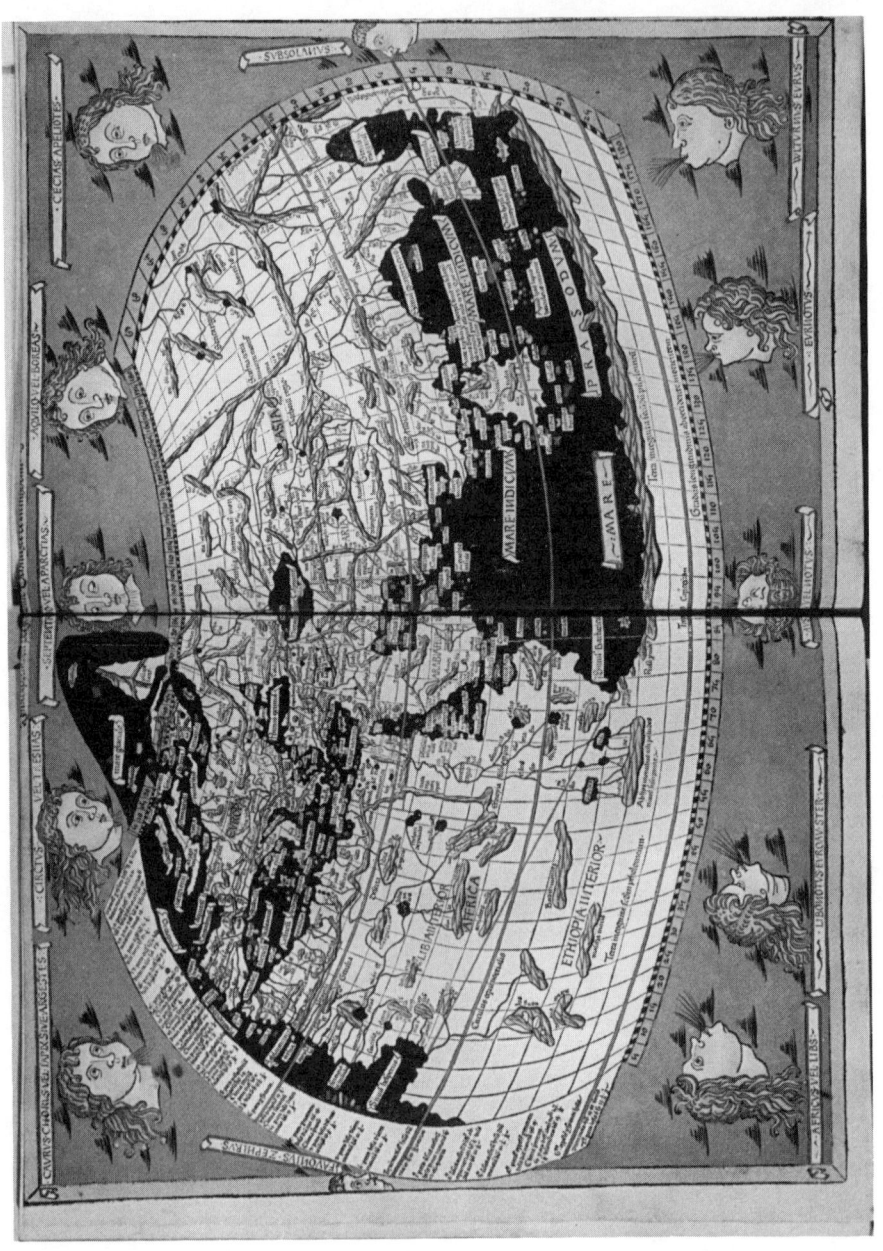

Figure 2.3. World Map, hand-colored woodcut with typeset place names, from Ptolemy, *Cosmographia*, Ulm,

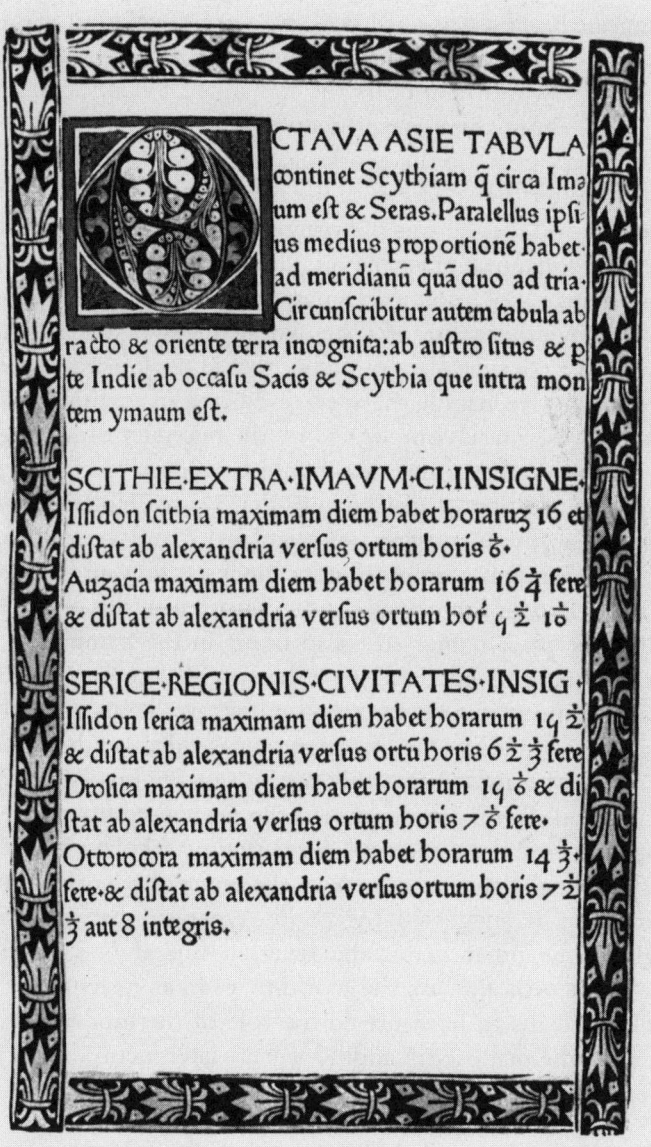

Figure 2.4. Descriptive Text for the Eighth Map of Asia, page of type with woodcut borders, Holle typeface #1, from Ptolemy, *Cosmographia*, Ulm, Lienhart Holle, 1482. Courtesy of the Newberry Library, Chicago.

maps cut from woodblocks. That this was an extraordinary project requiring the highest degree of skill and a great deal of time is implied by the unusual fact of the cutter's having signed his work; the upper margin of the world map bears the signature "Johannes Schnitzer of Armsheim." From this we can deduce several points: that Johannes was sufficiently proud of his work on the maps to sign his work; that he was the cutter (or *Schnitzer*) of the maps, as opposed to the designer or editor; and that he was not originally a native of Ulm. Whether or not this Johannes practiced in Ulm prior to his work on the Ptolemy maps is not known. His name, however, is not among those on Richard Muther's list of Ulm woodcutters of the late 1470s.[19] Thus we must consider the possibility that Holle looked outside Ulm for a cutter able to handle the specialized task of cutting these large, intricate blocks, a task complicated by the necessity of leaving spaces for the printed place names that would be added.

It is in the addition of place names that we see Holle's only major deviation from the manuscript of Nicolaus. A unique version of the world map, printed from a different block, is now preserved in the John Carter Brown Library at Brown University (fig. 2.5). On it are printed those place names that also occur in the manuscript. Additional place names, however, have been added to the woodcut by hand. This unique impression, then, indicates the hand of an editor, who sought to amplify the information provided by the manuscript model. It can be argued that this is proof of the involvement of the scribe Nicolaus in the production of the printed editions, something that has long been the subject of speculation by scholars.[20] The map is unsigned; that the cutting may nevertheless be the work of Johannes of Armsheim is suggested by an idiosyncrasy that is also found throughout the other maps: the reversed capital *N* as seen in the words "MARE INDICUM" on the world map. In any event, this unique woodblock seems to have played the role of the modern-day galley proof, since the manuscript additions were later incorporated into the final version of the world map.[21]

[19] Richard Muther, *German Book Illustration of the Gothic Period and the Early Renaissance, 1460–1530*, trans. Richard Shaw (Metuchen, N.J., 1972), p. 16. Muther's list is based on the Ulm tax books.

[20] Durand, like scholars before him, leaves open the question of Nicolaus' involvement in the printed editions. Durand, *The Vienna-Klosterneuberg Map Corpus*, p. 65.

[21] Several interpretations of the role of this unique woodcut have been made. In my opinion the most convincing argument—that it is indeed an intermediary block that served as a model for the final block—is made by Skelton, facsimile, p. vii.

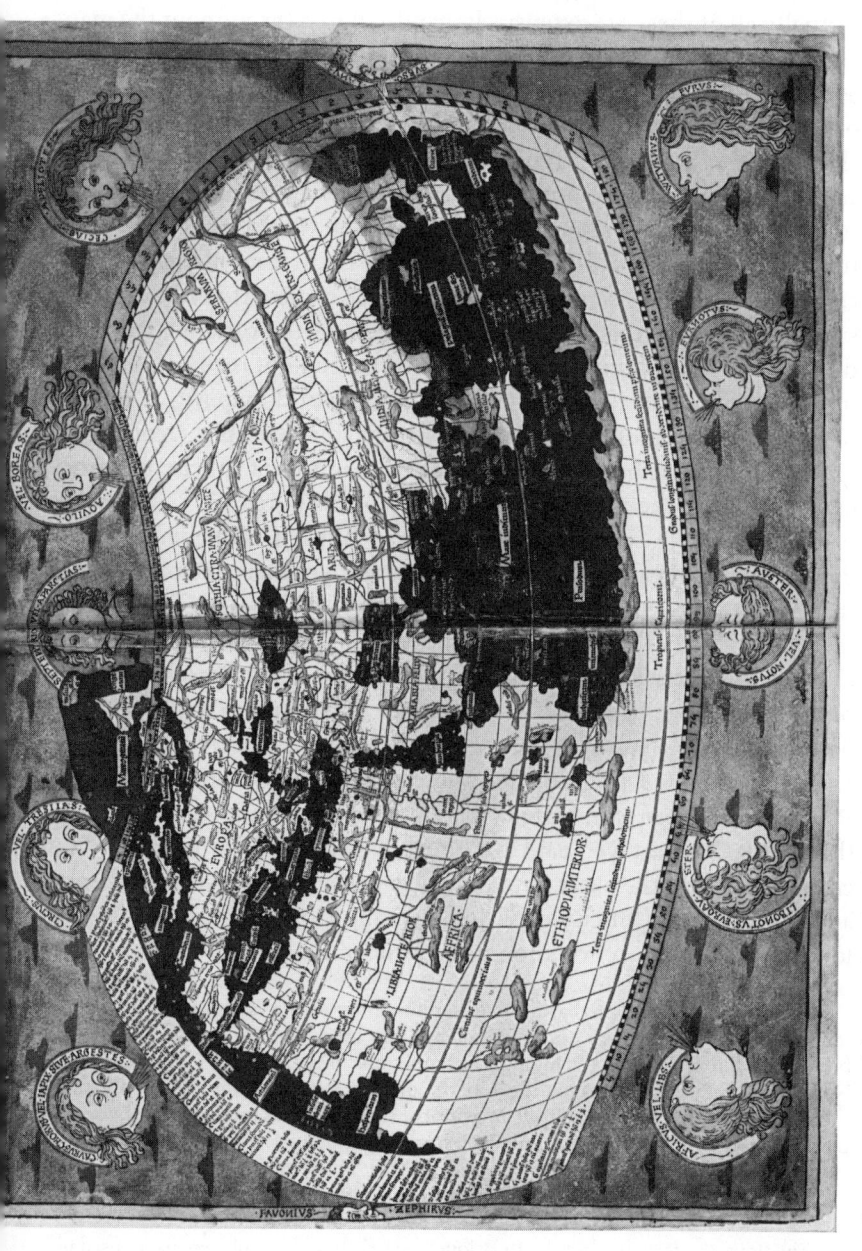

Figure 2.5. World Map, hand-colored woodcut with both manuscript and typeset place names, from Ptolemy, *Cosmographia*, Ulm, Lienhart Holle, 1482. Courtesy of the John Carter Brown Library at Brown University, Providence.

Approximately 120 copies of Holle's *Cosmographia* are still extant; virtually all of these are extensively hand-colored throughout the map and text sections.[22] Although no two copies are identical, there is a consistency in the application of pigments which suggests that parts of the edition received their coloration at one time and in the same shop, although almost certainly by a variety of hands. This in itself suggests a considerable outlay of capital. Twelve copies on vellum— no doubt intended as special presentation copies—also survive. These too are hand-colored but with a different decorative intention, and certainly not by the same hand as the paper copies. It is not entirely surprising to find that the printed character of the ornamentation is disguised in the vellum copies by the overpainting of the lines, as seen in a detail of one of the windheads from the world map (fig. 2.6). By having these copies "illuminated" rather than simply "colored," Holle brought the book even closer to its manuscript source, to some extent denying the actual printed nature of his book.

Lienhart Holle seems to have plunged himself immediately into debt in obtaining materials for the Ptolemy, yet there is no evidence that he tried to economize in that area either. His choice of paper for the edition is the best-documented instance of his business transactions of this sort. Through the book merchant Hans Harscher, Holle bought his paper from the city of Milan in late spring 1482. This is documented by a warning letter from the duke of Milan to the city of Ulm.[23] It is dated July 19, just three days after the printing of the Ptolemy had been completed. The letter informs the town council that Holle has not yet paid for the "Regalpapier" he used for his edition. Because the exact amount of his debt is not mentioned there, and because the Ulm city debt books dating from before 1486 are no longer extant, we do not know the extent of Holle's debt. It is none-

[22]To my knowledge there has been no serious study of the variant hand-colorings found in the 120 known copies of the Ptolemy. My own examination of copies at the New York Public Library (including a vellum copy in the Spencer Collection), the Newberry Library in Chicago, the Library of Congress, and the British Library suggests that their coloration is often quite consistent. For example, the Newberry Library has two virtually identical copies, clearly carefully planned by the same individual. Nonetheless, variations do exist; in the Thatcher Collection copy in the Library of Congress, the large areas of water on the maps are entirely painted in brown rather than the usual blue.

[23]The flower watermark, similar to Briquet 6560, is found in Milanese paper used in Reutlingen in the 1470s. The letter from the duke of Milan to the city of Ulm is cited by Amelung, *Der Frühdruck im deutschen Südwesten*, p. 264.

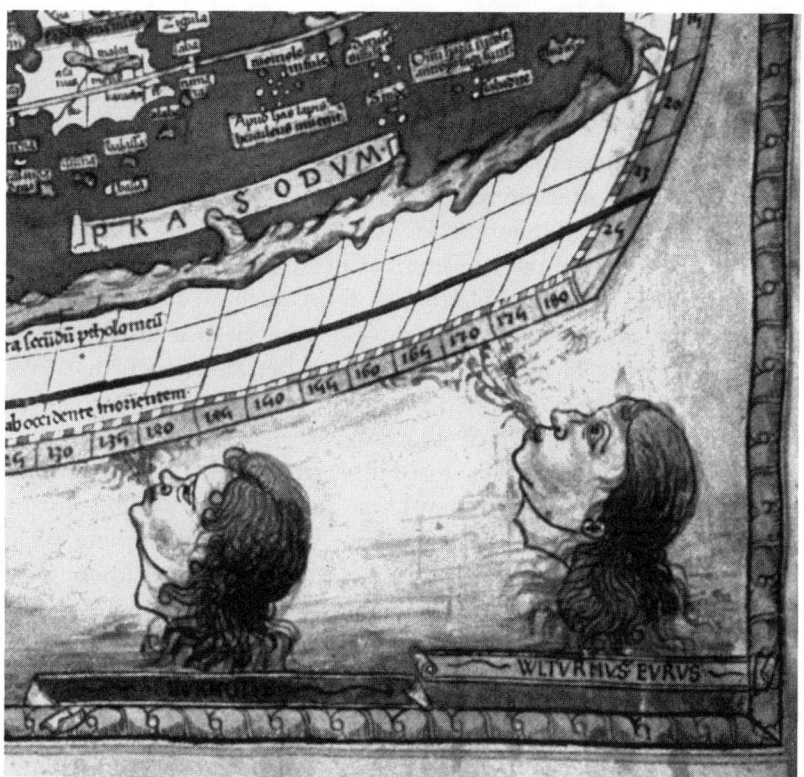

Figure 2.6. Windheads, detail from the World Map, hand-painted woodcut on vellum, from Ptolemy, *Cosmographia,* Ulm, Lienhart Holle, 1482. Spencer Collection, the New York Public Library, Astor, Lenox, and Tilden Foundations. Photo: Robert D. Rubic, New York.

theless possible to gain some idea of what kind of expenditure was entailed. From the account book of the printer Peter Drach of Speyer, we find that a bale—or about five thousand sheets—of this type of paper cost fifteen Rhenish guilders. This is the rough equivalent of the price of five bound, uncolored copies of the *Nuremberg Chronicle* or, according to Max Josef Neudegger's calculations of annual salaries, about half of the average per annum income for a printer.[24] At

[24]The famous account book of Peter Drach, first published by Ferdinand Geldner in 1962, is excerpted and translated into useful tables by Wilson, *The Making of the Nuremberg Chronicle,* p. 239. Wilson also reproduces Neudegger's salary calculations (p. 241). These can be found in their entirety in Max Josef Neudegger, *Die Hof-und StaatsPersonalitäts der Wittelsbacher in Bayern,* vol. 1 (Munich, 1889).

133 leaves per volume, Holle's edition of the Ptolemy, then, represented a major financial risk. That he was forced to purchase expensive materials on credit implies that Holle had little capital of his own and that he did not have a financial backer to advance him the necessary funds. Furthermore, there is evidence of Holle's increasing indebtedness, even after the publication of the Ptolemy. One individual who lent money to Holle was Jodocus Wind, an Ulm monk whose correspondence from the late summer of 1482 contains several references to Holle's debts. One letter mentions a debt of at least fourteen guilders, which, as we can see, is very near the price of a bale of Milanese paper.[25] That Holle was unable to repay his debts in cash is also implied by the correspondence of Wind, who sent a breviary to be bound by Holle in lieu of a cash debt.

There is little doubt, then, that Holle sank himself deep into debt during the production stages of his first book. We must assume by his publication of a fairly large edition (one could speculate about three hundred copies) that Holle believed he could recoup his losses with the sale of the books. The selling price of his book was no doubt high, reflecting the high cost of its production. This has been the usual interpretation of his failure. Yet Holle's inability to succeed with the Ptolemy edition is a more complex issue, and is based as well on the lack of a ready market for the kind of book he had produced.

On the most basic level, the lack of a market is borne out by Holle's own inventory. After his bankruptcy, much of Holle's stock was acquired by the Ulm printer Johannes Reger, who served as German agent for Justus de Albano of Venice. In addition to the Ptolemy blocks and type, Reger took possession of a number of unbound printed copies of the Ptolemy which remained unsold in Holle's inventory. Reger eventually reissued these copies with a supplement of his own.[26] Whatever the size of Holle's 1482 edition, it appears that the edition was too large for his market.

From a broader standpoint, it is important to recognize that an interest in cartography was, in this period, by no means widespread. Dana Bennett Durand's study of the Vienna-Klosterneuburg map corpus has shown that the study of geography and the related disciplines of astronomy and cartography were practiced in only a few

[25]Amelung, *Der Frühdruck im deutschen Südwesten*, pp. 264–65.
[26]On Johann Reger, see Amelung, *Der Frühdruck im deutschen Südwesten*, pp. 305–62.

northern universities—primarily Erfurt, Prague, and Vienna, and to a lesser extent also in Kracow, Leipzig, and Heidelberg—and in a select number of Benedictine houses such as Reichenbach and Tegernsee.[27] He concludes that the chief impetus in both the production and the study of maps in this period came from the clergy rather than from the laity, with the exception of small circles of humanist scholars.[28] One assumes that Holle would have succeeded in selling a number of copies of the Ptolemy to Benedictine monastic libraries in southwestern Germany, and indeed original bindings on several copies bear this out.

Yet Holle was not well situated to capitalize on this small demand for maps. Durand has shown that by the 1440s Nuremberg had become renowned as the "emporium" for scientific books and instruments.[29] By the second half of the fifteenth century, for example, that city already had a guild for compassmakers. Attracted by this reputation, the astronomer and mathematician Johannes Regiomontanus left the court of Budapest to settle in Nuremberg in the 1470s. Individuals wishing to acquire globes, measuring tools, or Hellenistic and Arabic scientific treatises knew that they might be found in Nuremberg. That such manuscripts could be acquired there for reasonable prices is also known; Durand cites the instance of Cardinal Nicolas of Cusa, who was for a time at the monastery of Tegernsee, and who attended the Diet of Nuremberg in 1444.[30] On that occasion he acquired for the total price of thirty-eight Rhenish florins an astrolabe, a large celestial globe, a torquetum, and no fewer than seventeen manuscripts dealing chiefly with science. Durand suggests that Cusanus felt he had made a great bargain. Certainly Holle's book would have been too expensive for many scholars; in addition, there is no evidence that he marketed his books in Nuremberg.

Ptolemy's *Cosmographia* was surely known in German humanistic circles before Holle's first printed edition, since manuscript copies were widely circulated in Italy after midcentury and presumably passed quickly to northern Europe.[31] It seems likely that the scribal tradition that allowed copies to circulate from one monastic or univer-

[27]Durand, *The Vienna-Klosterneuberg Map Corpus*, p. 65.
[28]Ibid., p. 90.
[29]Ibid., p. 88.
[30]Ibid., p. 88.
[31]The circulation of manuscript copies is discussed by Skelton, facsimile, pp. v–vii.

sity center to another was sufficient in the 1480s to satisfy the modest existing clientele. Holle's big, expensive book—while certainly an attractive novelty—did not satisfy the existing scholarly or scientific need for modern cartographic information and therefore found no ready market. It is interesting to note that the Rome Ptolemy, printed in 1478, also proved to be a financial failure for its publisher, thereby suggesting that even the larger humanistic circles of Italy could not support such an endeavor. Indeed, by the 1480s Ptolemy's work was outdated as a scientific tool and would probably have found its primary appeal among aristocratic collectors of deluxe books.

Holle's one documented success in selling the book turns out to have been a financial disaster, and demonstrates the lack of business sense that eventually drove his press to bankruptcy. The account book of Peter Drach of Speyer indicates that Drach ordered one hundred unbound copies of the Ptolemy from Holle. Amelung's careful reading of the account book has shown that Holle received no cash from this business transaction. Instead, Drach proposed to pay Holle only in kind, by printing for him at the Drach shop with paper supplied by Holle. The only cash to change hands went from Drach to Hans Harscher, presumably to settle the original paper debt with the city of Milan. Thus a large portion of the edition left Holle's shop without bringing in any revenue at all.

Holle's second ambitious publication is usually explained, like the Ptolemy, as an example of Holle's characteristic preference for heavily woodcut-illustrated texts. Yet it can be argued that the *Buch der Weisheit der alten Weisen* instead represents a very deliberate shift of strategy on the part of Holle. We have seen the difficulties he experienced in marketing a Latin scientific text which would at best have been of interest to only a wealthy, elite readership. It can be no coincidence that for his next book Holle selected a vernacular text clearly intended for a more popular audience, a text that, furthermore, had already appeared locally in a printed edition.

The *Buch der Weisheit der alten Weisen* is a German translation of John of Capua's *Directorium humanae vitae*.[32] This text, as the Latin title implies, was perceived as a type of mirror for princes. The fables, holding practical guidelines for moral conduct, are enacted—like

[32]For Holle's edition of the *Buch der Weisheit,* see Goff J-270; Hain 4029 (May 28, 1483), 4030 (July 24, 1483), and 4031 (June 2, 1484); Schramm VII, 14; *BMC* II, 538.

Aesop's fables—primarily by animals, with some exceptions, such as the tales of sexual morality centered on the actions of human beings. The *Directorium* is based on the collection of fables known as the *Kalilah wa Dimna* by Bidpai, an ancient Brahman philosopher of Kashmir. Transported from the East to the Arab world and from there to Spain, the fables had been known in the West since the thirteenth century and were ultimately translated into thirty-eight languages.[33] The German translation was made in 1470. Throughout this migration the *Kalilah wa Dimna* of Bidpai had retained its original nature as an illustrated text, in which the pictures were considered essential for the communication of its meaning. In electing to publish the *Buch der Weisheit*, Holle selected a text that virtually demanded illustration.

Holle issued his first printing of the Bidpai fables in May 1483. His edition postdated by about two years the first printed German edition, published by Conrad Fyner in nearby Urach with 127 woodcut illustrations.[34] One assumes that some of the appeal for Holle of the *Buch der Weisheit* was that, to use a modern term, its "marketability" had already been tested. A precedent had also been established by the popular woodcut-illustrated editions of Aesop, published by Johannes Zainer in Ulm in 1476 and reissued by Günther Zainer in Augsburg the following year. Yet Holle, perhaps fired by the ambition to better the Urach edition, did not capitalize, as the Zainers and so many other printers had done, on the preexistence of a woodcut program for his text. Rather than hire a cutter simply to copy the Urach illustrations, thereby eliminating the need for an artist to design new compositions, Holle embarked on a lavish and no doubt expensive decorative program which in no way echoes that of the Urach edition. For example, a comparison of corresponding illustrations from the

[33]The best study I have found on the literary migration of Bidpai's fables is Thomas Ballantine Irving, *Kalilah and Dimna: An English Version of Bidpai's Fables Based upon Ancient Arabic and Spanish Manuscripts* (Newark, N.J., 1980). Also, the integral role of illustrations in the various versions is discussed in Joseph Jacobs, *The Earliest English Version of the Fables of Bidpai* (London, 1888). An excellent recent study is Jill Sanchia Cowen, *Kalila Wa Dimna: An Animal Allegory of the Mongol Court. The Istanbul University Album* (Oxford, 1989).

[34]For Conrad Fyner's Urach edition of the *Buch der Weisheit*, see Goff J-269. Amelung devotes considerable attention to Zainer's Ulm Aesop in *Der Frühdruck im deutschen Südwesten*, pp. 93–102. See also the English translation of his chapter of the Zainer firm in Peter Amelung, *Johannes Zainer the Elder and Younger*, trans. Ruth Schwab-Rosenthal (Los Angeles, 1985).

Das·ij·Capitel·

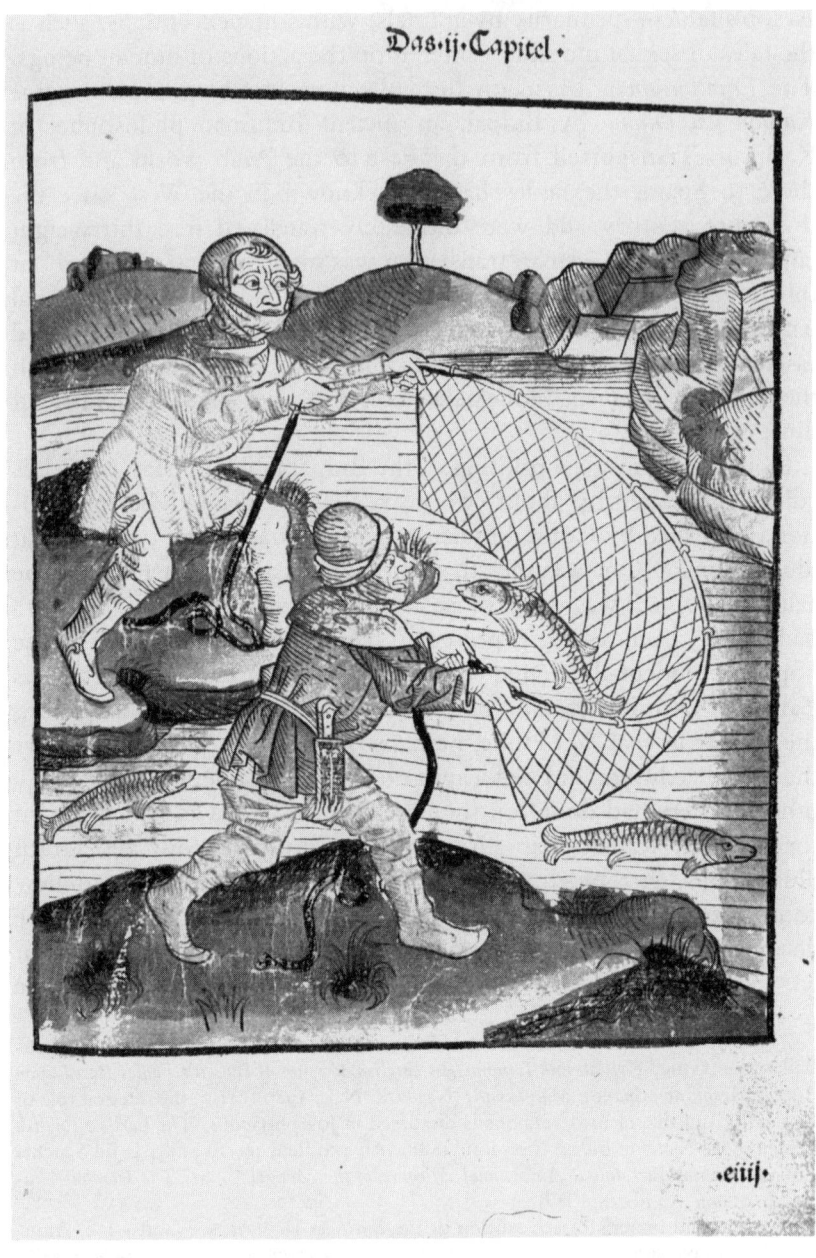

·eiiij·

Figure 2.7. The Fishermen Did Not Value Him and Threw Him Away, hand-colored woodcut, from Bidpai, *Buch der Weisheit der alten Weisen,* Ulm, Lienhart Holle, 1483. Courtesy of the Newberry Library, Chicago.

[58]

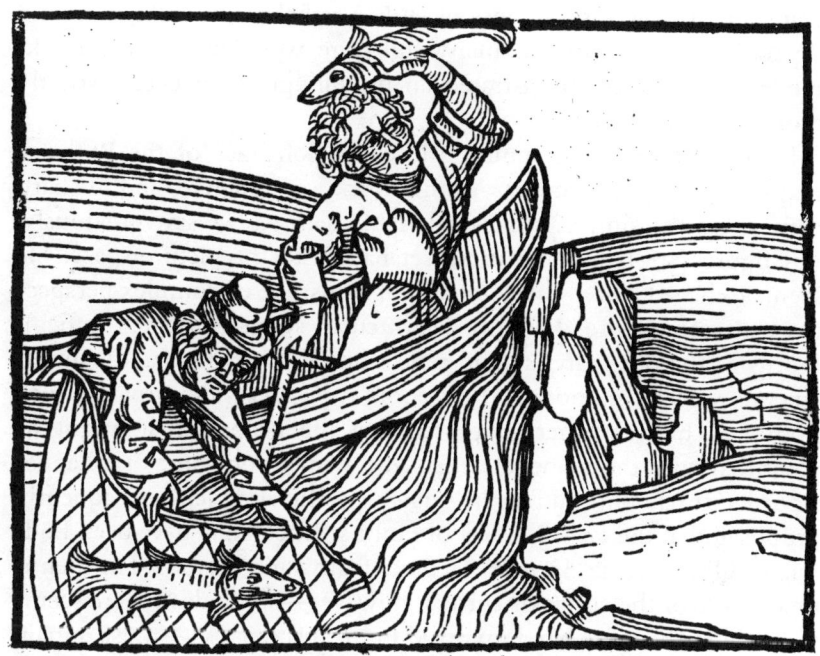

Figure 2.8. The Fishermen Did Not Value Him and Threw Him Away, woodcut, from Bidpai, *Buch der Weisheit der alten Weisen,* Urach, Conrad Fyner, 1482, PML 21785. Courtesy of the Pierpont Morgan Library, New York.

two editions demonstrates that, while clearly depicting the same fable, they are certainly independent artistic conceptions (figs. 2.7 and 2.8). Both the Urach *Buch der Weisheit* and the Aesop editions had employed small half-page illustrations which appeared embedded in the text. In contrast, Holle illustrated his book with 132 woodcuts, each occupying a full page.

There is some evidence that Holle did try to lower his production costs in this, his second endeavor. For example, the book is quarto rather than folio size, and he printed it on paper of local German manufacture, probably from Augsburg.[35] In addition, unlike the Ptolemy edition, most of the surviving copies of the *Buch der Weisheit* are not colored, the Newberry Library's impressive colored copy

[35]The paper bears the "deux clefs" watermark, similar to Briquet 3888, a rare watermark appearing principally in works issued by Günther Zainer and Johannes Baemler in Augsburg.

being one of the rare exceptions.[36] Nevertheless, in using a second typeface (fig. 2.9) and so many full-page woodcuts for the book, Holle once again demonstrated an unwillingness to take a strictly economical approach.

Holle's Bidpai artist, unlike the cutter Johannes of the Ptolemy maps, remains anonymous. Yet his work is distinctive, and in sharp contrast to the simple, small-scale fable pictures we saw previously. His figures are large, and often set back into the picture space. He seems to have favored the depiction of landscape or complex perspectives in architecture. He also delighted in suggesting such difficult motifs as the transparency and reflection of water (fig. 2.10), simultaneous view of indoors and outdoors (fig. 2.11), and ornately tiled floors. Richard Muther suggested that the Bidpai artist might be identified with the woodcut artist who worked on some of Johannes Baemler's early publications in Augsburg. Richard Field subsequently proposed that the *Formschneider* of Holle's Bidpai may have been Ludwig of Ulm, whose *Ars moriendi* dates from 1468–1470.[37] The identity and role of the cutter or cutters, however—and indeed there seems to be more than one hand involved in this production—must remain conjectural until the role of the model and its designer are also assessed. That model may well be manuscript 1389 in the Musée Condé, Chantilly, which was decorated about 1480 for Eberhard, duke of Württemberg. Unfortunately, at the time of this writing I have not yet been able to examine the manuscript.[38]

Certainly, as Muther recognized, there are large full-page woodcuts to be found in Augsburg books which share many stylistic characteristics with Holle's Bidpai cuts. Illustrations from Baemler's 1476 edition of the *Chronik von allen Kaisern und Konigen* display similarities with the Holle woodcuts in scale, handling of figures and architecture, and even details such as drapery folds. The cuts from Anton Sorg's *Seelentrost* of 1478 provide another example of this monumental style of Augsburg book illustration. The implication is that if

[36]The two other copies in the United States—in the Pierpont Morgan Library, New York, and the Rosenwald Collection, Library of Congress, Washington, D.C.—have also been examined for this study.

[37]Richard Field, *The Fable of the Sick Lion: A Fifteenth-Century Blockbook* (Middletown, Conn., 1974), p. 92 n. 1, p. 109.

[38]I am grateful to Eberhard König of the Free University, Berlin, for first bringing this manuscript to my attention. A page from the manuscript is illustrated in Christopher de Hamel, *A History of Illuminated Manuscripts* (Oxford, 1986), p. 157.

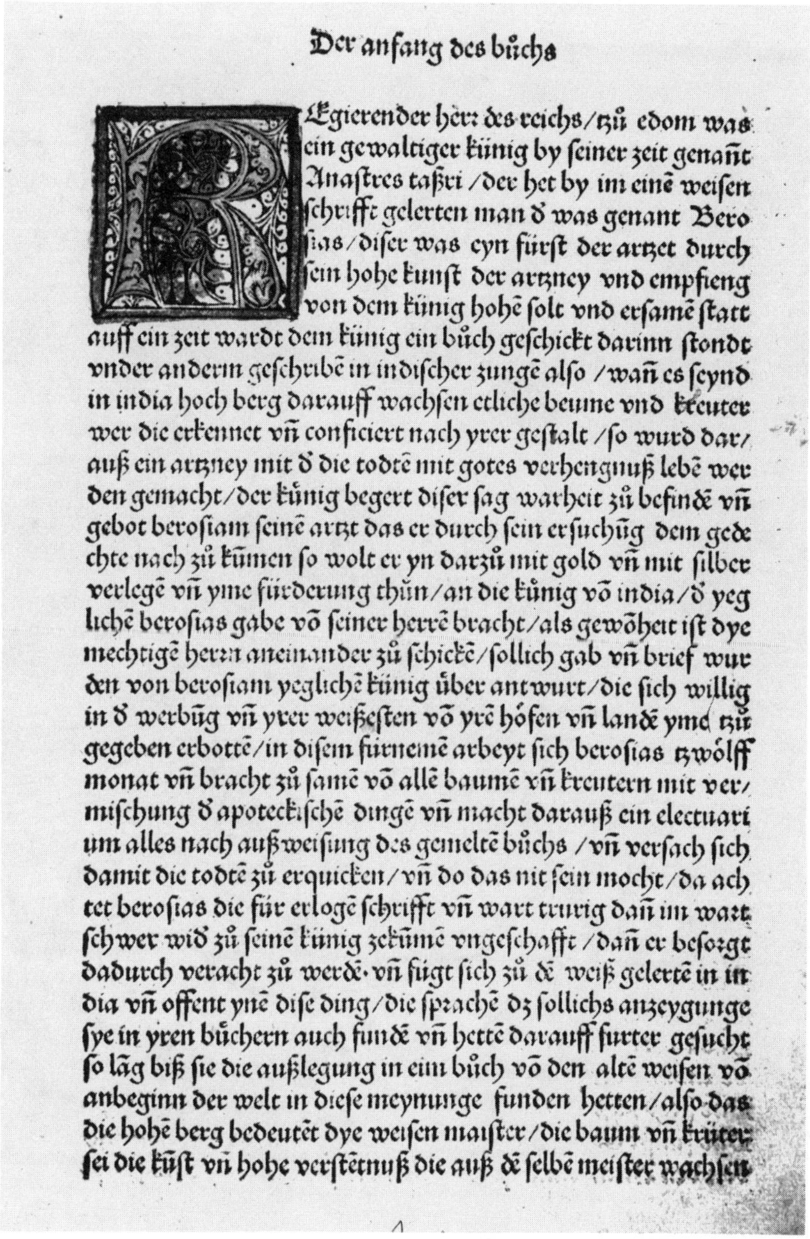

Der anfang des buchs

Egierender herr: des reichs/zů edom was ein gewaltiger künig by seiner zeit genant Anastres tasfri /der het by im eine weisen schrifft gelerten man d was genant Berosias /diser was eyn fürst der artzet durch sein hohe kunst der artzney vnd empfieng von dem künig hohe sold vnd ersame statt auff ein zeit wardt dem künig ein bůch geschickt darinn stondt vnder anderm geschribe in indischer zunge also /wann es seynd in india hoch berg darauff wachsen etliche beume vnd kreuter wer die erkennet vn conficiert nach yrer gestalt /so wurd dar/ auß ein artzney mit d die todte mit gotes verhengnuß lebe wer den gemacht/der künig begert diser sag warheit zů befinde vn gebot berosiam seine artzt das er durch sein ersuchüg dem gede chte nach zů kümen so wolt er yn darzů mit gold vn mit silber verlege vn yme fürderung thün/an die künig vo india/d yeg liche berosias gabe vo seiner herre bracht/als gewöheit ist dye mechtige herrn aneinander zů schicke/sollich gab vn brief wur den von berosiam yegliche künig über antwurt/die sich willig in d werbüg vn yrer weißesten vo yre höfen vn lande yme zů gegeben erbotte/in disem fürneme arbeyt sich berosias zwölff monat vn bracht zů same vo alle baume vn kreutern mit ver/ mischung d apoteckische dinge vn macht darauß ein electuari um alles nach außweisüng des gemelte büchs /vn versach sich damit die todte zů erquicken/vn do das nit sein mocht/da ach tet berosias die für erloge schrifft vn wart traurig dan im wart schwer wid zů seine künig zeküme vngeschafft /dan er besorgt dadurch veracht zů werde· vn fügt sich zů de weiß gelerte in in dia vn offent yme dise ding/die sprache ds sollichs anzeygunge sye in yren büchern auch funde vn hette darauff furter gesucht so lag biß sie die außlegung in ein bůch vo den alte weisen vo anbeginn der welt in diese meynunge funden hetten/also das die hohe berg bedeutet dye weisen maister/die baum vn kruter sei die küst vn hohe verstetnuß die auß de selbe meister wachsen

Figure 2.9. Preface, page of type with woodcut initial, Holle typeface #2, from Bidpai, *Buch der Weisheit der alten Weisen,* Ulm, Lienhart Holle, 1483. Courtesy of the Newberry Library, Chicago.

[61]

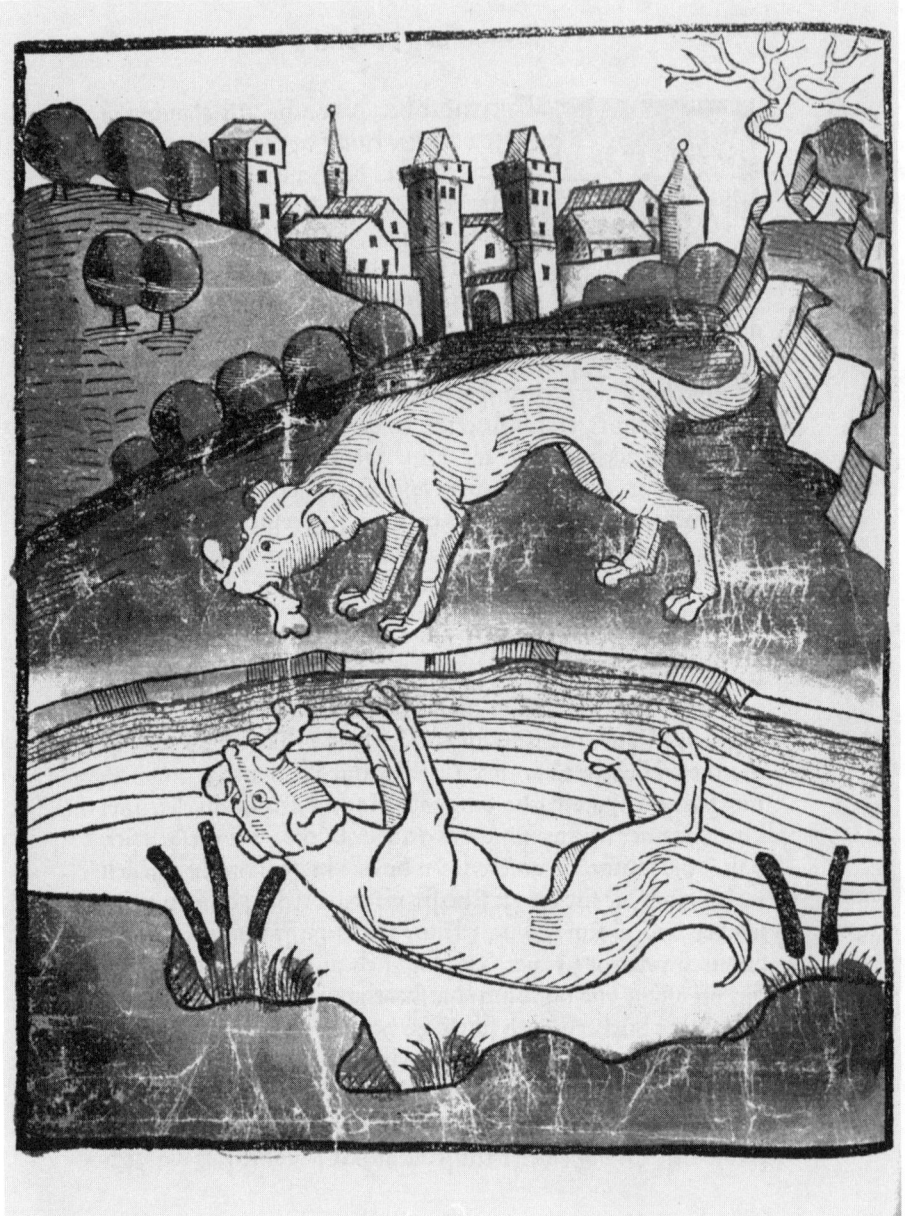

Figure 2.10. The Dog Carrying a Piece of Meat Sees His Reflection, hand-colored woodcut, from Bidpai, *Buch der Weisheit der alten Weisen,* Ulm, Lienhart Holle, 1483. Courtesy of the Newberry Library, Chicago.

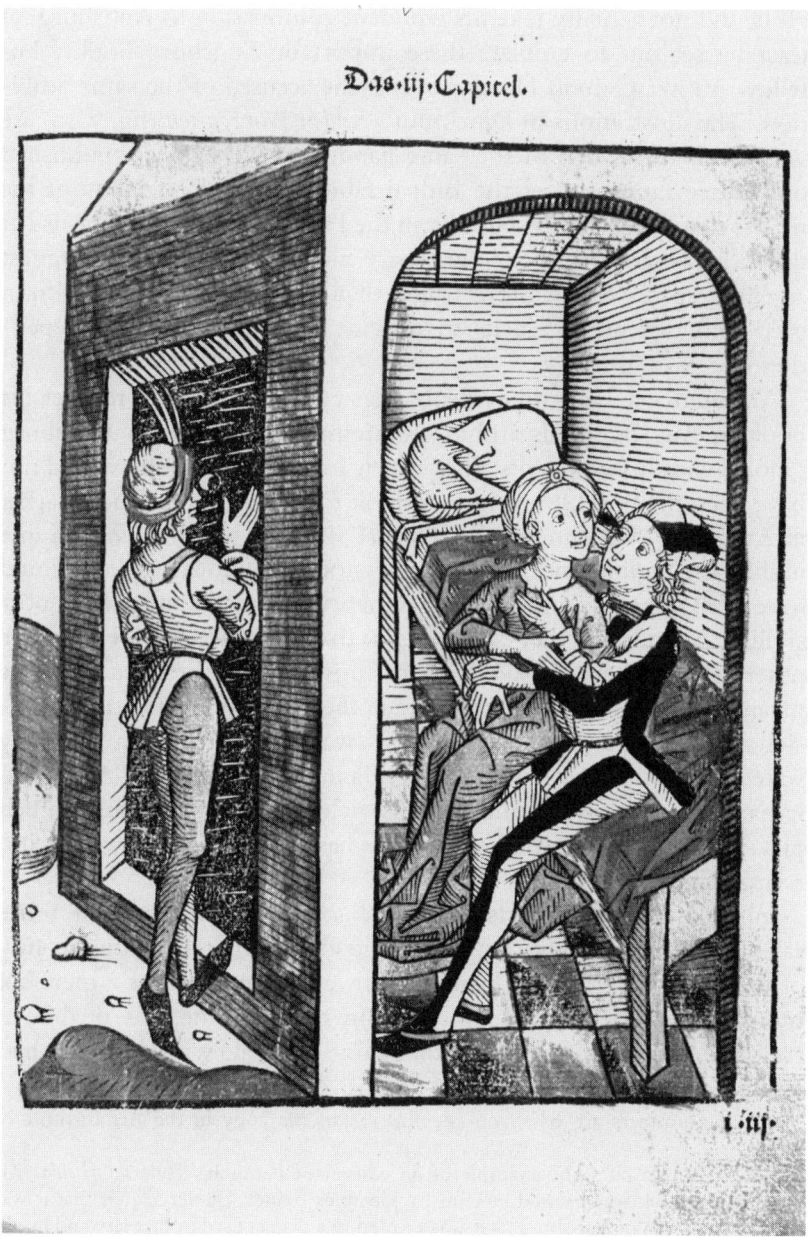

Das·iij·Capitel.

i·iiij·

Figure 2.11. The Woman Submits to Her Husband's Servant, hand–colored woodcut, from Bidpai, *Buch der Weisheit der alten Weisen,* Ulm, Lienhart Holle, 1483. Courtesy of the Newberry Library, Chicago.

Holle did not actually take his woodcut commission to Augsburg, at least he set out to emulate these important Augsburg books. His fellow printer Conrad Dinckmut may be accused of the same ambition. The illustrations in Dinckmut's *Seelen Wurzgarten* (fig. 2.12) are very likely the work of the same hand, and were in fact published only three months after the Bidpai fables. They share many of the motifs that have become familiar in the Holle book, such as the use of the archway to frame the picture space and of ceiling beams to suggest receding space. Much more frugal than Holle, however, Dinckmut used only seventeen blocks to provide 134 illustrations by repetition.[39]

Although we have no evidence that Holle intended to market his book in Augsburg, his ambitious attempt to produce an Augsburg "look" with his woodcuts allows such a conjecture. Holle would not have been the first Ulm printer to look for a larger and richer market in Augsburg.[40] Although the *Buch der Weisheit,* which is written in a highly intelligible and widely understood Danubian dialect, could have been appreciated by a wide audience, we may consider the possibility that in his aesthetic planning of this illustrated book Holle, like other Ulm printers, looked toward Augsburg and the greater private means that stimulated the book trade there.[41] The contrasting financial situation between the two cities was summarized, in the early sixteenth century, by Willibald Pirckheimer, who wrote: "Augsburg in particular has grown unbelievably rich. . . . Ulm has not so much private wealth as Augsburg, though it has a greater public wealth and a larger territory."[42]

Initial evidence suggests that the *Buch der Weisheit* was far more salable than the Ptolemy, since Holle issued a second printing in July of the same year. Holle's business, however, survived for a mere six months after this edition, and during that time he was unable to continue to produce works on the ambitious scale with which he had

[39]These numbers are based on examination of the copy in the Art Institute of Chicago.

[40]Curt Bühler cites the example of an edition of Petrarch's *Patient Griselda.* Although the book was printed in Ulm by Johannes Zainer, Bühler argues that it was intended for sale in Augsburg as it was printed in a dialect used in that city and not in Ulm. Curt F. Bühler, *The Fifteenth-Century Book* (Philadelphia, 1960), p. 59.

[41]I am grateful to Udo Strutynski, formerly of the German Department, Northwestern University, for this linguistic identification of the German text.

[42]Willibald Pirckheimer, quoted in Brady, *Turning Swiss,* p. 19.

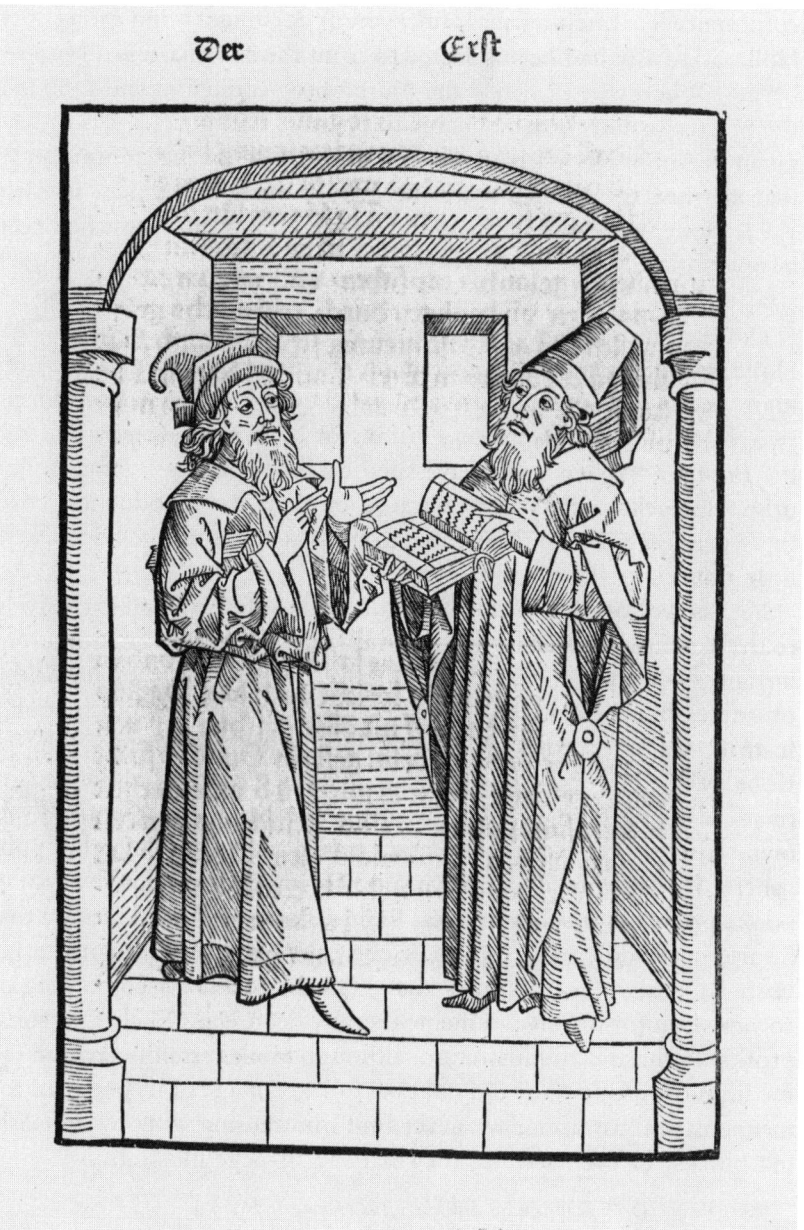

Figure 2.12. Dispute between a Jewish and a Christian Scholar, woodcut, from *Seelen Wurzgarten*, Ulm, Conrad Dinckmut, 1483. Gift of Mrs. Potter Palmer. Copyright ©1989 The Art Institute of Chicago. All rights reserved.

commenced. Amelung has uncovered documents indicating that Holle originally had been selected to print the city charter of Nuremberg.[43] When word reached the Nuremberg council in late 1483 that the printer would soon be unable to operate, the contract was instead given to Anton Koberger in Nuremberg. No doubt the circumstances that alarmed the council were the unpaid debts for which, in early 1484, Holle was banished from the city of Ulm.[44] His press had been in operation for less than two years.

Despite the brevity of his career, there can be little doubt that Holle's productions had an impact on his contemporaries and that the high quality of his editions was admired even in his own day. Within two years of his bankruptcy, editions of both the *Cosmographia* and the *Buch der Weisheit* had been issued by other printers using Holle's original blocks and type.[45] Because of their low production costs these printers were no doubt able to make a profit on the books with little financial risk to themselves.

Yet, as we have seen, Holle's failure cannot be ascribed exclusively to the expense he lavished on his productions, for there are numerous instances—such as the example of Koberger's *Nuremberg Chronicle*—of successful German publishers who produced ambitious books. Instead, we must consider a number of additional factors. Unlike Koberger in Nuremberg, or Johannes Zainer in Ulm, Holle had no financial backing to support his projects: the risk was entirely his own. Also, unlike Koberger, Peter Drach, and numerous other publishers, Holle seems not to have supplemented his income by selling books produced at other presses. Rather, there is some indication that he used a middleman, the bookseller Hans Harscher, to make his business deals. One assumes that Harscher received some sort of commission for his involvement, thereby decreasing Holle's personal profits. In the area of illustration, although Holle certainly favored the medium of woodcut, he did not take full advantage of its potential for inexpensive illustration; we never find him reusing or copying existing blocks, or even settling for smaller half-page illustrations.

[43]Amelung, *Der Frühdruck im deutschen Südwesten*, p. 267.

[44]The circumstances surrounding Holle's last two imprints remain puzzling. Both the third printing of the *Buch der Weisheit* (June 2, 1484) and the Golden Bull of Emperor Charles IV (September 6, 1484) were issued after Holle's bankruptcy and banishment had become official.

[45]Johannes Reger reissued the *Cosmographia* (Goff P-1085) in 1486; Conrad Dinckmut published the *Buch der Weisheit* (Goff J-271) using Holle's stock in 1485.

Finally, as we have seen, there is reason to believe that Holle's first book, the *Cosmographia* of Ptolemy, could not have succeeded on the local market, and that indeed there was no certain, preestablished market anywhere for such a printed book. His second book, the *Buch der Weisheit*, may be taken as Holle's recognition of this problem and as his attempt to enter into the more established area of popular literature. Yet his aesthetic ambitions placed even this book outside the range of inexpensive popular books. That Holle's productions were not typical of Ulm publishing also suggests a reason for his inability to survive there, and perhaps a lack of understanding of or interest in the essential characteristics of the Ulm book market.

This observation is confirmed by a closer look at the productions of Holle's fellow printers in Ulm at this time. The first clear distinction between him and the four other Ulm printers in operation before 1500 is in quantity and rate of production. Each of these printers produced more books per year than Holle; the two most successful, Johannes Zainer and Johannes Schäffler, produced eight and four books per year, respectively. We must also look at the subject matter of their publications: for both Zainer and Dinckmut, about two-thirds of their output was made up of theological texts, especially by Dominican authors, and books for religious use. These found a ready market in local monasteries and church schools. Johannes Schäffler, the only Ulm printer who never experienced serious financial difficulties, frequently published broadsides, which were apparently the economic mainstay of his operation.[46] Johannes Reger, too, produced nearly half of his output in this medium.[47] For the city of Ulm, with its extensive territorial holdings and dispersed population, the broadside would have filled a necessary practical function.

Thus it seems that Holle's ultimate mistake was to produce deluxe books intended for private, secular consumption in a town where public wealth and the clergy supported the printing trade. From his example we see that, evn in the early book trade, a crucial element of successful business practice was to supply a cost-efficient product to a well-established and tested market.

[46]This observation is made by Rosenthal, *Papers of the Bibliographical Society,* p. 224.
[47]Ibid., p. 226. Rosenthal provides a useful chart of Ulm productions, which shows half of Reger's output to have been broadsides.

[3]

The Career of Guy Marchant (1483–1504):
High Culture and Low Culture in Paris

Sandra Hindman

In the literature on the history of early printing, accounts of the career of Guy Marchant invariably present him as a successful printer of popular illustrated books.[1] Such accounts take as primary evidence the publication by Marchant of two illustrated works, both written in the vernacular, the *Danse macabre,* or the *Dance of Death,* and the *Compost et calendrier des bergers,* or the *Shepherds' Calendar.* These two works were published in multiple editions between 1486 and 1500, the *Dance* at least seven times and the *Calendar* at least six times (see appendix).[2] The *Dance of Death* is thought to reproduce murals of the same subject (with accompanying verses) painted on the walls of the Cemetery of the Innocents in Paris. The *Shepherd's Calendar* is a compendium of practical lore and spiritual knowledge, such as the signs of the zodiac, the labors of the month, the Credo, the Ten Commandments, the Seven Requests of the Damned, and so on. Both works were also published in versions with female instead of male protagonists, that is, the *Dance of Death for Women* and the *Shepherdesses' Calendar.*

[1]There has been no systematic study of Marchant's career, which is briefly discussed in the following: Anatole Claudin, *Histoire de l'imprimerie en France au XVe et au XVIe siècle,* 4 vols. (Paris, 1900–1914; reprinted, 1971), I, 335–406; Philippe Renouard, *Imprimeurs parisiens, libraires, fondeurs de caractères et correcteurs d'imprimerie, depuis l'introduction de l'imprimerie à Paris (1470) jusqu'à la fin du XVIe siècle* (Paris, 1898; reprinted, 1965), pp. 256–58; and *BMC* VIII, 55–70.

[2]Comparisons with illustrations of successive editions of these two works are found in Claudin, *Histoire de l'imprimerie,* I, 335–96. The editions are also recorded and described in Jacques-Charles Brunet, *Manuel du libraire et de l'amateur de livres* (Paris, 1863), II, cols. 490–93; II, cols. 202–7.

Largely because of these two works (or, actually, four), which are assumed to have reached a large audience, Marchant is credited with having made a new market for "popular printing" in Paris, when previously printers in Lyons had specialized in works of this nature, while printers in Paris concentrated on "scholarly printing" in the service of the court and of the university.[3] Marchant is even seen as a forerunner of the printers of the ancien régime who marketed the so-called *bibliothèque bleue,* the term used for certain books of general appeal that were distributed widely, often in the countryside by traveling salesmen.[4] He is also credited with having transformed the character of the early illustrated book in France, since the *Dance of Death* and the *Shepherds' Calendar* are generously illustrated on nearly every page with striking woodcuts. The implication of this version of his career is that Marchant's financial success was directly related to the success met by these editions. This version of the career of Guy Marchant is, at the very least, distorted.

Both the selection and the interpretation of the evidence are faulty in these accounts. In the course of his career Marchant published approximately 150 editions, among which the *Dance of Death* and the *Shepherds' Calendar* constitute only a small fraction. In focusing on the most celebrated editions and ignoring those that may be run-of-the-mill, the accounts thus fail to present an accurate overview of Marchant's career. They also assume that the content and appearance of Marchant's books holds the key to the definition of his audience, an assumption that Natalie Davis cautioned against in her seminal essay "Printing and the People."[5] In advising scholars to be wary of arguments that isolate the genre of a work on the basis of features inscribed within the work, Davis urged them to pursue alternative lines of investigation in order to come to terms with questions of audience: to supplement evidence contained in the texts with independent evi-

[3]On "popular" printing in Lyons, with specific comparisons to Paris, see Dominique Coq, "Les incunables: Textes anciens, textes nouveaux," in *Histoire de l'édition française,* vol. 1, *Le livre conquérant: Du Moyen Age au milieu du XVIIe siècle,* ed. Henri-Jean Martin and Roger Chartier in collaboration with Jean-Pierre Vivet (Paris, 1982), pp. 177–93, esp. pp. 185–88.

[4]On the *bibliothèque bleue,* see Robert Mandrou, *De la culture populaire aux XVIIe et XVIIIe siècles: La bibliothèque bleue de Troyes* (Paris, 1964). See also Rogert Chartier, *Figures de la queusérie* (Paris, 1982).

[5]Natalie Zemon Davis, "Printing and the People," in *Society and Culture in Early Modern France* (Stanford, 1975), pp. 191–226, esp. p. 192.

dence (for example, records of ownership and use) and to consider books as carriers of relationships.

The purpose of my essay is twofold. In the first part I attempt to reconstruct and then to reevaluate Marchant's career in order to understand the *Dance of Death* and the *Shepherds' Calendar* in a more accurate context. In the second part I try to identify the audiences for the *Dance of Death* and the *Shepherds' Calendar* by turning to new data such as owners' signatures and inventory records. From my investigation Marchant emerges as a very different sort of printer, one whose production, which was almost exclusively in Latin, is in line with that of earlier Parisian printers, especially Guillaume Fichet and Johann Heynlin, the official printers of the Sorbonne until 1473.[6]

Marchant's Career

In October and December 1483 Marchant published two books, Bonaventura's *Soliloquium* and the anonymous *De arte bene vivendi beneque moriendi tractatus,* or the *Ars moriendi,* respectively.[7] Although both are dated, neither is signed with his name. He was then apparently inactive as an independent printer until September 28, 1485,[8] when he issued the first copy of the *Dance of Death,* which is also the first book to mention him by name. A second edition of the *Dance of Death* appeared between June 6 and July 6, 1486. Then three and a half years later, in 1489/90, he published a second edition of Bonaventura's *Soliloquium.* During this three-and-a-half-year interlude he is

---

[6]On the Sorbonne Press with a list of its imprints, see Anatole Claudin, *The First Paris Press: An Account of the Books Printed for G. Fichet and J. Heynlin in the Sorbonne, 1470–1472* (London, 1898); and, with earlier bibliography, Jeanne Veyrin-Forrer, "Aux origines de l'imprimerie française: L'atelier de la Sorbonne et ses mécènes (1470–1473)," in *La lettre et le texte: Trente années de recherches sur l'histoire du livre* (Paris, 1987), pp. 161–87.

[7]Two works, occasionally ascribed to Marchant, may date from one year earlier: an imprint of Ariminensis' *Lectura,* ascribed to him by Marie L. C. Pellechet, *Catalogue général des incunables des bibliothèques publiques de France,* 26 vols. (reprinted, Nendeln, 1970), no. 5344; and an indulgence, *Le Grand Pardon . . . Reims,* of which there are two extant copies, both in Reims, Bibliothèque Municipale, 195 and 195 bis, ascribed to him by Jean M. Arnoult, *Catalogues regionaux des incunables des bibliothèques publiques de France,* vol. 1, *Bibliothèques de la Région Champagne-Ardenne* (Bordeaux, 1979), p. 145, no. 848.

[8]See the appendix to this essay for books sometimes ascribed to Marchant between 1483 and 1485.

thought to have worked for Antoine Vérard, because of the appearance of Marchant's typefaces in between two and five of Vérard's books.[9] It would be useful to know more about Marchant's career in the 1480s: Did he come from Paris or from Soissons, as has been suggested on the basis of one of his printer's marks? What did he do before he became a printer? How did he set himself up as a printer? Did he work initially for Vérard, as is sometimes assumed? Answers to these questions are not readily available.

The continuous series of books issued from Marchant's press in the 1490s (see appendix to this essay), and an analysis of this output, permits us to draw certain conclusions about his career. He often published as many as six to nine books a year; in good years, such as 1494, 1498, and 1499, he published as many as thirteen to fifteen. Certain generalizations can be offered about these publications. Most are in Latin (apart from the *Dance of Death,* the *Shepherd's Calendar,* and the few editions he did for Vérard in the 1480s, almost nothing is in the vernacular), and the texts include theological and humanist tracts. The majority are quarto in format, although the next-largest number are octavo. Nearly all are very short: thirty-six to forty leaves is the average length, while six to eight leaves is not uncommon. As might be suspected from these data, many of his texts were put together in tract volumes (a volume containing several, usually short, interrelated texts). In fact, we might justifiably see Marchant as a specialist in the tract volume. Many, nearly half, are sparsely illustrated with woodcuts of routine workmanship which are reused in other imprints. Many are offered for sale through the agency of others in the printing trade.

Typical of Marchant's small-format books is his edition of Gerson's *Conclusiones seu de Regulis mandatorum,* which was published five times in Paris, twice by Marchant.[10] In 1497 he published an octavo edition of the work (having published a quarto edition in 1489–90). The copy in the Newberry Library is bound with another work published by Marchant in 1499, a treatise erroneously attributed to Dionysius the

---

[9]Three of these books are alternatively ascribed to Antoine Caillaut; all five are illustrated. See *BMC* VIII, xxv and 55. On Vérard, see John MacFarlane, *Antoine Vérard,* Illustrated Monographs, no. 7 (1900; reprinted, Geneva, 1971).

[10]For Marchant's editions of this work, see Goff G-211, G-212; it was also published by Ulrich Gering, Martin Crantz, and Michael Friburger c.1473 (G-205); by Antoine Caillaut c.1485 (G-210); and by Georg Mittelhus in 1500 (G-213).

Carthusian, the *Speculum animae peccatricis*.[11] In the Newberry Library copy both imprints were made to be sold by Jean Petit, whose printer's mark appears on the title page of each work.[12] In other copies Marchant's printer's mark occurs, and some exist with variant colophons, which suggests that different formes were printed to reflect the different booksellers who handled the work. The simple woodcut of Adam and Eve, whose origin has not been traced, appears twice in the book, introducing each book in the volume (fig. 3.1). Since in the course of his career Marchant published two editions of this book, it may be surmised that he calculated the market well, selling out each edition. The fact that the two texts are bound together suggests that they were read together and thus thought of intellectually as complementary units.

Another example of a tract volume is more typical of the university audience at which Marchant's books were aimed. This volume, also in the Newberry Library, consists of five different works published between 1498 and 1501, bound together, and sold by the publisher-binder Denis Roce.[13] Four of the five works (not those of Marchant) are tracts on grammar and rhetoric by Philippus Beroaldus, who was a celebrated Italian humanist.[14] Although Beroaldus was born in Bologna in 1453 and died there in 1505, he enjoyed a short, impressive career in Paris, where he lectured in public. His lectures are said to have inspired a taste for ancient literature in France. The fifth work in the volume, the one published by Marchant, is an eight-page tract on letter writing by Guillermus Saphonensis, a French grammarian of the fourteenth century.[15] Its subject matter thus fits well with the tracts by Beroaldus.

[11]Chicago, Newberry Library, Inc. 8005A, bound with Inc. 8024.5 (*Speculum*), Goff S-649; see Pierce Butler, *A Check List of Fifteenth-Century Books in the Newberry Library and in Other Libraries of Chicago* (Chicago, 1933), p. 231.

[12]On Jean Petit, see Claudin, *Histoire de l'imprimerie*, II, 532–39; and Renouard, *Imprimeurs*, pp. 291–93.

[13]Chicago, Newberry Library, Inc. 8010.5; see Butler, *Check List*, p. 231. The contents is as follows: Philippus Beroaldus, *Orationes et poemata*, ed. Jodocus Badius Ascensius, Paris, [Michel Tholoze for] Denis Roce (or Jean du Pré), October 12, 1499, Goff B-494; Philippus Beroaldus, *De felicitate opuscula*, Gaspar Philippe for Denis Roce [after 1500], Goff B-486; Philippi Beroaldi, *De optimo statu*, Denis Roce, 1501; Philippi Beroaldi, *Opusculum eruditum*, Denis Roce, 1501, Goff B-473; and Guillermus Saphonensis, Guy Marchant for Denis Roce, September 24, 1498, Goff G-725.

[14]On Beroaldus, see Jules Paquier, *De Philippi Beroaldi junioris vita et scriptis (1472–1518)* (Paris, 1900).

[15]On Saphonensis, see *Nouvelle biographie générale*, XXII, 702 (under Maître Guillaume); and *Histoire littéraire de la France*, XXII, 26.

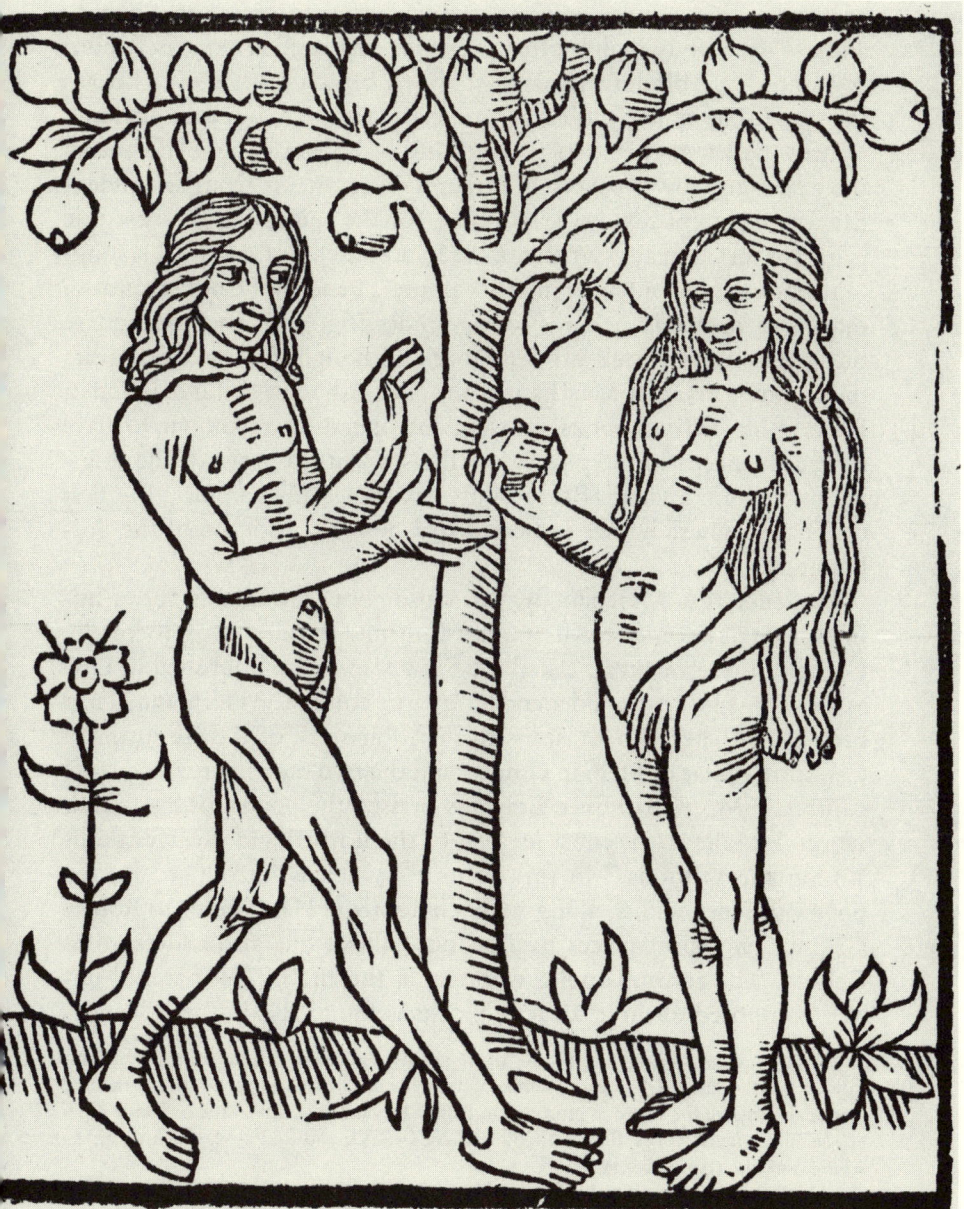

gure 3.1. Adam and Eve, from Gerson, *Conclusiones seu, de regulis mandatorum*, Paris, Guy
archant, 1497, Chicago, Newberry Library, Inc. 8005A, signature ai verso. Courtesy of the
ewberry Library.

[73]

Because this volume is intact, we can reconstruct its early history and use more fully than is often possible. Although in extremely poor condition, the binding is panel-stamped brown leather over boards (fig. 3.2). The spine, endbands, and clasp are gone, but four standing figures (perhaps representing saints and bishops) can be made out on the upper and lower covers.[16] Parchment fragments from an unidentified manuscript text serve as filling for the spine. On the first title page appears a neatly written note in a contemporary hand stating, "Five books are contained in this volume"; beneath the note appears a mark that probably belongs to the binder (fig. 3.3). Each of the five title pages bears Roce's printer's mark, although the last work bears the printer's mark of Marchant at the end. A bookseller and a binder, Roce published no books himself; his operation is known to have served the needs of the priests and the students of Paris.[17] The original owner, Ludovicus [Bor]basilius has signed his name on the first title page, where he has indicated that he is an associate of the Sorbonne.

Evidence that Marchant was in close contact with European humanist circles comes from another imprint, an edition of poems by Guilielmus Hermannus, called the *Silva odarum* and published in 1497 as a small, apparently independent quarto volume.[18] Hermannus had been a novitiate with Erasmus in the monastery of the Augustinian Canons Regular of Stejn in Gouda, and the two men maintained close contact.[19] More than once Erasmus praised the poetry of his friend, whom he called "the most learned of the learned and most virtuous among the virtuous." In this volume, which is introduced by the poetry of Hermannus, along with a letter from Hermannus to Robert Gaguin, two short pieces by Erasmus follow, one also addressed to Gaguin. The accompanying woodcut at the end of Harmannus' poetry composed of three separate blocks is found also in the Bonaven-

---

[16]Roce was apparently one of the most important Parisian booksellers who employed panel-stamped bindings, some of which bear his name, printer's mark, and device. Compare the Parisian bindings in Roger Devauchelle, *La reliure en France de ses origines à nos jours*, vol. 1 (Paris, 1959), pls. XIX–XXI; and Louis-Marie Michon, *La reliure française* (Paris, 1951), pl. X.

[17]On Roce, see Claudin, *Histoire de l'imprimerie*, II, 314–16, 323–24, 530–32; and Renouard, *Imprimeurs*, pp. 325–26.

[18]*BMC* VIII, 62–63; Goff H-65.

[19]On Hermannus with earlier bibliography, see Peter G. Bietenholz, ed., *Contemporaries of Erasmus: A Biographical Register of the Renaissance and Reformation*, 3 vols. (Toronto, c.1985–87), II, 184–85.

Figure 3.2. Panel-stamped binding, tract volume, including P. Beroaldus, *Orationes* etc., Paris, Denis Roce, c.1498–1501, Chicago, Newberry Library, Inc. 8010.5. Courtesy of the Newberry Library.

Figure 3.3. Title page, tract volume, including P. Beroaldus, *Orationes* etc., Paris, Den¡ Roce, c.1498–1501, Chicago, Newberry Library, Inc. 8010.5, signature ai recto. Cou¡ tesy of the Newberry Library.

tura, and we see it used again piecemeal in other imprints by Marchant, such as on the title page of the *Sphera mundi,* marketed by Jean Petit (fig. 3.4).[20] This work appears to be the only European printing of the poems of Hermannus. Some copies substitute the printer's mark of Denis Roce for that of Guy Marchant.

Marchant was apparently successful, to judge from documents of his property transactions.[21] A series of documents records various property transactions, among them Marchant's rental of substantially expanded quarters in 1498–99. He rented premises that took in a portion of the walls of the city between the gates of Bordelle and Saint-Victor, with the intervening three towers and the road. It is evident that he was, or became, a man of means.

Rather fancifully, some have even suggested that Marchant's apparent wealth comes from his family's trade, shoemaking.[22] Nothing is known of Marchant's background, but it is not impossible that his family were tradesmen, as his name ("merchant") implies, for other men involved in printing came from such backgrounds (for instance Jean Petit, the bookseller, whose father and grandfather had been butchers). In Marchant's case this hypothesis is based also on three of his six printer's marks, which show the patron saints of shoemakers, Crispin and Crispinian, making shoes (fig. 3.5).[23] In the third mark a book appears in the shield framed by the letters *G.M.* The concentration on the intriguing genre scene and its meaning has averted attention from the rebus, which is Marchant's motto, in the upper portion of the woodcut: "Sola fides sufficit" is taken from Thomas Aquinas' hymn "Pange lingua gloriosa" ("Sing, my tongue, the Savior's glory of his flesh"), composed in 1263 for the Office of the Corpus Christi.[24] The motto "Only faith suffices" and its source, one of the greatest theologians of the period and a master at the University of Paris, are entirely appropriate for the university audience of Mar-

---

[20]Published in February 1498; Goff J-418.

[21]For the documents on Marchant, see Jerome Pichon and Georges Vicaire, *Documents pour servir à l'histoire des libraires de Paris, 1486–1600* (Paris, 1895), pp. 14ff.

[22]*BMC* VIII, xxv.

[23]See Louis Polain, *Marques des imprimeurs et libraires en France au XVe siècle* (Paris, 1926), nos. 128, 129, 130; also described in *BMC* VIII, 56; and described and illustrated in Philippe Renouard, *Les marques typographiques parisiennes des XVe et XVIe siècles* (Paris, 1926), nos. 701–6, pp. 224–27.

[24]On the hymn, see John Julian, *A Dictionary of Hymnology* (London, n.d.), pp. 878–80. The hymn is set out in full at the end of the *Ars moriendi* of December 10, 1483.

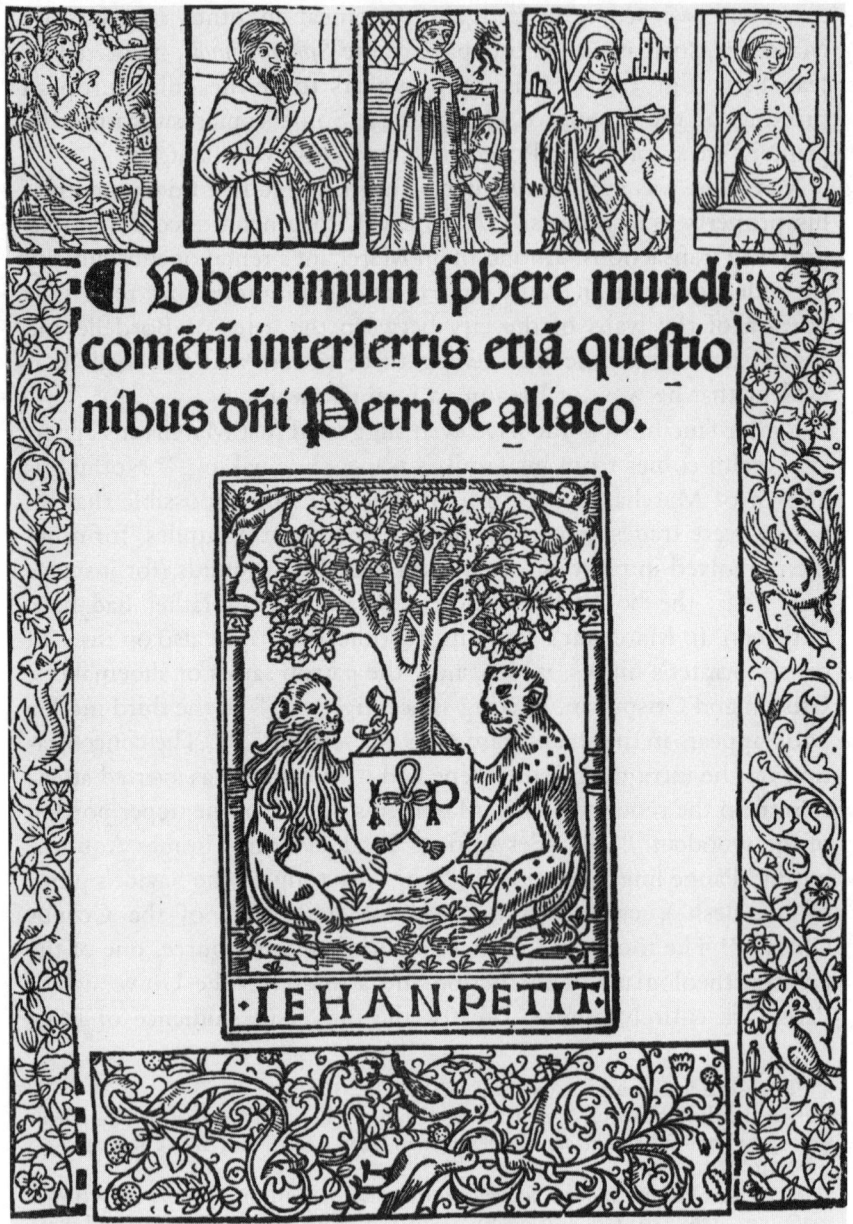

Figure 3.4. Title page, from Johannes de Sacro Busto, *Sphera mundi,* Paris, Guy Marchant, 1498, Chicago, Newberry Library, Inc. f8015. Courtesy of the Newberry Library.

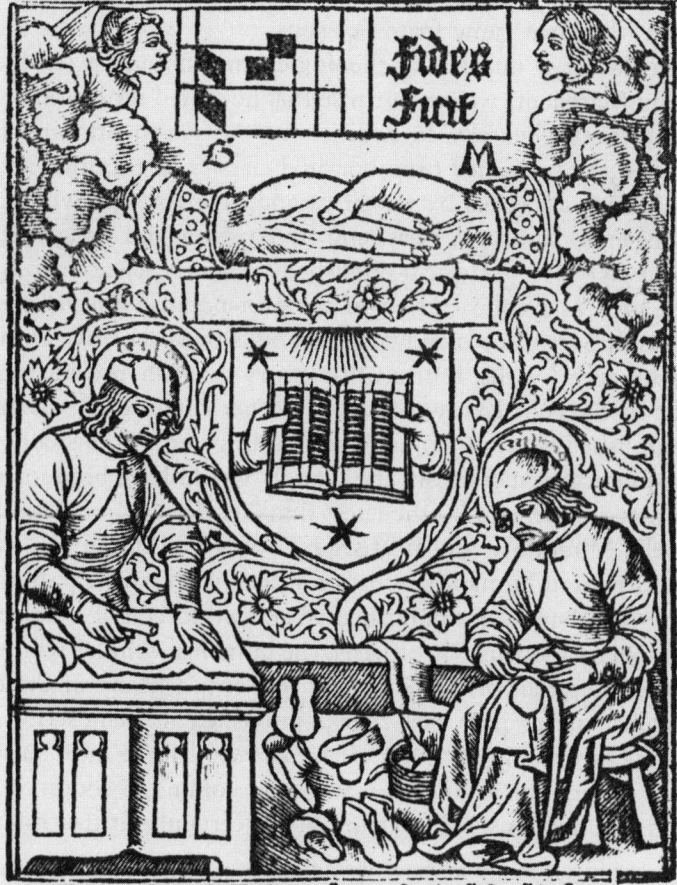

Figure 3.5. Printer's mark, Crispin and Crispinian, title page, from Guilielmus Hermannus, *Silva odarum,* Paris, Guy Marchant, 1497, Chicago, Newberry Library, Inc. 8003.5. Courtesy of the Newberry Library.

chant's books and are more important than the genre scene, which should probably be understood, as some scholars have done, simply as a clever word play on the name Marchant. The presence of these saints, who were especially venerated in Soissons, could simply indicate that Marchant came from Soissons.

From the large number of theological and humanist works published by Marchant, we can surmise that he aimed most of his works at a university clientele. In addition to the grammaticians already mentioned, he published time-honored classics in grammar and philosophy, such as works by Barzizius and Nebrissensis, who had recently been acclaimed in Paris, and by Aristotle and Diogenes, who were old favorites.[25] He also published books on science and mathematics, such as a folio edition of the ever-popular *Sphera mundi* by Johannes de Sacro Busto and two textbooks on speculative arithmetic and geometry by the fourteenth-century English prelate and theologian Thomas of Bradwardinus (no other copies of Bradwardinus were published before 1500, including in England).[26] This same circle of hypothetical readers from the schools would have been interested in the newest writings by the latest thinkers, letters by Erasmus and Pico della Mirandola, and treatises by Lefèvre d'Etaple, the Parisian pre-Reformation humanist, most of whose works were published in Paris by Marchant.[27] He published several works edited or containing postscripts by Jodocus Clichtoveus, the humanist-scholar who was to be named librarian of the Sorbonne in 1505.[28] Many of these new authors had never had their works published in manuscript form. Studies of printing in Strasbourg have shown that the most successful printers counted on selling their works in volume to educational and religious foundations.[29] Marchant would certainly fit that model for

[25]Marchant's role as a printer for the university is underscored by the fact that Barzizius' *Epistolae* was the first book printed by the Sorbonne press, in 1470; see Claudin, *First Paris Press*, pp. 49–50, *GW* 3675. Goff A-904 records no other editions of Nebrissensis' works in France except Marchant's.

[26]On Thomas of Bradwardinus, see Henry Crosby, ed., *Thomas of Bradwardine, "Tractatus de proportionibus": Its Significance for the Development of His Mathematical Physics* (Madison, 1955).

[27]For the life and works of Lefèvre d'Etaple, see Simone Guenée, ed., *Bibliographie de l'histoire des universités françaises des origines à la révolution*, vol. 1, *Generalités-Université de Paris* (Paris, 1981), pp. 327–29, nos. 1621–44.

[28]On Jodicus, see Jean-Pierre Massaut, *Josse Clichtove, l'humanisme et la réforme du clergé*, 2 vols. (Paris, 1968) (Bibliothèque de la Faculté de Philosophie et Lettres de l'Université de Liège, fasc. 183).

[29]Miriam Usher Chrisman, *Lay Culture, Learned Culture: Books and Social Change in Strasbourg, 1480–1599* (New Haven, 1982), pp. 81ff.

success. The fact that Marchant apparently obtained a degree of Master of Arts by 1497, when he first identifies himself in this way, underscores his day-to-day connection with the university.[30]

The placement of Marchant's first shop in a property known as the Hotel de Champ Gaillart behind the College of Navarre, to which it belonged, confirms that the printer had a close relationship with this institution. In 1499, while retaining his original location, Marchant opened new premises, the Hotel of Beauregard, which belonged to the College of Boncourt, itself part of the College of Navarre. No one has ever examined the relationship between Marchant and the College of Navarre.[31] Founded in 1304 by Jeanne of Navarre, wife of Philip the Fair, the College of Navarre was open to students of grammar, philosophy, and theology, which could explain the more or less equal concentration of books on these subjects among Marchant's editions. Marchant's specialization in tract volumes may also be understood better when we realize that the College was specifically intended to admit poor students, who received scholarships to pay for their education. Among the illustrious alumni of the college were Jean Gerson and Nicolas de Clamanges, both of whose works Marchant published. It would thus seem that Marchant's two locations were ideally situated for the market he made in books suitable for the faculty and students of the College of Navarre. We might even speculate as to the arrangement by which he published out of premises owned by the university. (Was his place a kind of Barnes and Noble, the firm that now has a monopoly on American college bookstores, for the College of Navarre?)

The statutes of the College of Navarre urged students to avoid luxury and to attend divine offices in the chapel, which was specially endowed with four chaplains and four clerics.[32] In this context Marchant's collaboration with Jean Le Munerat, cantor of the chapel

[30]Claudin, *Histoire de l'imprimerie*, I, 393 n. 1, publishes the text of a document that lists Marchant as a Master of Arts of the University of Paris.

[31]On the University of Paris during this period, see Jean Baptiste Louis Crevier, *Histoire de l'université de Paris depuis son origine jusqu'en l'année 1600*, 7 vols. (Paris, 1761); on the College of Navarre, especially around 1400, see Gilbert Ouy, "Le college de Navarre, berceau de l'humanisme français," in *Actes du 95e Congrès national des sociétés savantes, Reims*, vol. 1, 1970 (Paris, 1975), pp. 275–99 (Comité des travaux historiques et scientifiques, Section de philologie et d'histoire jusqu'à 1610); and on the library of the College of Navarre, which contained 2,400 volumes during the reign of Charles VIII, see Emile L. M. Chatelain, "Les manuscrits du college de Navarre en 1741," *Revue des bibliothèques* 11 (1901): 362–411.

[32]Crevier, *Histoire de l'université*, II, 212.

of the College of Navarre and theologian at the University of Paris, is understandable. In 1490 Le Munerat edited and amplified Usuardus' *Martyrologuim Gallicum,* according to the wishes of the bishop of Paris, to whom he addressed a special dedication and whose arms appear in the volume, which was published by Marchant.[33] Le Munerat appended a tract on the adaptation of music and words in hymns. The copy that belonged to Le Munerat himself, with an *ex dono* to the chapel of the College of Navarre, is still extant.[34] Six years later, in 1496, Le Munerat wrote a short tract entitled *De dedicatione ecclesie Parisiensis,* also published by Marchant. In addition to his affiliation with the College of Navarre, Marchant's vocation as a priest may help account for his relations with Le Munerat and his publication of these books.[35]

Although many of Marchant's books were sold on campus, as it were, a good many were also sold by local distributors, especially by Jean Petit and Denis Roce, and less frequently by Alexander Aliate and Geoffroy de Marnef,[36] all of whose bookstores were on the rue Saint-Jacques, closer to the Sorbonne proper. Marchant published at least twenty-four books for Jean Petit and nine books for Denis Roce. As we have seen, in many of these instances Marchant produced editions in which the title page varied, one part of the same edition having his own title page and another part having that of one of the distributors. This strategy entailed the extra time and cost involved in setting up part of one signature differently. But it ensured increased visibility with the same book on view and for sale in two locations. The practice of selling books through a distributor makes even more sense when we remember also that Marchant specialized in the short tract, which could be put together with other companion pieces by the prospective buyer. Roce's second calling as a binder was ideal, since he could assemble and bind these disparate books for individual customers, mostly priests and students. The end result, the tract volume, may be every bit as unique as the manuscript book, but it is rarely studied, since the history of printing has concentrated on the

---

[33]See Claudin, *Histoire de l'imprimerie,* I, 398–400.

[34]BN, Réserve B.186.

[35]See the two previously unpublished documents in Claudin, *Histoire de l'imprimerie,* I, 380–83, n. 1, and 406 n. 1.

[36]On Aliate and Marnef, see Claudin, *Histoire de l'imprimerie,* II, 342–47, 560 n. 53; Renouard, *Imprimeurs,* pp. 3, 260–61; and *BMC* VIII, 221–22.

uniformity of each imprint instead of on the uniqueness of the original book in which the imprint is found.

It is worth mentioning that Marchant's relationship with Petit is an especially intriguing one, for Petit was one of the most successful booksellers of the period. If Roce's shop specialized in books for priests and students, Jean Petit's was a kind of Kroch's or Brentano's (or its English variant, W. H. Smith's), where the customer might find anything—books in Latin or French, illustrated or unillustrated, secular or religious, expensive or cheap. Petit was also one of the four booksellers officially sworn in by the Sorbonne whose job it was to ensure that each school edition published (or written) was textually correct. What an advantageous business connection for a man who aimed much of his trade at the university!

Marchant's specialization in the short tract led him to publish other extremely short works, such as letters, consisting of only four to eight leaves, which could be printed in one or two formes, folded, and sold unbound. One such letter published by Marchant was clearly timely: the letter announcing Christopher Columbus' discovery of the New World.[37] When Columbus returned from the New World, he wrote a letter in Spanish, dated March 14, 1493, in Lisbon, telling what he had found. This letter was first published in Barcelona. Following its translation into Latin on April 29, the letter was rapidly printed throughout Europe, first in Rome in early May.[38] Marchant's first edition appeared shortly thereafter. Considered to be the forerunners of the modern newspaper, these letters were certainly meant to be folded because they have an actual title page. Marchant's title page reads in translation: "A Letter about the Islands lately discovered printed at Paris in the Gaillant Fields." The epigram of the bishop of Monte Peloso, R. L. de Corbaria, appears on the verso: "No region now can add to Spain's great deeds. / To such men all the world is yet too small. / An Orient land found far beyond the waves / Will add, great Betica, to thy renown. / Then to Columbus, the true finder, give / Due thanks; but greater still to God on high / Who makes new

[37]Printed in three variants by Marchant in 1493, of which there are only two recorded copies of each edition. See Goff C-761; and Wilberforce Eames, "Columbus' Letter on the Discovery of America," *Bulletin of the New York Public Library*, 28 (1924): pp. 595–99. The third edition has been published in facsimile: Cristoforo Colombo, *Epistola de insulis noviter repertis*, Harrisse facsimile, no. 6, 187—.

[38]For the Barcelona as well as other printed versions of the letter, see Goff C-756–C-762, and the more complete list in Eames, "Columbus' Letter," pp. 597–99.

kingdoms for himself and thee / Both firm and pious let thy conduct be."[39] Marchant added an illustration to his editions not found in those in Italy or Spain, a woodcut of the Annunciation to the Shepherds (fig. 3.6). He took the woodcut from a group of woodcuts that he reused from time to time and that are thought to come from a Book of Hours, which has yet to be identified.[40] Whatever the source, the woodcut is an apt illustration of the text, which urges the reader to "give due thanks . . . to God on high who makes new kingdoms for himself and thee." Again it is intriguing that Marchant published three variant impressions of Columbus' letter all in 1493 and all in the same format. He was the only French printer to publish the letter.

As in the case of the letter of Columbus, what makes Marchant so interesting is his apparent talent at identifying a market and his willingness therefore to deviate from time to time from his customary pattern of production. For example, in November 1499 he published a French translation of the *Mirabilia Romae vel potius historia et descriptio urbis Romae,* or *Les merveilles de Romme.*[41] This classic "pilgrim's guide" to the monuments in Rome was published in Latin throughout Europe over seventeen times before 1500. More than six German translations were published, and one Italian translation, the latter rather late (1510). Marchant's edition is the only French translation, and it is further distinguished from the others, which are mostly octavo in format, by being a duodecimo. Thus it is truly a pocket book. Only one smaller version was published, a twentyfourmo, published in Rome four months after Marchant's by Stephan Plannck.[42] It is tempting to see Plannck's publication as a response to the success of Marchant's.

Marchant marketed *Les merveilles de Romme* through another bookseller, Geoffroy de Marnef, presumably because this sort of publication was different from what he normally published and from what a prospective buyer would expect to find for sale in his shop. There

[39]Quoted from Eames, "Columbus' Letter," p. 596.

[40]Possibly from the *Horae,* of which only fragments of a single copy survive in Paris, BN, Réserve B.27814 (1).

[41]November 9, 1499, Goff M-607; for other printed versions, see Goff M-591–M-614; and Max Sander, *Le livre à figures italien depuis 1467 jusqu'à 1530: Essai de sa bibliographie et son histoire,* 6 vols. (New York, 1941).

[42]*Mirabilia Romae vel potius historia et descriptio urbis Romae,* Rome, Stephan Plannck, 1500; see Goff M-604.

Epigramma. N. L. de corbaria
Episcopi Montispalusti. Ad
Inuictissimũ Regem hispaniarũ.

Iam nulla hispanis tellus addenda triumphis
  At q̃ parum tantis viribus orbis erat.
Nunc longe eois regio deprensa sub vndis
  Auctura est titulos Betice magne tuos.
Vnde repertori merito referenda Columbo
  Gratia sed summo est maior habenda deo.
Qui vincenda parat noua regna tibiq̃ sibiq̃
  Teq̃ simul fortem prestat et esse pium.

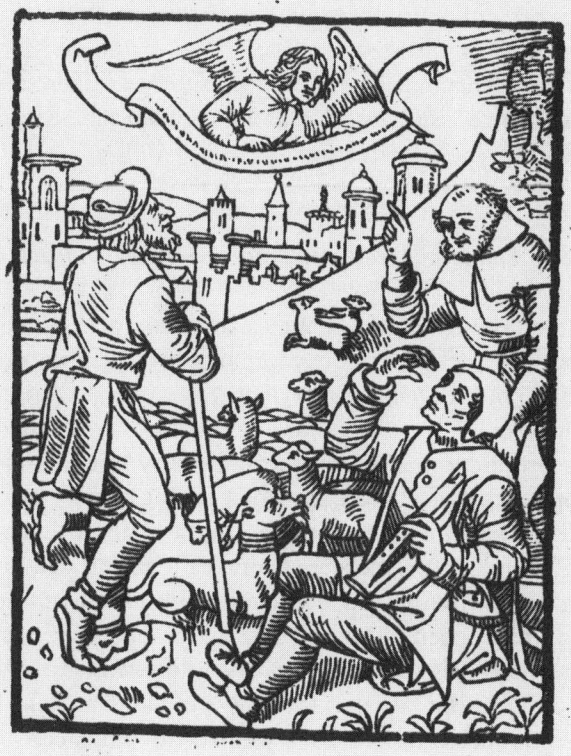

Figure 3.6. Annunciation to the Shepherds, from Christophorus Columbus, *Epistola de insula inventis,* Paris, Guy Marchant, 1493, New York Public Library, facsimile, Chicago, Newberry Library, Ayer 107.56 1493B. Courtesy of the Newberry Library.

[85]

were two advantages to using de Marnef instead of Jean Petit or Denis Roce, with whom Marchant most frequently collaborated during these years. De Marnef's shelves were full of this sort of "popular" vernacular book for the devout Catholic, bilingual copies in French and Latin of the Rule of Saint Benedict, bilingual copies of Saint Jerome's *Regle de dévotion,* several editions in Latin and in French of Sebastian Brant's *Ship of Fools,* and Books of Hours in the most popular liturgical uses, the Use of Paris and the Use of Rome. Just the right place for a pilgrim's guide in French! Furthermore, Geoffroy de Marnef worked with his two brothers, Jean and Enguilbert, who were also booksellers, and together they maintained provincial subsidiaries for the Paris bookstore in Poitiers, Angers, and Bourges. Small wonder that *Les merveilles de Romme* was not published by another printer either in Paris or the provinces, since it could be marketed so widely through the operations of the de Marnefs. Perhaps Marchant went to de Marnef for yet another reason: it was for de Marnef that he had also printed a Latin *Ars moriendi* with twenty-six woodcuts some nine years earlier.

The *Dance of Death* and the *Shepherds' Calendar*

Having reconstructed Marchant's career in such detail, I would now turn back to the original question: namely, the place of the *Dance of Death* and the *Shepherds' Calendar* in his career. It might initially appear that these two works are deviations from the norm of Marchant's production in much the same way that *Les merveilles de Romme* represents a deviation, but this is not exactly the case. *Les merveilles de Romme,* insofar as one can judge without having studied the original volumes or recovered any data about cost, must have been published in volume and at low cost for the tourist trade, and so it could not have been a luxury item. But much of the evidence consulted to date—the books themselves, inventories, owners' signatures—points to the fact that the *Dance of Death* and the *Shepherd's Calendar* were much admired by a well-to-do audience.

Although Davis pointed out that the king of France owned a copy of the *Shepherds' Calendar,* and thus concluded that this work was not consumed exclusively by "the people," she did not also point out the frequency with which these works occur in royal libraries, nor did she study the nature of the copies.[43] In conformity with the tradition followed in Vérard's enterprise (recall that Marchant is thought to have worked with him), some copies of the *Shepherds' Calendar* and the *Dance of Death* are on parchment instead of paper, and they are extensively illuminated.[44] They are thus personalized for a special patron, as is indicated by the copy of the *Shepherds' Calendar,* printed by Marchant for Vérard, on which the emblem and arms of King Charles VIII appear (fig. 3.7).[45] A copy of the *Dance of Death* published by Vérard with woodcuts inspired by but not copied from those in Marchant's version also comes from the library of Francis I at Blois.[46] It too is illuminated on parchment. A copy of the *Dance of Death for Women* was also in the library of the king (fig. 3.8).[47] Although this copy is on paper, it is carefully hand-painted. The copy of the *Dance of Death* owned by Anne of Brittany, twice queen of France, has not yet been identified, but chances are it was more lavish in materials and decoration than the "off-the-shelf" copies sold through Parisian booksellers.[48]

This information serves not only to confirm a wealthy audience for Marchant's so-called popular books but it also turns us again to questions about the reason for the success of his enterprise. Without concrete data on cost it is difficult to be certain, but I suspect that the exceptional commissioned sales of made-to-order copies of special materials for court patrons contributed substantially toward the profit

[43]Davis, "Printing and the People," pp. 197–99.

[44]For parchment copies of the *Dance of Death* (two in BN, one in Bibliothèque Municipale, Auxerre, and one in Lambeth Palace, London), see Joseph van Praet, *Catalogue des livres imprimés sur vélin de la Bibliothèque du Roi,* 6 vols. in 5 (Paris, 1822), IV, pp. 169–72, nos. 233, 234; and for parchment copies of the *Shepherds' Calendar,* see Praet, IV, p. 73, no. 104. See the illustrations in Claudin, *Histoire de l'imprimerie,* I, 368ff.

[45]BN, Réserve, VV. H.336m, with sixty-two miniatures, described in Praet, *Catalogue,* III, pp. 75–76, no. 104, and VI, p. 73, no. 104, reproduced in color in Claudin, *Histoire de l'imprimerie,* I, pp. 368 and 378. This copy was in the library of Francis I at Blois.

[46]BN, Réserve, Vélin.

[47]BN, Réserve Ye. 86, reproduced in facsimilie: *La danse macabre des femmes; (suivie de) La danse nouvelle des hommes; (augmentée du) Dit des trois morts et des trois vifs; (du) Débat d'un corps et d'une ame; (et de la) Complainte d'une ame damnée* (Paris, 1977).

[48]On Anne of Brittany's copy, see Alphonse M. Chazaud, *Enseignements d'Anne de France: Inventaire des meubles estans en la maison de Monseigneur le duc de Bourbonnais et d'Auvergne estant en sa ville d'Aiguesperses* (Paris, 1507), as quoted by Schutz, *Vernacular Books,* pp. 44 and 74.

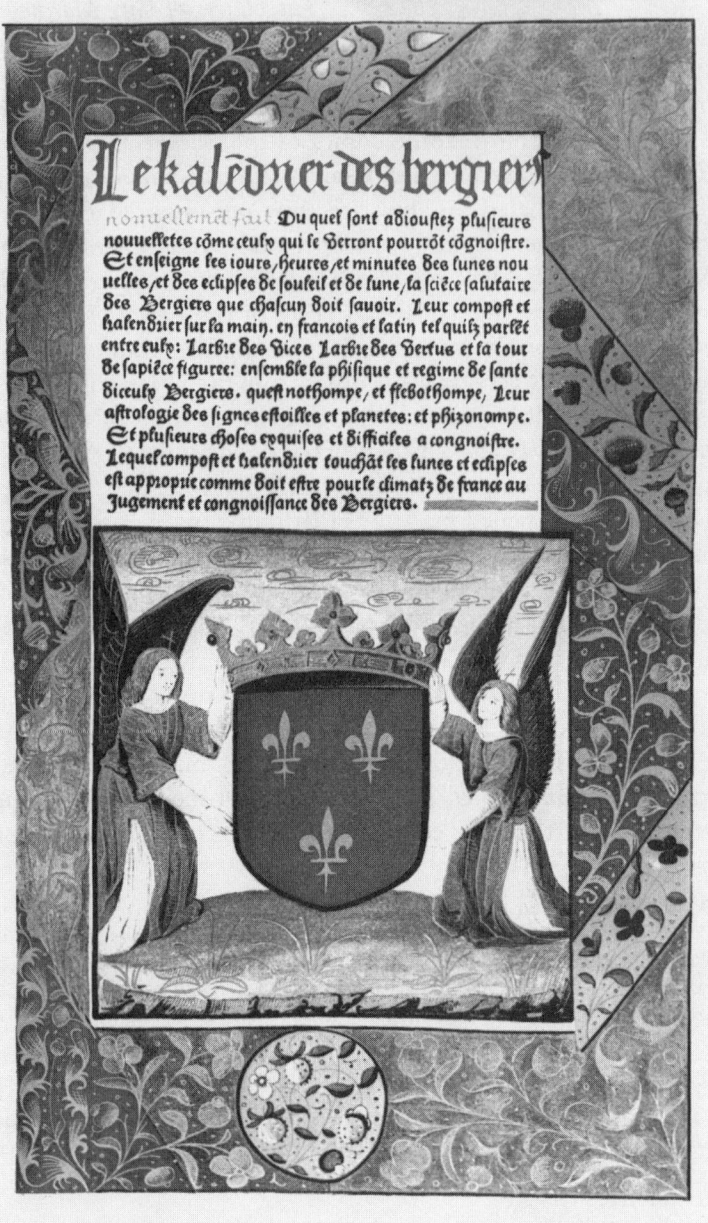

Figure 3.7. Title page, *Shepherds' Calendar,* Paris, Guy Marchant for Antoine Vérard, 1493, BN, Réserve VV. H.336m. Photo: Anatole Claudin, *Histoire de l'imprimerie en France au XVe et au XVIe siècle* (Paris, 1900–1914; reprinted, 1971), I, opp. p. 369. Courtesy of the Newberry Library, Chicago.

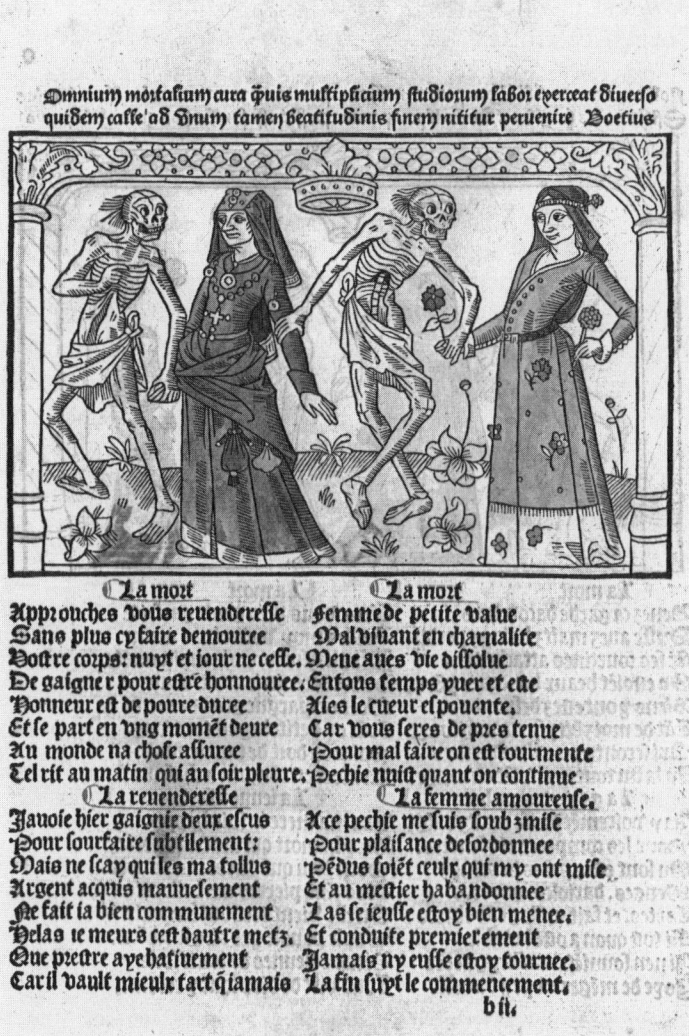

Omnium mortalium cura quis multiplicium studiorum labor exerceat diuerso
quidem calle ad unum tamen beatitudinis finem nititur peruenire Boetius

La mort

Approuches vous reuenderesse
Sans plus cy faire demouree
Vostre corps nuyt et iour ne cesse
De gaigner pour estre honnouree
Honneur est de poure duree
Et se part en vng momet deure
Au monde na chose asseuree
Tel rit au matin qui au soir pleure

La reuenderesse

Jauoie hier gaignie deux escus
Pour sourfaire subtilement:
Mais ne scay qui les ma tollus
Argent acquis mauuesement
Ne fait ia bien communement
Helas ie meurs cest dautre metz.
Que prestre aye hatiuement
Car il vault mieulx tart q iamais

La mort

Femme de petite value
Mal viuant en charnalite
Mene aues vie dissolue
En tous temps yuer et este
Ales le cueur espouente.
Car vous seres de pres tenue
Pour mal faire on est tourmente
Pechie nuit quant on continue

La femme amoureuse.

A ce pechie me suis soubz mise
Pour plaisance desordonnee
Pedus soiet ceulx qui my ont mise
Et au mestier habandonnee
Las se ieusse estoy bien menee.
Et conduite premierement
Jamais ny eusse estoy tournee.
La fin suyt le commencement.
b ii.

Figure 3.8. The Resaleswoman and the Prostitute, from the *Grand danse macabre des femmes,* Paris, Guy Marchant, 1491, BN, Réserve Ye. 86, fol. Bii. Photo: Bibliothèque Nationale, Paris.

Marchant realized on the edition. If even a hand-colored copy on paper cost twice as much as a plain copy, then how much more was a parchment copy richly illuminated in gold and azure worth?[49] If my reconstruction is correct, then, the sale of so-called popular books to royal and aristocratic patrons ironically may have been the basis for Marchant's success with these works.

Parenthetically, the simulation of the manuscript as it occurs in these examples for aristocratic patrons certainly relates these works to scribal culture, more so than any of Marchant's other publications. It may be worth asking whether their content was considered more "medieval," more appropriate to the medium of the manuscript, especially when one realizes that works by Erasmus, Lefèvre d'Etaple, and Jodocus Clichtoveus do not survive in similar dual editions. In any event, such evidence for Marchant's participation in scribal culture should be juxtaposed with the documentary evidence of his apparently close association with an illuminator, Jehan Le Cousturier of the place Maubert, with whom he went into business in 1486, the very year of the publication of the first extensively illustrated version of the *Dance of Death*.[50]

Ownership of the *Dance of Death* and the *Shepherds' Calendar* was of course not restricted to the aristocracy, as a survey of more than 220 inventories after death reveals.[51] Bourgeois families owned half the copies of the 1485 edition of the *Dance of Death*, whereas only one-quarter of the copies were in the hands of the royalty or the aristocracy.[52] One-third of the copies of the *Shepherds' Calendar* were in the hands of the nobility. Among the bourgeois owners of the *Dance of Death*, three-quarters were women, although this fact is difficult to interpret.[53] It does not necessarily mean that the audience for the work consisted largely of women, since men were often a generation older than their wives during this period and frequently predeceased

[49]For relative prices, see, with further references *Pen to Press,* pp. 196–99.

[50]Pichon and Vicaire, *Documents,* p. 14.

[51]See Alexander H. Schutz, *Vernacular Books in Parisian Private Libraries of the Sixteenth Century According to the Notarial Inventories,* University of North Carolina Studies in the Romance Languages and Literatures, no. 25 (Chapel Hill, 1955); also Albert Labarre, *Le livre dans la vie amienoise du seizième siècle: L'enseignement de inventaires après décès, 1503–1576,* Publications de la Faculté des Lettres et Sciences humaines de Paris-Sorbonne, Série Recherches no. 66 (Paris, 1971).

[52]Schutz, *Vernacular Books,* p. 44.

[53]Ibid. pp. 77, 80, 82: Claude Cousin, wife of a *docteur regent* of the University of Paris: Jeanne Labbé of Amiens, and Jacqueline Martin of Amiens.

them, thus leaving the inventories in the name of their wives. The breakdown by class of owners of the *Shepherds' Calendar* (any edition) is almost identical to the data presented for the *Dance of Death*, with the exception of a slightly larger fraction of owners from the nobility.[54] One-third of the owners of the *Dance of Death* also owned the *Shepherds' Calendar*, so it would seem that the two works were considered comparable by the book buyers and readers of the period.

Conspicuously absent as owners of either the *Dance of Death* or the *Shepherds' Calendar* is the new group of book owners, the noveaux riches of the period, who came from the upwardly mobile social classes in Paris made up of counselors at court, members of parliament, financial officers, attorneys, and notaries.[55] What the nouveaux riches owned in abundance were works such as Bartholomeus Anglicus' *Propriétés des choses* and Boccaccio's *Cent nouvelles,* that is, works that had a longstanding deluxe manuscript tradition under the sponsorship of individuals in royal and noble circles.[56] These data too are difficult to interpret. They could mean that, in aspiring to emulate the aristocracy, this class of book owners shied away from new works that cut so clearly through the social spectrum in favor of established works that were known to be favorites among the elite. By contrast, the aristocracy, in purchasing the *Dance of Death* and the *Shepherds' Calendar,* were breaking with their own buying habits and setting new patterns of taste.

In two respects the inventories show up the *Dance of Death* differently from the *Shepherds' Calendar.* The *Shepherds' Calendar* continues to appear in inventories until around midcentury, whereas the *Dance of Death* ceases to appear, except in inventories of booksellers, after about 1525.[57] It would seem, then, that the popularity of the *Shepherds' Calendar* endured, whereas the taste for the *Dance of Death* wore out. One other detail supports this interpretation. Inventories of booksellers as late as 1551 record multiple copies in stock of the *Dance*

[54]Ibid. p. 39.

[55]See, however, a copy of the *Shepherds' Calendar* now in the Houghton Library, Harvard University, signed by Noel de Aloncourt, attorney for the king at Sens, referred to by Davis, "Printing and the People," p. 326 n. 6.

[56]See, for example, the inventory of 1518 of Antoine de Cocquerel, attorney and counselor to the bishop at Amiens, in Labarre, *Le livre,* pp. 272–77. Nearly all his books are in the vernacular; he owned a mixture of printed books and manuscripts; and chronicles and romances, along with works of popular piety and devotion, predominate.

[57]Schutz, *Vernacular Books,* pp. 39, 44.

of Death—one hundred copies each in two cases and fifty copies in a third—which suggests, along with the data from the inventories of ordinary households, that booksellers were having a hard time marketing the work.[58] Parenthetically, it also indicates something about the large size of the original editions of the *Dance of Death* and gives cause for some puzzlement about the scarcity of copies in modern times.

So far I have focused almost exclusively on the middle and upper classes in an urban environment (the inventories come from Amiens and Paris), for which far more data about patterns of ownership (and consequently readership) exist than for the countryside or for the lower classes. There remains the question of the likelihood of a rural French peasant's possessing (and reading) a copy of the *Dance of Death* or the *Shepherds' Calendar*. Davis has pointed to a few such instances for the *Shepherds' Calendar*, to which I can add another instance.[59] A copy of the 1499 edition of the *Shepherdesses' Calendar* in the British Library records the names of members of a family from Essex with a note in English proclaiming that the present owner stole the book at Morlaix in Brittany.[60] On the flyleaf appears another note in French of the death of Beatrice de Maly at La Roge (La Roche) which is dated earlier, August 15, 1506. La Roche is a tiny inland village some 40 kilometers from Morlaix in Brittany. Although I have been unable to identify these particular families and therefore know nothing about their social status, here is a concrete example of rural ownership of the *Shepherdesses' Calendar* (and, incidently, pride in theft, which would not seem to be an upper-class characteristic!). It would appear, then, that the *Dance of Death* and the *Shepherds' Calendar* had a variable audience—perhaps more variable than the audiences imaginable for Marchant's tract volumes but perhaps not more numerous.

What kind of portrait of Marchant the printer emerges from this two-part reassessment of his work? First and foremost, Marchant stands out as a printer of short, simply produced humanist and theological works in Latin for a market in university and religious cir-

---

[58]In 1522 Janot had fifty copies; and in 1551 Galiot du Pré had one hundred copies, according to Schutz, *Vernacular Books*, p. 44.

[59]Davis, "Printing and the People," pp. 197–99 and n. 26, a seventeenth-century curate.

[60]*Compost et calendrier des bergieres*, August 17, 1499, in *BMC* VIII, 67.

cles. Having successfully identified this market, he made a number of astute business decisions: he was careful to restrict his press runs so that his editions sold out, to produce books that could go together in different combinations, and to sell his books through more than one outlet. He typically included sparse pictorial adornments in his editions so as to enhance their visual appeal, and he reused woodcuts frequently so as to cut design costs. His affiliation with the College of Navarre must have ensured a steady clientele for these volumes. At the same time, he appears to have kept his eye on the vernacular market, printing from time to time unillustrated works such as *Les merveilles de Romme* and illustrated works such as the *Dance of Death* and the *Shepherds' Calendar,* for which he has come to be known as a printer of "popular" books. Most of these books were marketed by other booksellers. But the "popular" works for which he is best known, the *Dance* and the *Calendar,* are anomalous in his career. And the audience for the luxury versions of these works was located in court circles, which calls into question previous characterizations of the works. Without further knowledge of the day-to-day operations of Marchant's business, one might thus provisionally argue that Marchant's success must have been the result of his calculation not of a popular "low culture" market but of a continuing market for "high culture" books for the university of an urban capital.

Preliminary List of Imprints: Guy Marchant

No checklist of the imprints published by Marchant exists in the literature on early printing. The following preliminary listing constitutes an initial step toward establishing such a checklist in which the following details are specified: date, place of publication, whether printed for a bookseller, author, title, size of the volume, and Goff number. Brackets indicate that the details are not printed in the volume but rather have been ascertained by other means. The list constitutes a concordance of Goff, the supplement to Goff, the *BMC,* Marie L. C. Pellechet, *Catalogue général des incunables des bibliothèques publiques le France.* 26 vols. (reprinted Nendeln, 1970), and other sources.

1. Sept. 9, 1492, Paris, [Guy Marchant or Louis Martineau], Gregorius Ariminensis, *Lectura super primum librum Sententiarum,* folio (G-480).
2. [Before Oct. 17, 1482], [Paris, Guy Marchant], *Le grand pardon de Notre Dame de Reims,* 2º.

3. [After Aug. 30, 1483], [Paris, Guy Marchant], *Remonstrances faites au feu roi Louis XI,* 4° (R-145).

4. [Oct. 1483], Paris, [Guy Marchant], Bonaventura, *Soliloquium,* 4°.

5. Dec. 10, 1483, Paris, [Guy Marchant], *Ars moriendi,* 4° (A-1094).

6. [C.1483], [Paris, Guy Marchant], Anianus, *Compotus cum comment (avec mode d'emploi envers français).*

7. [C.1484], [Paris, Guy Marchant], Johannes Gerson, *De ecclesiastica potestate et De origine juris et legum tractatus,* 4° (G-226).

8. [C.1484], Paris, [Guy Marchant], Thomas Aquinas, *Confessionale,* 4°.

9. Sept, 28, 1485, Paris, Guy Marchant, *Danse macabre,* folio.

10. After Sept. 28, 1485 and before June 7, 1486, Paris, Guy Marchant [for Antoine Vérard], *Danse macabre,* folio.

11. Between June 7 and July 7, 1486, Paris, Guy Marchant, *Danse macabre des hommes, Danse macabre des femmes, Le débat du corps et de l'ame, et La complainte de l'ame damné,* folio.

12. [C.1485–90?], [Paris, Guy Marchant?], *Ars notariatus,* 4°.

13. June 26, 1488, Paris, [Antoine Caillaut or Guy Marchant for Antoine Vérard], Christine de Pizan, *Faits d'armes et de chevalerie,* folio (C-471).

14. Aug. 8, 1488, Paris, [Guy Marchant or Antoine Caillaut for Antoine Vérard], Oliver de la Marche, *Le chevalier deliberé,* 4° (L-29).

15. Sept, 8, 1488, Paris, [Guy Marchant or Antoine Caillaut for Antoine Vérard], Aristotle, [*Ethica ad nicomachum.* Trans.] *Les ethiques en francoys,* 2°.

16. [C.1488], [Paris, Guy Marchant], Nigellus Wirecker, *Speculum stultorum* (W-64).

17. [C.1488?], [Paris, Guy Marchant], Guillermus Tardivus, *Antibalbica,* 4°.

18. Jan. 5, 1489/90, [Paris, Guy Marchant] for Antoine Vérard, *Horae* [in Latin and French].

19. Mar. 6, 1489/90; Paris, Guy Marchant, Gerson, *Conclusiones De diversis materiis moralibus, sive De regulis mandatorum,* 4° (G-211).

20. Aug. 8, 1489, Paris, [Guy Marchant for] Antoine Vérard, Aristotle, *Le livre de politiques,* (trans. N. Oresme), folio (A-1027).

21. March 12, 1489/90, Paris, Guy Marchant, Bonaventura, *Soliloquium,* 4°.

22. March 1490, Paris, Guy Marchant, *Ars moriendi,* 4°.

23. July 31, 1490, Paris, Guy Marchant, Usuardus, *Martyrologium Gallicum* (ed. with additions by Johannes Le Munerat), 2°.

24. Aug. 16, 1490, Paris, Guy Marchant, Odo, *Expositio canonis missae,* 4o.

25. Sept. 4, 1490, Paris, Guy Marchant, Nicolaus de Clamangiis, *Latinum super duabis materiis contrariis* [trans. of two poems by Philippe de Vitry], 4°.

26. [Oct. 1,] 1490, Paris, Guy Marchant, Publius Faustus Andrelinus, *Livia.*

27. Jan. 20, 1490/91, Paris, Guy Marchant, *Danse macabre.*

28. Oct. 15, 1490, Paris, Guy Marchant for Geoffrey de Marnef, *Chorea ab eximio macabro versibus alemanicis edita* (ed. Petrus Desrey), folio (D-21).

29. [C.1490], Paris, Guy Marchant, *Regimen sanitatis salernitanum,* 4° (R-64).

30. [C.1490–1492], Paris, Guy Marchant, *Aie memoire de la mort.*

31. [C.1490–1495], [Paris, Guy Marchant, and/or Poitiers, Jean Bouyer and Guillaume Bouchet], Henricus de Septimello, *Liber elegiorum* (H-48).

32. [C.1490], [Paris], Guy Marchant, Antonius Farenus, *Confessionale,* 4° (F-51).

33. [C.1490], [Paris, Guy Marchant], Saint Isidorus Hispalensis, *De ortu et obitu prophetarum et apostolorum,* 4°.

34. [C.1491], Paris, Guy Marchant, Nicolaus de Clamengis, *De filio prodigo exhortans peccatorem ad poenitentiam.*

35. April 15, 1491/92, May 3, 1492, May 22, 1492, Paris, Guy Marchant, *Danse Macabre,* folio (D-20).

36. April 30, 1491, Paris, Guy Marchant, *Danse macabre des femmes, Les trois morts et les trois vifs.*

37. [Between 1491 and 1500], Paris, Guy Marchant, Nicolas Du Mesnil, *Le maniere.*

38. June 23, 1492, Paris, Guy Marchant, Horatius, *Sermones,* 40 (H-481).

39. [Between 1492 and 1496], Paris, Guy Marchant, Michel Bureau, *Tractatus.*

40. April 18, 1493, Paris, Guy Marchant [in part for Antoine Vérard], *Compost et kalendrier des bergiers,* folio (C-54).

41. [After April 29, 1493], Paris, in campo Gaillardi [Guy Marchant], Christophorus Columbus, *Epistola de insulis nuper inventis,* 4° (C-761).

42. July 18, 1493, Paris, Guy Marchant, *Compost et kalendrier des bergiers,* folio (C-55).

43. [Aug. 16,] 1493, Paris, Guy Marchant, Augustinus Datus, *Elegantiolae,* 4°.

44. Sept. 3, 1493, Paris, Guy Marchant, Phalaris, *Epistolae* (trans. Fr. Aretinus), 4° (P-563).

45. Sept. 5, 1493, Paris, Guy Marchant, Isidorus Hispalensis, *De summo bono,* 8° (I-198).

46. [C.1493], [Paris, Guy Marchant for Antoine Vérard], *Compost et kalendrier des bergieres,* folio.

47. [C.1493], Paris, [Guy Marchant or Antoine Caillaut], Jacobus Publicus, *Ars conficiendi epistolas,* 4° (P-1091).

48. Feb. 6, 1494, Paris, Guy Marchant, Bonaventura, *Sermones de morte,* 4° (B-943).

49. April 3, 1494, Paris, Guy Marchant, Andrelinus, *Elegiae* (A-691a).

50. May 16, 1494, Paris, Guy Marchant, Isidorus Hispalensis, *Synonyma de homine et ratione, seu Soliloquia,* 8° (I-207).

51. July 2, 1494, Paris, Guy Marchant, Odo, Bishop of Cambrai, *Expositio canonis missae*, 8º (O-24).

52. July 31, 1494, Paris, Guy Marchant, *Ars moriendi*.

53. Aug. 16, 1494, Paris, Guy Marchant, Bonaventura, *Soliloquium*, 8º.

54. Sept. 6, 1494, Paris, Guy Marchant, Johannes Consobrinus, *De iustitia commutativa* (C-862).

55. Oct. 15, 1494, Paris, Guy Marchant, Alliaca, *Tractatus exponibilum*, 4º (A-486).

56. Oct. 24, 1494, Paris, Guy Marchant, Jacobus Lupius, *Fructus sacramenti penitentiae*, 8º (L-398).

57. Nov. 21, 1494, Paris, Guy Marchant, Petrus Paulus Vergerius, *De ingenius moribus*, 8º (V-138).

58. [1494], Paris, Guy Marchant, Julian Quinion, *Epistola*.

59. [C.1494], Paris, [Guy Marchant], *Stella clericorum*, 4º (S-780).

60. [After 1494], Paris, Guy Marchant, Jacobus de Gruytrode, *Colloquium peccatoris et crucifixi Jesu Christi*, 8º (J-58).

61. [C.1494], [Paris], Guy Marchant, Johannes Chrysostomus, *Liber de eo quod nemo laeditur ab alio nisi a semetipso fuerit laesus*, 8º (J-292).

62. [C.1494], [Paris, Guy Marchant], Marcus Tullius Cicero, *Synonimorum libellus*.

63. Feb. 1495, Paris, Guy Marchant, Thomas Bradwardinus, *Arithmetica speculativa*, 4º (B-1071).

64. March 12, 1495/96, Paris, Guy Marchant, Hieronymus, *Prologi in Bibliam*, 8º (H-188).

65. May 20, 1495, Paris, Guy Marchant, Thomas Bradwardinus, *Geometria speculativa*, folio (B-1072).

66. May 27, 1495, Paris, Guy Marchant, Bonaventura, *De triplici via* (B-971).

67. June 5, 1495, Paris, Guy Marchant, Werner Rolewinck, *Sacramentum missarum*, 8º (R-300).

68. [C.1495], [Paris, Guy Marchant], Hieronymus Balbus, *Epigrammata*, 4º (B-19).

69. Jan. 4, 1496/97, Paris, Guy Marchant [in part for Denis Roce], Odo, Bishop of Cambrai, *Expositio canonis missae*, 8º (O-25).

70. Jan. 7, 1496/97, Paris, Guy Marchant [in part for Jean Petit], *Compost et kalendrier des bergiers*, folio (C-56).

71. Jan. 30, 1496/97, Paris, Guy Marchant, *Modus poenitendi*, 8º (M-773).

72. May 10, 1496, Paris, Guy Marchant, Publius Faustus Andrelinus, *De influentia siderum et querela Parisiensis pavimenti*, 4º.

73. May 16, 1496, Paris, Guy Marchant, Jean Le Munerat, *De dedicatione ecclesiae parisiensis*.

74. Aug. 6, 1496, Paris, Guy Marchant, Hieronymus Savonarola, *Revelatio de tribulationibus nostrorum temporum*, 4º (S-238).

75. [Aug. 31,] 1496, Paris, Guy Marchant for Jean Petit, Publius Faustus Andrelinus, *De Neapolitana victoria,* 4°.

76. [Aug. 9, 1496], Paris, Guy Marchant, Ovidius, *De nuce.*

77. Aug. 9, 1496, Paris, Guy Marchant [for Jean Petit], Publius Faustus Andrelinus, *Elegiae,* 4° (A-692).

78. Oct. 24, 1496, [Paris], Guy Marchant, Faber (= Lefèvre d'Etaples), *Introductiones in diversos libros Aristotelis* (ed. Jodocus Clichtoveus, Guillermus Gonterius, and David Lauxius), 4° (F-15).

79. Nov. 14, 1496, Paris, Guy Marchant, Johannes Consobrinus, *De iustitia commutativa,* 8° (C-863).

80. Dec. 30, 1496, Paris, Guy Marchant, *Flores legum secundum ordinem alphabeti* (F-212).

81. [C.1496], [Paris, Guy Marchant], Andreas de Escobar, *Modus confitendi* (A-673).

82. [Jan. 20, 1497], [Paris, Guy Marchant], Guilielmus Hermannus, *Silva odarum,* 4° (H-71).

83. March 5, 1497/98, Paris, Guy Marchant, *Le livret des consolacions contre toutes tribulacions,* 8° (L-256).

84. March 22, 1497/98, Paris, Guy Marchant for Jean Petit, Gerson, *Conclusiones de diversis materiis moralibus, sive De regulis mandatorum,* 8° (G-212).

85. March 29, 1497, Paris, Guy Marchant pour Jean Petit, Jacobus de Gruytrode, *Colloquium peccatoris et crucifixi Ihesu Christi.*

86. April 2, 1497, Paris, Guy Marchant, Isidoros Hispalensis, *Synonyma de homine et ratione, seu soliloquia,* 8° (I-208).

87. April 10, 1497, Paris, Guy Marchant, in part for Jean Petit, *Ars moriendi,* 8° (A-1099).

88. June 17, 1497, Paris, Guy Marchant, Bonaventura, *Soliloquium,* 8° (B-955).

89. Oct. 12, 1497, Paris, [Guy Marchant], Jacobus Faber Stapulensis (= Jacques Lefèvre d'Etaple), *Introductiones in diversos libros Aristotelis* (ed. Jodocus Clichtoveus, Guillermus Gonterius, and David Lauxius), 4° (F-16).

90. Nov. 4, 1497, Paris, Guy Marchant, in part for Jean Petit, Werner Rolewinck, *Sacramentum missarum,* 8° (R-301).

91. Nov. 9, 1497, Paris, [Guy Marchant for Jean Petit], Matthaeus de Cracovia, *Dialogus rationis et conscientiae de frequenti usu communionis,* 8° (M-370).

92. 1497, Paris, "In vico sancti Jacobi ad intersignium Ursi prope sanctum Maturinum," Hieronymus Brunschwig, *Isagogicon moralis disciplinae* (trans. Brunus Aretinus), 4° (B-1253).

93. Jan. 29, 1498/99, Paris, Guy Marchant [in part for Jean Petit], Petrus de Alliaco, *Conceptus insolubilia,* 4°.

94. Feb. 16, 1498/99, Paris, Guy Marchant, Gasperinus Barzizius, *Epistolae,* 4° (B-266).

95. Feb. 1498, Paris, Guy Marchant for Jean Petit, Johannes de Sacro Busto, *Sphaera mundi,* 4° (J-418).

96. [After April 19, 1498], [Paris, Guy Marchant], Picus de Mirandula, *Conseil profitable contre les ennuis et tribulations du monde* (trans. R. Gaguin), 4°.

97. Aug. 7, 1498, [Paris], Guy Marchant [in part for Denis Roce], Hieronymus, *Vita et transitus: Epistola de monte,* Augustinus Hieronymi, *Epistola de magnificentiis Hieronymi,* Cyrillus, *De miraculus Hieronymi,* 4° (H-245).

98. Aug. 7, 1498, Paris, Guy Marchant, Pseudo Cremonensis Eusebius, *Epistole.*

99. Aug. 8, 1498, Paris, Guy Marchant, in part for Jean Petit, Athenagoras, *De resurrectione* (trans. Marsilius Ficinus) (A-1176).

100. Sept. 11, 1498, Paris, Guy Marchant, Stephanus Fliscus, *Synonyma,* Gasparini Barzizii, *Opusculum de eloquentia* (with a postscript by Jodocus Clichthoveus).

101. Sept. 20, 1498, Paris, Guy Marchant [in part for Denis Roce], *Dialogus inter clericum et militem* (alt. title = *Disputatio . . .*), 4° (D-157).

102. Sept. 24, 1498, [Paris], Guy Marchant, in part for Denis Roce, Guillermus Saphonensis, *Modus epistolandi* or *Modus conficiendi epistolas,* 4° (G-725).

103. Dec. 11, 1498, Paris, Guy Marchant, Augustinus Datus, *Nomina magistratum dignitatumque romanorum cirium* (comment, Jodocus Clichtoveus), Franciscus Niger, *Regulae XXX elegantiarim* (comment, Jodocus Clicthoveus).

104. Dec. 18, 1498, Paris, Guy Marchant, J. Lupi Rebello, *Tractatus fructus sacramenti poenitentiae,* 8°.

105. [C.1498], [Paris, Guy Marchant], Picus de Mirandula, *Lettre à François de Mirandole,* 8° (P-643).

106. [C.1498], [Paris], Guy Marchant, Antonius de Raymundia, *Libellus contra beneficiorum reservationes,* 4° (A-916).

107. [C.1498–1500], [Paris, Guy Marchant], Seneca, *Flores [ex diversis libris excerptae], Sententiae [ex diversis libris excerptae], De remedus fortuitorum,* 8°.

108. [C.1498], Paris, [Guy Marchant], Hugo de Sancto Victore, *Regula S. Augustini,* 8° (H-533).

109. [C.1498], [Paris], Guy Marchant, *Articuli fidei* (A-1153).

110. [C.1498], [Paris, Guy Marchant], Jacobus de Gruytrode, *Colloquium peccatoris et crucifixi Jesu Christi,* 8° (J-59).

111. Feb. 19, 1499/1500, Paris, Guy Marchant for Denis Roce, Jacques Faber Stapulensis (Lefèvre d'Etaple), *Ars moralis,* 4° (F-13a).

112. March 3, 1499/1500, Paris, Guy Marchant for Alexandre Aliate], Proba Falconia, *Camina sive certones vergilii,* 4° (P-989).

113. April 6, 1499, Paris, Guy Marchant, in part for Jean Petit, Raymundus Lullus, *De laudibus B.V. Mariae,* folio (L-390).

114. April 10, 1499, Paris, Guy Marchant for Jean Petit, Raymundus Lullus, *De laudibus B.V. Mariae* (ed. LeFèbvre d'Etaple); folio (L-391).

115. June 10, 1499, Paris, Guy Marchant (for Jean Petit), Werner Rolewinck, *Sacramentum missarum,* 8º (R-302).

116. June 17, 1499, Paris, Guy Marchant, [*Poenitas cita*].

117. June 19, 1499, Paris, Guy Marchant for Jean Petit, Odo, Bishop of Cambrai, *Expositio canonis missae,* 8º (D-26).

118. July 29, 1499, Paris, Guy Marchant, in part for Jean Petit, Bonaventura, *Soliloquium,* 8º (B-956).

119. Aug. 17, 1499, Paris, Guy Marchant, in part for Jean Petit, *Compost et kalendrier des bergieres,* folio (C-58).

120. Aug. 23, 1499, Paris, Guy Marchant, in part for Jean Petit, *Ars moriendi.*

121. Sept. 2, 1499, Paris, Guy Marchant, [Johannes Gerson], *Alphabetum divini amoris,* 8º (A-531).

122. Sept. 24, 1499, Paris, Guy Marchant, in part for Jean Petit, Dionysius Carthusiensis, *Speculum animae peccatricis,* 8º (S-649).

123. Nov. 9, 1499, Paris, [Guy Marchant] for G. de Marnef, *Les merueilles de romme* (trans. of *Mirabilia Romae, vel potius historia et descriptio urbis Romae*), 12º (M-607).

124. Nov. 16, 1499, Guy Marchant, Jean Raulin, *Collatio.*

125. Nov. 16, 1499, Paris, Guy Marchant, in part for Enguilbert, Jean, and Geoffrey de Marnef, Johannes Raulinus, *Collatio de perfecta religionis planta-tione* (ed. S. Brant), with Pius II, *Carmen sapphicum in Passionem christi,* 8º (R-31).

126. Dec. 24, 1499, Paris, Guy Marchant, Paulus Niavis, *Latinum idioma pro parvulis editum,* 8º (H-38).

127. Jan. 9, 1500/01, Paris, Guy Marchant, Augustine, *De vita christiana,* 8º (A-1361).

128. April 4, 1500/01, Paris, Guy Marchant for Alexander Aliate, Pseudo Aristotle, *Problemata "Omnes homines,"* 4º (A-1044).

129. Jan. 23, 1500/01, Paris, [Guy Marchant], Laurentius Valla, *Elegantiae linguae latinae. De Pronomine sui. Add. Antonius Marcinellus: Lima quaedam laurentii vallensius,* 4º.

130. Sept. 10, 1500, Paris, Guy Marchant for Jean Petit, *Compost et kalendrier des bergers,* folio (C-57).

131. Oct. 7, 1500, Paris, Guy Marchant, *Modus poenitendi,* 8º (M-776).

132. Oct. 12, 1500, Paris, Guy Marchant, Nicolaus Horius, *De assumptione beatissimae Mariae Virginis,* 8º.

133. Oct. 21, 1500, [Paris], Guy Marchant, Cardinal Bessarion, *Epistolae et orationes,* 8º (B-520).

134. Nov. 19, 1500, Paris, Guy Marchant for Denis Roce, Antonius

Nebrissensis, *Introductiones latinae,* with additions by Julianus Garces, 4°
(A-904).

135. [C.1500], [Paris, Guy Marchant], Albertus Fantinus, *Liber terminorum,*
4°.

136. [C.1500?], [Paris, Guy Marchant], S. Hieronymes, *Psalterium.*

137. [Before 1501], Paris, [Guy Marchant?] for D. Roce, Thomas Aquinas,
De modo confidendi et puritate conscientiae, 8° (T-310?).

138. [C.1503], Paris, Guy Marchant for Jean Petit, Publius Faustus Andrelinus, *De Neapolitana fornovien sique victoria.*

139. [C.1503], Paris, [Guy Marchant] for Jean Petit, Publius Faustus Andrelinus, *Eligiae.*

140. [C.1505], [Paris, Guy Marchant], Saint Bonaventura, *De praeparatione
ad missam cum orationibus III,* 8°.

141. [C.1500], Paris, [Guy Marchant?], Petrarca, *De vita solitaria,* 4°.

142. [C.1495], Paris, Guy Marchant, Petrus Sanchez Ciruelus, *Arithmetica
practica seu algorismus.*

143. [N.d.], [Paris, Guy Marchant] for Denis Roce, Theodolus, *Ecloga The-
oduli.*

144. [N.d.], [Paris, Guy Marchant?] for Jean Alexandre and Charles de
Bougne of Angers, Dante, *Elegantiolae* (D-87).

145. [N.d.], Paris, [Guy Marchant? for] E., G., and J. de Marnef, Diogenes
Laetius, *Vitae et sententiae philosophorum* (trans. Ambrosius Traversarius),
4° (D-227).

146. [C.1499], [Paris, Guy Marchant], H. Herpf, *Directorium ad consequendum
vitae perfectionem* (with other tracts).

147. [N.d., c.1508?], [Paris, Guy Marchant for] Jean Petit, Diodorus
Siculus, *Bibliothecae historicae libri VI* (trans. Gianfrancesco Poggio Brac-
ciolini, ed. Aegidius de Maserus), 4° (D-215).

148. [N.d.], [Paris, Jean or Guy Marchant for Denis Roce], Diodorus
Siculus, *Bibliothecae historicae libri VI* (trans. Gianfrancesco Poggio Brac-
ciolini, ed. Aegidius de Maserus), 4° (D-214).

149. [After Dec. 1507], [Paris], Guy Marchant for Jean Petit, M. Junianus
Justinus, *Epitomae in Trogi Pompeii historias,* 4° (J-623).

PART II

AUTHORS AND ARTISTS

[4]

Text, Image, and Authorial Self-Consciousness in Late Medieval Paris

Cynthia J. Brown

In this essay I propose to clarify how the advent of printing affected French writers of vernacular works in the late fifteenth and early sixteenth centuries. I investigate the relationship of writers to their literary enterprise by examining in the books themselves verbal and visual representations of authors and the rapport between the two. The works of André de la Vigne (c. 1470–c. 1515) and Pierre Gringore (c. 1475–c. 1539) represent two case studies of a group of French poet-historians known as the *rhétoriqueurs,* whose literary activity, which spanned the years 1460 to 1530, provides useful models for the period of transition from manuscript to print in France. Centered in Paris at the beginning of the sixteenth century, each of these writers was directly or indirectly associated with the French royal courts of King Charles VIII or his successor, Louis XII.

The literary production of André de la Vigne offers particularly useful information for an investigation into the author's consciousness of his artistic craft and of the ways it may have been shaped by the advent of printing. As we shall see, the relationship between the physical presentation of La Vigne's major work, *La ressource de la Chrestienté,* and the writer's image of himself evolves in a significant manner in the transition from the manuscript to the printed versions of the work. These developing stages provide sources for tracing a change in literary authority that likely occurred on a more general scale in the shift from manuscript to print.

It is important to understand that the *Ressource de la Chrestienté* constitutes an allegorical polemic written in support of Charles VIII's anticipated military expedition to Italy to capture Naples in August 1494. I try to demonstrate how, through its different versions over the course of some twenty-five years, La Vigne's status as author develops within the same text from a conventionally medieval secondary stance into a growing authoritative presence, and how at the same time his patron Charles VIII changes from a dominant, personalized authority to a more absent, ambiguous persona. The transition from script to print seems to have played a central role in this evolution, attested to by textual changes and documented by illustrations. In other words, the history of the publication of the *Ressource de la Chrestienté* offers the modern reader a view of the working out of the author's relationship to his work as a consequence of the invention of printing.

At least three phases in this process can be observed; these coincide with the chronological evolution of the versions of the *Ressource*. The first involves the royal manuscript presentation copy (BN, MS fr. 1687), possibly the earliest extant version of the text, dating from 1494, and a contemporaneous manuscript belonging to the Count of Angoulême (BN, MS fr. 1699); the second stage is represented by the first printed edition of the work, which came out a year later in Angoulême (Aix-en-Provence, Bibliothèque Méjanes, Inc. D 14–15); the third centers on a series of early-sixteenth-century Parisian imprints of an anthology, the *Vergier d'honneur,* which contains the *Ressource* as its introductory piece.[1] Overlapping with the second and perhaps third stage, moreover, are two anonymous manuscript adaptations of La Vigne's work (BN, MSS fr. 20055 and 15215).

In examining the facing folios that open the royal manuscript of the *Ressource* (figs. 4.1 and 4.2), the viewer perceives at the left a writer as he offers his closed, finished book to a seated royal figure: the former is on his knees, a characteristic posture of the author in a presentation miniature; the latter, presumably his patron, is crowned and enthroned. Those versed in the interpretation of royal signs would recognize in short order the visual tribute to King Charles VIII of

---

[1]For details on these editions and their relationship to the other versions, see Cynthia J. Brown, "The Evolution of André de la Vigne's *La Ressource de la Chrestienté:* From the Manuscript Tradition to the *Vergier d'honneur* Editions," *Bibliothèque d'Humanisme et Renaissance* 45 (1982): 115–25, as well as idem., the critical edition of the *Ressource de la Chrestienté* (Montreal, 1989). All references in the text are to this edition.

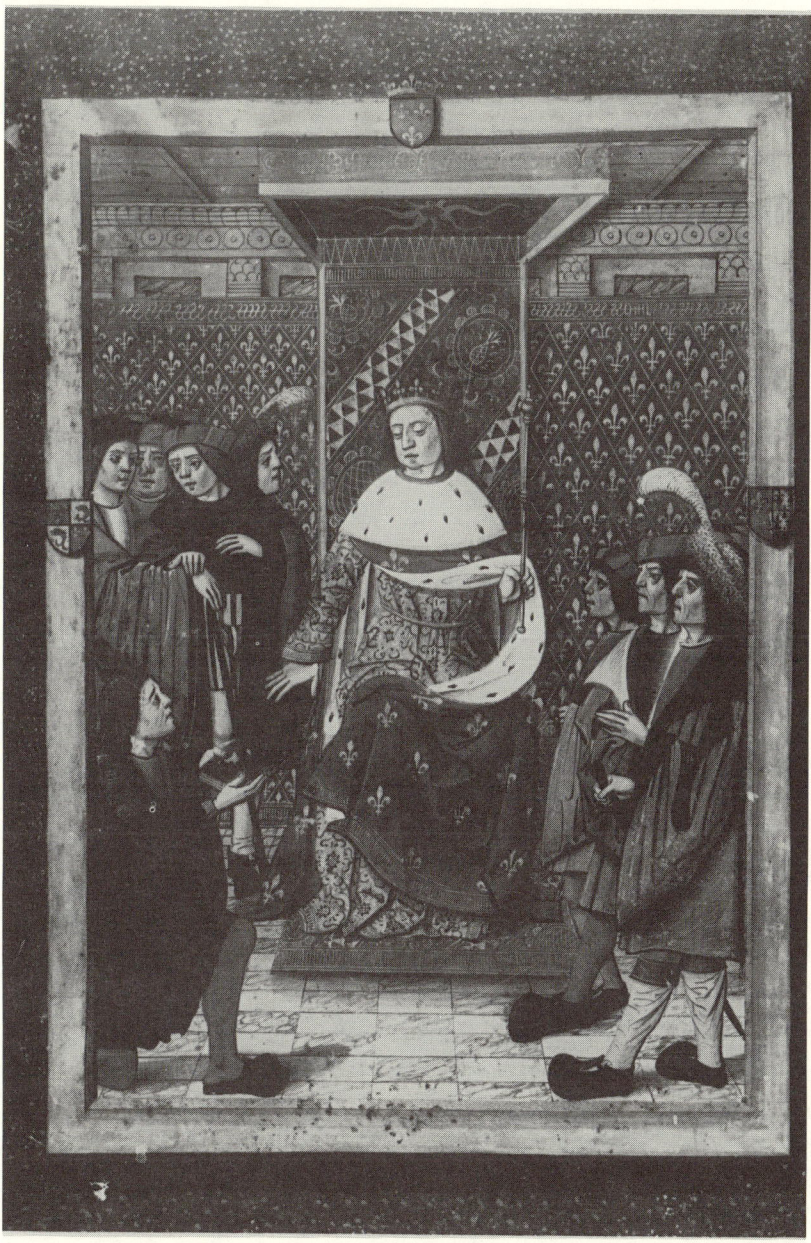

Figure 4.1. Poet Offering His Work to King Charles VIII, frontispiece, from *La ressource de la Chrestienté*, BN, MS fr. 1687. Photo: Bibliothèque Nationale, Paris.

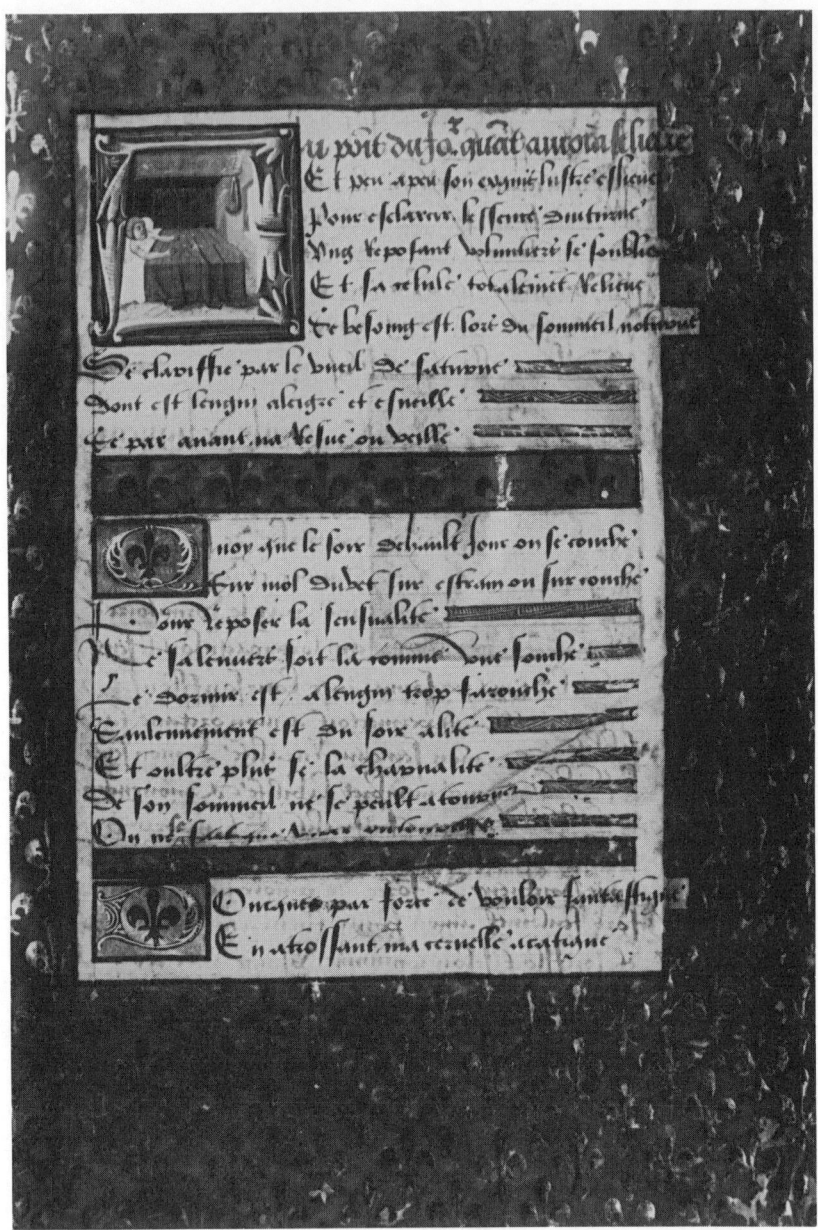

Figure 4.2. Historiated initial of Dreaming Poet, from *La ressource de la Chrestienté,* BN, MS fr. 1687, fol. 2r. Photo: Bibliothèque Nationale, Paris.

France, his queen, Anne of Brittany, and their son, the dauphin. The fleur-de-lis motif of the backdrop and robe, exquisitely echoed on the facing folio at the right (fig. 4.2) by its identically decorated margins, which all but engulf the text from without and within, signals that the monarch hails from the House of France, whereas the three marginal shields portray a French coupling with the ermine devices of Brittany (right) and those of a dauphin (left). These anticipate in point of fact the decorative program of the entire manuscript: on each and every folio the text is surrounded by an alternating pattern of the same heraldic devices.

By contrast, the other characters in the frontispiece are unidentified and unidentifiable. The author figure represents one of a multitude of anonymous dedicators of works. Here, then, from the outset we observe in symbolic terms the very political relationship of the patron and poet: the writer is beholden to the protector for financial retribution and directly or indirectly for the subject of his work; the patron, the object of the dedication, dominates in many ways the poet's literary enterprise.[2] While we do not know if Charles VIII actually commissioned the *Ressource de la Chrestienté*, securing the king's patronage was clearly La Vigne's goal and reward for writing this work, for French royal political aims—support for the anticipated Naples expedition—constitute the raison d'être of the book, and this particular manuscript was specially decorated for the king's viewing. As it turned out, La Vigne subsequently accompanied the king as secretary during the Naples expedition.

Although the opening verses of the text present a first-person voice, who describes his state of insomnia and ensuing heavy, nightmarish sleep,[3] no sign, verbal or visual, clearly identifies the speaker or establishes any connection between him and the kneeling figure in the presentation miniature. The initiated reader might well connect the scene of the man sleeping in the first historiated letter on the second folio (fig. 4.2) with the ever-influential *Roman de la Rose* tradition, which similarly and repeatedly dramatized the narrator-pro-

---

[2]For a discussion of the relationship between the *rhétoriqueurs* and their patrons, see Paul Zumthor, *Le masque et la lumière* (Paris, 1978); and Cynthia J. Brown, *The Shaping of History and Poetry in Late Medieval France: Propaganda and Artistic Expression in the Works of the Rhétoriqueurs* (Birmingham, 1985).

[3]See *Ressource de la Chrestienté*, vv. 10–27.

tagonist of the text.[4] Even though a certain authority is thereby accorded his word, particularly since it is associated with a dream vision,[5] at the same time, this conventional pose ensures a certain anonymity because it links the narrator figure to a traditional literary representation.

It is only at the very end of the work some 1,500 lines later that the reader discovers the relationship between the speaker in the text and the figure in the frontispiece, for there the former declares (emphasis added):

> Et pour conclure, je vous pry, treschier sire
> Que le traicté vous plaise avoir en grace,
> Quoy que n'y soit la scïence Porphire,
> Ne la prudence de Virgille ou Bocace.
> Se mon engin eust plus grant efficace,
> J'eusse trop mieulx labouré et enté
> La Ressource de la Chrestïenté,
> Qui a vous, sire, de presenter n'est digne,
> Ne plus ne moins que le fruyt *De la vigne.*
>
> [vv. 1461–69]

> [And in conclusion, I pray, my beloved lord,
> That it please you to hold this treatise in favor,
> Even though Porphry's wisdom cannot be found in it,
> Or the prudence of Virgil or Boccaccio.
> If my abilities were more effective,
> I would have labored on and grafted much more
> The *Ressource de la Chrestienté*
> Which is not worthy of being presented to you, sire,
> Any more or less than the fruit of the vine.]

[4]See David Hult's landmark study of Guillaume de Lorris' part of the *Roman de la Rose* entitled *Self-Fulfilling Prophecies: Readership and Authority in the First Roman de la Rose* (New York, 1986), in particular pp. 74–82, where he provides details regarding the image of the sleeping poet in the *Rose* iconography.

[5]See Hult, *Self-Fulfilling Prophecies,* pp. 127–37, where he talks about how the dream vision magnifies the narrator's authority. On p. 127 he states: "The transfer from a phenomenal universe of divine prophecy to one of narrative prophecy suggests an oscillation within the dream construct between a God-centered theological universe and the writer-oriented universe of fiction, where the author replaces God as the omniscient controlling figure." Many other works from the fourteenth and fifteenth centuries open with a dreaming-poet scene and miniature.

With a coincidence of time and action, as the presentation of the completed work is made, the "I" and "you" of these verses clearly hark back to the dedication scene of the opening miniature. A contemporary audience would have recognized the coincidence of the first-person voice and the metaphoric signature of André *De la vigne*. While the "you" is not specifically named here, the emblems of the opening miniature have long since signaled the identity of the enthroned dedicated figure; furthermore, as an endorsement of this visual code and insurance that this recognition be maintained throughout the text, two series of illuminated acrostics within the work specify the name Charles of Valois.[6] Thus, as was often the case in the manuscript-produced work of La Vigne's predecessors, identification of the creator of the text receives secondary attention, deferred as it is until the very end of the composition.[7] Significantly, the author's name is not illuminated. It is nonetheless worthy of note that the last words are presented visually as a signature, at once part of the metaphor in verbal terms (fruyt *De la vigne*) and separate as a conscious authorial sign in visual terms (fig. 4.3).

In point of fact, the precise identification of the two principal figures in the frontispiece depends on a visual assimilation of the text. While literature was still orally transmitted at this late date—and the extensive rhyme and prose play of much of the *Ressource* attest to its oral affiliations—the role of the acrostics and of La Vigne's signature in the work underlines the importance the author placed on its visual reception as well.

[6]The first series of acrostics spells out CHARLES DE VALOIS in a number of ways (vv.678–719), while the second contains the following acrostic: CHARLES HVITJESME ET DERNJER DE CE NOM PAR LA GRACE DE DJEV ROY DE FRANCE A QVJ DJEV DOINT BONNE VJE ET LONGVE ET PARADIS A LA FIN (vv.1364–1445).

[7]See for example, the works of Jean Molinet (1435–1507), such as *La complainte de Grèce* (1464):

> Cest ouvrage,
> Lourt, sauvaige,
> Sans parage, ou riens n'est net,
> Mollu d'un gros *mollinet*.

(ed. N. Dupire, *Les faictz et dictz* [Paris, 1936], I, 26) or *Le Temple de Mars* (c. 1475):

> Pour Dieu, excusés ma simplesse,
> S'il est obscur, trouble ou brunet:
> Chascun n'a pas son *molin net*.

(Dupire, *Faictz et dictz*, p. 76), where Molinet "signs" in a similar manner.

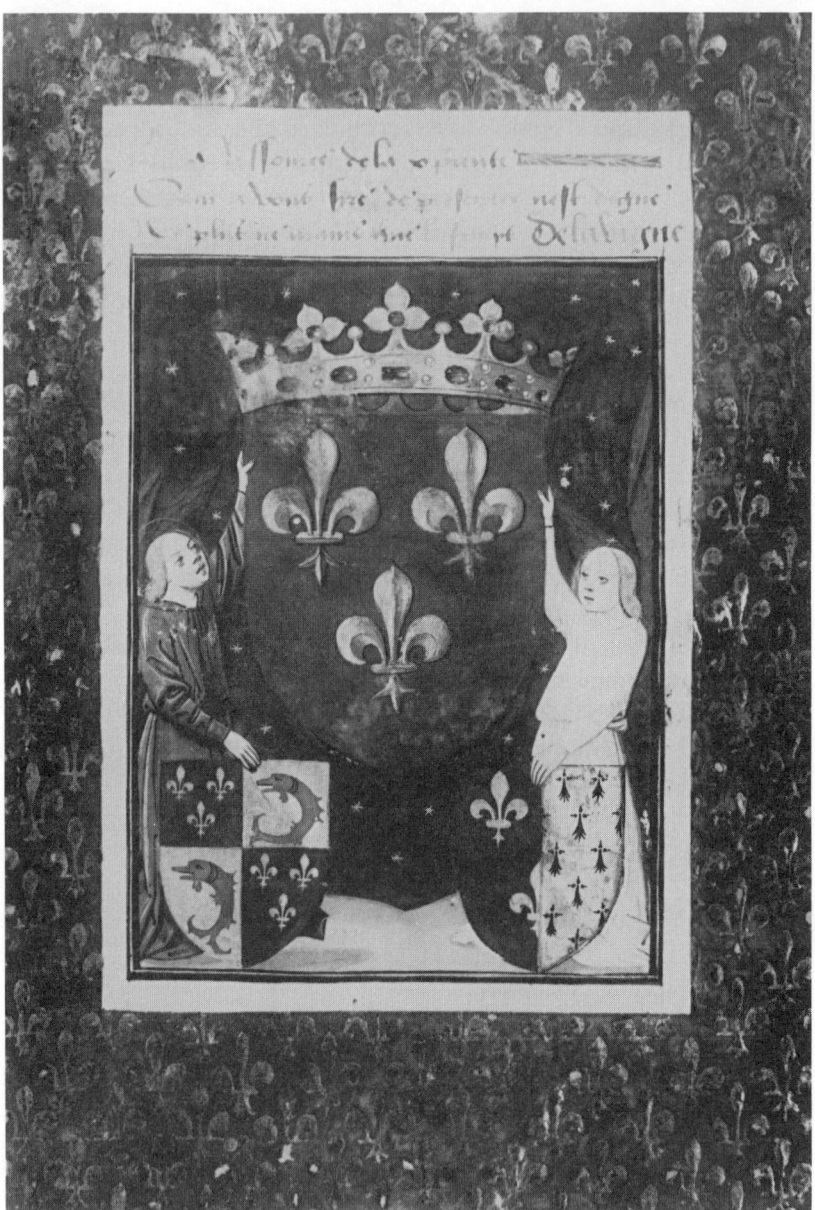

Figure 4.3. André de la Vigne's metaphoric signature followed by the Royal Coat of Arms of King Charles VIII and Queen Anne of Brittany, from *La ressource de la Chrestienté*, BN, MS fr. 1687, fol. 46r. Photo: Bibliothèque Nationale, Paris.

In returning to the first two leaves of manuscript 1687 (figs. 4.1 and 4.2), we become aware that essential temporal and character differences between the illustration at the left and the opening of the text at the right undermine the possibility of a verbal-visual "dialogue" between the two. Whereas the miniature depicts the finished work and its dedication or "publication,"[8] as it were, the initial lines of the text set the stage for the action, which, as we shall see, concerns the process of the creation of that very work, for an allegorical drama is first imagined into existence, then witnessed, and finally recorded. The tradition of placing a dedication miniature before the text, and perhaps too the desire to stamp the king's presence everywhere in this particular manuscript, likely dictated this disruption of communication between text and image at the beginning of the volume. This is resolved only in the last few lines, where, in a self-conscious stance, La Vigne steps outside his text, names himself elliptically, and directly addresses Charles VIII in what can be described as a "metacursive dialogue,"[9] depicted in concrete form in the frontispiece. Like the miniature, these last lines remain external to the rest of the narrative.

On the one hand, then, from the first to the last folio of manuscript 1687 of the *Ressource,* the specific presence of Charles VIII dominates the poetic composition both visually, as the acrostics and illustrations show, and verbally, since the work strongly encourages support of royal policy. The author's image remains traditionally anonymous until the end, where even his metaphoric signature is undermined by the invading presence of the joint royal coats of arms below it (fig.

---

[8]See Robert K. Root, "Publication before Printing," *PMLA* 28 (1913): 428, where he explains that the act of presenting a work to a patron was equivalent to the formal act of publication.

[9]Hult, *Self-Fulfilling Prophecies,* p. 113, uses this term in reference to the *Roman de la Rose.* "The Narrator's self-conscious stance, his direct address to the reader—constitutive parts of the literary prologue—will initiate an implicit or explicit metadiscursive dialogue with the reader/listener." In fact, in the *Ressource,* La Vigne first addresses the more general reader, albeit more indirectly through third-person usage, in the three preceding lines by means of a conventional humility topos:

> En supplïant tous ceulx qui cy aprés
> Le vauldront lire, a payne ou de leger,
> Que les faultes leur plaise corriger.
> [vv. 1458–60]

> [Beseeching all those who hereafter
> Will want to read it, with difficulty or ease,
> That they please correct any errors.]

[111]

4.3). Moreover, the manuscript producers—scribe, illuminator, and miniaturist—remain completely anonymous contributors to the manuscript book of the *Ressource.* Their goal, like the author's, was apparently dictated directly or indirectly by that of the king. [10]

On the other hand, it is true that the illustrator of manuscript 1687 manifests and maintains an interest in authorial—or rather narrative—presence throughout: the images he paints reflect the ubiquitous first-person narrator in the text, but, as a result in part of the legacy of the *Roman de la Rose,* this presence remains ambiguous. In the *Ressource,* what appear to be the authentic words of the author, André de la Vigne—those that we "heard" in the final verses and which are doubtless to be associated with the kneeling figure in the initial illustration—become confused if not lost through the first-person voices of the text. This is because the creative figure is himself fictionalized. [11] Before proceeding to a study of the relationship between text and image of the author within the narration, let us examine the source of this ambiguity.

As in many medieval works, especially from the *Roman de la Rose* on, the presentation of the author occurs in a complex layering of subjectivities, which proceed from a kind of external authoritative figure, as the final verses of the *Ressource* demonstrate, to a more internal fictional one. [12] This is complicated by the commonly adopted dream framework, whose pseudoautobiographical dimension makes all the more ambiguous the role of the author in the working out of the narrative strategy. [13] It is Guillaume de Lorris' use of the autobiographical "I" in the early-thirteenth-century part of the

[10]See Gaston Duval, "Notes sur quelques manuscrits exécutés dans l'atelier d'Antoine Vérard," *La correspondance historique et archéologique* 7 (March 1900): 71–72, who suggests that this manuscript was produced in the Parisian workshop of Antoine Vérard.

[11]Hult, *Self-Fulfilling Prophecies,* p. 62, describes the first-person voice of the *Rose* in these terms.

[12]Ibid., p. 2.

[13]For further thoughts regarding the dream motif in French vernacular works of the fourteenth and fifteenth centuries, see Pierre-Yves Badel, "Songes et apparitions," in his *Roman de la Rose au XIVe siècle* (Geneva, 1980), pp. 331–409; Christiane Marchello-Nizia, "Entre l'histoire et la poétique: Le 'songe politique,'" *Revue des sciences humaines* 55, 183 (July–September 1981): 39–53; and Jeannine Quillet, "Songes et songeries dans l'art de la politique au XIVe siècle," *Les études philosophiques* 3 (July–September 1975): 327–49.

Roman de la Rose and Jean de Meung's continuation of it in the 1270s that altered the role of the self-conscious authorial voice in vernacular fictional French literature.[14] Previously it had been relegated to distinctly defined positions outside the text, to prologues and epilogues, as can be seen in the works of Chrétien de Troyes or Marie de France. In the *Rose*, however, the persona of the first-person voice is multiplied in an intricate meshing of narrative levels as the narrator occupies positions before, during, and after the recounted events.[15] In other words, the author's role and identity become ambiguous because of their linking with the narrative voice within the fictional framework of the text. The latter recounts the tale not in the third person but in the first person because he is also a participant in the action. How does the use of illustrations, nonverbal in nature, reflect this change? The answer appears to lie in the use of the dreaming-poet motif.

In returning to the opening lines of the *Ressource* text and the first historiated letter (fig. 4.2), we can now understand that the illustrator has depicted here the dreaming poet whose vision, as convention would dictate, will eventually provide the setting and action of the work. It is at this moment, then, that the fictionalized creator starts to shift into his role as narrator, speaking with a voice that does not coincide, at least temporally, with the figure in the dedication miniature or with the words at the end of the text because logically it precedes those moments. As the fitful sleeper prepares the stage for his nightmarish vision, his versified words set this moment apart from his prose remarks during the actual vision that follows. In symmetrically

[14]For analyses of the first-person voices in the *Roman de la Rose*, see Charles Dahlberg, "First Person and Personification in the *Roman de la Rose:* Amant and Dangier," *Mediaevalia: A Journal of Medieval Studies* 3 (1977): 37–58; Roger Dragonetti, "Pygmalion ou les pièges de la fiction," in *Orbis mediaevalis: Mélanges de langue et de littérature médiévales offerts à Reto Raduolf Bezzola* (Bern, 1978), pp. 89–111; David Hult, "Closed Quotations: The Speaking Voice in the *Roman de la Rose*," *Yale French Studies* 67 (1984): 248–69; Stephen G. Nichols, Jr., "The Rhetoric of Sincerity in the *Roman de la Rose*," in *Romance Studies in Memory of Edward Billings Ham*, California State College Publications (Hayward, Calif., 1967), pp. 115–29; Rupert T. Pickens, "*Somnium* and Interpretation in Guillaume de Lorris," *Symposium* (Summer 1974): 175–86; Paul Strohm, "Guillaume as Narrator and Lover in the *Roman de la Rose*," *Romanic Review* 59 (1968): 3–9; Karl D. Iutti, "From *Clerc* to *Poète*: The Relevance of the *Romance of the Rose* to Machaut's World," in *Machaut's World: Science and Art in the Fourteenth Century*, ed. M. P. Cosmand and B. Chandler (New York, 1978), pp. 209–16; and E. B. Vitz, "The *I* of the *Roman de la Rose*," *Genre* 6 (1973): 49–75.

[15]Hult, *Self-Fulfilling Prophecies*, p. 137.

completing the exterior narrative framework, the first-person voice shifts from prose back to poetry at the end of the dream to describe his awakening and eventual recording of the debate and action just witnessed. At this point in the text the reader discovers a historiated scene that visually translates the verse passage in which the poet records the observed and/or dreamed events (fig. 4.4).[16] The unmade bed in the background recalls the initial historiated scene, while focus is placed on the poet's transcription after his awakening of what had ostensibly transpired in his mind. The juxtaposed rubric *L'Acteur,* which essentially means author,[17] further emphasizes this role. Thus, although still expressed in conventional terms and placed in traditional prologue and epilogue framing positions, the verse text and the last historiated initial in particular call attention to moments in the creative process. La Vigne's self-conscious discussion about the composing of his work, placed within the text itself,[18] has been emphasized through illustration. By a kind of "contamination," because of its symmetrical positioning with the final historiated scene and its juxtaposition within the text, the initial dreaming-poet illustration comes to signify the intellectual or imaginative part of the creative process as much as the narrator's crossing of the fictional barrier does in the *Rose.* Thus, as far as the construction of the narrative framework of the *Ressource* is concerned, text and illustration together reinforce the idea of the fictionalized creator. While La Vigne's identity is deferred, unlike his future patron's, and relegated to a position outside the main action, emphasis is nevertheless placed on the creative process as a prerequisite to and a result of the action within the vision. In this sense La Vigne imitates his

---

[16]See *Ressource de la Chrestienté,* vv. 1447–57.

[17]For a study of the evolution of the term in Latin, see M. D. Chenu, "Auctor, Actor, Autor," *Bulletin du Cange* 3 (1927): 81–86.

[18]The *Rose* iconographic tradition does not emphasize this creative aspect as much. It is true that the change of authors is highlighted through illustration (see Hult, *Self-Fulfilling Prophecies,* pp. 77–89), as are Jean de Meung's self-reflexive passages, but the creative role itself is not particularly emphasized. La Vigne and his contemporaries developed much more extensively the actual nature of the dream and protagonist's preceding state. In the same way, emphasis is placed at the end on its transcription. In the *Rose* the narrator speaks briefly in the beginning of composing the work, which he has apparently not yet undertaken, drawing more attention to its audience (like La Vigne in the last verses of the *Ressource*) and its "matiere" than the act of composing (ll. 32–44, ed. D. Poirion [Paris, 1974]). The last line only cursorily speaks of the awakening.

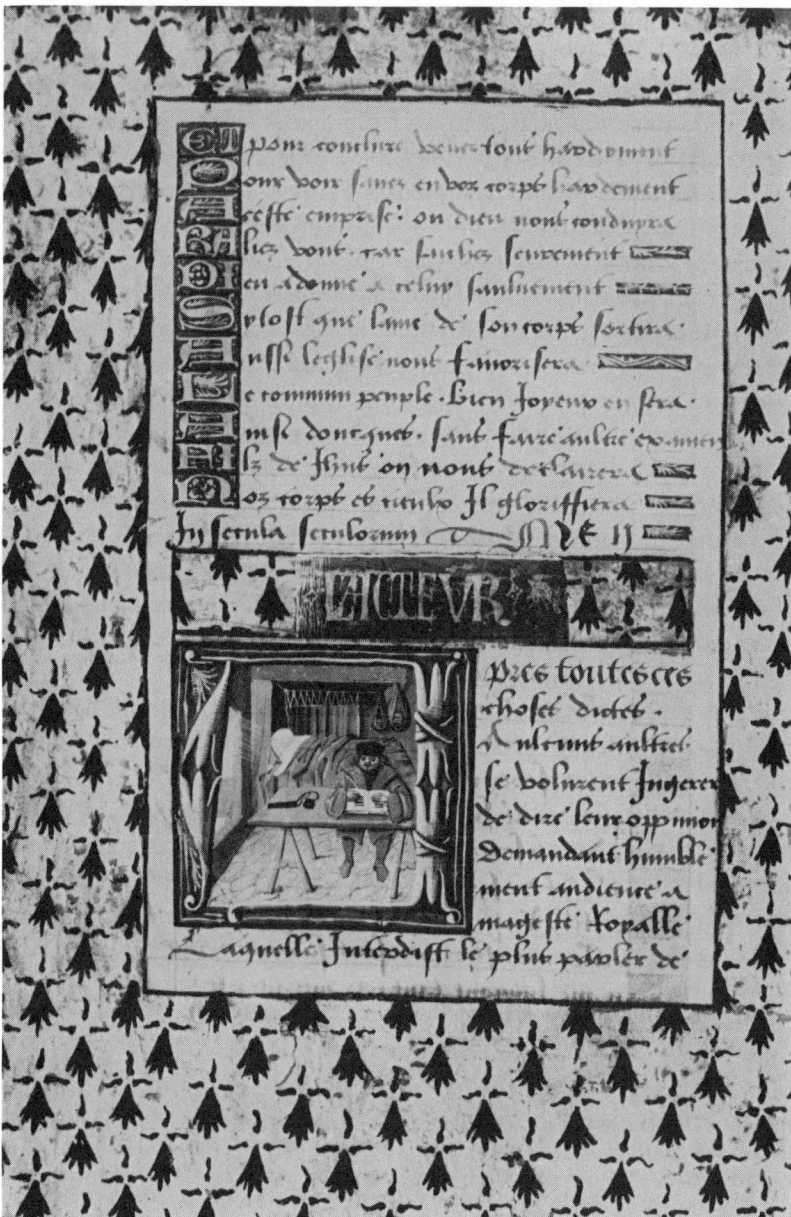

Figure 4.4. Historiated initial of the Poet Recording the Allegorical Scenario of His Dream, from *La ressource de la Chrestienté,* BN, MS fr. 1687, fol. 44v. Photo: Bibliothèque Nationale, Paris.

immediate contemporaries, such as Jean Molinet, and his more distant, revered predecessor Alain Chartier.[19]

This emphasis on the creative function of the first-person voice disappears once the main action of the dream begins, however, and the illustrator of manuscript 1687 traces that change in focus as the narrator becomes a secondary witness figure who overhears the complaint of Lady Christianity and then surreptitiously follows her to the Garden of Honor, where he eavesdrops on the subsequent discussion and debate with Lady Nobility, Good Counsel, Royal Majesty, and I-Don't-Know-Who. Two historiated initials document this new first-person-witness role, and in an amusing fashion the disappearing *acteur's* face is depicted peeking through the bushes (see BN, MS fr. 1687, fols. 2v, 10r).[20] From this point until his awakening the speaker merely introduces the personified figures. His reduced textual participation is reflected by his complete absence in the five following historiated initials, in which the figure of Royal Majesty, the allegorical counterpart of Charles VIII, dominates the stage (fig. 4.5). Not only does her enthroned stance recall that of the king in the dedication miniature, but also her two speeches are literally generated by the acrostics of the monarch's name (see note 6).

In this way, the emphasis on the French king outside of the action is strengthened visually and verbally from within the work. Just as Charles VIII is at the center of the artistic presentation of the *Ressource,* so too is his alter ego, Royal Majesty, the focal point of the action in the allegorical vision. Just as the political theme and subject dominate the action in the text itself, so too the patron's political stature tends to overshadow the poet's creative function. But the two do coexist, albeit somewhat tenuously, and, generally speaking, the reader observes a strong rapport between text and illustration.

The second *Ressource* manuscript does not furnish such a rich mine

---

[19]For a discussion of Jean Molinet's framing self-consciousness, see Cynthia J. Brown, "The Rise of Literary Consciousness in Late Medieval France: Jean Lemaire de Belges and the Rhétoriqueur Tradition," *Journal of Medieval and Renaissance Studies* 13, 1 (Spring 1983): 53–58. Alain Chartier, in his 1422 *Quadrilogue invectif,* a prototype of the *rhétoriqueur* dream allegory, focuses more on the development of the setting of the framework than on the subject of composition. While Christine de Pizan's works provide several examples of this motif, the *rhétoriqueurs* never mention her as one of their revered predecessors.

[20]The very scenes illustrated here are similar to those represented in the *Rose* iconographic program. See Hult, *Self-Fulfilling Prophecies,* p. 111 n. 10.

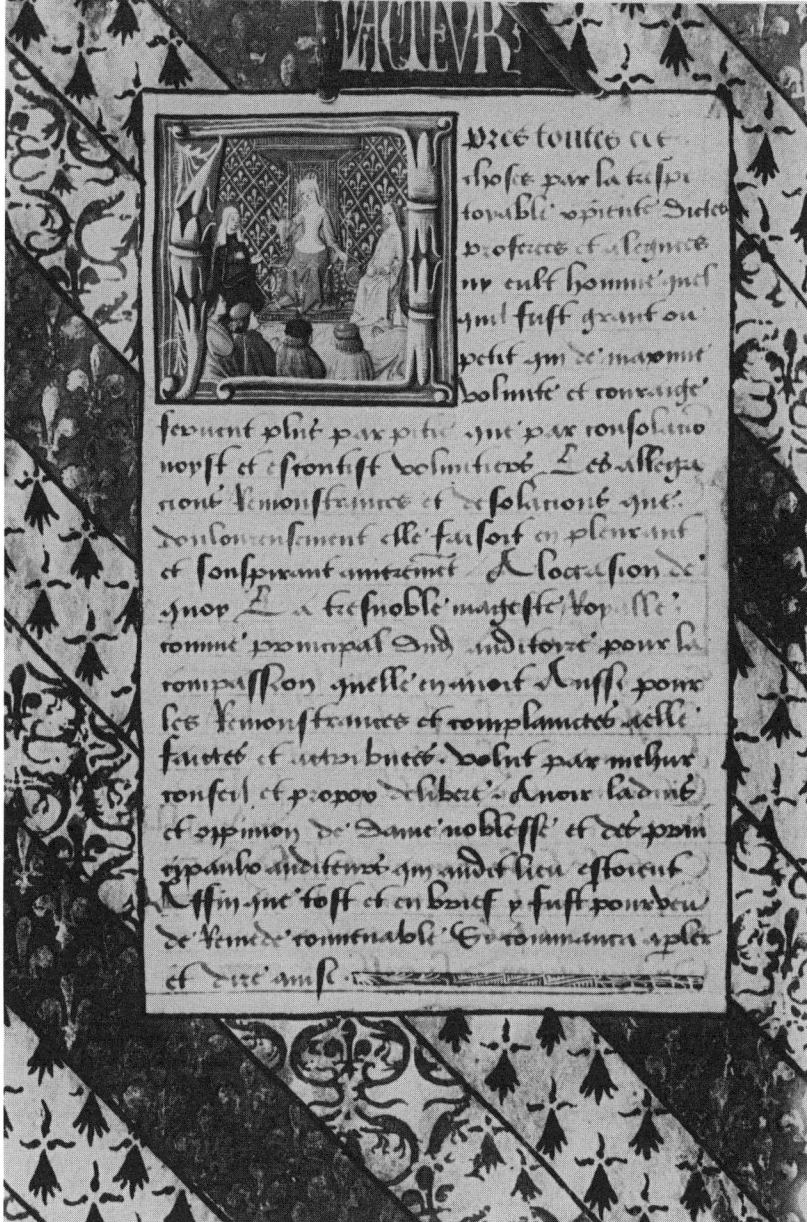

Figure 4.5. Historiated initial of Royal Majesty Enthroned with Lady Christianity at Her Right and Lady Nobility at Her Left, from *La ressource de la Chrestienté,* BN, MS fr. 1687, fol. 23v. Photo: Bibliothèque Nationale, Paris.

of information regarding the relationship of the poet to his text and to his patron. The Angoulême coat of arms on the first folio, the only decorated leaf, indicating the ownership of Duke Charles of Angoulême, and the illuminated acrostics of the name Charles of Valois, whose visual presence is otherwise reduced, tend to overshadow the author's metaphoric signature.

Two anonymous manuscript reworkings of the *Ressource* from about the same time completely usurp La Vigne's role and identity, while homage is still paid to Charles VIII through retention or reforming of the acrostics.[21]

A more neutralizing effect is achieved with the first printed edition of the *Ressource,* published in Angoulême in 1495. Not only does the complete lack of illustration, symbolic ornamentation, and emphasized acrostics in this version virtually erase the visibility accorded the French king in the manuscript versions, a visibility never again quite regained, but, despite the use of a title page, the authorship of the work also goes unacknowledged. Even La Vigne's metaphoric signature, clearly set off in the final line of the manuscript versions, is in no way emphasized at the end of the Angoulême edition, thereby lending near anonymity to the work. Moreover, the producers of this edition remain unnamed, as in the manuscript tradition, for no printer's mark or colophon is displayed.[22] Printing in this version, whether intentional or not, acted as an equalizing agent in regard to

---

[21]BN, MS fr. 20055, contains only the second set of acrostics relating to Charles VIII, but it omits the last seven verses of La Vigne's version, thereby cutting off the highlighted message in the middle of the word PARADIS. The following Latin acrostic is added: KAROLUS OCTAVUS REX RECTIET PACIS AMICUS. Because these constitute the last verses of the text, the reference to La Vigne has also been eliminated. BN, MS fr. 15215 imitates 20055 in this respect. See *Ressource de la Chrestienté,* appendices III and IV.

[22]The printers of the Angoulême edition were Pierre Alain and André Cauvin; see Brown, "Evolution of La Vigne's *Ressource de la Chrestienté,*" p. 115. Significantly, this printed edition is more closely affiliated with the manuscripts of the *Ressource* than with the later *Vergier d'honneur* editions. According to Rudolf Hirsch, "Title Pages in French Incunables, 1486–1500," *Gutenberg Jahrbuch* (1978): 63, title page usage was slow to catch on, except in France, and especially in Paris, Lyons, Poitiers, and Rouen after 1486, where 70 percent of the imprints (compared with 45.3 percent overall) made use of title pages. He notes on p. 63: "In manuscripts the name of the scribe, locality and date were given only rarely, for obvious reasons. There was neither clear need for, nor benefit derived from, this type of identification in the singly produced codex. Conditions changed with the production of multiple, identical copies by letter press, but progress was slow and irregular." Hirsch adds that, "following the scribal tradition, titles were apparently considered more important than authors" (n. 3).

all persons associated with the making of the book. As a result, attention is brought to the word of the text alone, and the strongly rhetorical flavor of the composition, which surfaces in the sections where exhortations to support the king's expedition and condemnation of pacifist leanings are made, dominates this no-frills stage of reproduction.

It is evident, then, that the illustrations in the *Ressource* versions discussed thus far play a critical role in the transmission of the author's image. Not only reinforcing more or less explicit textual references, they also provide memorable, concrete images of the very names contained in the text. This becomes all the more apparent when the illustration is absent. While the advent of printing may have resulted in a less ambitious decorative program, at least in this case, it precipitated other modifications that eventually offered a writer other forms of visibility.

This change can be seen in the *Vergier d'honneur* versions of the *Ressource de la Chrestienté,* printed in at least six different editions in Paris sometime after May 1498 up until 1525. These mark a renewed emphasis on the author figure and bring attention to the printer as well. While the royal acrostics are more or less emphasized in all of the *Vergier* editions by an added space between the first and second letters, those in the second speech of the fifth edition are not highlighted. Both sets remain unemphasized in the sixth edition. Charles VIII, who by this time had died, is, however, prominently named on the title page, which describes at length how his actions constitute the focus of the first two compositions in the *Vergier* compendium (emphasis added):

> Le Vergier d'honneur nouvellement imprimé a Paris. De l'entreprise et voyage de Napples. Auquel est compris commant le roy *Charles huitiesme de ce nom* a banyere desployee passa et rapassa de journee en journee de puis Lyon jusques a Napples et de Napples jusques a Lyon. Ensemble plusieurs aultres choses faictes et composees par reverend pere en Dieu *monseigneur Octovien de Sainct Gelais,* evesque d'Angolesme, et par *Maistre Andry de la Vigne,* secretaire de monsieur le duc de Savoye avec aultres.[23]

[23]This constitutes the title of the first edition of the *Vergier d'honneur* (see note 24 for information on the other editions). In this and all subsequent citations taken directly from the original editions abbreviations have been expanded, capital letters have been

[The Garden of Honor, recently printed in Paris. Concerning the enterprise and voyage of Naples. Which explains how King Charles VIII with unfurled banner traveled day by day from Lyons to Naples and from Naples to Lyons. Along with several other works composed by the Reverend Father in God, Monseigneur Octovien de Saint Gelais, bishop of Angoulême, and by Master André de la Vigne, secretary of Monsieur the Duke of Savoy, with others.]

Along with his deceased patron, the author is given credit. For the first time André de la Vigne is named on the title page before the text of the *Ressource* and specifically designated as the secretary of the duke of Savoy.[24] Yet, La Vigne shares authorial glory with his more celebrated peer, Octavien de Saint-Gelais (1468–1502), whose name actually precedes his.[25] The final verses of the *Ressource* itself, however, come to the author's rescue, for here La Vigne is named directly instead of through a play on words, as in the manuscripts and Angoulême edition. In order to announce the composition that follows, the last verses of the *Ressource* had to be changed, with the result that La Vigne is identified as the king's "orateur" and as the author of the next work (the emphasized portions indicate the changes from the first version):

> Si mon engin eust plus grant efficace,
> J'eusse trop mieulx *e(s)t sans nulle reprise*
> *Mis en avant de Napples l'ent[r]eprise,*
> *Que vous presente en vers, coupletz et ligne*
> *Vostre treshumble orateur,* De la Vigne.
> [vv. 1465–69]

---

added to mark the beginning of a proper name, the use of *i* and *j, u* and *v* has been modernized, apostrophes have been used to indicate elided vowels, and acute accents and punctuation have been added or modified when necessary. Brackets indicate an added letter, and parentheses enclose an incorrect letter.

[24]In the five other editions of the *Vergier d'honneur* the words "de la Royne et" have been added immediately after the word "secretaire," indicating that these were printed after La Vigne had become the queen's secretary in 1504.

[25]As a result, this title page information is somewhat misleading about the authorship of the different compositions contained in the *Vergier d'honneur* anthology. Because Saint-Gelais is named first, bibliographers have credited him as the main author of the volume. In point of fact, he composed only one piece of the collection, while acrostics indicate that La Vigne wrote at least five other works in the compendium. It has not yet been possible to determine who the "aultres" may have been.

[If my abilities were more effective,
I would have *put forward* in better fashion,
And without any reprimand, the Naples enterprise,
Which is presented to you in verse, stanza, and line
By your very humble orator, De la Vigne.]

Here the author's identity, function, and relationship to his text are clarified, whereas this was not the case in the final verses of the manuscript and Angoulême versions. Moreover, his rapport with his dedicatee is less obsequious.[26] Curiously, in this context Charles VIII's identity has become somewhat ambiguous. While reflecting the change from the original version of the work in La Vigne's status vis-à-vis his patron—he had since been hired as an official spokesman for the king—these lines were in fact printed after the death of Charles VIII. Would the reader, who was likely to have been somewhat distant from the royal circle, understand that La Vigne's earlier connection with Charles VIII was being alluded to, or would he assume the dedicatee to be the duke of Savoy, as advertised on the title page, or even King Louis XII?[27]

The use of illustrations tends to reinforce these textual changes, which emphasize La Vigne's presence over Charles VIII's. In every edition of the *Vergier* version of the *Ressource* a woodcut of the author can be found, and in five of the six it is placed as a frontispiece on the verso side of the title page. Instead of being portrayed in a subordinate position, on his knees, offering his work to his patron, the author is in fact depicted alone, contemplating or reading his book (figs. 4.6 and 4.7). While the author figure is indeed placed in greater visual prominence than in the previous *Ressource* versions, these representations are not linked specifically to the *Ressource* text, for the same woodcuts appear in other printed works of the time and are thus less intimately

---

[26]The phrase "Qui a vous, sire, de presenter n'est digne" (which is not worthy of being presented to you) has been replaced by "Que vous presente en vers, coupletz et ligne" (Which is presented to you in verse, stanza, and line), and the word "sire" is eliminated.

[27]Through La Vigne's patroness Queen Anne of Brittany. Dominique Coq, "Les incunables: Textes anciens, textes nouveaux," in *Histoire de l'édition française,* vol. 1, *Le livre conquérant* (Paris, 1982), p. 192, suggests that the editions of the *Vergier d'honneur* were strategically timed to coincide with Louis XII's and Francis I's military campaigns in Italy.

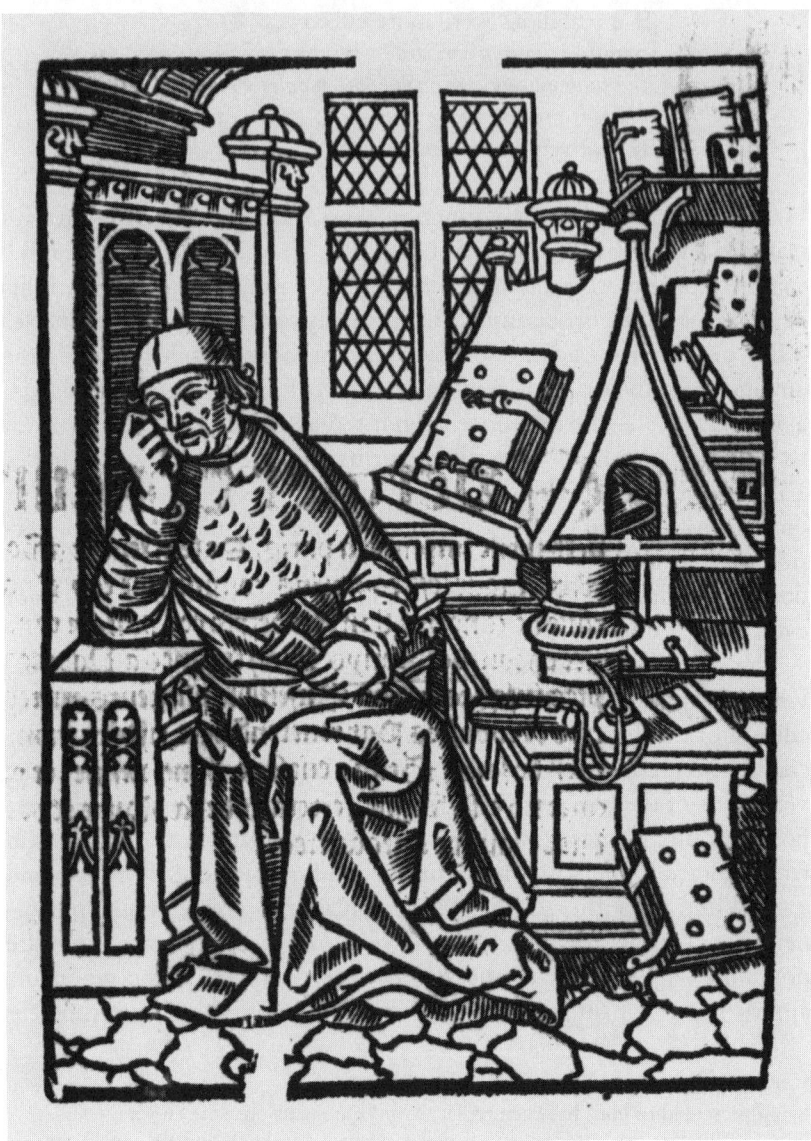

Figure 4.6. Author woodcut, from *Le vergier d'honneur,* 2d ed., BN, Réserve 4° Lb²⁸ 15A, title page verso. Photo: Bibliothèque Nationale, Paris.

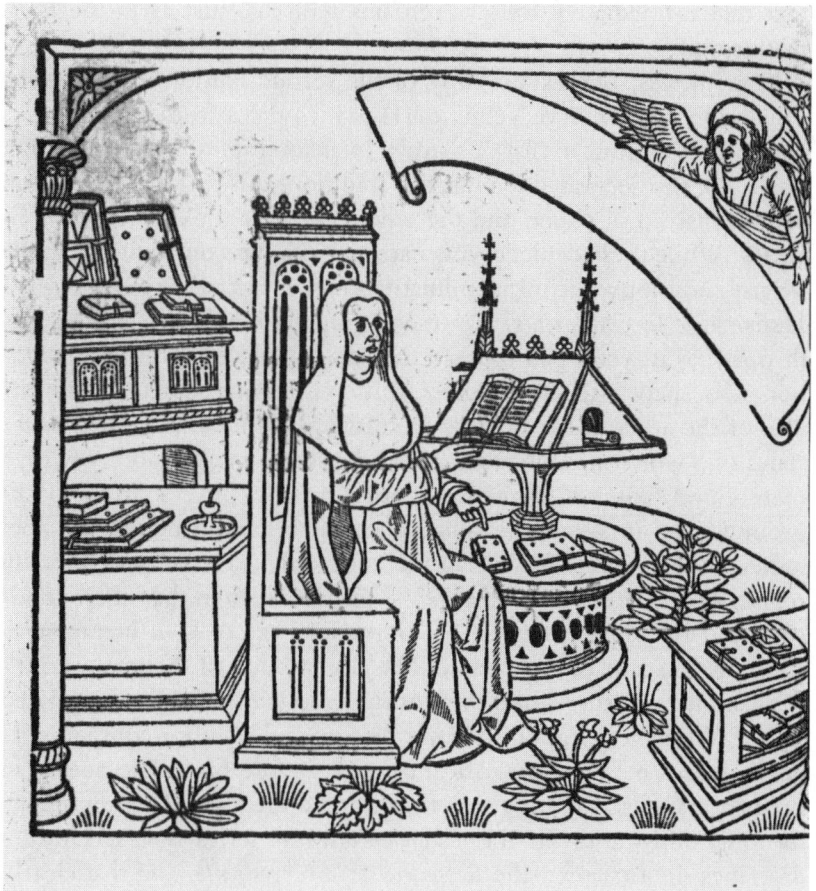

Figure 4.7. Author woodcut, from *Le vergier d'honneur,* 5th ed., BN, Roth-schild 479. Photo: Bibliothèque Nationale, Paris.

associated with the work itself. It is the idea of authorship that appears to be emphasized here more than the image of a particular author.[28] Since the figure in question reads or contemplates an ostensibly finished, bound book, the rapport between the illustration and the

[28]Given that the name of Saint-Gelais precedes La Vigne's on the title page, it is conceivable that the author figure represents the bishop of Angoulême, as his religious attire (and, in the second woodcut, religious inspiration) would seem to suggest. Yet the frontispieces of works by writers without apparent religions affiliation contain similar images.

text that immediately follows remains tenuous, just as in the royal manuscript.

Nonetheless, one extant copy of the second edition of the *Vergier d'honneur* (BN, Réserve Vélins 2241), which dates from after 1504, is particularly significant for our study. In an attempt to imitate the high quality of the decorated manuscript tradition, this text was printed on vellum instead of paper, and the woodcuts were replaced with miniatures. While these depict events narrated in other compositions in the *Vergier* anthology, the initial miniature does in fact relate to La Vigne's *Ressource de la Chrestienté*. It presents not the king but the poet, enthroned, as it were, pen in hand (fig. 4.8). Unlike any other illustration associated with the *Ressource,* this frontispiece coincides with the idea of the artist in the process of creating, for in front of the writer stand two women, doubtless Ladies Christianity and Nobility, with a man, Good Counsel, while three other parties converse in the background. The imagined personified characters stand before the poet rather than before Royal Majesty. Not only has the poet literally replaced the patron on the throne, as we have seen in the other woodcuts, but the subject chosen for portrayal is a scene of literary creation, not a scene of dedication. The closed book of the manuscript's dedication miniature—and even of the woodcuts—has been replaced by the unfinished, unbound leaves on which the author composes, as he visualizes his own allegorical creation before him. The poet is in the process of writing his as yet unfinished creation. This represents the only illustration in the *Vergier d'honneur* series that specifically describes the first text, the *Ressource de la Chrestienté,* and that clearly depicts La Vigne himself. It is in this hybrid copy of the printed *Vergier,* then, that the author and his creation are accorded the most attention. Visually the decoration is more personalized, recalling the manuscript tradition, except that the author figure rather than the patron is the focal point. Yet the author's identity depends on verbal highlighting from the print tradition through the use of title pages and the altered final lines of the *Ressource* text. The two coexisting forms of book reproduction have powerfully merged in this instance to produce the most individualized image of the creating writer.

With the author's presence more often and more visibly advertised, the role and identity of the printer in the production of the *Ressource de la Chrestienté* came to rival that of the author and in a way replace that of his former patron. While the early editions of the *Ressource* contain

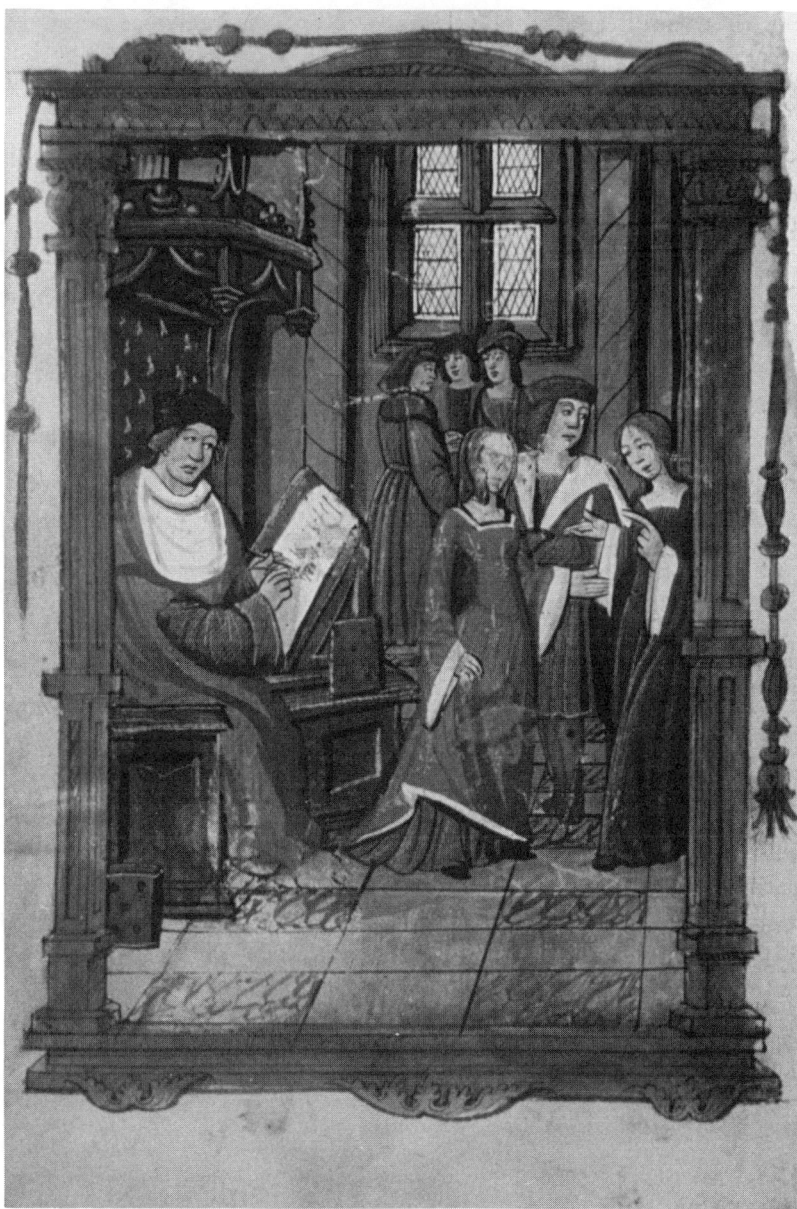

Figure 4.8. Poet Composing His Work with His Created Characters, Lady Christianity, Lady Nobility, and Good Counsel, before him, from *Le vergier d'honneur,* 2d ed., BN, Réserve Vélins 2241, title page verso. Photo: Bibliothèque Nationale, Paris.

no information about its printers,[29] it did eventually come to be attached to the work itself because of a developing competition among printers and booksellers.[30] In point of fact, with the third edition of the *Vergier d'honneur,* published between 1506 and 1509, the printer's presence became more manifest. While this edition bears no opening woodcut of the author figure, as in the first two editions, Jean Trepperel, acting as printer and bookseller, placed his name and address in a colophon at the end of the volume, followed by his printer's mark. With his identity more manifest, Trepperel's presence vied with the author's, whose name nevertheless remained prominently displayed on the title page. Curiously enough, Trepperel printed at the very end of the work a woodcut depicting an author dictating to a scribe (fig. 4.9). Was this image chosen because it dignified the book through reference to its "more noble" origin in the manuscript version?

Some six years later, in 1512, Jean Petit placed his bookseller's mark directly on the title page, displaying his own name in letters three times the size of the title which carried Charles VIII's, La Vigne's, and Saint-Gelais's (fig. 4.10).[31] The fifth and sixth editions of the work by Philippe Le Noir demonstrate a similar consciousness: the former (1521–22) bears his name and address as bookseller on the title page; in the colophon he is described as "libraire juré de l'Université" (sworn bookseller of the University), and his printer's mark is displayed at the end. The last edition, published in 1525, also exhibits Philippe Le Noir's address below the title and his initials above, as well as the sign ⨎ , which supposedly confirmed owner's rights (fig. 4.11),[32] with similar identification in the colophon. The Renaissance-like engraved framework, which dominates the title page, much as

[29]See note 22. It is thought that the first two editions of the *Vergier d'honneur* were printed in Paris by Pierre Le Dru. The ubiquitous Vérard seems to have had his hand in the enterprise as well. See the *Catalogue des incunables* (Paris, 1982), II, fasc. 1, pp. 159–60.

[30]Hirsch, "Title Pages in French Incunables," p. 64, states that "sales promotion was one important purpose of title pages," and explains on p. 65: "Keen competition among the many members of the book trade favored an arrangement by which the client was informed at a glance of the contents, and the supplier. The custom of advertising through the use of carefully designed title pages (widely accepted soon thereafter) was born in France."

[31]Hirsch, "Title Pages in French Incunables," p. 64, points out that Jean Petit was one of the most active users of title pages.

[32]Robert Brun, *Le livre français illustré de la Renaissance* (Paris, 1969), pp. 38–39.

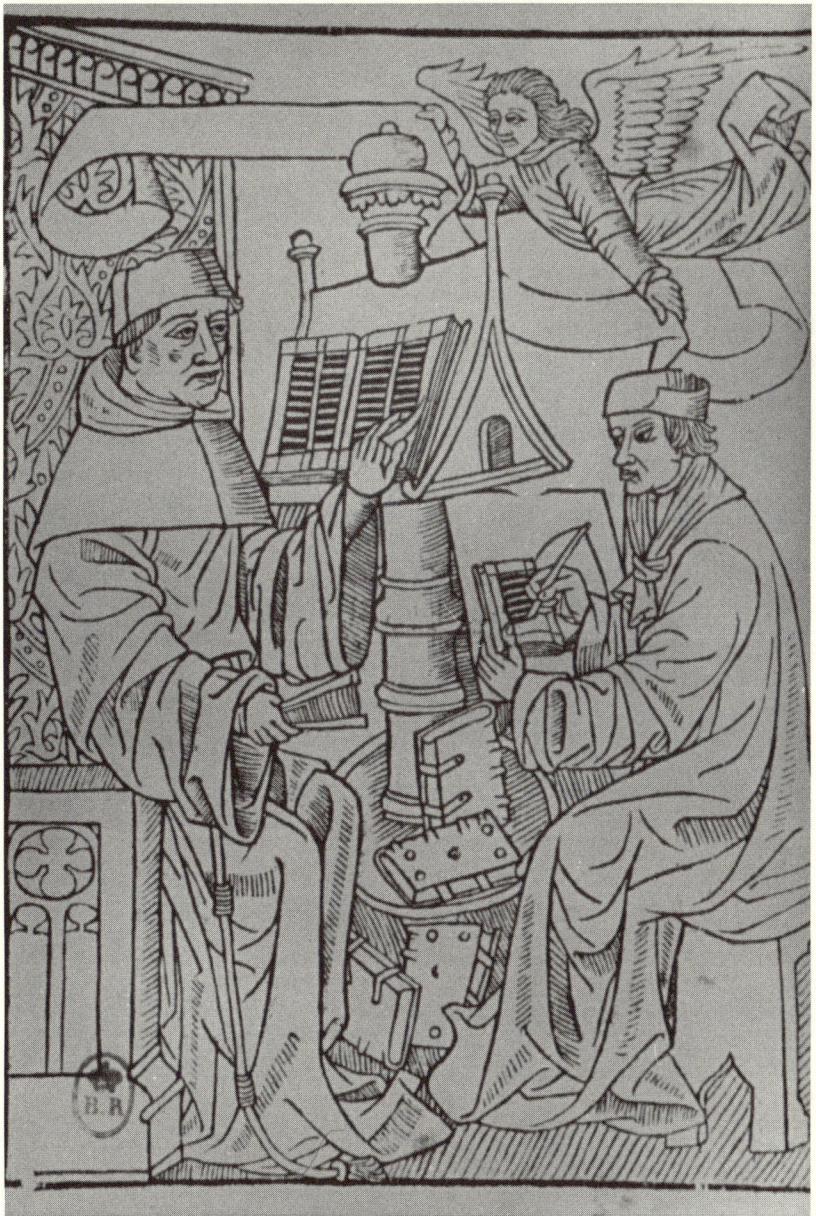

Figure 4.9. Author Dictating His Work to a Scribe, from *Le vergier d'honneur*, 3d ed., BN, Réserve 4° Lb²⁸ 15B, fol. 182r. Photo: Bibliothèque Nationale, Paris.

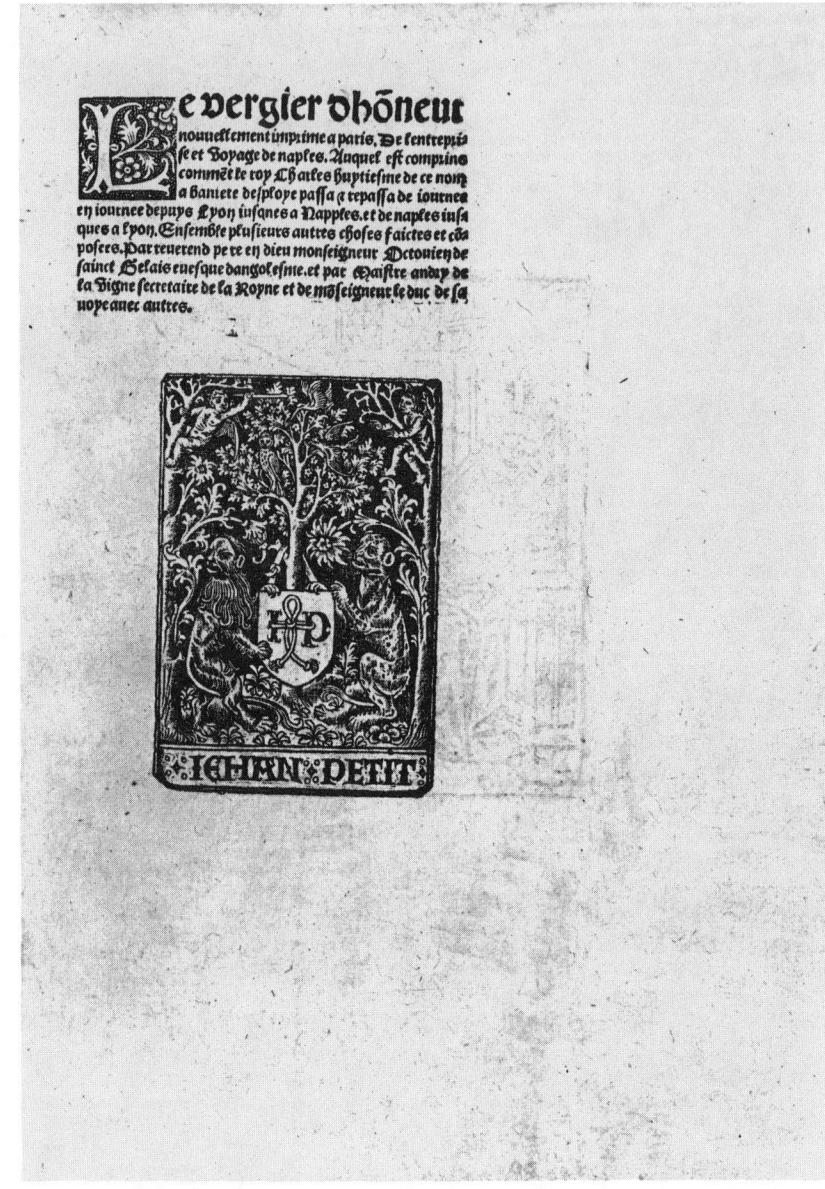

Figure 4.10. Mark of Jehan Petit, bookseller, from *Le vergier d'honneur*, 4th ed., Cambridge, Mass. Harvard University, Houghton Library FC.Sa.233.500.VC, title page. By permission of the Houghton Library.

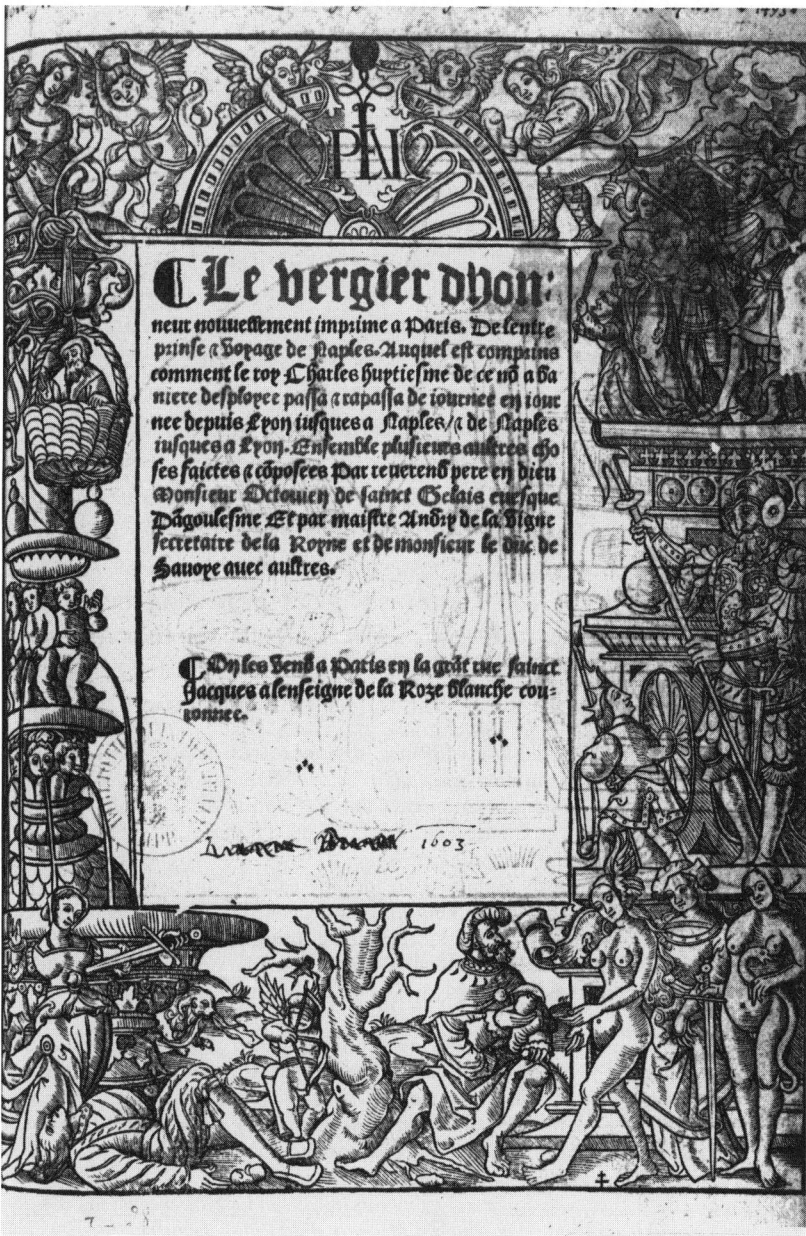

Figure 4.11. Initials and address of Philippe Le Noir, printer–bookseller, from *Le vergier d'honneur*, 6th ed., BN, Réserve K. 70 (2), title page. Photo: Bibliothèque Nationale, Paris.

the royal decoration did in manuscript 1687, may represent the printer's attempt to attract the book purchaser's eye with fashionably up-to-date decoration. These developments suggest a growing consciousness on the part of the printers and booksellers of the importance of advertisement and self-identification. While the author may have been freer of the patronage system,[33] he now had to confront another authority in the bookmaking process—the printer, who controlled to a large degree the physical presentation of his work.

This tension between author and printer, implicit in the placement of names on the title page and in the colophon, appears to have surfaced in Paris in the early years of the sixteenth century, when writers began to react to the phenomenon of pirated editions, that is, those printed without authorial permission. In 1504 André de la Vigne himself stood up to this situation by filing a lawsuit against Michel Le Noir, who was about to print *Le vergier d'honneur*. In the end, the author gained rights to the publication of his own work over the printer[34] in one of the earliest such lawsuits. La Vigne was obviously conscious of and concerned about protecting his literary rights, so much so that he became actively involved in the production of his text. Probably as a result, La Vigne's other printed works not only publicize his authorship but reflect royal protection as well.[35]

[33]The patronage system did not, of course, disappear with printing. In fact, printing probably fostered its continuation in many ways. We know, for example, that La Vigne was still seeking royal protection after the first edition of the *Vergier d'honneur*, that is following the death of Charles VIII in May 1498. This he obtained sometime in 1504 when he became secretary to Queen Anne of Brittany. La Vigne's royal association is thereafter prominently displayed on the title pages of his printed works (see note 35). In point of fact the French king himself depended on his propagandists and the wider distribution of their works through the printing press (see Brown, *Shaping of History and Poetry*). Nevertheless, *rhétoriqueurs* such as Jean Lemaire, Jean Bouchet, and Pierre Gringore did have seemingly independent involvement with the printing of their own works.

[34]For details regarding the lawsuit, see Cynthia J. Brown, "Du manuscrit à l'imprimé en France: Le cas des Grands Rhétoriqueurs," in *Actes du Ve Colloque international sur le moyen français*, Milan, May 6–8, 1985, I, 117 n. 37. Jean Bouchet was involved in La Vigne's lawsuit against Le Noir, who, along with Vérard, had in the same year printed his work *Les regnars traversans* without the author's permission (see Jennifer Britnell, *Jean Bouchet* [Edinburgh, 1986], pp. 304–5). Another *rhétoriqueur*, Jean Lemaire de Belges, was apparently a victim of Michel Le Noir as well in the same year (see Henri Hornik, ed., *Le Temple d'Honneur et de Vertus* [Geneva, 1957], p. 14). From 1509 on he obtained royal privileges for the rest of his printed works (see Jacques Abelard, *Les illustrations de Gaule et Singularitez de Troye de Jean Lemaire de Belges: Étude des éditions, genèse de l'oeuvre* [Geneva, 1976], pp. 59–60).

[35]While there does not appear to be any officially stated connection between La Vigne's legal victory and the subsequent advertisement of his royal ties, it is clear that

The literary production of other *rhétoriqueurs* centered in Paris at the same time as André de la Vigne reflects a similar developing authorial consciousness, which appears to be related to the rise of printing. One of the most prominent figures in this regard is Pierre Gringore, whose involvement with the print culture was even more pronounced than La Vigne's, owing perhaps to his relatively independent status vis-à-vis royal patronage.[36] Whereas La Vigne's legal rights to the *Vergier d'honneur* remained more or less hidden in the Paris Parlement records of the day, Gringore's participation in the publication of his works and control over their printing and distribution came to be advertised more and more explicitly on the title pages of the editions themselves. Most of his works, which are as a rule strongly moralistic and often polemical and which were written about the same time as La Vigne's compositions, have come down to us in print form alone.[37] As a culling of title page and colophon information reveals, within a period of some five to ten years, during the first decade of the sixteenth century, whether by editorial policy or authorial deci-

he did obtain the protection of Anne of Brittany sometime between the conclusion of the lawsuit in June 1504 and November 18–19, 1504, when he witnessed her *sacre* and entry into Paris, which he eventually rendered into verse, signing as her secretary by means of an acrostic in the final stanza. See Henri Stein, "Le sacre d'Anne de Bretagne et son entrée à Paris en 1504," *Mémoires de la Société de l'Histoire de Paris et de l'Ile de France* 29 (1902): 268–304, for a copy of the text, which was apparently never printed at the time. For details on the announcement of La Vigne's name and royal association in four later works, see Brown, *Shaping of History and Poetry,* pp. 163–86.

[36]There is no evidence that Gringore's works were officially commissioned or subsidized by the House of France, despite the fact that many espoused royal policy. Archival records show, however, that along with a certain carpenter named Jean Marchant he received payment for the construction of sets, composition of "Mystères," stage decoration, costumes, and the like on the occasion of several *entrées royales* into Paris between 1502 and 1515 (see *Oeuvres complètes de Gringore,* vol. 2, *La vie de Monseigneur Saint Louis par personnages,* ed. A. de Montaiglon and J. de Rothschild [Paris, 1877; reprinted, Geneva, 1970], pp. xx–xxii).

[37]Two of the extant manuscripts of Gringore's works involve royal ceremonials— *L'entrée de la Reine Mary Tudor* (1514; BL, Cottonian MS Vespasian B. II), and *Le Couronnement, sacre et entrée de la Royne a Paris* (1517; Bibliothèque de Nantes, MS 1337)—and were never printed until the twentieth century. *La vie de Monseigneur Saint Louis* (n.d. [1498–1515]; BN, MS fr. 17511) was not printed until the nineteenth century. Nonetheless, sixteenth-century manuscript versions of *L'entreprise de Venise* (Bibliothèque de Soissons, MS 204), *Les abus du monde* (PML, MS 516), *L'obstination des Suysses* (BN, MS fr. 2336), and a portion of *Les menus propos* (BN, MS fr. 2274, fols. 4–10r) exist along with printed editions of the same texts; some of the manuscripts were apparently copied from the imprints. Some twenty other works by Gringore have come down to us in print form alone, suggesting that he relied most often on the printing press for the reproduction of his compositions.

sion or both, Gringore's identity with his works and his control of them became significantly more manifest.

The printer's and/or bookseller's name and address are nearly always indicated on the title page of Gringore's first work, the *Château de labour,* printed in Paris some ten times between 1499 and 1532.[38] Yet the author's name never appears. Despite changes in this configuration in other later compositions, subsequent editions of the *Château de labour* were never modified accordingly. Gringore's next three works (the *Château d'amour, Lettres de Milan,* and *Complainte de la Terre Saint*), all printed around 1500, as well as his *Complainte de Trop Tard Marié* of 1505, follow a similar pattern, whereby the printer's and/or bookseller's presence preempts the author's, at least on the title page, or, like the author's, is missing altogether. Is it to be presumed that Gringore's name did not yet elicit recognition among readers in the early years of the sixteenth century, as Saint-Gelais's and La Vigne's probably did, and was therefore not placed in the position of most prominence?

Whatever the explanation, it is noteworthy that in each of these early compositions, and in fact in nearly all of his numerous works, Pierre Gringore made use of an acrostic signature in the last stanza of his composition to such an extent that it became a personal trademark.[39] The rubric "L'Acteur" often sets this stanza apart from the

---

[38]The *Château de labour* title page bears the name of the Parisian printer Philippe Pigouchet in large letters beneath his mark, along with the name and address of the bookseller, Simon Vostre, in three extant editions dating from October 1499, March 1500, and May 1500. Other edition title pages bear the name and mark of the printers Jacques Le Forestier (Rouen, November 1500) and Gaspard Philippe (Paris, n.d. [1500–1510]), and the name and mark of the booksellers Nicole de la Barre (n.d. [1519]) and Gailliot du Pré (May 1532). The 1509 Paris edition of Gilles Couteau and the undated Jean Trepperel Paris editions bear no name on the title page, although these printers are identified along with their addresses in the colophon. For bibliographical information on Gringore's works, see Charles Oulmont, *La poésie morale, politique et dramatique à la veille de la Renaissance: Pierre Gringore* (Paris, 1911), pp. 29–66; and Avenir Tchémerzine, *Bibliographie d'éditions originales et rares d'auteurs français des XVe, XVIe, XVIIe et XVIIIe siècles* (Paris, 1933), VI, 25–100.

[39]The use of the acrostic merits further study, for it may have become more prevalent in the print culture because it necessitated a visual decoding as opposed to the earlier metaphorical signatures of a Jean Molinet or André de la Vigne, which seem to have had a more firmly entrenched place in the manuscript culture. One finds an acrostic in the following: *Le Château de labour* (1499); *Le Château d'amour* (c.1500; see note 42); *Lettres nouvelles de Milan* (c.1500); *La piteuse complainte de la Terre Sainte* (c.1500); *La complainte de Trop Tard Marié* (1505); *Les folles entreprises* (1505); *L'entreprise de Venise* (1509); *Les abus du monde* (1509); *L'union des princes* (c.1509); *La chasse du Cerf des Cerfs* (c. 1510); *La coqueluche* (1510); *L'espoir de paix* (c. 1510); *L'obstination des Suysses* (c.1512); *Les fantasies de Mère Sotte* (1516); *Les menus propos* (1521); *Le testament*

rest of the verses in the text, and in some cases the reader is specifically directed to look for his name—one finds the rubric "L'Acteur et
surnom d'icel mis" (The author's last name placed herewith)—or
reconstruct the vertical text containing his signature by the announcement "Le surnom de l'Acteur sera trouvé par les premieres lettres de
ce couplet" (The author's last name will be found in the first letters of
this stanza).[40] Unlike the more ambiguous metaphoric signatures
characteristic of his predecessors such as Jean Molinet[41] and André de
la Vigne, which risked greater anonymity once the text reached readers outside the literary circle that would have recognized them,
Gringore's use of the acrostic, especially in its position of closure,
brought further assurance that his authorship would be recognized
and remain associated with the text. In other words, just like La
Vigne, whose identity was specified in the last verses of the *later*
versions of the *Ressource,* Gringore did not have to rely solely on title
page or colophon information, presumably the jurisdiction of the
printer, for advertisement of his authorship. It is significant that what
kept the patron's identity alive in the *Ressource* text, the acrostic, was
adopted by the author, Gringore, for similarly effective ends.[42]

---

de Lucifer (1521?); *Le blazon des heretiques* (1524); *La complainte de la Cité Crestienne* (c.
1525); *La quenoulle spirituelle* (c.1525); *Les heures de Nostre Dame* (c.1525); *Notables,
enseignemens* (1528).

[40]The rubric "L'Acteur" precedes the acrostic stanza in Gringore's *Labour, Lettres
nouvelles, Trop Tard Marié, Entreprise, Abus, Coqueluche, Fantasies* (where one finds
PIERRE GRINGORE spelled out in a two-stanza acrostic), *Menus propos,* and *Blazon.* In *La
quenoulle* one reads "Incitation de l'acteur," and in *Cité Crestienne* "Conclusion de
l'acteur." The rubric "Le surnom de l'acteur qui a fait et composé ce livre par les
premieres lettres de ce couplet" precedes the acrostic stanza in Pigouchet's edition of
the *Château d'amour,* while "Le surnom de l'Acteur sera trouvé par les premieres lettres
de ce couplet" announces the last stanza of the *Folles entreprises.* Finally, the *Notables,
enseignemens* offers these details: "Fin et conclusion de ce present livre laquelle monstre
et enseigne par la premiere lettre de chacun vers le surnom de l'acteur."

In some works Pierre Gringore's name was announced either on the title page (*La
chasse du Cerf des Cerfs* [1510]; *L'espoir de paix; Heures de Nostre Dame; Para-
phrase . . . Pseaumes* [1541]) or in a colophon at the end (*Trop Tard Marié; Le jeu du
Prince des Sotz* [1512]; *Menus propos; Notables, enseignemens*).

[41]See Cynthia J. Brown, "L'eveil d'une nouvelle conscience littéraire en France à la
grande époque de transition technique: Jean Molinet et son moulin poétique," *Le
moyen français* 22 (1988), *Actes du Colloque international,* "Du manuscrit à l'imprimé,"
McGill University, Montreal, October 3–4, 1988: 15–35.

[42]Nevertheless, another attempt by the printer Michel Le Noir to subvert an author's
control over his own work involves Gringore's *Château d'amour.* For details, see Cynthia
J. Brown, "The Confrontation between Printer and Author in Early Sixteenth-Century
France: Another Example of Michel Le Noir's Unethical Printing Practices," *Bibliothèque d'humanisme et Renaissance* 53 (1991): 105–19.

The content of these stanzas coincides with its physical emphasis as well, for in nearly every instance Gringore's voice addressed his general readers outside the text, often exhorting them to certain moral behavior.[43] This is not the ambiguous, ever-changing first-person speaker of La Vigne's *Ressource*. The moralizing "I" of these final exhortative stanzas is the same voice heard throughout nearly all of Gringore's works.

The numerous editions of Gringore's satirical *Folles entreprises,* which attack all forms of ambition, oppression, and debauchery, mark a significant change from his earlier works in the presentation of authorial image and identity. While only the mark, not the name, of the Parisian printer Pierre Le Dru (the same one who had printed the first two *Vergier* editions) adorns the title page of two of three issues of the 1505 *Folles entreprises* edition, verses at the bottom of the page

[43]Examples of these acrostic stanzas of exhortation are found, for example, in *Les lettres nouvelles de Milan,* ed. E. Balmas (Milan, 1955), p. 91; and *L'union des princes,* ed. Anna Slerca (Milan, 1977), p. 72, respectively:

G   entilz francoys, soyez de la victoire
R   emercians Jesus le createur;
I   l nous appert que l'euvre meritoire
N   ous vient du Ciel, Dieu est nostre adjuteur.
G   loire, triumphe, magnificence, honneur
O   nt conquesté à Milan gens d'Armes;
R   egretz, souspirs Ludovic en cueur
E   n a souvent, et pleure maintes larmes.

G   ardez vous bien que laches ne soyez,
R   egraciez celluy qui vous a faictz,
J   oyeusement estandars desployez.
N   'ayez doubte que avec vous Dieu ne ayez,
G   loire donne a ceulx qui sont parfaictz;
O   stez l'erreur que les payens infectz
R   emidrent sus par Macomet herite:
E   n bien faisant son devoir Dieu gens quicte.

The acrostic stanza at the end of the *Quenoulle spirituelle* is preceded by the rubric "Incitation de l'acteur" (BN, Collection Rothschild 498, fol. [C vii verso]):

G   lorifions le nom de Jhesucrist,
R   ememorons sa saincte passion.
J   oygnons noz cueurs au benoist Saint Esprit,
N   otons les maulx et dure affliction,
G   randes douleurs, abhomination,
O   u Jhesus fut souffrant douleur cruelle,
R   [e]sveillons nous, fillons d'affection
E   n la quenoulle dicte spirituelle.

provide the bookseller's address as that of Mère Sotte, or Mother Folly; Parisian contemporaries would immediately have recognized this name as that of the character played by Pierre Gringore himself in dramatic presentations by the theater troupe known as the Enfants sans Souci:

> Qui en veult avoir se transporte
> Sans deshonneur et sans diffame,
> Pres du bout du pont Nostre Dame,
> A l'enseigne de Mere Sotte.

> [He who wishes to obtain copies should go,
> Without dishonor or infamy,
> To the sign of Mother Folly,
> Near the end of the bridge of Our Lady.]

First presented as a bookseller on the title page, Gringore eventually names himself as author in his trademark acrostic at the end of the work,[44] while the colophon clarifies that Pierre Le Dru printed it for him. Curiously, on the title page of one extant version of a 1505 Le Dru edition of the *Folles entreprises,* one discovers the image of Mère Sotte (fig. 4.12) instead of the printer's mark. Thus, the implicit tension between author and printer-bookseller is dispelled, for Gringore has usurped the position of bookseller for himself, while the identity of the printer is deferred until the colophon. Could it be that the years 1504–5 represented in Paris a critical period during which authors asserted themselves more and more vigorously against printers, whose practices were increasingly viewed as unethical? In nearly every case, the Mère Sotte illustration appears on the title page of the remaining editions of the *Folles entreprises,* even though the

---

[44]"Le surnom de l'acteur sera trouvé par les premieres lettres de ce couplet":

G   rans et petitz le livre en gré prenez,
R   ongez ces motz a vostre entendement
J   oyeusement, les faultes reprenez,
N   otez que l'ay composé simplement;
G   races en rens a Dieu devotement,
O   u j'ay recours en composant tout oeuvre,
R   ememorant que sans luy nullement
E   ntendemens choses offusques n'euvre.

(ed. Le Dru [Paris, 1505], fol. h iv verso).

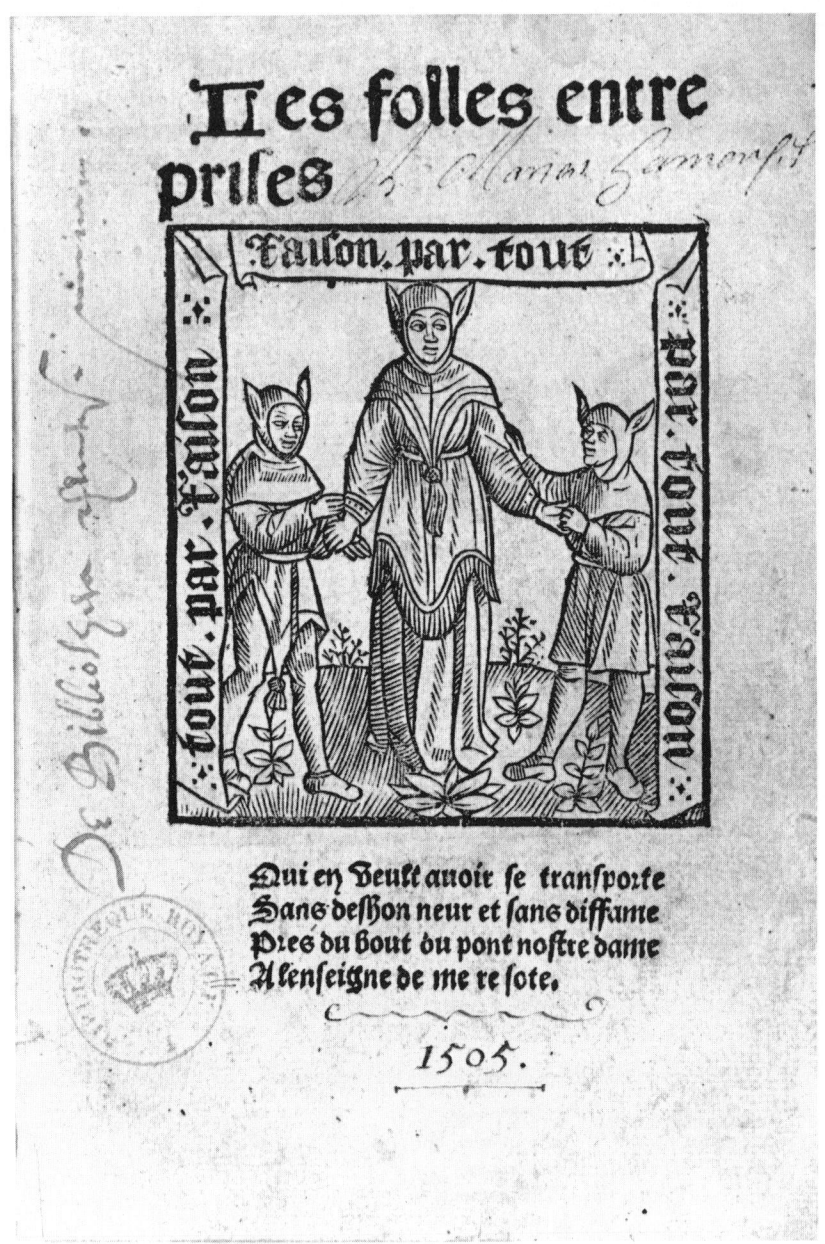

Figure 4.12. Mère Sotte (= Pierre Gringore), woodcut with Gringore's address as bookseller, from *Les folles entreprises*, BN, Réserve Ye, 1321, title page. Photo: Bibliothèque Nationale, Paris.

advertised address is no longer that of Gringore's theatrical alter ego.[45] This development implies that the Mère Sotte woodcut became Gringore's personal trademark, not in his capacity as bookseller so much as in his function as actor-author. In fact, this same illustration decorates the title page of most of Gringore's other major works.[46] The author's theatrical persona, probably more recognizable than his own name, thus came to play the same role in visual terms as the verbal designation of La Vigne's authorship on the *Vergier d'honneur* title page. In other words, an advertising technique related to the practical aspects of printing and selling was eventually used to enhance the image of the author and to elicit recognition of his identity.[47]

Of even greater significance than Gringore's ubiquitous acrostic signature and Mère Sotte woodcut is the fact that each of the Le Dru

---

[45]One finds either the address of the widow of Jean Trepperel (Paris, [1506], 1510):

> En rue neufve, ou pent l'escu de France,
> Vous trouverez les Folles Entreprises,
> Ou les faultes de plusieurs sont comprises:
> A tous venans on les vent et delivre

that of Jean Marnef (Paris, 1506; January 6, 1507; January 30, 1507):

> Au pellican rue sainct Jaques ce livre,
> Intitulé les Folles Entreprises,
> Ou les faultres de plusieurs sont comprises:
> A tous venans on les vent et delivre

or that of an unidentified Lyons bookseller (1507):

> En rue Me[r]ciere pres de confort ce livre
> [Intitulé] les Folles Entreprises,
> [Ou les] faultes de plusieurs sont comprises:
> [. . .]as Lyon on le vent et delivre.

[46]These tend to be nonpolitical and nonreligious works: the first edition of *Les abuz du monde*, *La coqueluche*, *Le jeu du Prince des Sot* (as might be expected, since Gringore played the role of Mère Sotte in it), nine extant editions of *Les fantasies de Mère Sotte*, and six surviving editions of *Les menus propos*.

[47]In some cases one does find dedication woodcuts, with the poet on his knee offering a book to a royal figure, on the verso side of the title page. See, for example, the miniature in a 1505 version of the *Folles entreprises* (Paris, Pierre Le Dru), and the woodcut in a 1507 Lyons edition and 1507 Paris edition (Marnef) of the same work; the title page of a 1525 Paris edition of *Les abus du monde* (J. Trepperel); the last folio of a c. 1509 Lyons edition of *L'entreprise de Venise* (P. Maréchal and B. Chaussard) and the title page of a c. 1509 Paris edition of the same work; and the title page of *L'union des princes* (c. 1509, Paris). These may well have been editions that were subsidized by or offered to King Louis XII himself, since they specifically supported his policies.

issues of the *Folles entreprises* of 1505 bears a so-called *ordonnance* at the end, which stipulates that no one has the right to sell or distribute the work or have it printed for one year without the author's permission:

> Il est dit par l'ordonnance de justice que l'acteur de cedict livre nommé Pierre Gringore, a privileige de le vendre et distribuer du jourdhuy jusques a ung an, sans ce que autre le puisse faire imprimer ne vendre, fors ceulx a qui il en baillera et distribuera, et ce sur peine de confiscacion des livres et d'amende arbitraire.

> [It is proclaimed by judicial ordinance that the author of this book, named Pierre Gringore, has the right [privilege] to sell and distribute it for one year beginning today, without which no one else can have it printed or sold, except those to whom he will give and distribute it, and this holds under penalty of confiscation of the books and a fine.]

What La Vigne had obtained through a lawsuit in June 1504, namely acquisition of rights to the printing and selling of the *Vergier d'honneur* for one year, had become a validated part of the publication process for Gringore just eighteen months later. It is doubtless significant that, from this point on, the first editions of Gringore's works contained some kind of authorial protection.[48]

While scholars have noted in general terms that concerns about literary ownership surfaced in the sixteenth century,[49] the actual sys-

---

[48]Gringore's June 1509 edition of the *Abus du monde* bears an *ordonnance* similar to that of the *Folles entreprises* for one year. The only known edition of the *Union des princes* (c. 1509) gives Gringore selling and distribution rights to the work "jusques au jour Sainct Jehan Baptiste" (June 24). That of the *Chasse du Cerf des Cerfs* (c. 1510) gives the author printing and selling rights "jusques au jour de Noel prochain venant"; *La coqueluche* of 1510 does so for a period of one month. All these *ordonnances* appear at the end of the printed text.

A c. 1509 Lyons edition of *L'entreprise de Venise* bears a woodcut of the royal arms on the verso of its title page, although no *ordonnance* is to be found. One edition of the *Espoir de paix* of 1510 likewise displays the royal arms on the title page, but one also finds the expression "Cum privilegio," the first time this designation occurs in any of Gringore's extant works. The verso of the title page explains that the work was composed by Pierre Gringore in honor of King Louis XII. These signs suggest that the *Espoir de paix* was protected and/or commissioned by royal authorities. It is an *ordonnance* at the end of the same work that sets down terms similar to those found in the 1505 edition of the *Folles entreprises*.

[49]Elizabeth Eisenstein, *The Printing Press as an Agent of Change* (New York, 1979), I, 120, states, for example: "By 1500, legal fictions were already being devised to accommodate the patenting of inventions and the assignments of literary properties. . . .

tematic use of copyrights did not really take hold until later in the seventeenth and eighteenth centuries.[50] Details regarding the history of the institution of *privileges* in Paris during the first decades of the sixteenth century still remain somewhat vague. While an awareness of the importance of some kind of control dates from the late fifteenth century,[51] the examples of these two *rhétoriqueurs* offer early evidence indeed of the growing confrontation between author and printer-bookseller over ownership rights to a book. Information in Gringore's early works and La Vigne's lawsuit suggest that one year was often the time period during which an author was initially granted rights over the publication of his work.[52]

Another phase in the ownership history of Gringore's works, which began with the 1505 edition of his *Folles entreprises,* was apparently initiated with the first printing in 1516 of the *Fantasies de Mère Sotte,* a long moralistic narrative against vice. Below the ever-present woodcut of Mère Sotte one reads, "Cum privillegio regis," implying that royal authority had by this point become attached to the idea of what was now called a *privilege.*[53] Moved up to the front of the book, that very *privilege,* printed on the verso side of the title page, granted rights to Pierre Gringore, this time for *four* years, a substantial increase over previous *ordonnances* in the allotted time of authorial control. The printer is never mentioned. Two early editions of the *Fantasies* bear the author's address—Gringore once again has become

Competition over the right to publish a given text also introduced controversy over new issues involving monopoly and piracy. Printing forced legal definition of what belonged in the public domain."

[50]See Lucien Febvre and Henri-Jean Martin, *The Coming of the Book,* trans. David Gerard (London, 1976), pp. 162–66.

[51]According to Elizabeth Armstrong, whose book *Before Copyright: The Book-Privilege System 1498–1526* (Cambridge, 1990) enlightens scholars on these matters, the first French *privilege* was obtained in Lyons in 1498. A number of years passed, however, before others were sought and granted. Her research corroborates my findings that Pierre Gringore played a central role in the development of the *privilege* system in France.

[52]See note 48. Gringore was given rights to *La coqueluche* for only one mouth. But the first editions of *Fantasies* (1516), *Menus propos* (1521), *Heures de Nostre Dame* (1527), and *Notables, enseignemens* (1528), for example, all contain *privileges* granting Gringore rights to these works for four years.

[53]See Armstrong, *Before Copyright,* pp. 22–33; and Abelard, *Illustrations,* pp. 59–60, for details regarding Jean Lemaire's royal *privilege* of 1509. Gringore's *Fantasies, Menus propos, Heures de Nostre Dame,* and *Notables, enseignemens* contain royal *privileges.*

bookseller—while another adds a new Gringore device at the beginning of the text.

The title page of a fourth edition, which may have come out in
1518,[54] explains that it was printed for the bookseller Jean Petit
(bookseller of the fourth edition of the *Vergier d'honneur*), to whom
Gringore had apparently given selling rights:

> Imprimees a Paris pour Jehan Petit libraire juré de l'université dudict
> lieu. Ayant par transport le privilege dudict Mere Sotte, autrement dit
> Pierre Gringore. Et se vendent a l'enseigne de la fleur de lys d'or en la
> rue sainct Jacques pres des Maturins.

> [Printed in Paris for Jean Petit, sworn bookseller of the university of said
> place. Having obtained by transfer the privilege of so-called Mother
> Folly, otherwise known as Pierre Gringore. And sold at the sign of the
> golden fleur-de-lis on Saint Jacques Street near the Mathurins.]

This announcement reflects quite obviously how the chosen printer
or bookseller benefited from the *privilege* protection system as much
as the author. It is thought that Gringore authorized Petit to sell his
books since he had left or was about to leave Paris and was no longer
in a position to supervise the continued sale of the *Fantasies*.[55] Even
though the "Cum privilegio" disappears after the four-year time limit
and the bookseller's address changes, the Mère Sotte woodcut remains on the title page of the *Fantasies de Mère Sotte* up through
around 1530, probably because of its association with the title.

Although illustrations continued to play an important role in the
early years of printing, it seems apparent, from the preceding studies of
La Vigne and Gringore, that the relationship of image and text changed
during the transition from manuscript to print. Instead of focusing on
narrative authority within the work, illustrations helped develop more
and more the author's image outside the text. The Mère Sotte woodcuts are one example of this. Other features of printing—title pages,
colophons, the use of *privileges,* authors' doubling as booksellers—
reinforced the new nonfictionalized presence and independent authori-

---

[54]Pierre Gringore, *Les fantasies de Mère Sote,* ed. R. L. Frautschi (Chapel Hill, 1962),
p. 28.
[55]Ibid.

ty of the author as well. It comes as no surprise, then, to discover that the ambiguous, more medieval-like complex of first-person voices of a dreaming narrator, typified in La Vigne's *Ressource de la Chrestienté*, disappears in the works of later *rhétoriqueurs* such as Gringore.[56] His authorial voice, for example, remains one-dimensional and essentially less fictionalized, in part because he does not invoke the traditional dream framework, at least in the same manner, as earlier *rhétoriqueurs*.[57] The historical author's ideas no longer needed the validation of an allegorical dream. In other words, a clearer distance came to be maintained between creating writer and fictional characters, for the first-person voice no longer participated so actively in their discourse. Whereas the subject of artistic creation came to invade the literary text from within in the production of a contemporary *rhétoriqueur* such as Jean Lemaire de Belges (1475–c.1515) (see note 56), in most of Gringore's works the author's voice itself, through its moralistic exhortations, tends to dominate the narrative. Both reflect a new direction in the relationship between the author and his literary enterprise.

In this comparison of the works of André de la Vigne and Pierre Gringore, which were printed and sold by the same Parisian book producers during the first decades of the sixteenth century—Pierre Le

---

[56]See details about another *rhétoriqueur*, Jean Lemaire, in Brown, "Rise of Literary Consciousness," pp. 64–71, and in *Shaping of History and Poetry*, pp. 150–51.

[57]While several of Gringore's earlier works, such as the *Château de labour* and *Château d'amour*, present a scenario similar to that of La Vigne's in the *Ressource*, whereby allegorical figures interact and are witnessed by an *acteur-narrateur*, a dream framework is never adopted in these compositions. Furthermore, the narrator is not a withdrawn, secondary figure whose identity and functions change according to the dynamics of the other characters. The speaker in Gringore's works is always a moralizing one who is directly involved with the characters in the text—sometimes he is the main character, as in the *Château de labour*—and at the same time with the readers outside it, whom he directly admonishes or counsels. The mythological opening of the *Chasse du Cerf* prepares the reader for a dream sequence, through association with other *rhétoriqueur*-like texts, yet Gringore undermines that very convention by presenting a nonallegorical, supposedly realistic account of his experiences. While the dream does find its way into the *Folles entreprises,* its traditional structure is subverted here as well. The first-person voice is "reposant de nuyt" at the outset, but does not actually fall asleep until halfway through the work. Despite the existence of a dialogue between allegorical figures and the topos of the awakening poet who proceeds at the end of the work to record his vision, the narrator's character in the *Folles entreprises* has been established from the beginning as a moralizing one, and it does not change once the dream has officially commenced. Gringore's latest works, such as the *Fantasies de Mère Sotte,* demonstrate an even greater distance between first-person narrator and fictional characters.

[141]

Dru, Jean Trepperel, Jean Petit, and Philippe Le Noir—we can observe a gradually developing self-consciousness. On the one hand, this is manifest within the text itself: La Vigne clarifies his role in the later versions of the *Ressource,* although the narrative voices still enmesh ambiguously; Gringore eventually abandons the medieval-like narrative voice altogether. On the other hand, the exterior presentation reflects too a greater focus on authorial image: after some ten years, La Vigne's authorship is advertised in print on the title page; Gringore's authority is stamped there prominently just five years after his first work is published and is validated and protected thereafter by *privileges.* No longer anonymously or ambiguously depicted in illustrated form, as was La Vigne throughout the history of the *Ressource de la Chrestienté,* Gringore, through his personalized woodcut image as Mère Sotte, came to dominate the exterior packaging of his printed works, as did his one-dimensional, nonfictionalized voice from within.

While it is difficult to ascertain the initial source of this change, it seems reasonable to conclude with the suggestion that the advent of print and its development in the late fifteenth and early sixteenth centuries played no small part in the rise of authorial self-consciousness among vernacular writers in Paris. It may ultimately have effected a change in the concept of literature itself.

[5]

New Perspectives on the History of Mainz Printing: A Fresh Look at Illuminated Imprints

Eberhard König

From the earliest stages of the bibliographical description of manuscripts, the approach has existed which in recent decades has been designated with the now fashionable term *codicology*[1]: the collaboration of textual historians, liturgists, paleographers, librarians, and art historians. Yet in the study of the fifteenth-century book a peculiar distinction is still maintained: art historians study decoration in the handwritten book but pay less attention to the printed illustrations in printed books or to printed decorations. The mixed form, which is so often encountered in the incunable period—printed books with decorations painted by hand—has attracted mainly the interest of incunabulists, and they, naturally, are concerned primarily with the work of the printer. Eloquent witness to this can be found in collections of reproductions such as those compiled by Carl Wehmer, where from the wealth of extant copies those selected were ones that were not "disfigured" by decorations made by hand.[2] Art historians, by contrast, could not pretend to

Part of the discussion in this essay was published in a different form under the title "The History of Art and the History of the Book at the Time of the Transition from Manuscript to Print," in Lotte Hellinga and John Goldfinch, eds., *Bibliography and the Study of 15th-Century Civilisation*, British Library Occasional Papers, no. 5 (London, 1987), pp. 154–84 (originally translated by Lotte Hellinga); another part of the discussion will appear as the introduction in a forthcoming "leaf book" on the 1462 Bible.

[1]See Léon Gilissen, *Introduction à la codicologie* (Brussels, 1987); from the extensive literature on the subject I shall merely refer to *Pen to Press*.

[2]Carl Wehmer, *Deutsche Buchdrucker des 15. Jahrhunderts* (Wiesbaden, 1971).

much enthusiasm for material that, although infinitely rich and varied, gave room only occasionally to pictorial illustration, since the printers usually left space only for initials, other decorations having to be confined to the margins.[3] The art historian is thus conditioned to expect visual material in incunabula to be mainly ornamental rather than pictorial.

Many aspects of printed books can, however, provide valuable information for the art historian. The art historian should systematize the initials and borders, and above all localize them. In only a few cases is it possible to attach names to illuminators; this is almost entirely confined to Augsburg, where Johann Bämler, to name but one, illuminated a considerable number of incunables from Strasbourg.[4] Yet even without names it is still possible to arrive at interesting insights on art historical grounds. The book, once produced in black and white in the printing house, had to be finished by hand, and we gain insight into trade relations by identifying the places where this handwork was carried out, for the unfinished books were often transported over many hundreds of miles before being illuminated. The history of art can also benefit from the fact that is it usually possible to attach either a known date or an approximate dating to printed books, as well as a place of publication, whereas in fifteenth-century manuscripts it is unusual to find dates for decoration. Even when dates of publication in printed books can function only as *termini post quem* for the work of the illuminators, they offer many more fixed points in a chronology than can ever be found among manuscript material. The place of printing may also be of interest to the art historian, even in those cases in which the illumination took place in an entirely different location.

My proposed enterprise—the study of the illustrated incunable printed in Germany—confronts uncertainties owing to the lacunae in our knowledge. A coherent history of book illumination in the German-speaking countries of the Holy Roman Empire does not exist.[5] It is therefore impossible to fit what can be observed in in-

---

[3]For a survey of the subject, see Curt F. Bühler, *The Fifteenth-Century Book: The Scribes, the Printers, the Decorators* (Philadelphia, 1960).

[4]See Sheila Edmunds, "The Place of the London Haggadah in the Work of Joel Ben Simeon," *Journal of Jewish Art* 7 (1978): 24–34, esp. pp. 32–34.

[5]The best survey so far is Albert Boeckler, *Deutsche Buchmalerei der Gotik* (Königstein i. T., 1959).

cunabula into any neat system for localization. Manuscripts and incunabula must complement each other in order eventually to construct a comprehensive history of fifteenth-century German book
illumination.[6]

Contributions to the Study of Incunabula
by Art History

Since the art historian's research is confined to what happened to
books after they left the presses, it might initially seem that this
research does not touch upon the main concerns of the study of
incunabula. But what happened to books subsequent to their printing
does have implications for the study of incunabula, as much as for the
history of all books of this period. When we can demonstrate that two
copies of the 42-line Bible traveled from the Rhine to the Thames
before being illuminated, we undermine the frequently cited cliché
that England did not admit the products of the new art of printing
until 1474.[7] This evidence thus contributes to our view of the conditions in England that made it receptive to printed books. For the
history of printing in Mainz this evidence also testifies to the fact that
at an early date the new invention had aroused interest even as far
away as London.

It is not particularly difficult for an art historian to recognize English decoration in a book printed in Mainz; this applies also to other
distinct styles of decoration, such as borders painted in Bruges or

---

[6]A first, all-too-bold attempt to investigate the illumination of books, at least in the
area between Mainz and Heidelberg in the first decades of printing, was presented by
Elgin Vaassen, "Die Werkstatt der Mainzer Riesenbibel in Würzburg und ihr Um-
kreis," *Archiv für Geschichte des Buchwesens* 13 (1973): cols. 1121–1428. Equally over-
ambitious was my own attempt to present a survey of the illumination of the 42-line
Bible: E. König, "Die Illuminierung der Gutenbergbibel," *Johannes Gutenbergs 42
Zeilige Bibel: Kommentarband zur Faksimile-Ausgabe,* ed. Wieland Schmidt and
Friedrich-Adolf Schmidt-Künsemüller (Munich, 1979), pp. 69–125; this work is part-
ly revised in later articles, for instance, "Möglichkeiten kunstgeschichtlicher Beiträge
zur Gutenberg-Forschung: Die 42 zeilige Bibel in Cologny, Heinrich Molitor und der
Einfluss der Klosterreform um 1450," *Gutenberg Jahrbuch* (1984): 83–102.

[7]One volume in Lambeth Palace Library and a fragment of a leaf in the British
Library; see E. König, "A Leaf from a Gutenberg Bible Illuminated in England,"
British Library Journal 9 (1983): 32–50; for the view that printing began late in England,
see Elizabeth Armstrong, "English Purchases of Printed Books from the Continent,
1465–1526," *English Historical Review* 94 (1979): 268–90.

Paris.[8] It is more difficult, and therefore more interesting for the incunabulist, to establish these connections nearer the printing house, where many more copies were decorated. The illumination of books in Mainz during the early years of printing has mainly been investigated by Elgin Vaassen.[9] If we can provide evidence, however, that there was not only "in-house binding" but also "in-house decoration" in the Fust and Schoeffer workshop, art history will have made a significant contribution to our understanding of these printers.[10] We cannot be certain yet whether incunabulists will be able to refrain from seeing in Johannes Fust the evil villain who wanted to deprive Gutenberg of the fruits of his successful invention; instead they may come to consider him an active partner in the first printing venture, even if he did not share the practical work: a man who was inventive in his own right. In this view it was he who would have stimulated experiments with printed forms of decoration and who had a number of copies of each edition decorated by a single skilled illuminator of his own choice.[11]

The history of art, however, has possibilities beyond a crude and large-scale distribution of styles over culturally distinct areas of western Europe and Italy, or the (almost anecdotal) connection of illuminators with one particular partner in the earliest printing house. If we chart the dissemination of the earliest printed books together with particulars of individual copies, we are led to a hypothesis about what buyers the printers in Mainz had in mind when they decided on

[8]Not until 1462 with the illumination of copies of the 48-line Bible (B48), printed by Fust and Schoeffer, did Bruges and Paris come to play a significant role. Luxurious Bruges decoration in the style of Vrelant can be found in the Madrid copy of the 48-line Bible, and many French libraries (Paris, Tours, and others) have copies of the B48 illuminated in France; there are also Italian copies of this edition in Chantilly, Milan, and so on.

[9]See Vaassen, "Die Werkstatt."

[10]On Fust, see E. König, "Für Johannes Fust," in *Ars Impressoria: Entstehung und Entwicklung des Buchdrucks: Eine internationale Festgabe für Severin Corsten zum 65. Geburtstag,* ed. Hans Limburg et al. (Munich, 1986), pp. 285–313; and on "in-house" binding by these printers, see Hermann Knaus, "Uber Verlegereinbande bei Schoeffer," *Gutenberg Jahrbuch* (1938): 97–108, and Vera Sack, "Über Verlegeseinbände und Buchhandel Peter Schöffërs," *Archiv für Geschichte des Buchwesens* 13 (1973): 249–88.

[11]Particularly interesting and in need of further research are copies purchased in Mainz, apparently in large numbers, by the congregation of Santa Giustina in Padua, illuminated in Padua and distributed over the affiliated houses, of which there are examples in the British Library; Musée Condé, Chantilly; New York Public Library; and elsewhere.

the text of the first major book they were to produce.[12] The primary question that must be asked is: What need was there at all for a Latin Bible of the size of the 42-line Bible?

The Decision to Print the Vulgate First

The question of *who* made the decision to print the Vulgate as the first major text to be published using the new technique need not be answered here, although I must declare my conviction that Fust's influence was decisive. The question of *why* the Bible was chosen, insofar as it has been asked at all, has led to some astonishing historical misconceptions. The Protestant theologian Heinrich Karpp, for example, asserted as recently as 1981 that even before the Reformation one could speak seriously of a *Schriftprinzip,* the fundamental significance of the Scriptures.[13] Gutenberg (the only person to whom historiography grants an active role) would have intended the Scriptures to be the ultimate foundation and the yardstick for Christian thought and action. According to Karpp, the textura style of typography and script belongs to "the Bible used in worship," and he concluded that Gutenberg's intention was that his printed Bible be used in church.[14]

A complete Bible in church, if any were found at all, would be in the vernacular, to be read privately. There is, of course, no liturgy without quotation of Bible texts, but it would hardly be possible to locate in a complete text of the Vulgate the short texts that were in daily use in the service as lections, antiphons, and so on. It is not until the introduction of the Protestant service that we find the Bible on the altar. Up to the present day the only book that the Roman Catholic service requires here is the missal, which is frequently pictured in contemporary panel paintings of church services.[15]

It can hardly have been the intention of Gutenberg and Fust to revolutionize the Roman Catholic rite. Historians conversant with the Mass have therefore refrained from trying to find a positive explana-

---

[12]See König, "Möglichkeiten," pp. 83–102.

[13]See Heinrich Karpp, "Die Kirchengeschichtliche Bedeutung der Gutenbergbibel," *Zeitschrift für Theologie und Kirche* 76 (1979): 310–30.

[14]Ibid., p. 311.

[15]On the pictorial evidence for types of books employed during church services, see E. König, "The History of Art and the History of the Book," esp. pp. 156–58.

tion for the selection of the Vulgate. They have instead taken the view that it must have been chosen by default, that the printers had really wished to print a missal. The three distinct type sizes in textura style, which were available in 1457–58 for the printing of the first Psalter and the *Canon Missae,* were surely designed for this project; but in the end the printers must have balked at the technical difficulties involved in printing a missal.[16]

This explanation for the printing of the Vulgate remains a tempting theory, for it takes account of the reality of religious life as well as the types available in the printing house. But were there really technical grounds for deciding in favor of the Vulgate, which required, of course, only one size of type? Furthermore, what technical refinements might have been made in the short period between the printing of the Bible and the Psalter?[17]

To make it possible for the late medieval book trade to sell a work in an unheard-of number of copies at a high price (as was economically inevitable with the first or very first printed works) there had to be a particular attraction to lure buyers to an old, well-known, and widely available text presented in a new form. Most of the first owners of the 42-line Bible and its early successors had one remark-

[16]Most recently summarized by Severin Corsten, "Die Drucklegung der 42zeiligen Bibel: Technische und chronologische Probleme," in Schmidt and Schmidt-Künsemüller, *Kommentarband,* pp. 33–67, esp. pp. 41–42; Gottfried Zedler had pointed out that the initials *W* and *K,* present in the typeface used for the 42-line and 36-line Bibles, are not required in the printing of a Vulgate Bible, but are indispensable for printing a missal in a German-speaking country; see G. Zedler, *Die sogenannte Gutenbergbibel sowie die mit der 42zeiligen Bibeltype ausgeführten kleineren Drucke* (Mainz, 1929), pp. 9–14; Rudolf Blum revived Zedler's argument in *Der Prozess Fust gegen Gutenberg: Eine Interpretation des Helmaspergischen Notariatsinstruments im Rahmen der Frühgeschichte des Mainzer Buchdrucks (Beiträge zur Buch-und Bibliotheksgeschichte)* (Wiesbaden, 1954), pp. 89–102. Corsten, "Die Drucklegung," p. 41, expressed reservations, as did Ferdinand Geldner, "Das Helmaspergische Notariatsinstrument in seiner Bedeutung für die Geschichte des ältesten Mainzer Buchdrucks," in *Der gegenwartige Stand der Gutenberg-Forschung,* ed. Hans Widmann (Stuttgart, 1972), pp. 91–121, esp. pp. 111–13. In the same volume Widmann, p. 23, seems to agree with these authors; but Friedrich-Adolf Schmidt-Künsemüller, p. 137, speaks of "geplanten Missale" (planned missal): see also his article "Der Streit um das Missale speciale," *Aus der Welt des Bibliothekars: Festschrift für Rudolf Jochhoff* (Cologne, 1961), pp. 51–89, esp. p. 76.

[17]Even the two-color decorative initials used in the Psalters could also have been used in the 42-line Bible, as William Scheide has pointed out in "A Speculation Concerning Gutenberg's Early Plans for His Bible," *Gutenberg Jahrbuch* (1973): 129–39.

able thing in common: they already possessed Bibles.[18] It is unthinkable that monasteries such as Saint Blasius or Melk would not already have owned a manuscript of the Vulgate.[19] It cannot have been the curiosity value of the new technology that persuaded the abbot of such a house to spend a considerable sum of money; he must have had more substantial reasons.[20] We would face similar questions if the missal had been planned as the first book, and the answers would perhaps be even less ambiguous, for a new missal would be bought only when the old one became obsolete, or when one wished to offer a donation for the salvation of one's soul. Only in response to a reform of the Mass would a large number of missals—such as print can supply—need to be produced. There is no trace of an archiepiscopal reform around 1450 to support the assumption that the first book to be printed was to be a Mainz missal. At the time when Gutenberg and Fust were making plans for their first book, however, there was a movement to reform the Mass, and it may even have been active in Mainz: in 1450 the Benedictine House of Saint James (which later owned a 42-line Bible) was incorporated into the Bursfeld congregation. One of the main objects of the congregation was to standardize the church service.[21] Unfortunately, the decisions of the General Chapter of the congregation do not survive for the period critical to these considerations (1450–1455), but the second extant agreement, for the year 1459, reports that a new missal was accepted, and this received the *approbatio* of the chapter in the following year.[22] Work on this missal must have been carried out in the preceding years. It is not beyond belief that by 1450 a start had been made, and that Gutenberg and Fust had in mind a Bursfeld reformed missal

[18]The only contemporary price we know for a 42-line Bible is the incredibly high sum of one hundred Rhenish guilders (*cent[u]m flor[enos] Rene[n]ses*) for the—albeit splendidly illuminated—volumes on vellum in the H. E. Huntington Library, San Marino, California; see Ilona Hubay, "Die bekannten Exemplare der zweiundvierzigzeiligen Bibel und ihre Besitzer," in Schmidt and Schmidt-Künsemüller *Kommentarband*, pp. 127–55, no. 36.

[19]Saint Blasius in the Black Forest is the provenance of the copy now in the Library of Congress, Washington, D.C. (Hubay, "Die bekannten Exemplare," no. 35); Melk of the copy in the Beinecke Library, Yale University (ibid., no. 41).

[20]BN, on vellum (Hubay, "Die bekannten Exemplare," no. 15).

[21]See Walter Ziegler, *Die Bursfelder Kongregation in der Reformationszeit: Dargestellt an Hand der Generalkapitelsrezesse*, Beiträge zur Geschichte des Alten Mönchtums und des Benediktinerordens, no. 29 (Münster, 1986).

[22]See P. Volk, *Die Generalkapitels-Rezesse der Bursfelder Kongregation* (Sieburg, 1957), I, 101, no. 7, and 104, no. 3.

when they developed the three sizes of type which were used in the Psalter and the *Canon Missae*. The fact that the second Psalter, printed in 1459, followed the use of the Bursfeld congregation is also an argument in favor of this speculation.[23] The printers' technical achievement could then have been engaged in the promotion of one of the principal ideas of the monastic reform: that identical texts should be present in all monasteries. The art of printing could guarantee this, as not even the most accurate scribe could. This surely strengthens the hypothesis of the planning of a missal at an early date. It would not have been technical obstacles that defeated the printers and wrecked the project but the slowness of the monks' progress in deciding on a uniform text.

The fact that no missal was printed in 1460, soon after the confirmation of the General Chapter, also requires an explanation. Several conditions had changed: the Mainz partnership had been reconstituted after Gutenberg's departure; the initial experience with the marketing of editions (in many copies) of printed books may well have led to changes in pricing; and finally, the monks on whom the printers had counted in the early phase of the project may by 1460 no longer have been alive.

Yet this speculation on why a missal was not printed does not explain the choice of the Vulgate as the first printed book. The 42-line Bible presents itself as belonging to the tradition of large Bibles in folio, limited almost entirely to monastic use, where they were used exclusively for reading aloud during meals in the refectory.[24] Many

[23]The Fust and Schoeffer editions of the Psalter can be divided into two groups, according to their liturgical use: the editions of 1457, 1502, and 1515 were for the use of the diocese of Mainz; the editions of 1459, 1490, and 1516 were for the congregation of Bursfeld. Only the edition of 1516 is thus designated, with the title *Psalterium ordinis S. Benedicti de Observantia Bursfelden(se)*. The same text was printed in Speyer in 1496 by Peter Drach. The edition of 1459 contains an indication of the connection between the Mainz house of Saint James with the Bursfeld congregation: the colophon includes the words (not present in the 1457 edition) "ad laudem Dei ac honorem S. Jacobi." The liturgical aspect was discussed by Franz Falk, "Die Mainzer Psalterien von 1457, 1459, 1490, 1502, 1515, und 1516 nach ihrer historisch-liturgischen Seite," *Festschrift zum 500 jährigen Geburtstage von Johann Gutenberg* (Mainz, 1900), pp. 257–60.

[24]Such Bibles in folio are mainly from the thirteenth century; but some existing examples are known from the fifteenth century as well; see Leipzig, University Library, MS 1, decorated by the same shop that illuminated the copies of the B42 in Berlin and San Marino; for illustrations, see D. Debes, *Leipziger Zimelien: Bücherschätze der Universitätsbibliothek* (Weinheim, 1989), p. 114 and color pl. 63.

features in individual copies of the 42-line Bible, and also its immediate successors, show that they were used for just this purpose.[25] The Bursfeld reform movement, and also similar movements in southern Germany (Melk and Tegernsee) and in Italy (Santa Giustina in Padua), not only revised the missal but also addressed the custom of reading at meals. The difficulties encountered here manifest themselves as early as the first agreement of the General Chapter of Bursfeld: their seventh decision (1458) reads: "It would please the fathers that the wooden sign be placed before the wandering eyes of the brothers in the refectory, 'Avert your eyes, lest they see vanity,' so that thus blushing it restrains the sight and directs the mind toward the readings."[26]

In such a context we can expect a thorough reconstitution of the contents of a monastic library in every case where a monastery had adopted the reform and become a member of the Bursfeld or Melk congregations. The function of the "corrector of the readings at meals" (*emendator lectoris mensae*)—to censor what was read at the table—gained in importance. Libraries were examined critically; much was discarded, and new books with improved texts were bought.[27] The contents of the libraries and the priories of what was to be read in the refectories show us that it was here that the Vulgate came into its own, or rather was preferred above all other texts. The *Consuetudines* of Tegernsee, for example, state: "One should read at meals the Bible, the sermons and homilies of the holy fathers, the *Moralia* of Gregory, and other tracts and writings of the doctors."[28] If

[25]There are many traces of sections marked for reading in the refectory, and explicit indications such as "hic continueter in refectorio" in the Göttingen copy (Hubay, "Die bekannten Exemplare," no. 2), fol. 142, vol. 2.

[26]Volk, *Die Generalkapitels-Rezesse,* I, 95, no. 7: "Placuit patribus, ut fratribus in refectorio vagis visu existentibus apponatur signum ligneum, in quo erit scriptum: 'Averte oculos tuos ne videant vanitatem,' ut sic erubescens visum contineat et lectiones intendat."

[27]An example is described dramatically by Wilhelm Wittwer, *Catalogus abbatum* (1493), where he maintains that the Abbot Melchior von Stamhaim had all service books for the monastery of Saints Ulrich and Afra in Augsburg replaced by purchasing new ones or by having them recopied in the scriptorium; see Erich Steingräber, *Die Kirchliche Buchmalerei Augsburgs um 1500* (Basel, 1956), p. 46.

[28]See Joachim Angerer, *Die Bräuche der Abtei Tegernsee unter Abt Kaspar Ayndorffer, verbunden mit einer textkritischen Edition der Consuetudines Tegernseenses* (Munich, 1968), p. 166, ll. 16–17: "Legatur ad mensam 'de biblia,' de sermonibus sanctorum patrum et homeliis, de Moralibus Gregorii et aliis doctoribus tractatibus et scriptis."

we set aside Peter Schoeffer's interest in legal and canonical texts, this passage from the *Consuetudines* reads almost like a publishing program for his enterprise at Mainz.

In the reformed monasteries, the renewed value attached to reading at table also stimulated interest in their collections of other books. At Saints Ulrich and Afra in Augsburg, the first abbot to head the monastery after its reformation, Melchior von Stamhaim, not only discarded the old books but established a scriptorium for producing new books, a process that included illumination.[29] Elsewhere I have sought to demonstrate that the Bodmer 42-line Bible at Cologny near Geneva was illuminated at Augsburg, and that this is directly connected with Melchior von Stamhaim's efforts to provide his monastery with better books.[30] Melk and Brixen are two other important centers of the reform movement of about 1450, and both were early owners of copies of the 42-line Bible, of which the Vienna copy was illuminated in Vienna for the famous Bishop Nicholaus Cusanus of Brixen (fig. 5.1).[31] I also remain firm in my belief that the copy of the 42-line Bible at the Bayerische Staatsbibliothek in Munich had been destined by the monastery of Tegernsee for their new foundation at Andechs and was illuminated either at Tegernsee or at Andechs.[32]

Another example has come to my attention which may serve as a further witness to the connection between the reform movement and the early printing of Bibles, and shows that this connection continued to motivate the production of other editions that followed the 42-line Bible. The Bibliotheca Philosophica Hermetica in Amsterdam owns a copy of Heinrich Eggestein's first Latin Bible, printed at Strasbourg no later than 1468, which beyond a doubt was illuminated by a monk

[29]See Steingräber, *Die Kirchliche Buchmalerei.*

[30]König, "Die Illuminierung"; idem., "Möglichkeiten."

[31]The Abbey of Melk is the origin of the B42 in the Beinecke Library, Yale University (Hubay, "Die bekannten Exemplare," no. 41), Brixen of the copy in the ONB (ibid., no. 27).

[32]Hubay, "Die bekannten Exemplare," no. 5; originally I assumed that the Munich copy was illuminated in Brixen, since stylistically it appears closely related to the Brixen style; Elmar Hertrich, however, objected in "Die Gutenberg-Bibel neu kommentiert," *Aus dem Antiquariat Börsenblatt,* Frankfurt 72 (1980), pp. A 360–6, esp. p. 364. In König, "Möglichkeiten," pp. 83–102, I have accepted his arguments. Yet it does appear to me that a painter is at work here who moved from Brixen to Tegernsee, and from there, possibly in a short time, to Andechs, as Anton Pelchinger is known to have done; see Virgil Redlich, *Tegernsee und die deutsche Geistesgeschichte im 15. Jahrhundert,* Schriftenreihe zur bayerischen Landesgeschichte, no. 9 (Munich, 1931).

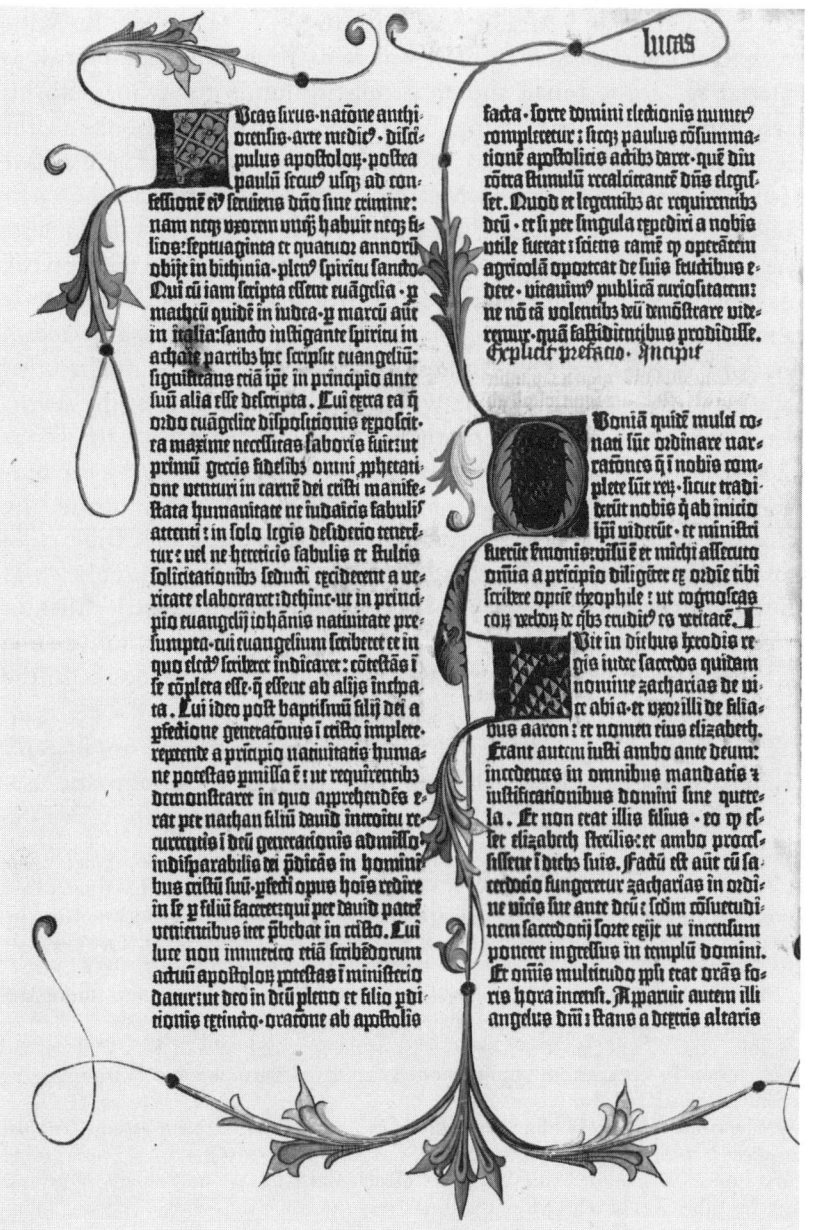

Figure 5.1. Leaf illuminated in Vienna for Brixen, from the B42, ONB, Inc. 3 B 14, II, fol. 217v. By permission of the Österreichische Nationalbibliothek, Vienna.

of Saints Ulrich and Afra in Augsburg (fig. 5.2).[33] In Wilhelm Wittwer's *Catalogus abbatum* (1493), a certain Pater Johannes Franck is
entered as "a good man and an excellent illuminator who, with his
own hands, illuminated choir books and many other books in the
convent."[34] As he died in 1472, we can infer that Franck must have
been present in 1458 when Melchior von Stamhaim had the choir
books of the abbey replaced; the signature "franck" shows that at least
one of the antiphonaries from Saints Ulrich and Afra is his work
(Bayerische Staatsbibliothek, Munich, MS clm 4305).[35] Thus his style
can be identified unambiguously, and it can be easily recognized in
this copy of the Eggestein Bible. A note of ownership on the first text
page establishes that the Bible was in the abbey in at least the seventeenth or early eighteenth century.[36] It is not likely that the scriptorium in the abbey would have undertaken commissions for out-
siders. In contrast with the many Eggestein Bibles illuminated by
Johannes Bämler, also at Augsburg,[37] Franck's Eggestein Bible is an
isolated piece of work. We therefore must assume that the abbey was
still buying printed Bibles in the mid-1460s to be used either in
priories or at the main abbey itself. The Eggestein Bible would be one
of those books designated by Wittwer as "many other books in the
convent."

There is hardly any evidence for individual or private use of early
printed Bibles to balance the abundant traces of their monastic use.

---

[33]*GW* 4205; see *The Fifteenth-Century Book: Incunabula from Eighty-Nine Presses*,
H. P. Kraus Catalogue, no. 173 (New York, 1986), pp. 19–22, no. 12.; Margaret Lane
Ford, *Christ, Plato, Hermes Trismegistus: The Dawn of Printing*, Catalogue of the Incunabula in the Bibliotheca Philosophica Hermetica I, 1 (Amsterdam, 1990), no. 40,
pp. 88–89.

[34]Steingräber, *Die Kirchliche Buchmalerei*, p. 46: "Bonus vir et optimus illuminstra
qui, suis manibus, illuminavit libros chori et alios plurimos in conventu."

[35]Ibid., fig. 2, and pp. 56–57, with a list of the service books of Saints Ulrich and
Afra, found in libraries at Munich and Augsburg, containing many paintings by
Johannes Franck.

[36]The contemporary binding, as recorded in Ernst Kyriss, *Verzierte gotische Einbände
im alten deutschen Sprachgebiet*, 3 vols. (Stuttgart, 1951–1956), no. 89, is a further
indication of Augsburg and even Saints Ulrich and Afra; we may therefore assume
that the Bible was purchased by the monastery "in black and white," and was rubricated, illuminated, and bound there.

[37]See Edmunds, "The Place of the London Haggadah"; the British Library copy of
Eggestein's third Bible (*GW* 4208), c.14.d.I., decorated with paintings only at the
beginning of the two volumes and at the beginning of Genesis 1:4, as was Bämler's
habit; elsewhere it is decorated in Bämler's characteristic style.

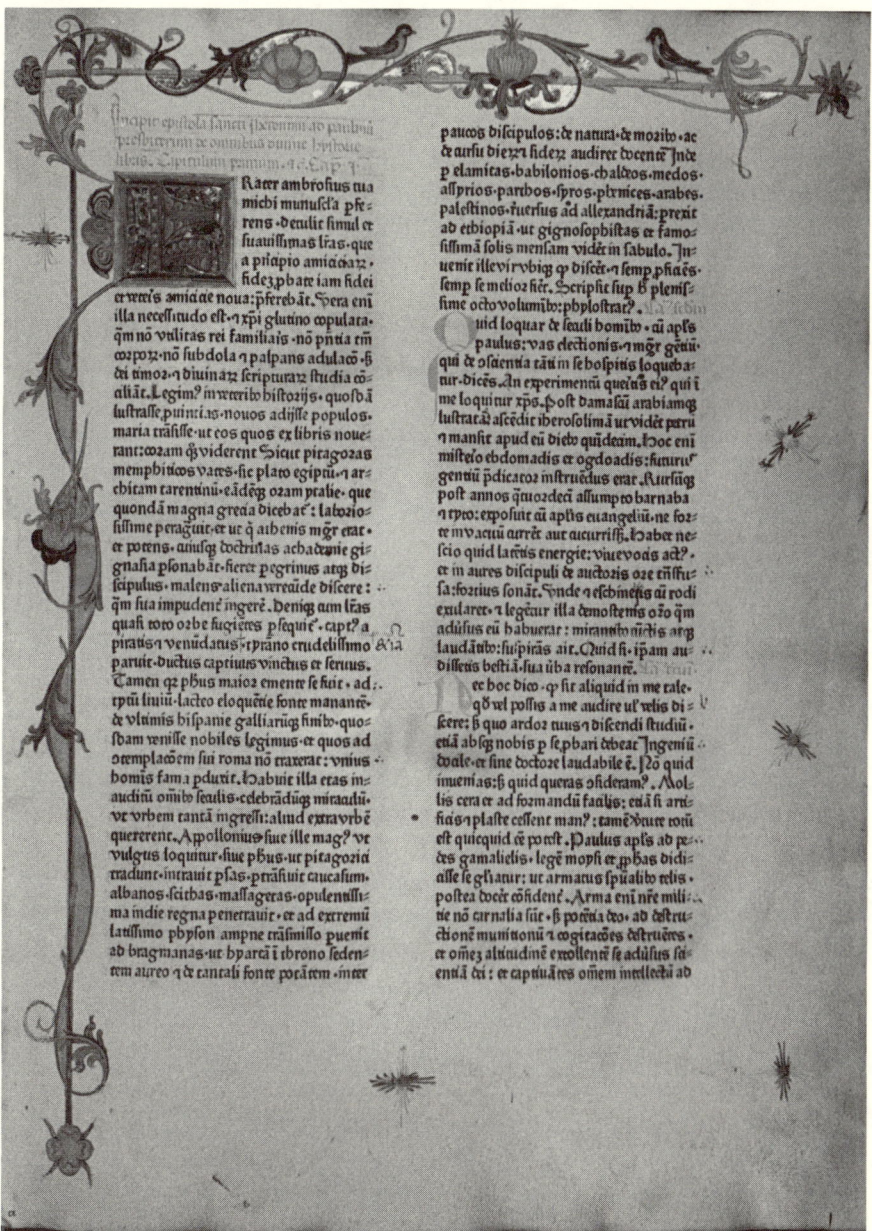

Figure 5.2. Leaf illuminated by Johannes Franck, Augsburg, from the Eggestein Bible, Strasbourg, Heinrich Eggestein, 1468, Private Collection, I, fol. 1. Photo: H. P. Kraus, New York. Courtesy of Amsterdam, BPH.

Aeneas Silvius, of course, in the rediscovered letter of October 1454, contemplates buying one, but that is for the use of a person of such exceptional standing as Cardinal Carvajal.[38] One of the first private owners of an early printed Bible on record is Dr. Knorr, pastor of one of the main churches in Nuremberg and canon of the cathedral at Bamberg, whose chapter financed the printing of the 36-line Bible. Knorr would have been in an exceptional position since he belonged to the small circle of clerics who had instigated the printing of Bibles in Bamberg.[39]

To sum up, we can now assemble the views of the various positions taken in the history of printing (to which art history could make several contributions) to build up a new picture: a real stimulus to the printing of the Vulgate was the assurance of the regular market provided by the reformed monasteries. Prior to the Vulgate there may have been plans for a monastic missal for the same developing market: the Bursfeld congregation (not the archdiocese of Mainz as was originally thought). Yet the delay in preparing the text rather than the technical difficulties in producing it prevented the execution of this plan. A large-format Vulgate would not serve for private reading (except perhaps for elderly gentlemen such as Cardinal Carvajal, who would not need his spectacles to read it, as Aeneas Silvius pointed out), and was not required for church services, but was the most important text for reading in the refectory required by the (reformed) rules of monastic houses. An authoritative text was indispensable in discussions about liturgical reform.

The identification of illumination and calligraphy in copies of the 42-line Bible makes three specific contributions: it shows that it is likely that Fust as publisher had a number of copies prepared to be ready for use by in-house illuminators at Mainz; it highlights the preponderance of monastic houses as first owners of the Bibles; and finally it shows that part of the edition was sent far abroad and illuminated only when it reached Flanders, London, or Italy. There are indications that, after the obvious economic significance of Frankfurt

[38]Erich Meuthen, "Ein frühes Quellenzeugnis (zu Oktober 1454?) für den ältesten Buchdruck," *Gutenberg Jahrbuch* (1982): 108–18.

[39]Ferdinant Geldner, "Ein neuer Hinweis auf Bamberg als Druckort der 36zeiligen Bibel: Das Wappen des Peter Knorr im Exemplar der Bibliothèque Nationale," *Gutenberg Jahrbuch* (1964): 48–51.

am Main, ports and trading centers with fairs, such as Bruges, Lübeck, and Leipzig, were of importance in the marketing of the Bible.[40] It is clear that the printers did not merely rely on their first objective, the reformed monasteries, but expected to attract a wider market that could absorb novelties of every kind.

Illumination and Calligraphy of the 48-Line Bible

Only in the case of the 42-line Bible has the variety of possibilities of illumination and calligraphy been surveyed, even if insufficiently.[41] Research for this essay could not include an examination of all extant copies of the 48-line Bible, especially as the Second World War has made the location of a substantial number of copies difficult, while others have changed hands after such sales as those of the holdings of the General Theological Seminary in New York and the Edward Doheny Memorial Library in Camarillo, California.

Nevertheless, the short survey presented here is based on a study of nearly fifty copies, almost three-quarters of them on vellum. Most of these copies are complete and bound in two volumes, in rare cases four.[42] Nearly all volumes have been stripped of their original binding; one beautiful Nuremberg binding still adorns the Stuttgart copy, while a defective Flemish binding still covers the 48-line Bible formerly in the Doheny Library.[43] Bindings therefore rarely provide an aid to localizing the early owners.

I know of one copy, in the University Library of Würzburg, which is almost devoid of any decoration. Work on this Bible was inter-

[40]See König, "Möglichkeiten"; decorated in Bruges are the copies formerly at the Buchmuseum, Leipzig (Hubay, "Die bekannten Exemplare," no. 48), and the vellum copy at the Pierpont Morgan Library, New York (ibid., no. 37); at Lübeck the copies at Pelplin (ibid., no. 28) and also perhaps Copenhagen (ibid., no. 13); at Leipzig the copies at Berlin (ibid., no. 3) and the H. E. Huntington Library, San Marino, California (ibid., no. 36).

[41]König, "Möglichkeiten."

[42]For instance, an interesting copy in the Bodleian Library, Oxford (Auct. M.1.4).

[43][Paul Needham], *The Estelle Doheny Collection*, pt. 1, *Fifteenth-Century Books Including the Gutenberg Bible*, sale catalogue, Christie's, New York, October 22, 1987, lot 5, has erroneously included the Darmstadt copy (K. H. Staub, *Buchkunst des Mittelalters: Cimelien der Hessischen Hochschul- und Landesbibliothek Darmstadt* [Wiesbaden, 1980]) as one with a contemporary binding.

rupted after the completion of minor decoration, and the illumination of the larger initials, the responsibility of a specialized craftsman, was never carried out.

The number of copies adorned only with calligraphy is very small compared with the other early Bible issues, and poor calligraphy is to be found only in paper copies such as those in Bonn and Göttingen. Some of the copies with calligraphic decoration range from the finest works of virtuoso calligraphers—such as the incomplete paper copy in the Bibliothèque Nationale in Paris—to the solid but by no means extravagant copies in Munich or Mainz, of which the latter—composed of two volumes from different sets—is the only example still preserved in the city.

Among the illuminated 48-line Bibles are four that have been executed by a brilliant illuminator. He has tentatively been identified as Fust's painter, or the Fust Master, who for some time worked exclusively for the publisher, and whose hand can be identified in certain copies of all the books printed by Fust, excluding the Psalters, which did not need to be completed by hand.[44] The Fust Master decorated two copies of the Gutenberg Bible, and no fewer than eight copies of the *Durandus,* faithfully reproducing the same design, apparently with the help of stencils (fig. 5.3). With this edition the idea of producing identical decoration reached its peak.[45] In the 1462 Bible the Fust Master changes his practice by varying his motifs, thus providing one more reason to believe that variety was a major aim when this Bible was designed (fig. 5.4).

The Fust Master is the only illuminator to be located with certainty in Mainz and who was entrusted with copies of the 48-line Bible. There is no trace of the style of the Göttingen model book in any of

[44]See König, "Für Johannes Fust." Three of these copies are on vellum. The one in the Scheide Library, Princeton, and the one in the Pierpont Morgan Library, New York, were both already known to Adolph Goldschmidt, who was the first to assemble work of this illuminator and recognize that he had been closely connected with Fust ("The Decoration of Early Mainz Books," *Magazine of Art* 31 [1983]: 519–22). The third Bible is in the University Library, Cambridge. The fourth example, the second volume, on paper, is preserved in the University Library, Giessen, and has only recently come to my attention.

[45]The importance of exact repetition even in illumination of incunabula was first discussed in my article "The Influence of the Invention of Printing on the Development of German Illustration," *Manuscripts in the Fifty Years after the Invention of Printing: Some Papers Read at a Colloquium at the Warburg Institute on 12–13 March, 1982,* ed. J. B. Trapp (London, 1983), pp. 85–96.

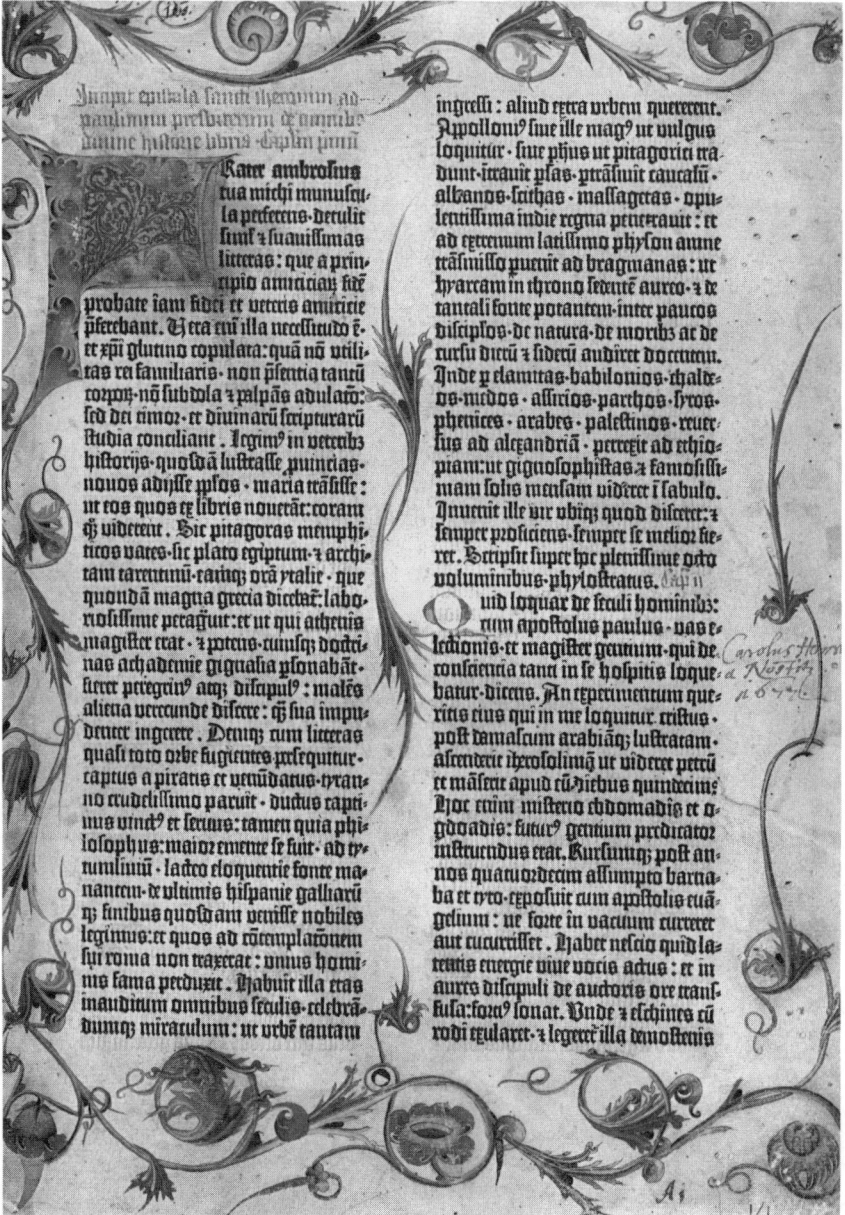

Figure 5.3. Leaf illuminated by the Fust Master, Mainz, from the B42, PML 12, I, fol. 1 verso. Courtesy of the Pierpont Morgan Library, New York.

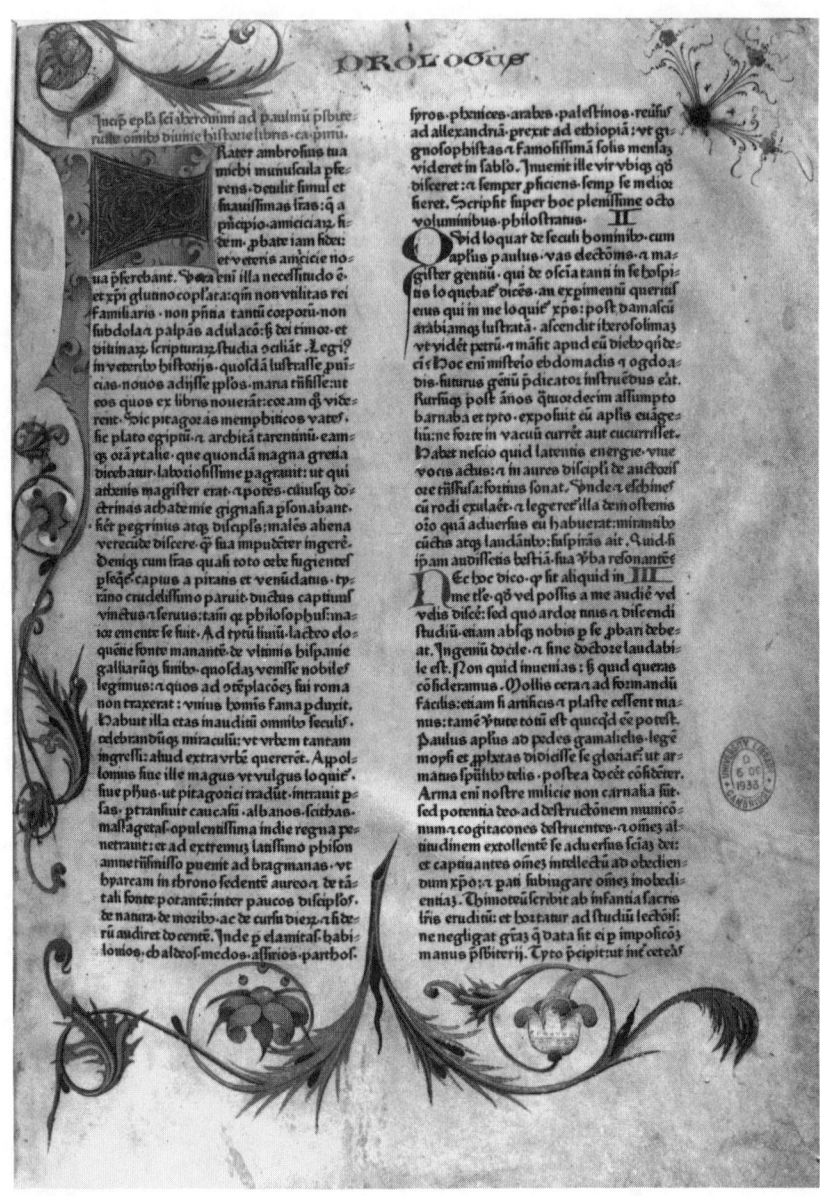

Figure 5.4. Leaf illuminated by the Fust Master, Mainz, from the B48, Cambridge University Library, I, fol. 1. By permission of the Syndics of Cambridge University Library.

his copies,[46] nor indeed of any other hand easily identifiable as working in Mainz. Only some of the copies with calligraphy may be safely localized in Mainz. No Mainz binding of a 48-line Bible is recorded.[47]

A second important group excels in the beauty of its illumination, often with historiated initials. Gold leaf in elegantly sprayed panicles and decorative spheres in blue, red, and green characterize the border design together with the colorful, leafy, but always strictly stylized plants. Comparisons with illuminated manuscripts allow us to locate these kinds of borders in Cologne. Belonging to this group are the Palatina copy in the Vatican, the New Testament in Darmstadt, and a Bible that was in the possession of the municipal authorities in Frankfurt for many centuries and is now part of the Stadt- und Universitätsbibliothek (fig. 5.5).[48] The most splendid example is the copy in London which includes the original owner's name and device in the decoration (fig. 5.6). Conradus Doleatoris is named in the border of the second frontispiece.[49] This man, with the German name of Konrad Bender, matriculated at Cologne in 1466 and became dean of the Collegiate Church of Saint Bartholomew in Frankfurt (today called the Dom), the church that served as the place of election of the German kings. Bender owned a considerable library, parts of which are still in Frankfurt,[50] and is representative of the type of person who purchased a folio Bible for his own personal use—that is, the class of men for whom the 1462 issue was partly conceived.

[46]See Hellmut Lehmann-Haupt, *The Göttingen Model Book* (Columbia, Mo., 1972), pp. 83ff. and fig. 12. The vellum copies of the Gutenberg Bible in Göttingen and the Bibliothèque Nationale in Paris are illuminated in this style.

[47]Three copies of the 42-line Bible have Mainz bindings; see Otto Mazal, "Die Bucheinbände der erhaltenen Exemplare der zweiundvierzigzeiligen Bibel," in Schmidt and Schmidt-Künsemüller, *Kommentarband*, pp. 157–75, esp. p. 160: the copies are in Mainz, Immenhausen, and formerly Camarillo, California, now Maruzen, Tokyo.

[48]See Kurt Ohly and Vera Sack, *Inkunabelkatalog der Stadt- und Universitätsbibliothek und anderer öffentlicher Sammlungen in Frankfurt am Main* (Stuttgart, 1966), no. 506, and *Bibliotheca Publica Francofurtensis*, ed. Klaus Dieter Lehmann, (Frankfurt, 1985), pl. 31, with commentary by Gerhard Powitz; see also König, in "The History of Art & The History of the Book," esp. pp. 172ff.

[49]BL, Inc. 102; see the description in *BMC*, vol. 1.

[50]See Ohly and Sack, *Inkunabelkatalog*, nos. 194, 1288, 1720, and 1904, concerning his library and for more information about Doleatoris. He was canon of Saint Bartholomew when he matriculated at Cologne; Hermann Keussen calls him Vasbender; see *Die Matrikel der Universität Köln*, 3 vols. (Bonn, 1928–1931), I, 743, no. 309, 58.

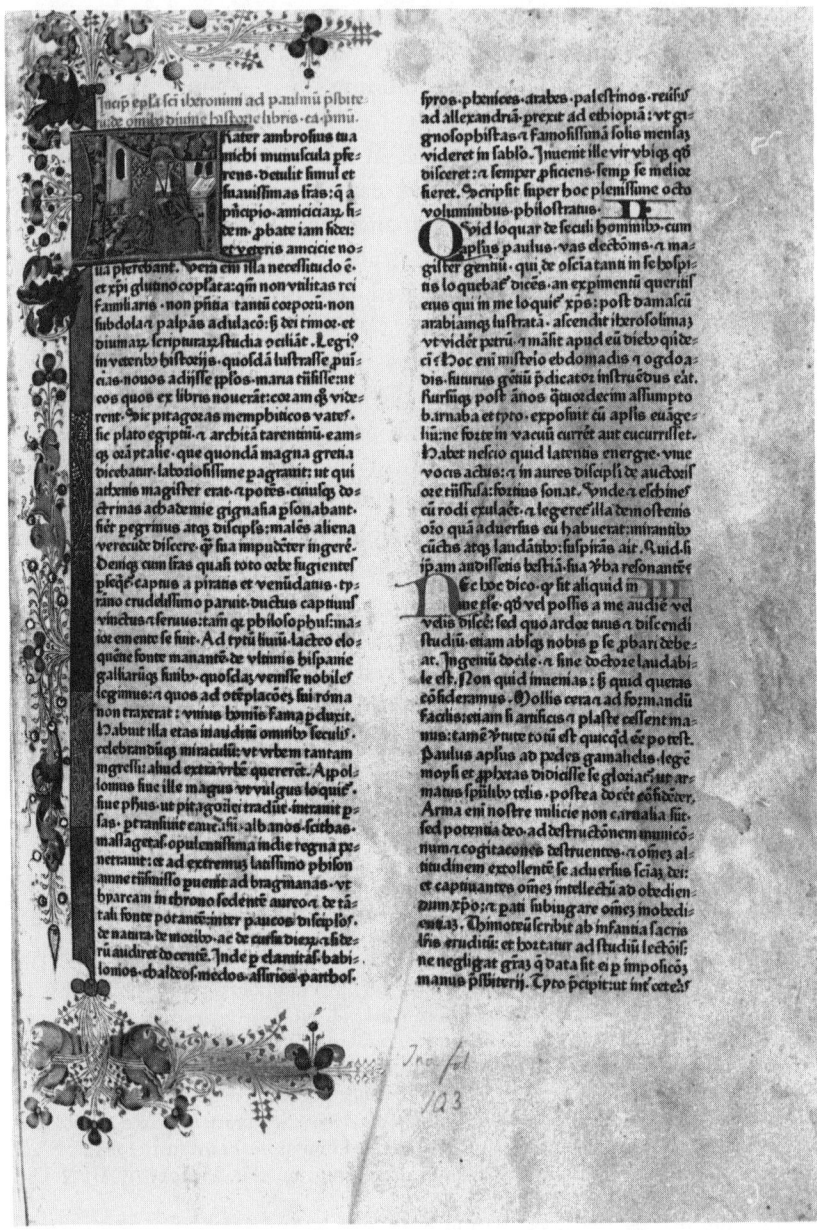

Figure 5.5. Leaf illuminated in Cologne, from the B48, Frankfurt, Stadt-und Universitätsbibliothek, I, fol. 1. Courtesy of Stadt- und Universitätsbibliothek, Frankfurt.

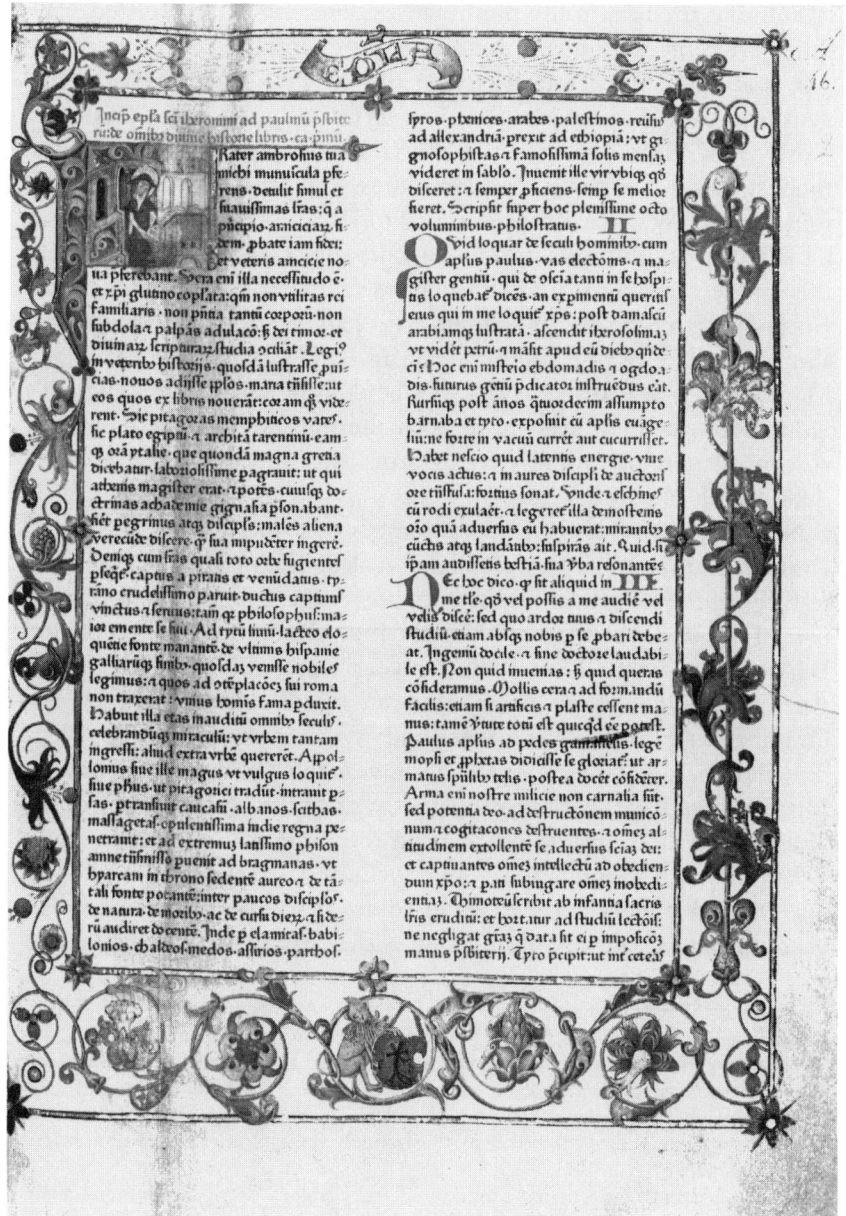

Figure 5.6. Leaf illuminated in Cologne from the B48, BL, Inc. IC 102, I, fol. 1.
By permission of the British Library.

Some of the beautifully illuminated copies are rather isolated. The Stuttgart Bible with its old Nuremberg binding has decent illumination and came from the library of the German order at Bad Mergentheim to its present location. It is stylistically so close to monastic work from Nuremberg that it must have originated in one of the monasteries in the town.[51] A well-known illuminator's hand can be found in a copy in San Marino,[52] that of Johannes Bämler, who began his career as an illuminator of incunabula (fig. 5.7). He decorated only this single example from Mainz, however, after which he dealt exclusively with Strasbourg printers who sent their books to his workshop in Augsburg to be illuminated (fig. 5.8).[53] In the case of the San Marino copy, it is obvious that the book was finished in a layman's workshop and may even have been illuminated without a specific customer in mind, for a coat of arms was added soon after by a different illuminator.

Not very many of the other copies show typical characteristics of German illumination. A splendid two-leaf fragment at Cambridge testifies to the loss of an important copy from Cologne, or it may be part of the same copy from which the New Testament has survived in Darmstadt. The Bible in Braunschweig represents decoration from that town. Of German origin, but more difficult to locate, is the illumination in copies at Florence and Washington, D.C. The splendid illuminator of the unfinished copy at the University Library in Munich may have worked in Regensburg,[54] the best example of his work being the Rosenwald Cicero in the Library of Congress.

But German illumination is not predominant in copies of the 48-line Bible. I know of at least eight copies that show a distinct Italian makeup and are lavishly illuminated with a great variety of historiated

---

[51]For a color reproduction, see Christiane and Gerhard Römer, *Bibelhandschriften. Bibeldrucke. Gutenbergbibel in Offenberg. Katalog zur Ausstellung* (Offenburg, 1980), no. 8. For comparisons in Nuremberg, see Karl Fischer, *Die Buchmalerei in den beiden Dominikanerklöstern Nürnbergs* (Nuremberg, 1928), with further literature.

[52]See Roland Baughman and Robert O. Schad, *Great Books in Great Editions* (San Marino, 1954; rev. ed., 1973), no. 2, pl. II. Strangely enough, this lavishly illuminated copy is on paper.

[53]Sheila Edmunds is preparing a monograph on Bämler's activity as illuminator and rubricator; in the meantime, see Edmunds, "The Place of the London Haggadah," with a summary account of Bämler as illuminator on pp. 32ff.

[54]See the entries by Robert Suckale in the exhibition catalogue, *Regensburger Buchmalerei: Von frühkarolingischer Zeit bis zum Ausgang des Mittelalters* (Munich, 1987), pp. 70–110.

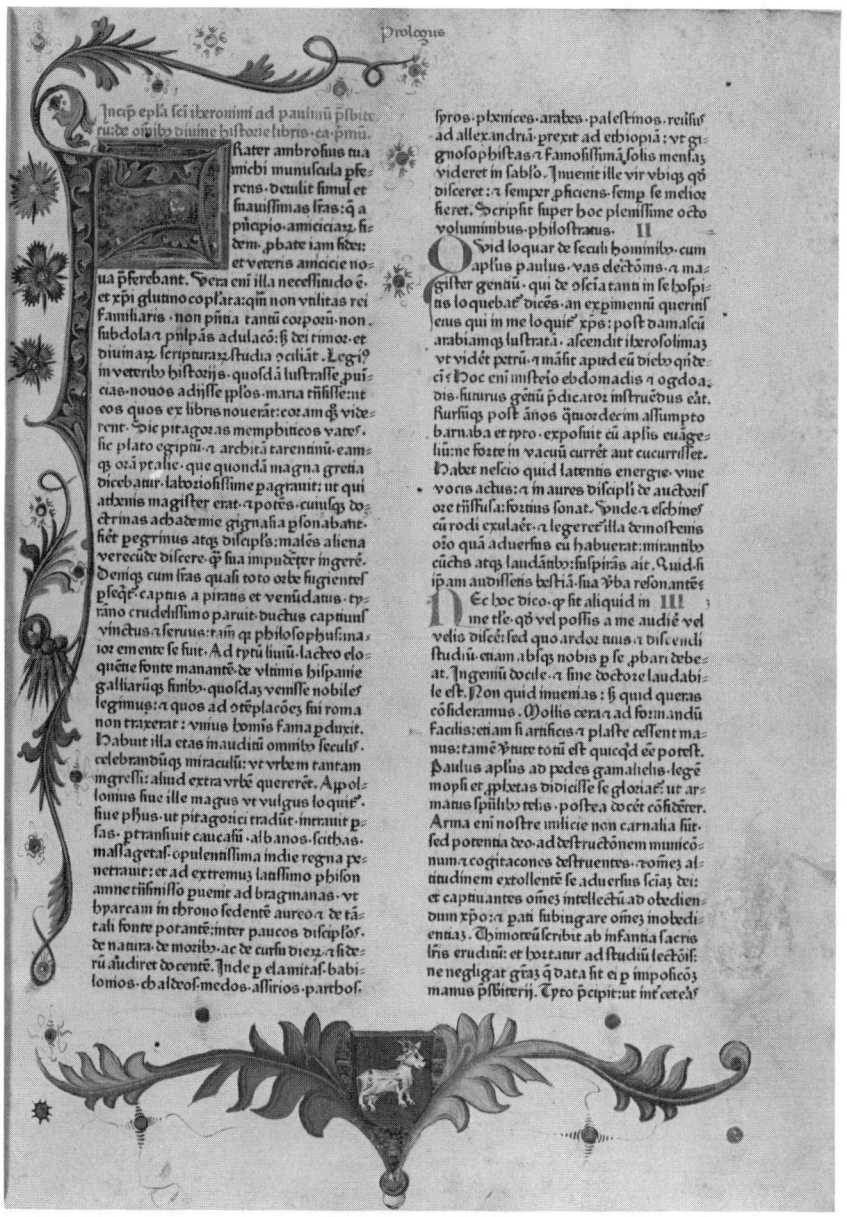

Figure 5.7. Leaf illuminated by Johannes Bämler, Augsburg, from the B48, San Marino, Calif., Huntington Library, I, fol. 1. By permission of the Huntington Library.

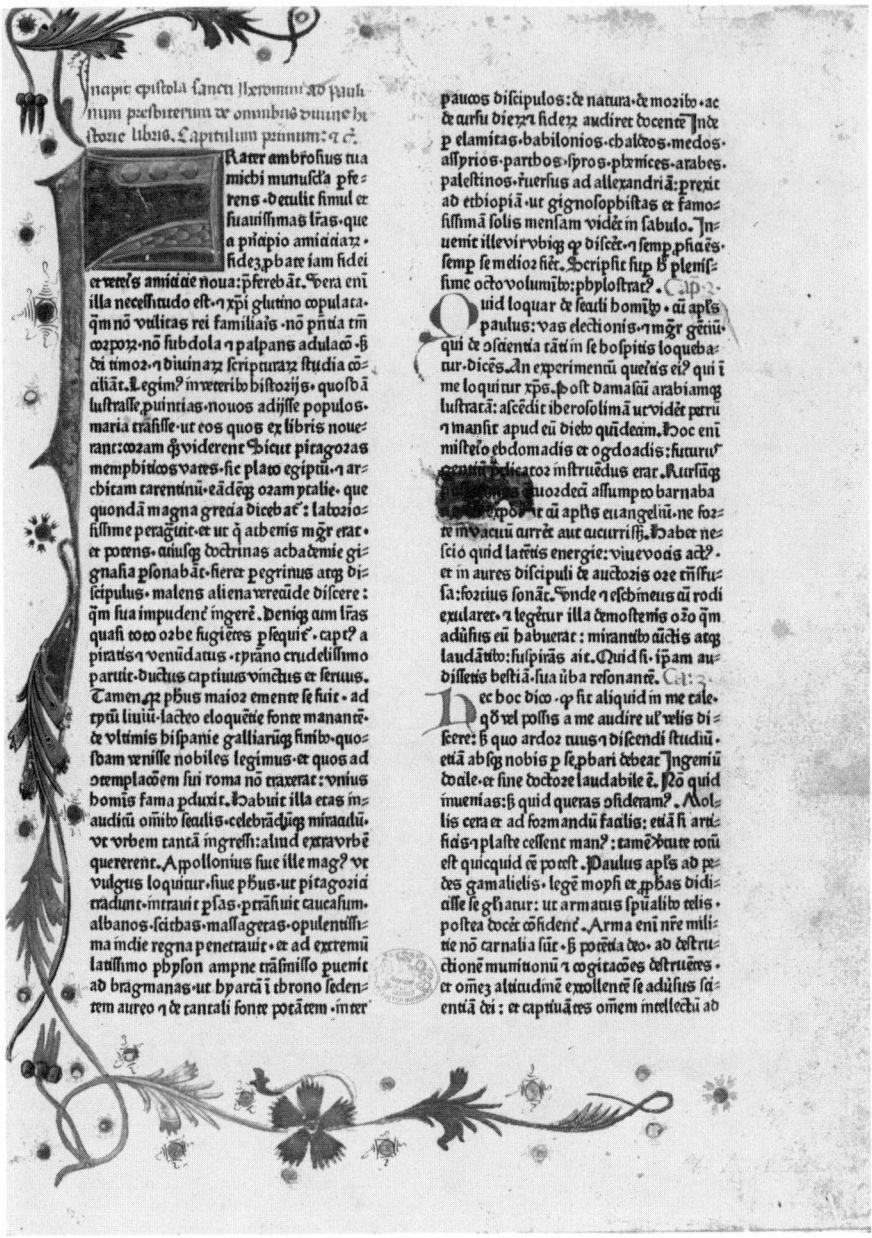

Figure 5.8. Leaf illuminated by Johannes Bämler, Augsburg, from the Eggestein Bible, Strasbourg, Heinrich Eggestein, 1468, BL, Inc. C14.d.1, I, fol. 1. By permission of the British Library.

initials.[55] At least one of these copies can be traced back to an important first owner: the copy in Chantilly has been marked with the ex libris of the congregation of Santa Giustina in Padua, and although erased, the inscriptions are easily identifiable when compared with other well-preserved ex libris of the congregation, for example one in a *Durandus* of 1459. Stylistic comparisons with a fragment containing the New Testament, now in the British Library, prove that this copy also belonged to the same congregation. It was the special practice at Santa Giustina that the congregation responsible for library acquisitions catalogue the books centrally but deposit them in the various houses of the congregation. Other extant copies with Italian decoration may have been destined for the same library, and it is evident that Santa Giustina, as in the case of the *Durandus,* bought more than one copy of the 1462 Bible in order to use the edition to augment the libraries of certain monasteries within the congregation. Apparently the Benedictine reform as one of the major impulses for early printing continued to guarantee that large numbers of this Bible edition were sold immediately.[56]

The most enigmatic copy still in Italy is the 48-line Bible in Naples. Calligraphy and makeup are surely by an Italian hand.[57] But the frontispiece, with its brilliant border miniature of the penitent Saint Jerome and the bright colors of the acanthus decoration point to France, and the style is reminiscent of the art of Jean Fouquet. Thus, this copy of the 1462 Bible constitutes an irritating example of France and Italy meeting in Naples—strangely enough, here in an incunable from Mainz.[58]

Another illuminator's name may be cited in connection with the copy now in Madrid. William Vrelant, an outstanding illuminator from Bruges in Flanders, painted in the same style. His influence on other artists was so great, however, that it is practically impossible to

[55]These are not identical with the eight copies cited by Wehmer, *Deutsche Buckdrucker,* no. 13, as evidence for the success of the issue in Italy; Wehmer collected only the copies still in Italian collections.

[56]On the library of the congregation, see P. Schmitz, *Histoire de l'ordre de saint Benois* (Maredsous, 1948–1956), III, 157–174; and I. Tassi, *Ludovico Barbo, 1381–1443* (Rome, 1952).

[57]This unpublished copy has been brought to my attention by Bodo Brinkmann of Berlin.

[58]A good survey of such north-south connections is provided by Nicole Reynaud, *Jean Fouquet: Les dossiers du département des peintures* (Paris, 1981).

isolate his work, and he no longer plays a role as an independent artist in recent research.[59] Bruges pen flourishes and initial painting are clearly discernible in the copy formerly in the Doheny Library, an attribution that is well supported by the old binding, undoubtedly of Flemish origin (figs. 5.9 and 5.10).[60]

The distinction between French and Flemish work is frequently unclear.[61] In all, about ten copies have Franco-Flemish decoration; some of these were evidently executed in Paris and central France, an attribution based less on stylistic evidence and more on knowledge of their early owners, who are identifiable by their coats of arms. The copy now in the Bibliothèque Sainte-Geneviève in Paris once belonged to the Carthusians of Rouen, while the copy in the Bibliothèque Mazarine in Paris was given to the Parisian College de Navarre in 1515. One of the Arsenal copies is stylistically close to illumination executed at the court of René d'Anjou and Jeanne de Laval, who also bought a 1457 Psalter. A further example was illuminated for Jean de Wailly, dean of Orléans, but the most prominent provenance for a French copy is that of the Bible still in Tours, originating from the most famous French Benedictine abbey, Saint-Martin in Tours.[62]

In general, the Italian illuminators of 48-line Bibles did not confine themselves to mere ornamental decoration but liked to include some figures in the initials. Examples such as the New Testament fragment in the British Library include a portrait of the evangelist at the beginning of every Gospel. French illuminators, by contrast, were more reluctant to include figures in the makeup of an imprint. This in itself characterizes the two different book cultures. Italian illuminators were more accustomed to the initial's providing the major opportunity for the figural or narrative. In France the miniature had developed at a very early stage into an independent decorative form. For these reasons Italian illuminators were more adept at using the small space left

[59]The Vrelant question is thoroughly discussed by James Douglas Farquhar, *Creation and Imitation: The Work of a Fifteenth-Century Manuscript Illuminator* (Fort Lauderdale, Fla., 1976). See also the oeuvre list by Georges Dogaer, *Flemish Miniature Painting in the Fifteenth and Sixteenth Centuries* (Amsterdam, 1987), pp. 99–106. These authors did not include incunabula.

[60]See Needham, *Estelle Doheny Collection*.

[61]See my contribution to the *Estelle Doheny Collection* sale catalogue, "Illuminated Incunabula in the Doheny Collection," pp. 284–302, esp. pp. 291–93.

[62]All information about early ownership is taken from unpublished entries in the different copies. An illustration of the copy in Tours with a baroque ex libris of Saint Martin is included in my "Illuminated Incunabula in the Doheny Collection," fig. 5.

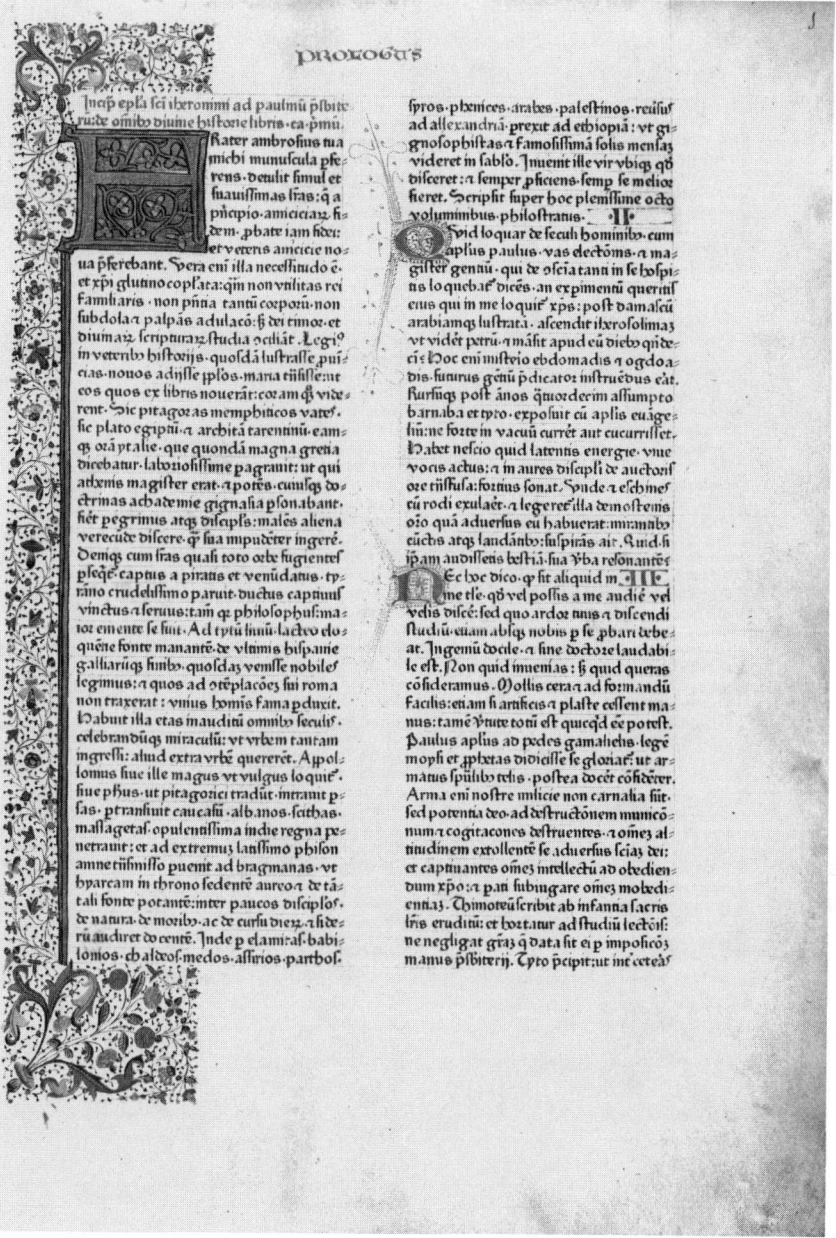

Figure 5.9. Leaf illuminated in Bruges, from the B48, Tokyo, Maruzen, I, fol. 1. By permission of Maruzen.

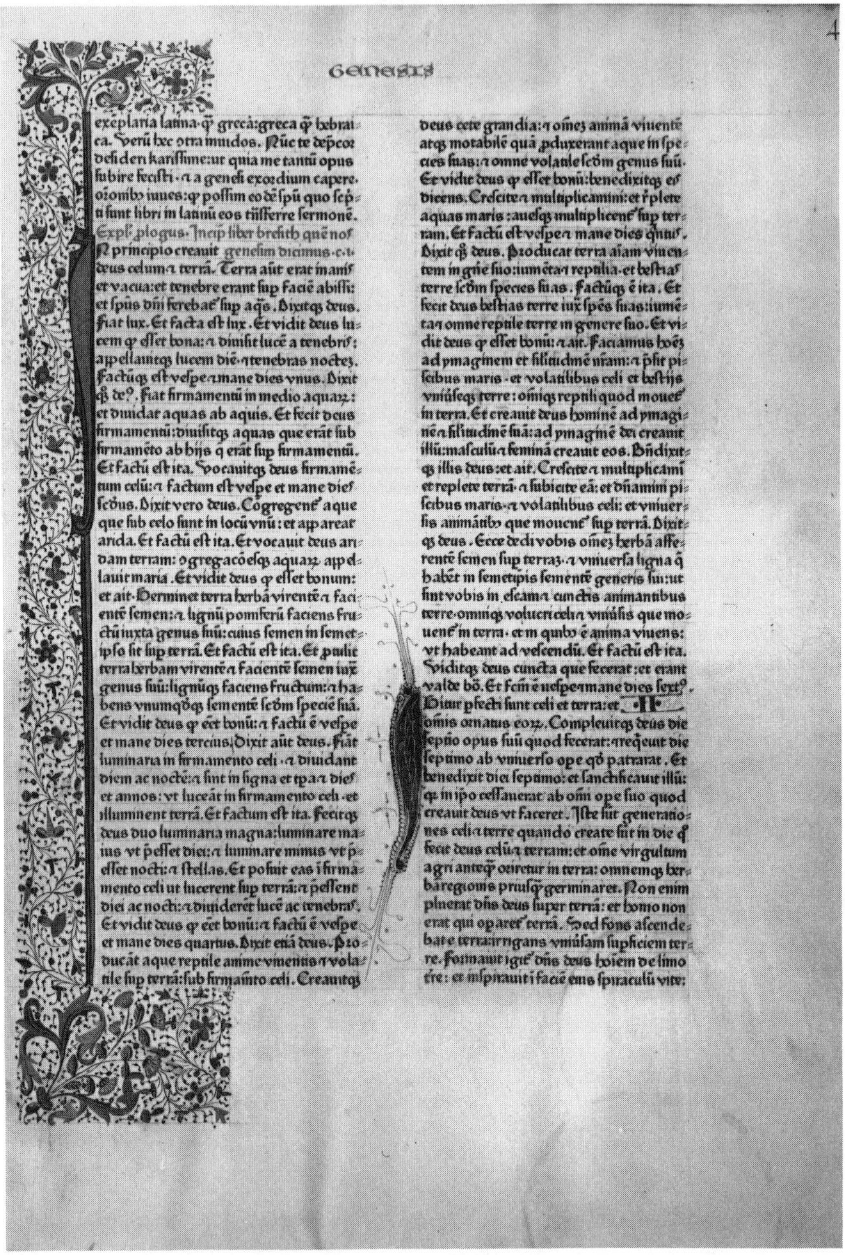

Figure 5.10. Leaf illuminated in Bruges, from the B48, Tokyo, Maruzen, I, fol. 4. By permission of Maruzen.

blank for the narrative scenes, whereas the French, less practiced in dealing with the historiated initial, would regularly apply only ivy leaf and acanthus to initials when no space had been made available for miniatures.

The European Success of the 48-Line Bible

Unlike any other printed Bible, the 48-line edition met with success throughout Europe. Even today the original pattern of distribution may be understood by looking at the present location of the copies.[63] Fewer than half of the locations listed in the *Gesemtkatalog der Wiegendrucke* are German or Austrian towns (only twenty-four). France is particularly rich, with fourteen copies, eleven of which are in Paris; even Italy with eight copies is well represented, and most of the imprints in these two countries have very old provenances. Countries farther east or north figure less significantly; no copy is mentioned in a Scandinavian collection or in Poland, if one accepts Breslau as belonging historically to Germany.

No doubt the 1462 Bible was not conceived solely for the German market. Large regions that played an important role in the distribution of the three Bibles printed earlier do not appear in the statistics for the 48-line Bible.[64] Erfurt, Leipzig, Strasbourg, and the entire upper Rhine area including Switzerland can be ignored in connection with the 48-line Bible. Even Augsburg is represented by only a single copy, and neither Austria nor the Tirol plays a role. The distribution in Mainz and the surrounding region was much smaller than in the case of the 42-line Bible.

We can thus conclude that a large share of the German market must have been satisfied by the first Bible issues. Mainz and the region ranging from the middle Rhine to Erfurt were supplied with the 42-line Bibles, which were also distributed in Leipzig, the major market city to the east, well known for its commercial fairs and its important

---

[63]Wehmer, *Deutsche Buchdrucker,* has already taken this approach.

[64]In a forthcoming book I shall try to give a precise idea of what may be said about the distribution of the first printed edition of the Latin Bible. A rather premature sketch for the 42-line Bible is given in my article "Die Illuminierung," which has already been revised in part in later articles, as in "The History of Art and the History of the Book" and "Möglichkeiten."

university. The city was also aware of the 36-line edition, which was published in Bamberg.[65] Strasbourg and the upper Rhine were the ideal market for Mentelin and his successor in the printing of Bibles, Heinrich Eggestein. Strasbourg was soon to dominate a second large market, that of the city of Augsburg, which was an important junction for two old trade routes, the one following the river Danube to Austria and the east, and the one going south to the Tirol and northern Italy and including the large mountainous region of the Alps.[66]

When Fust and Schoeffer published their 48-line Bible they must have been aware of this situation. Accordingly they may have developed their sales strategy to overcome any oversupply in the German market for Bibles. Therefore, the only intelligent alternative was to seek new customers either in regions still resisting the new technology or abroad, a competitive attitude that met with great success. In Germany itself they conquered the last important market, Cologne. In that town and the surrounding regions nobody had been very keen to purchase a 42-line Bible from Mainz, probably because people there were used to the text compiled by Thomas à Kempis for the Windesheim congregation. This may explain the reluctance of Cologne to buy copies of the first Bibles.[67] What remains unexplained is what persuaded buyers in the 1460s to change their minds.

With their astute sales strategy Fust and Schoeffer proved that Mainz was still the universally accepted cradle and hub of printing. In contrast to the time of the printing of the first Bible, Italy and France now opened up as suitable markets for such great printers and publishers. And the success of the 48-line Bible in Italy, France, and Flanders reinforced the position of Gutenberg's successors in Mainz as the leading German printers of the time.

[65]Evidence from bindings, illumination, and early provenance shows that the 36-line Bible was distributed in Franconia from Würzburg to Nuremburg and Bamberg; Leipzig, with its important fair, was the only place farther east to which it was exported.

[66]Augsburg illumination in Mentelin's Bible can be identified in copies in Vienna and Cambridge. The copy in the Biblioteca Angelica in Rome was completed by an Augsburg illuminator; its very beautiful illuminations show that a first attempt to have it decorated in Strasbourg must have failed. The loss of the Strasbourg Library in the Franco-Prussian War has made the identification of genuine Strasbourg illumination in incunabula difficult. Examples of average quality are the Eggestein Bibles in the Bibliothèque Mazarine in Paris and at Manchester, illuminated by the same people who finished the 42-line Bible in Cambridge.

[67]See König, "The History of Art and the History of the Book," pp. 172ff.

Only the 42-line Bible had been distributed on a similar scale; but the number of copies sold abroad must have been much smaller than copies of the 1462 Bible, as there is only one copy each in Italy and in Holland, two in Flanders, and none in France; this, of course, may also be due to the uncertain survival of such books. Nonetheless, two full copies must have been exported to England in the first years after the 42-line Bible had been published.[68] Compared with this issue, the 36-line edition from Bamberg and Mentelin's 49-line Bible can only be described as regionally restricted phenomena, since just one copy of the first Strasbourg edition was exported to a region outside Germany; the one now in Cologne possibly came through Flanders.

Thus we gain an even more clearly defined picture for the editions of the Bible that were printed after the 42-line Bible. The monasteries maintained their position as the chief purchasers, and we perceive a pattern developing that relates places of printing to their market. Mainz served, as it were, the whole world. The 48-line Bible of 1462 was illuminated in France, in the southern and northern Netherlands, and in Italy—competition being encountered only nearer home. Styles of illumination found in the 42-line Bible are no longer evident in the later Mainz editions; Bamberg provided Leipzig, where at least three copies of the 36-line Bible were illuminated.[69] Augsburg illuminated books from Strasbourg; Bämler illuminated only one 48-line Bible,[70] but he and other Augsberg illuminators decorated most of the Strasbourg Bibles, which were to find their destinations in southern Germany and Austria by way of Augsburg.[71]

[68]See König, "A Leaf from a Gutenberg Bible."

[69]Copies at Leipzig, Jena, and Greifswald; see König, "Die Illuminierung," p. 112, figs. 28–29.

[70]Copy at H. E. Huntington Library, San Marino, California; see Baughman and Schad, *Great Books,* pp. 8–9, no. 2.

[71]It is striking that there are no significant groups of Strasbourg illumination in early Strasbourg books; the largest group so far consists of three books: the B42 in the Cambridge University Library together with two copies of Latin Eggestein Bibles (Bibliothèque Mazarine, Paris, and John Rylands University Library, Manchester). Early provenance of Strasbourg books with Augsburg book decoration indicates many of the great Bavarian and Austrian monasteries, with the exception of Klosterneuburg.

[6]

The Impact of Printing on
Miniaturists in Venice after 1469

Lilian Armstrong

T he Venetian Renaissance is one of the best-studied periods of European art, and yet numerous masterpieces that were literally in the hands of Venetian patricians are little known. Among the thousands of books printed in Venice in the late fifteenth century are many whose hand-painted frontispieces are dated works of art of the highest artistic quality.[1] The

I am grateful to the Department of Art History, University of Warwick; to the Bibliographical Society, London; and to the School of Library and Information Science, University of California, Los Angeles, for opportunities to present versions of the lecture that resulted in this paper. I also wish to express my gratitude to the J. Paul Getty Museum and particularly to Thomas Kren, Curator of Manuscripts, for inviting me to be a Visiting Scholar to the museum for a period in 1988 when I was able to work on this material. Additionally, I gratefully acknowledge the support of an American Philosophical Society Research Grant. Peter Fergusson of Wellesley College gave much-valued editorial assistance. This paper was completed in February 1988, although some subsequent references have been added to the notes.

[1]Many examples are considered in the fundamental work of Giordana Mariani Canova, *La miniatura veneta del Rinascimento* (Venice, 1969), and I am very grateful to the author for sharing with me her profound knowledge of Italian manuscript and book decoration.

More recent publications of unknown or little-known frontispieces of major importance include *Schatten van de Koninklijke Bibliotheek* (The Hague, 1980–81), p. 146; Lilian Armstrong, *Renaissance Miniature Painters and Classical Imagery: The Master of the Putti and His Venetian Workshop* (London, 1981), frontispiece and figs. 43, 59, 89; "Fine Printed Books," Sotheby Parke Bernet, New York, June 25, 1982, lot 113, color plate on cover (now PML, no. 77565); Lilian Armstrong, "The Agostini Plutarch: An Illuminated Venetian Incunable," in *Treasures of the Library, Trinity College Dublin* (Dublin, 1983), figs. 56, 59, 61; Nigel Thorp, *The Glory of the Page: Medieval and Renaissance Illuminated Manuscripts form Glasgow University Library* (London, 1987), pls.

classicizing style of the frontispieces and historiated initials added to these volumes perpetuated a taste that was developing simultaneously in the monumental arts.[2] Greater familiarity with this genre can thus broaden our understanding of the origins of the Venetian Renaissance in the visual arts. Furthermore, the study of hand-decorated Venetian incunables can reveal how illuminators responded to the revolutionary new invention of printing, and shed light on the diverse processes of finishing and distributing the earliest Venetian printed books.[3]

In this essay I analyze the visual evidence found in individual Venetian incunables of the 1470s which I believe supports two hypotheses: first, that miniatures were working under pressure to speed up the processes of decorating books; and second, that the printers and booksellers organized some of the hand embellishment for printed books prior to sale rather than, as in the more traditional situation, the buyer's arranging for the decoration after purchase was guaranteed. The individual books themselves thus become primary documents revealing complex relationships between printers, miniaturists, and patrons in Renaissance Venice.

39–40 and pp. 149–66; Angela Dillon Bussi et al., *La collezione di Angelo Maria d'Elci* (Florence, 1989), nos. 94, 98; Alberto Petrucciani, *Gli incunaboli della Biblioteca Durazzo*, Atti della Società Ligure di Storia Patria, n.s., vol. 28 (102), fasc. 2 (Genoa, 1988), nos. 156, 256.

[2]Pioneering efforts to relate book illumination to the monumental arts in the Veneto include Maurizio Bonicatti, *Aspetti dell'umanesimo nella pittura veneta dal 1455 al 1515* (Rome, 1964); and Millard Meiss, *Andrea Mantegna as Illuminator* (New York, 1957).

[3]On Venetian printing, see Horatio F. Brown, *The Venetian Printing Press* (London, 1891); Carlo Castellani, *La stampa in Venezia dalla sua origine alla morte di Aldo Manuzio* (Venice, 1889); Victor Scholderer, "Printing at Venice to the End of 1481," *The Library*, n.s., 5 (1924): 129–52; Leonardas V. Gerulaitis, *Printing and Publishing in Fifteenth-Century Venice* (Chicago, 1976); Martin Lowry, *The World of Aldus Manutius* (Ithaca, 1979); and Neri Pozza, ed., *La stampa degli incunaboli nel Veneto* (Vicenza, 1984).

I am very grateful to Martin Lowry for the opportunity to read his book in typescript: *Nicholas Jenson and the Rise of Venetian Publishing in Renaissance Europe* (Cambridge, 1991). See also Martin Lowry, "The Social Background of Nicolas Jenson and John of Cologne," *La bibliofilia* 83 (1981): 193–218; idem., "Humanism and Anti-Semitism in Renaissance Venice: The Strange Case of the *Decor Puellarum*," *La bibliofilia* 88 (1985): 39–54; and a publication appearing after this essay was completed, Mary A. Rouse and Richard H. Rouse, *Cartolai, Illuminators, and Printers in Fifteenth-Century Italy: The Evidence of the Ripoli Press*, UCLA University Research Library, Department of Special Collections, Occasional Papers, no. 1 (Los Angeles, 1988).

In an effort to make known as many hand-illuminated incunables as possible, the illustrations in the present article will be examples not previously reproduced, except for figure 6.4.

Miniaturists in Venice in the Decade before Printing

In comparison with Florence or Milan, Venice and Padua were not major centers of manuscript production or illumination in the first half of the fifteenth century.[4] The Gothic style of Cristoforo Cortese prevailed in the early Quattrocento, and by the late 1450s Leonardo Bellini had emerged as the most important miniaturist in Venice.[5] The latter illuminated official Venetian *commissioni* and religious and humanist texts in a style that mixed conservative floral borders of Ferrarese derivation with more up-to-date Mantegnesque putti and other figures in perspectival settings. Leonardo Bellini was a cousin of the famous monumental painters Giovanni and Gentile Bellini, and thus was a part of one of the great artistic families who dominated Venetian art in the later Quattrocento.

The relative paucity of distinguished miniaturists active in Venice and Padua on the eve of the age of printing is suggested by the fact that important commissions went to non-Venetian artists throughout the 1460s. The Lombard artist Girolamo da Cremona worked in Mantua in 1461, but in the mid-1460s he illuminated liturgical books destined for Santa Maria della Misericordia in Padua and for San Giorgio Maggiore in Venice. His large historiated initials show familiarity with the spatial configurations and *all'antica* vocabulary of Andrea Mantegna's frescoes in the Eremitani Church in Padua, as well as exquisite light effects adapted from Flemish art.[6] In 1470, however,

[4]Jonathan J. G. Alexander, "Artists and the Book in Padua, Venice, and Rome in the Second Half of the Fifteenth Century," Sandars Lectures, Cambridge University, June 1985. I wish to thank the author for providing me with a typescript of his Sandars lectures. See also Giordana Mariani Canova, "La miniatura a Padova nella prima metà del Quattrocento: Bilancio di un'experienza illustrativa," in *Miniatura italiana tra Gotica e Rinascimento,* Atti del II Congresso di Storia della Miniatura Italiana, Cortona, September 24–26, 1982, ed. Emanuela Sesti (Florence, 1985), I, 355–88.

[5]A comprehensive study of Cortese is still lacking. See, however, Carl Huter, "Cristoforo Cortese in the Bodleian," *Apollo* 111 (1980): 11–17; and Giordana Mariani Canova, "Cristoforo Cortese," in *Arte in Lombardia tra Gotico e Rinascimento* (Milan, 1988), 230–39.

For Leonardo Bellini, see Mariani Canova, *La miniatura veneta,* pp. 11–32; and Ursula Bauer-Eberhardt, "Die Rothschild Miscellanea in Jerusalem: Hauptwerk des Leonardo Bellini," *Pantheon* 42 (1984): 229–37.

[6]Giordana Mariani Canova, "I manoscritti miniati dei monasteri benedettini padovani," in *I benedettini a Padova e nel territorio padovano attraverso i secoli* (Treviso, 1980), pp. 75–87; idem., "Girolamo da Cremona in Veneto: Una nuova ipotesi per

Girolamo is no longer in the Veneto, but is documented in Siena illuminating *corali* for the cathedral.[7]

Franco de' Russi of Mantua was also active in the Veneto in the decade before the coming of printing.[8] After working on the *Bible of Borso d'Este* in Ferrara from 1455 to 1461, he appears to have gone to Venice or Padua, where he also illuminated in an avant-garde style inspired by Mantegna. In the frontispieces of a *Gratulatio di Bernardo Bembo a Cristoforo Moro* destined for Cardinal Ludovico Trevisan and executed between 1463 and 1465, Franco enclosed the text with an architectural structure hung with classical swags; he alluded to Roman sarcophagi with monochrome reliefs and crowded his borders with exuberant angels, putti, lions, and peacocks.[9]

Yet other Lombard miniaturists, probably including Belbello da Pavia, illuminated a set of *corali* for the Benedictine monastery of San Giorgio Maggiore at the very end of the 1460s.[10] Thus, despite the high quality of works by the Venetian Leonardo Bellini and by a few distinguished non-Venetians such as Girolamo da Cremona and Franco de' Russi, one is still left with a fairly modest quantity of books illuminated in Venice and Padua in the 1460s.

Lacking evidence to the contrary, it should be presumed that the patronage of miniaturists such as Franco de' Russi and Leonardo Bellini fitted a traditional pattern. The coats of arms on the manuscripts they illuminated are those of prestigious Venetian families who would have commissioned the illuminations directly from the miniaturists. This pattern of patronage is one of the aspects of book illumination thrown into question by the advent of printing.

---

l'antifonario dei santi Cosma e Damiano," in *Studi di storia dell'arte in memoria di Mario Rotili* (Naples, 1984), pp. 331–43.

[7]Hans-Joachim Eberhardt, *Die Miniaturen von Liberale da Verona, Girolamo da Cremona und Venturino da Milano in den Chorbüchern des Doms von Siena: Dokumentation—Attribution—Chronologie* (Munich, 1983); Maria Grazia Ciardi Dupré, *I corali del Duomo di Siena* (Milan, 1972).

[8]Mariani Canova, *La miniatura veneta*, pp. 24–30 and 104–6; idem., "Girolamo da Cremona in Veneto"; and Jonathan J. G. Alexander, "A Manuscript of Petrarch's Rime and Trionfi," *Victoria and Albert Museum Yearbook* 2 (1970): 27–40.

[9]BL, Add. MS 14787, fols. 1v and 6v (Mariani Canova, *La miniatura veneta*, figs. 20–21).

[10]Giordana Mariani Canova, "Il recupero di un complesso librario dimenticato: I corali quattrocenteschi di S. Giorgio Maggiore a Venezia," *Arte veneta* 27 (1973): 38–64.

Lilian Armstrong

The Arrival of Printing in Venice

Leonardo Bellini's dominance of book illumination in Venice changed drastically in the years immediately following 1469. In that year the new invention of printing arrived in Venice. Johannes Gutenberg had perfected the printing of books with movable type in Germany by at least 1450. By 1465 printing had been brought to Italy, to Subiaco outside Rome, and four years later a German named Johannes de Spira opened the first press in Venice.[11] Ultimately this invention led to the demise of the scribal and miniaturist professions, but the immediate situation was a very different one.

The industry of printing grew in Venice with astonishing rapidity. In the first five years about fifteen printing firms were established in Venice, which printed a total of over 130 editions. By 1480 about fifty printers had printed at least one book. And by 1500 over one hundred firms had been active, collectively producing between 3,000 and 4,000 editions.[12] Within thirty years Venice had become the largest center of book production in all of Europe. In contrast to manuscript production, vastly increased numbers of a given text appeared. Documents indicate that many editions ran between 100 and 400 copies each in the earliest years, but by the mid-1470s editions of around 1,000 copies are recorded.[13] In the five-year period from 1469 through 1473, a very conservative estimate of 130 editions at 100 copies each would mean a *minimum* of 13,000 volumes printed; doubling this number would doubtless be more realistic.

The earliest books printed in Venice were distinguished by their large size and by the beauty of their typeface and layout (figs. 6.1, 6.3–4, 6.7, 6.9, 6.11).[14] Initially printers adopted a layout for the page

---

[11]See note 3 and additionally Rudolf Hirsch, *Printing, Selling, and Reading, 1450–1550* (Wiesbaden, 1974); and Ferdinand Geldner, *Die deutschen Inkunabeldrucker*, 2 vols. (Stuttgart, 1968–1970).

[12]Estimates on numbers of editions printed in Venice in the fifteenth century vary considerably. Scholderer, "Printing at Venice," estimates the number at just over 3,000 (p. 74), and Gerulaitis, *Printing and Publishing*, suggests 4,500 (p. 64).

[13]Hirsch, *Printing*, pp. 65–67; and Florence Edler de Roover, "Per la storia dell'arte della stampa in Italia: Come furono stampati a Venezia tre dei primi libri in volgare," *La bibliofilia* 55 (1953): 110–11.

[14]Measurements of a few early editions underline the assertion about size; the following are cited from *BMC*, vol. 5.: Johannes de Spira, Pliny, 1469, 410 × 278 mm (p. 153); Johannes and Vindelinus de Spira, Augustine, 1470, 398 × 275 mm (p. 153);

which resembled the layout of manuscripts; lines were left blank for chapter headings, and others were indented, leaving room for capital letters to be added by hand. In further imitation of manuscripts, a few copies of most editions were also printed on parchment. Although printers soon began to set chapter headings in type, they continued to leave blank spaces for capitals throughout the 1470s. Thus, in addition to being collated and gathered, the newly printed books needed to be rubricated, and if they were to be purchased by a wealthy person, there would also be a demand for some kind of decoration in order to look "finished."

The significance of these facts for the immediate future of rubricators and illuminators was very great. Rubrication and painted decoration would certainly have been easier to execute before the book was stitched than afterward, implying, I believe, that the illuminators worked in relatively close proximity to the location where the books were printed and collated. Books printed by the two firms of Johannes and Vindelinus de Spira (the latter soon joining forces with Johannes de Colonia and Johannes Manthen) and of Nicolaus Jenson appear to have the highest proportion of hand-illuminated copies in the early 1470s. But our ignorance of who organized these processes, where the work took place, and how soon after printing the handwork was executed is accentuated by the huge numbers of books that did indeed receive some degree of rubrication or embellishment.[15]

Vindelinus de Spira, Livy, 1470, 409 × 285 mm (p. 154); *Biblia italica,* 1471, 399 × 281 (p. 157); Boccaccio, *Genealogiae deorum,* 1472, 319 × 217 mm (p. 162); Nicolaus Jenson, Eusebius, *De evangelica praeparatione,* 1470, 330 × 224 mm (p. 167); Quintilian, 1471, 327 × 227 mm (pp. 168–69); Tortellius, 1471, 409 × 288 (p. 170); Macrobius, 1472, 326 × 219 (p. 172); Pliny, 1472, 406 × 273 (p. 172); *Scriptores rei rusticae,* 1472, 333 × 233 (p. 173).

[15]Rough statistics supporting the notion that Nicolaus Jenson and the De Spira-Colonia and Manthen group in particular drew on the services of trained illuminators are beginning to accumulate. The following numbers are suggestive; all pertain to incunables printed by 1481, decorated by miniaturists working in the Veneto: Mariani Canova, *La miniatura veneta:* thirty-four out of the forty-five illuminated incunables in the catalogue were printed by Jenson or by the De Spira-Colonia and Manthen group; Armstrong, *Renaissance Miniature Painters:* twenty-six out of thirty-nine were printed by the same firms; Lilian Armstrong, "Il Maestro di Pico: Un miniatore veneziano del tardo Quattrocento," *Saggi e memorie di storia dell'arte* 17 (1990): thirty-eight out of fifty-two come from the two firms. In his Sandars lectures, Alexander stressed the importance of Jenson's books as the focus of illumination.

A Hierarchy of Decoration

A hierarchy can be postulated to describe the degree of finish for Venetian incunables of the early 1470s. At the bottom, at least from the artistic point of view, are the thousands of books that never received any additions by hand, and which exist to this day with empty spaces where initials should be. Next would be the thousands of books that were indeed rubricated, that is, had the appropriate initials and chapter headings added by hand in red and blue ink. Figures 6.3, 6.6, 6.9, and 6.11 show chapter headings added by hand. In many cases the rubricated initials were also flourished with penwork in a contrasting color, blue ink for the red letters and purple for the blue letters.[16] Keepers of incunable collections, dealers in rare books, bibliophiles, and scholars who handle incunables can attest to the thousands of volumes that have been rubricated throughout, although efforts to quantify this knowledge face enormous difficulties.[17]

Still other books received painted and gilded capital letters in some or all of the blanks left for them, in addition to being rubricated. It is at this point in the hierarchy that one shifts from persons trained exclusively as scribes to those who had to know how to apply paint and gold leaf to parchment or paper, and thus to artists or craftsmen with at least a minimum of training as illuminators. Several types of painted initials appear in the earliest Venetian printed books, the most common of which are the so-called white vinestem initials, or *bianchi girali*. The letter is gold leaf on a prepared surface surrounded by a pattern of white vines which are actually the surface of the paper or parchment itself. The interstices between the vines are painted green, blue, and red or violet, and triads of tiny white dots further enliven the colored surfaces (figs. 6.1–3, 6.9).[18]

[16]Alternating red and blue initials can be seen in the color plates reproducing folios of a *Breviarium romanum* (Venice, Nicolaus Jenson, 1478) and an Avicenna, *Canon medicinae* (Venice, Petrus Maufer, 1486), in Thorp, *Glory of the Page,* pls. 29 and 30; in addition to being rubricated throughout, these incunables have paragraph markers, underlining, and painted frontispieces.

[17]Computerization and statistical analysis should eventually assist the study of this problem, but at present even estimates are difficult if not impossible. Margaret Smith is undertaking some quantitative studies of the rubrication of incunables.

[18]For a classic example of a rubricated book title and white vinestem initial, see Pliny, *Historia naturalis* (Venice, Johannes de Spira, 1469), illustrated in *The Art of the Printed Book, 1455–1955: Masterpieces of Typography through Five Centuries from the Collections of the Pierpont Morgan Library, New York,* with an essay by Joseph

Other frequently found initials are gold letters against rectangles of solid color from which acanthus leaves extend into the margins; these often alternate with colored letters on gold rectangles, also enhanced with acanthus.[19] Both these common types of initials derive directly from manuscript illumination of earlier decades. Books might receive one large painted initial on the opening page of text but otherwise be only rubricated, or sometimes not finished further at all. Alternatively, many volumes have all of their large initial spaces painted with white vinestem or acanthus embellished initials.

Observation of books with sequences of painted initials leads to an intriguing fact. In a number of cases the books are painted with initials in one style while the first page of text is either decorated in another style or not decorated at all. Sometimes the differences are simply between two types of Italian decoration, but in other examples the change may be from Italian initials to a frontispiece in a northern European style. This anomaly is one indication that books were being decorated before sale to a specific client was guaranteed. In these examples the initial spaces, which would be difficult of access once the book was gathered and stitched, presumably were painted in anticipation of sale. The first folio, or an important page of text near the beginning of the book which was more accessible to the miniaturist, would remain unpainted. In order to acquire a fully "finished" volume, the buyer would then need only arrange for a more or less elaborate frontispiece, depending on his or her pocketbook and taste.[20]

Blumenthal (New York, 1973), pl. 8; and for other examples, see Marino Zorzi, "Stampatori tedeschi a Venezia," in *Venezia e la Germania* (Milan, 1986), figs. 122, 126, 128–29, 132.

[19]Several initials of this type are illustrated in color in Thorp, *Glory of the Page,* pl. 29.

[20]A few examples with discrepancies between the decoration of the first page of text and the rest of the incunable must suffice. Master of the Putti and Master of the London Pliny: Armstrong, *Renaissance Miniature Painters,* cat. nos. 11 (vol. 1), 16, 17, 30, 35, 36, 41; Franco de' Russi: Antonio M. Adorisio, "Carlo Crivelli, Girolamo da Cremona e Franco de' Russi in incunaboli miniati della Biblioteca Casanatense," *Accademie e biblioteche d'Italia* 40 (1972): 33–34, fig. 7. Other examples: Italian initials and Dutch frontispiece: Thorp, *Glory of the Page,* cat. no. 88; German imprint with German initials and additions by the Venetian Pico Master: A. Barzon, *Codici miniati: Biblioteca Capitolare della Cattedrale di Padova* (Padua, 1950), pl. LXXI, a; Parma imprint with contrasting styles of frontispiece and initials: Paul Meyvaert, "The Duke Pliny," *Duke Library Notes* 42 (1971): 23–34; Antonio Maria da Villafora initials and French borders: BN, Vélins 96, *Biblia italica,* Venice [Adam de Ambergau], 1471.

The next step up in the hierarchy are books in which the first page of text received a handsome but relatively standardized border. Here, too, the most common types of borders came directly out of the manuscript tradition. Variations of white vinestem borders appear frequently in Venetian incunables of the early 1470s.[21] In a folio from a Pliny *Historia naturalis* printed by Nicolaus Jenson in 1472, now in Paris, the white vinestems have been transformed into putto heads and curving horns (fig. 6.1), but in many other examples the motifs are actual vines.[22] In this type of frontispiece the border fills three margins and is enclosed by narrow lines of red and gold; a circular area surrounded by a green wreath or a line of gold is reserved in the bottom margin for the addition of a coat of arms. If figural motifs are included, the border can sometimes be attributed to a specific miniaturist. In the Paris Pliny, the rather frail boneless figures and the predilection for pink in the costumes and the modeling are characteristic of an artist known as the Master of the Pico della Mirandola Pliny, or the Pico Master,[23] but in many examples the patterns are too standardized to identify an artist or a workshop.

A second border frequently found is a type that had been used by illuminators in Ferrara, especially in the famous *Bible of Borso d'Este,* but which had been popularized in Venice by Leonardo Bellini by the 1460s.[24] The motifs are regularly spaced red and blue flowers and gold dots surrounded by delicate spiraling penwork: they may be enclosed by red and gold lines (fig. 6.2), or be unframed and taper at

[21]For examples of white vinestem borders in addition to those discussed herein, see Mariani Canova, *La miniatura veneta,* figs. 25, 26, 67, 73; Otto Pächt and Jonathan J. G. Alexander, *Illuminated Manuscripts in the Bodleian Library, Oxford,* vol. 2, *Italian School* (Oxford, 1970), pl. LXXXVI, pr. 63, and pl. LXXXVIII, pr. 70, pr. 82; Dillon Bussi, *La collezione . . . d'Elci,* pl. xiv; Zorzi, "Stampatori tedeschi," figs. 126, 132.

[22]For a color reproduction of the standard type, see H. P. Kraus, *Early Books Printed on Vellum,* catalogue 156 (New York, 1980), pl. 2 (Augustinus, *De civitate Dei,* Venice, Johannes and Vindelinus de Spira, 1470, copy on parchment with Loredano of Venice arms).

[23]Armstrong, "Il Maestro di Pico," includes a catalogue of seventy-six illuminated manuscripts and incunables attributed to the miniaturist; the Pliny is cat. no. 20, BN, Réserve S. 414.

[24]Adolfo Venturi, ed., *La Bibbia di Borso d'Este,* 2 vols. (Milan, 1937), facsimile. For Leonardo Bellini manuscripts, see Mariani Canova, *La miniatura veneta,* color pls. 3 and 4 and figs. 10 and 18; floral borders in Venetian incunables of the 1470s are pl. 8 (Master of the Putti) and fig. 22 (Franco de' Russi). See also Thorp, *Glory of the Page,* no. 96 (arms unidentified); Zorzi, "Stampatori tedeschi," fig. 133 (color); and Alan G. Thomas, *Catalogue Forty-Three* (London, 1981), color pl. I (Pliny, *Historia naturalis,* Venice, Nicolaus Jenson, 1472, border by the Pico Master [Armstrong, "Il Maestro di Pico," cat. no. 25]; arms of the Granfioni of Padua).

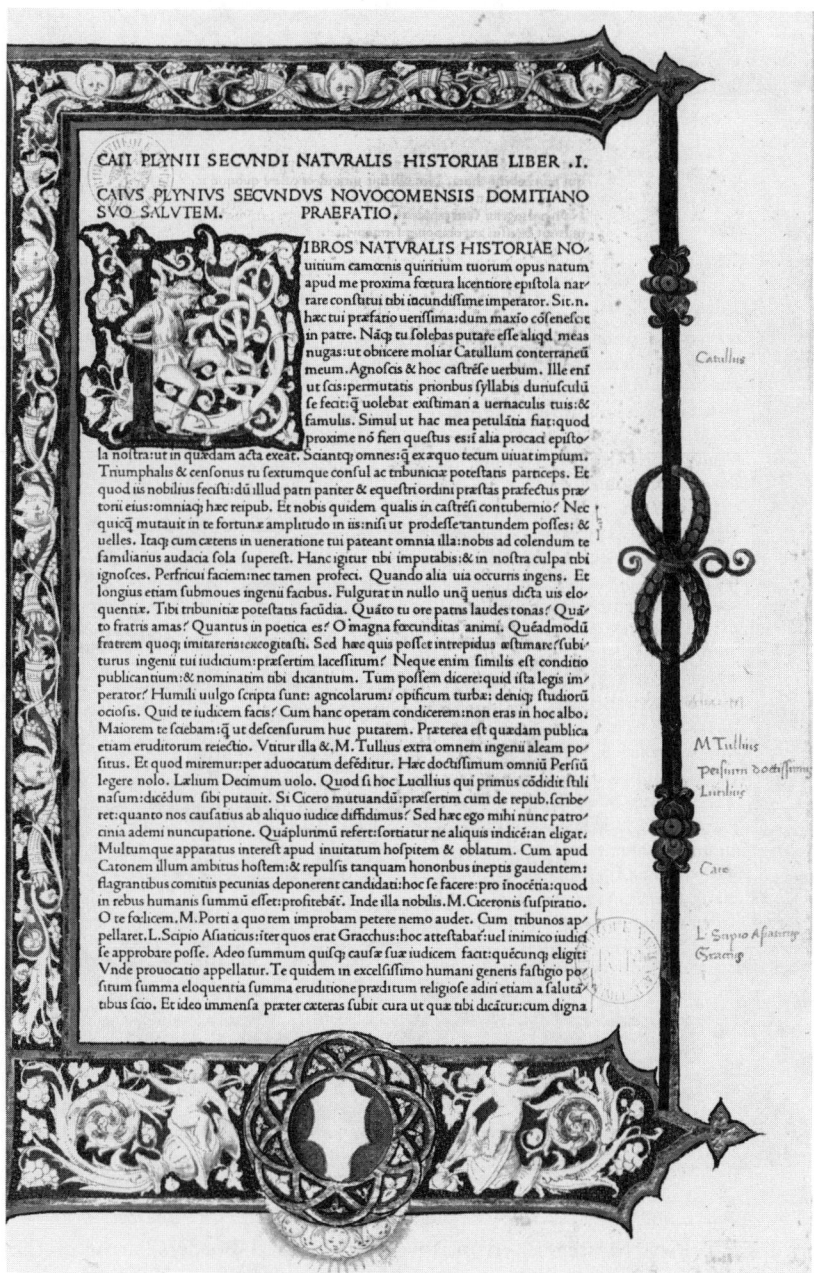

Figure 6.1. Pico Master, frontispiece with white vinestem borders, arms not added, from Caius Plinius Secundus, *Historia naturalis*, Venice, Nicolaus Jenson, 1472, BN, Réserve S. 414, bk. 1. Photo: Bibliothèque Nationale, Paris.

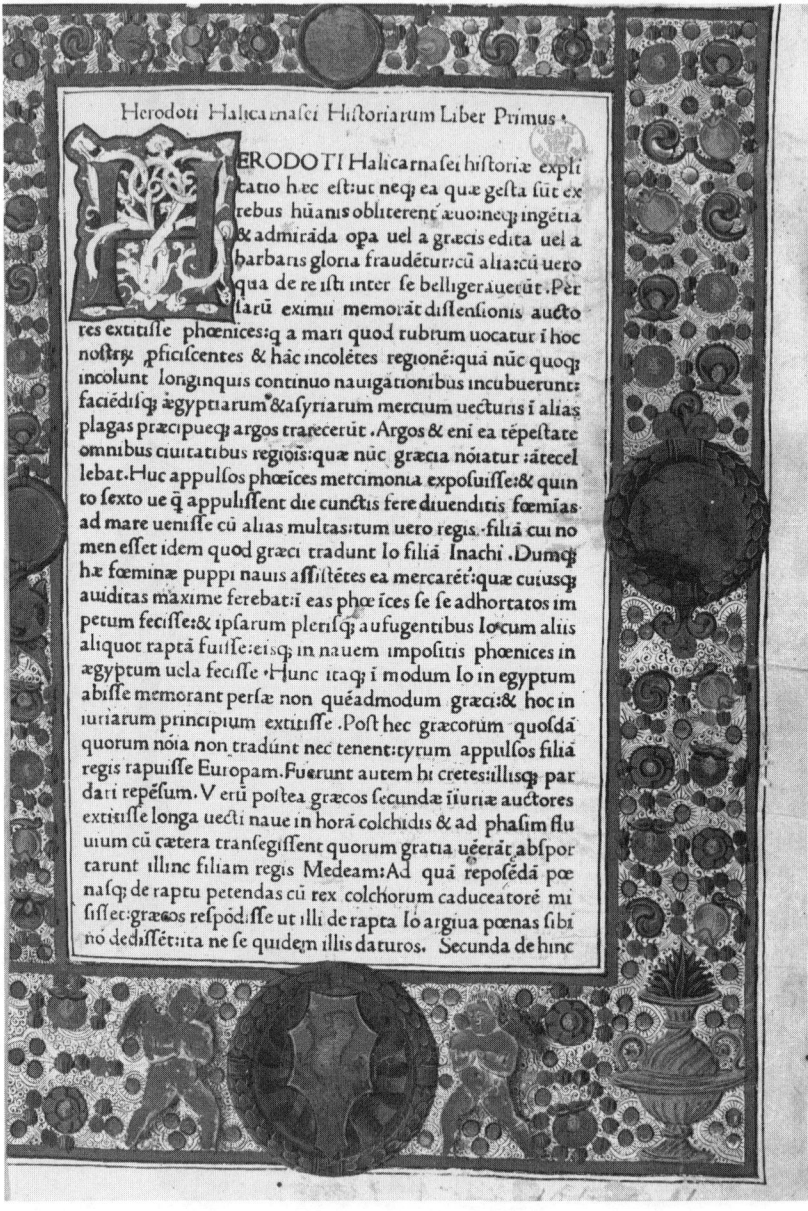

Figure 6.2. Pico Master (?), frontispiece with floral borders, arms of the Pisani of Santa Marina of Venice, from Herodotus, *Historiae,* Venice, Jacobus Rubeus, 1474, BL, C.1.c.3, fol. 2 (on parchment). By permission of the British Library Board.

the extremities. Like Venetian white vinestem borders, floral and gold dot borders often include roundels with tiny scenes of animals in landscapes or heads *all'antica* in monochrome. No exact counterpart of this type of border seems to have been developed for initials, as was the case for white vinestem borders; the Herodotus printed by Jacobus Rubeus in 1474, shown in figure 6.2, is thus typical in using a white vinestem first initial in combination with floral borders.[25]

Yet another motif is common for borders in the earliest books printed in Venice: a straight garland of laurel, sometimes bound by ribbons or interrupted by rings of fruit. This type of border can be seen in a handsome Jenson Eusebius of 1470 illuminated by the Pico Master and destined for the Benedictine monastery of San Giorgio Maggiore of Venice (fig. 6.3).[26]

White vinestem, floral, and laurel borders can often be very beautiful but are quite standard and repetitious. Depending on the price the patron was willing to pay, they could fill one, two, three, or four margins, and they could incorporate figural work or not. To execute them would have required training as an illuminator rather than as a scribe, but a competently trained illuminator of even middling talent could certainly have ground them out with considerable rapidity because of the patternlike nature of the motifs. If a book had already been otherwise "finished" with rubrication, the printer-bookseller could guarantee the client a personalized first page of text in a relatively short period of time.

That there were far richer variants of painted borders can be seen by observing copies of a Macrobius of 1472 and a Plutarch of 1478, both printed by Nicolaus Jenson (figs. 6.4–5). The Macrobius belonged to Giovanni Pico della Mirandola, while the Plutarch bears arms of which the sinister side is Fregosa of Genoa.[27] The layout of the frontispiece is similar, with framed borders interrupted by rectangles in the corners and roundels in the middle of the margins. The decorative patterns are vines or interlace in brilliant colors painted against gold

[25]BL, C.1.c.3, fol. 2 (Armstrong, "Il Maestro di Pico," cat. no. 27, on vellum, arms of the Pisani of Santa Marina of Venice). The Pliny mentioned in note 24 also combines floral borders with a white vinestem first initial.

[26]BL, IB 19261A (Eusebius, *De Evangelica praeparatione*, Venice, Jenson, 1470; Armstrong, "Il Maestro di Pico," cat. no. 7). I am grateful to Lotte Hellinga for having brought this incunable to my attention.

[27]Respectively, Cambridge, Trinity College Library, Trin. Vi.18.52, on parchment; and BN, Réserve J. 101–2, on paper (Armstrong, "Il Maestro di Pico," cat. nos. 15, 47).

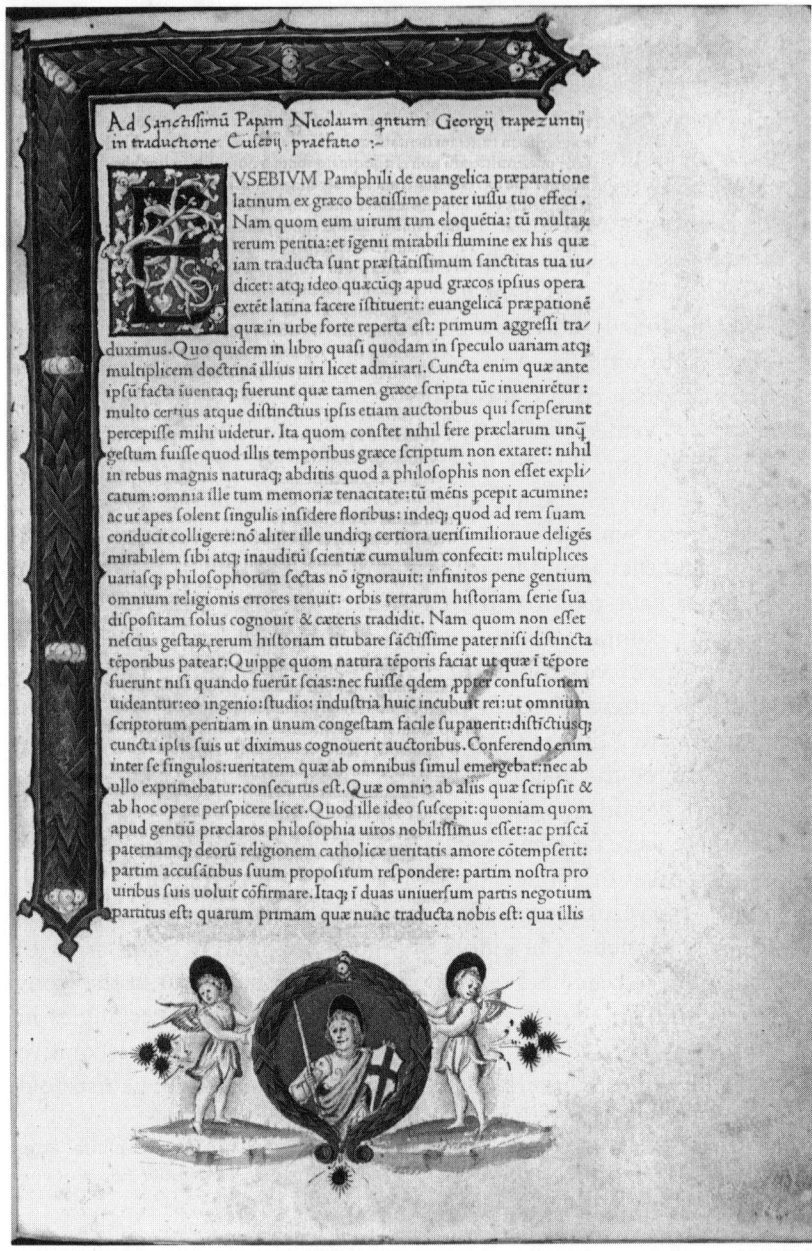

Figure 6.3. Pico Master, frontispiece with laurel borders and image of Saint George, from San Giorgio Maggiore, Venice, from Eusebius, *De evangelica praeparatione,* Venice, Nicolaus Jenson, 1470, BL, IB 19261A, fol. 1. By permission of the British Library Board.

[186]

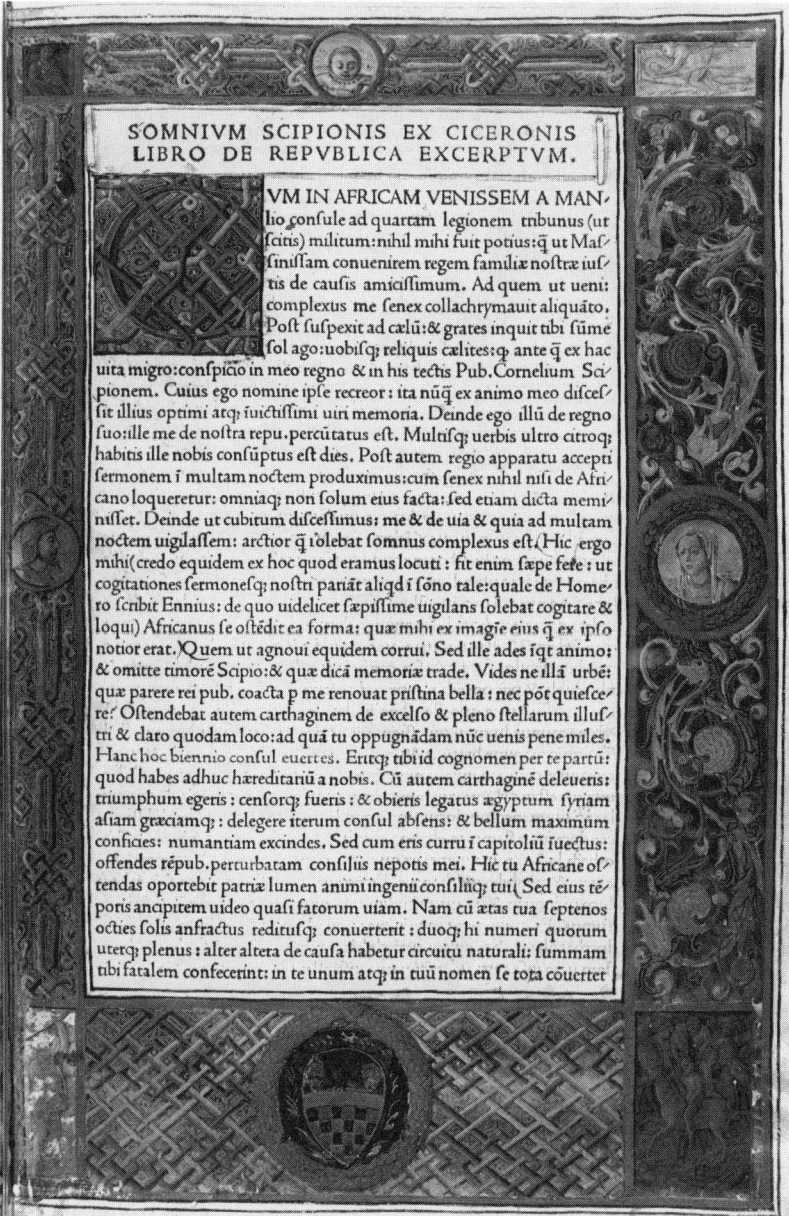

SOMNIVM SCIPIONIS EX CICERONIS
LIBRO DE REPVBLICA EXCERPTVM.

VM IN AFRICAM VENISSEM A MAN-
lio confule ad quartam legionem tribunus (ut
scitis) militum:nihil mihi fuit potius:q ut Maf-
sinissam conuenirem regem familiæ nostræ iuf-
tis de caufis amicissimum. Ad quem ut ueni:
complexus me senex collachrymauit aliquáto.
Post sufpexit ad cælu:& grates inquit tibi súme
sol ago:uobisq; reliquis cælites:q ante q ex hac
uita migro:conspicio in meo regno & in his tectis Pub.Cornelium Sci-
pionem. Cuius ego nomine ipfe recreor: ita núq ex animo meo discef-
sit illius optimi atq; iuictissimi uiri memoria. Deinde ego illú de regno
fuo:ille me de nostra repu.percútatus est. Multisq; uerbis ultro citroq;
habitis ille nobis confúptus est dies. Post autem regio apparatu accepti
fermonem í multam noctem produximus:cum fenex nihil nisi de Afri-
cano loqueretur: omniaq; non folum eius facta:fed etiam dicta memi-
niffet. Deinde ut cubitum difcessimus: me & de uia & quia ad multam
noctem uigilassem: arctior q íolebat somnus complexus est.(Hic ergo
mihi(credo equidem ex hoc quod eramus locuti: fit enim fæpe fete:ut
cogitationes fermonesq; nostri pariat aliqd í fóno tale:quale de Home-
ro scribit Ennius: de quo uidelicet fæpissime uigilans folebat cogitare &
loqui) Africanus fe ostédit ea forma: quæ mihi ex imagie eius q ex ipfo
notior erat. Quem ut agnoui equidem corrui. Sed ille ades iqt animo:
& omitte timoré Scipio:& quæ dicá memoriæ trade. Vides ne illá urbé:
quæ parere rei pub. coacta p me renouat pristina bella: nec pót quiefce-
ref Ostendebat autem carthaginem de excelfo & pleno stellarum illuf-
tri & claro quodam loco:ad quá tu oppugnádam núc uenis pene miles.
Hanc hoc biennio conful eueries. Eritq; tibi id cognomen per te partú:
quod habes adhuc hæreditariú a nobis. Cú autem carthaginé deleueris:
triumphum egeris: censorq; fueris: & obieris legatus ægyptum syriam
afiam græciamq;: delegere iterum conful abfens: & bellum maximum
conficies: numantiam excindes. Sed cum eris curru í capitoliú fuectus:
offendes répub.perturbatam consiliis nepotis mei. Hic tu Africane of-
tendas oportebit patriæ lumen animi ingeniiconsiliiq; tui(Sed eius ré-
poris ancipitem uideo quasi fatorum uiam. Nam cú ætas tua septenos
octies folis anfractus reditufq; conuerterit: duoq; hi numeri quorum
uterq; plenus: alter altera de caufa habetur circuitu naturali: summam
tibi fatalem confecerint: in te unum atq; in tuú nomen fe tota cóuertet

Figure 6.4. Pico Master, frontispiece with interlace borders, figural motifs, and arms of Giovanni Pico della Mirandola, from Macrobius, *In somnium Scipionis expositio: Saturnalia,* Venice, Nicolaus Jenson, 1472, Cambridge, Trinity College Library, Trin. VI.18.52, fol. 1 (on parchment). By permission of the Master and Fellows of Trinity College.

[187]

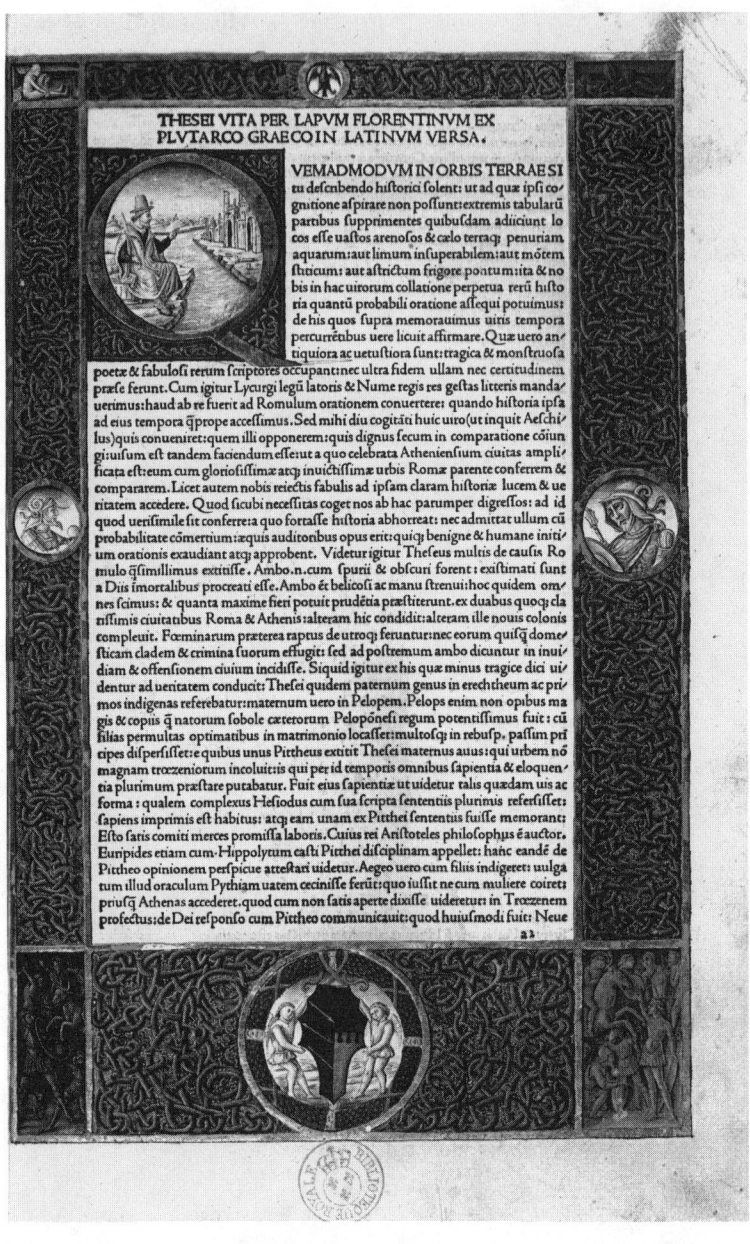

Figure 6.5. Pico Master, frontispiece with green vine on gold ground borders, roundels with soldiers *all'antica*, arms dexter unidentified impaled with Fregosa of Genoa, historiated initial of a Greek (Theseus or Plutarch) seated outside a city, from Plutarchus, *Vitae parallelae*, Venice, Nicolaus Jenson, 1478, BN, Réserve J. 101, fol. 1. Photo: Bibliothèque Nationale, Paris.

[188]

leaf. Heads are drawn or painted in the roundels, and similar eques-
trian scenes painted in monochrome in the lower corners permit an
attribution to the Pico Master. These two frontispieces also help to
refute a commonly held misapprehension that only the incunables
printed on parchment were elaborately painted. Despite the similar
degree of decoration of the two volumes, the Plutarch, like many
other hand-decorated incunables, is printed on paper (see also figs.
6.1, 6.3, 6.6–8).

Even in borders as rich as these can be found a curious feature. The
area in the bottom margin prepared for a coat of arms is quite often
still blank. Such omissions can be noted in figures 6.1, 6.9, and 6.10,
as well as in another copy of the 1472 Jenson Pliny now in Paris with a
full border painted by the Pico Master.[28] In all these cases the arms
have not been painted over or scraped but simply were never added,
thereby contributing to the sense that incunables were being prepared
"on spec" in anticipation of sale, rather than for a commission.

Borders, Techniques, and Formulae Used by Named Artists

At the top of the hierarchy of hand decoration in Venetian books
are the highly original frontispieces and initials with figurative components by named artists or by anonymous artists identifiable by
stylistic groups. Studies of these works have stressed attribution,
iconographic problems, and the search for sources in ancient and
contemporary monumental art. The continuing need for these studies
is evident when it is realized that even very original artists remain
completely unknown. A find in the Huntington Library of a three-
volume Livy printed by Vindelinus de Spira in 1470 and decorated
with frontispieces painted by a hitherto unknown artist exemplifies
this situation.[29] The Huntington Livy has a frontispiece of the most

---

[28]BN, Vélins 498, on parchment (Armstrong, "Il Maestro di Pico," cat. no. 19, fig.
9). See also Dillon Bussi, *La collezione . . . d'Elci,* pl. XIV.

[29]San Marino, California, Huntington Library, no. 90971. Each volume has a frontispiece in pen and ink with some areas of tempera; woodcut white vinestem initials
have been added throughout after the printing and painted in gold and colors. The
erased arms are perhaps Zorzi of Venice. Another miniaturist whose illuminated
incunables are unpublished is the artist who illuminated an Ovid manuscript in Rimini
(Giordana Mariani Canova, Piero Meldini, and Simonetta Nicolini, *I codici miniati
della Gambalunghiana di Rimini* [Milan, 1988], pp. 192–95, SC-MS 108); he added an

distinctive type developed in the Veneto in this period, that is, the "architectural frontispiece" (fig. 6.6).[30] The margins have been filled with architectural elements in a classicizing vocabulary. On the base of the monument hang green swags and a damaged coat of arms, and at the right is a Roman soldier holding a spear. Also characteristic of this illusionistic composition is that the area nearest the lines of text is painted to look as if it were the curling edge of a piece of parchment. The parchment thus appears to be suspended in front of the monument, and the soldier is sandwiched between the page and the architecture. The artist has maintained the integrity of the printed page as a flat surface while still exhibiting a Renaissance fascination with the illusion of three-dimensional space.

In contrast to the Huntington incunable are those painted by artists to whom names and groups of works have already been assigned. But even in major works by these identified miniaturists, there is evidence that the artists were pushed by the arrival of printing to experiment with less time-consuming artistic processes. Virtually all of the named artists working in printed books in the 1470s used two different techniques, including Franco de' Russi, Girolamo da Cremona, the Putti Master (figs. 6.7, 6.9), the Master of the London Pliny, the Pico Master (figs. 6.4–5, 6.8), Benedetto Bordone, and Antonio Maria da Villafora. Some compositions were executed in tempera with gold leaf and gold paint, while others were drawn in pen and ink and lightly touched with watercolor (figs. 6.7–8).[31] Occasionally both

---

architectural frontispiece to a Petrarch *Canzoniere* (Venice, Leonard Wild, 1481 [Venice, Biblioteca Marciana, Inc. V. 549]) and illuminated other incunables now in Padua, London, Dublin, and Milan. I hope to reconstruct the oeuvre of this artist in the near future.

[30]The sources and significance of the architectural frontispiece have been treated by Otto Pächt, "Notes and Observations on the Origins of Humanist Book Design," in *Fritz Saxl: A Volume of Memorial Essays,* ed. Donald J. Gordon (London, 1957), pp. 184–94; Margery Corbett, "The Architectural Title Page," *Motif* 12 (1964): 49–62; Giordana Mariani Canova, "Le origini della miniatura rinascimentale veneta e il Maestro dei Putti (Marco Zoppo?)," *Arte veneta* 20 (1966): 73–86; Jonathan J. G. Alexander, "Notes on Some Veneto-Paduan Illuminated Books of the Renaissance," *Arte veneta* 23 (1969): 9–20; Armstrong, *Renaissance Miniature Painters,* pp. 19–26; and Alexander, "Artists and the Book."

[31]The following sources contain examples of the two techniques by a given artist: Franco de' Russi: Mariani Canova, *La miniatura veneta,* color pl. 9 and figs. 22–26; and Adorisio, "Carlo Crivelli, Girolamo da Cremona e Franco de' Russi," fig. 7; Girolamo da Cremona: Mariani Canova, *La miniatura veneta,* color pls. 19–21; *Bibli-*

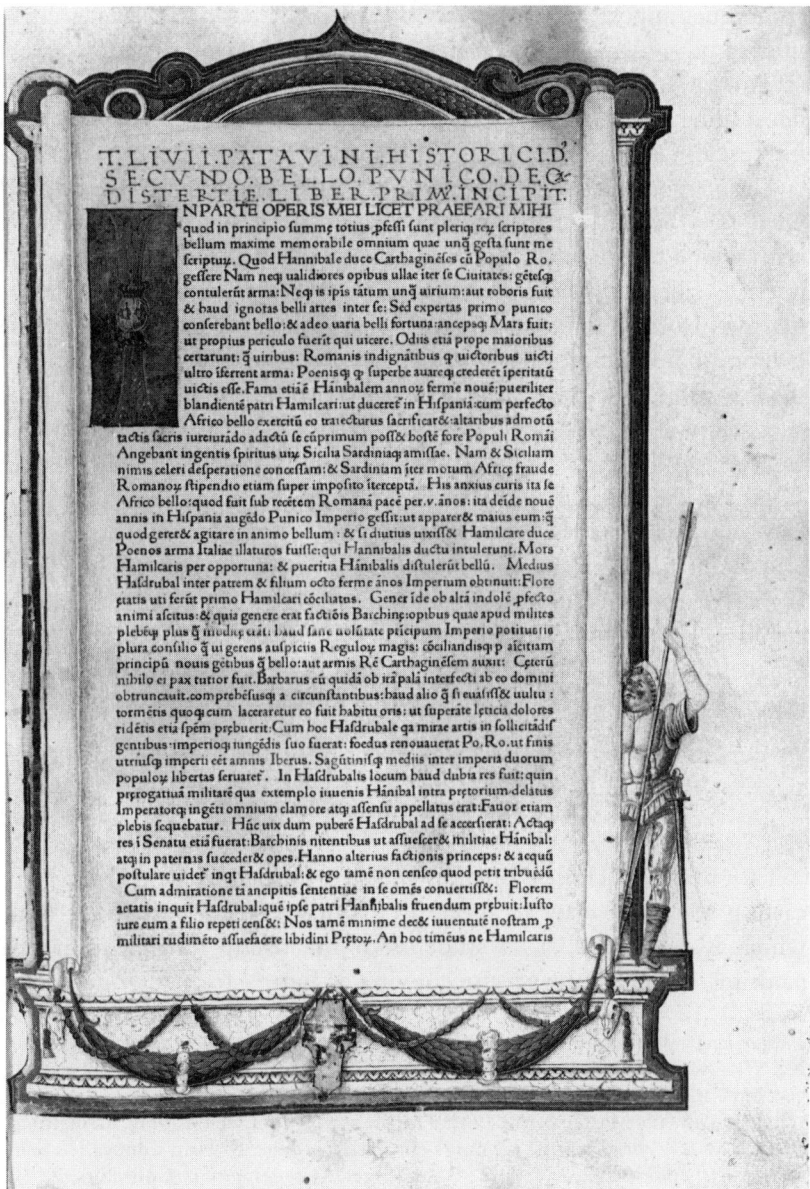

Figure 6.6. Architectural frontispiece with soldier *all'antica,* damaged arms (Zorzi of Venice?), from Titus Livius, *Historiae romanae decades,* Venice, Vindelinus de Spira, 1470, San Marino, Calif., Huntington Library, no. 90971, vol. 2. By permission of the Huntington Library.

techniques appear in a single frontispiece. The pen and ink technique, while still a demanding one requiring expertise as a draftsman, is somewhat less time-consuming than tempera. The motivation for developing compositions in pen and ink may in part have been an interest in faster execution.

The named miniaturists working in this period also all developed what may be called the historiated initial plus coat of arms formula with which to decorate an opening page of text. The blank area of the initial is filled with a classical or *all'antica* motif, while in the lower margins isolated fantastic creatures support the coats of arms of the owners. For example, in a 1472 Jenson Macrobius by the Master of the Putti a nude woman accepts fruit from a bowl held out by a putto, and below a Triton defends the arms (fig. 6.7). In the initial area of a Boccaccio *Genealogiae deorum*, printed by Vindelinus de Spira also in 1472, the Pico Master sketches a putto fighting a dragon; two sirens and whimsical fuzzy trees flank the shield in the lower margin (fig. 6.8).[32] In this minimal formula the owner is complimented by his family blazon; his appreciation of an avant-garde style is modestly suggested. The first page is "finished" without undue investment. Small wonder that printers and buyers alike were pleased with the inventiveness of these masters.

Other Streamlining Efforts

Two further technical phenomena suggest that there was a certain casting about for ways to speed up the decorative process. The first, which is very familiar to students of manuscript illumination and painting, is simply the precise copying of figures from a model draw-

othèque *Joseph Martini, première partie,* August 27–29, 1934 (Milan, 1934), lot 325, pls. XXXIII–XXXIV (Suetonius, *Vitae Caesarum,* Venice, Jenson, 1471, now PML 79000); Carlo Castellani, *L'arte della stampa nel Rinascimento,* vol. 1, *Venezia* (Venice, 1894), pp. 18–19; Master of the Putti and Master of the London Pliny: Armstrong, *Renaissance Miniature Painters,* passim; Benedetto Bordone: Mariani Canova, *La miniatura veneta,* color pls. 29–30; H. A. Feisenberger, "Contemporary Collectors, XLIV: The Henry Davis Collection, II, The Ulster Gift," *The Book Collector* 21 (1972): 348 and figs. 6a,b; Antonio Maria da Villafora: Mariani Canova, *La miniatura veneta,* color pls. 40–41 and figs. 150, 153, 186–200.

[32]The Macrobius is a detached leaf, one of several with historiated initials by the Master of the Putti (Francesco Radaeli, Bredford Libri Rari SA, Lugano); the Boccaccio is BL, C.5.d.I/I (Armstrong, "Il Maestro di Pico," cat. no. 13).

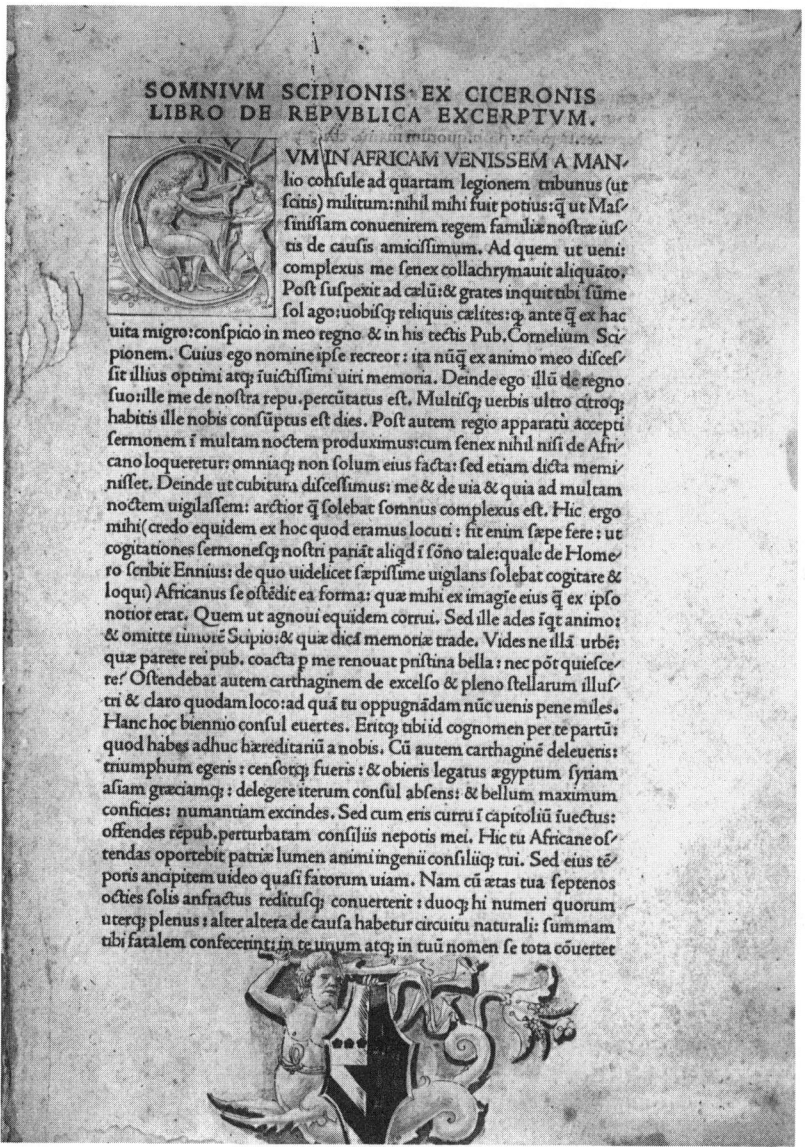

Figure 6.7. Master of the Putti, first text page with historiated initial and a Triton supporting an unidentified coat of arms, from Macrobius, *In somnium Scipionis expositio: Saturnalia,* Venice, Nicolaus Jenson, 1472, detached folio. Courtesy of Francesco Radaeli, Bredford Libri Rari SA, Lugano.

Genealogiç deorum gentilium Ioannis boccatii de certaldo Ad Vgo
nē inclytum Hierufalem & cypri regem.Eiufdem libri probçminm.

I fatis ex relatis Donini Parmēfis egregii militis tui ue
ra percepi .Rex inclyte fūmope cupis Genealogiā deoz
gentilium & heroū ex eis iuxta fictiones ueterum defcē
dentiū:atqɜ cū hac quid fub fabularum tegmine illuftres
quondam fenferūt uiri:Et me a cçlfitudine tua quafi exp
tiffimū atqɜ eruditiffimū hominem in talibus fe lectuɜ tanto operi au
ctorem.Sane ut omiferim defyderii tui admirationem(nō enim paruū
hominem decet quid tegem moueat perfcrutari)aduerfus electionem
mei quid fentiam:dicere ptermittam.Ne dum infufficientiam meam
monftrauero per fubterfugia arbitreris impofiti laboris onus euitem:
Anteɡ̃ ad fententiam meam circa impofitum opus deuentā:lib& Sere
niffime regum apponere.Et fi non omnia:quçdam faltem quç inter do
ninum infignem militem tuū:dum iuffa tuç cçlfitudinis explicaret :&
me iteruenere uerba:ut eis perlectis fatis iudicium tuum de me uideas
& temeritatem meam:dū inobedientiam tuç maieftatis deuenio.Cuɜ
igitur ille facundo ore facra maieftatis tuae ftudia:& opera regalis ofti
cū admirāda:necnon & infignes atqɜ gloriofos quofdā tui nois titulos
lōga dicacitate explicuiffet :eo deuenit:ut conatu plurimo me in tuaɜ
fententiam deducere conaretur:non unica tantū ratione:fed multis:ex
quibus fateor ualidç uidebantur quçdam.uerū poftɡ̃ tacuit: & mihi re
fpondendi copia facta ē:fic dixi.Arbitrat͡ forfan facunde miles feu rex
tuus de pximo nofter futurus pftāte deo:hāc infaniā ueteruɜ fcilicet cu
pientium fe habere diuino procreatos fanguine angulū terrç modicuɜ
occupaffe: & tanɡ̃ ridiculum quoddam:ut erat:paruo tēporis pfeueraſ
fe tractu:& ueluti etiam recentiffimū opus facile colligi poffe .Attamē
(bona femper tua pace dicam)aliter lōge ē.Nā ut omtraɜ cycladas & re
lıquas aegei maris infulas:Achaiam:Illiricam:atqɜ Thraciaɜ:quas peñ
fomenta huius ftultitiç emicuere plurimū:& potiffine dū grçcorū Res
pu.floruit.Euxini maris bellefponciaci Meonii icarii Pamphilii Cylı
cis phçnicis & Syrii atqɜ Aegyptiaci littora fua cōtagione infecit.Nec
Cyprus noftri regis infigne decus ab hac labe fuit immunis.Sic & ōeɜ
libyç atqɜ Syrtiuɜ & numidiç oram labefactauit:& atlantiacos occiduiqɜ
maris finus & remotiffimos hefperidū hortos.Nec mediterranei tātū
maris fuit contenta littoribus:quinimo & ad icognitas maris nationes
etiam penetrauit.Decidere etiam in pernitime hanc cū littoralibus ac
colç omnes nili fonte carentis & bateng libycae una cum fuis peftibus
& antiquiffimarū thebaɜ folitudines.Necnon & fuperiores Aegyptii
atqɜ garamātes feruidi & calētes nimium hirfutiqɜ Aethiopes & odori

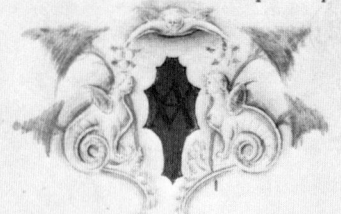

Figure 6.8. Pico Master, first text page with historiated initial and sirens flanking a repainted coat of arms (originally Priuli of Venice),
from Boccaccio, *Genealogiae deorum,* Venice, Vindelinus de Spira, 1472,
BL, C.5.d.I/I, fol. 11. By permission of the British Library Board.

ing. Three incunables are known that have exactly the same centaur family drawn in the lower margin.[33] In two cases the family, consisting of a fanciful centaur with a nymph and a putto on his back, appears twice, once on either side of a heraldic shield (fig. 6.9). The format of the two volumes, an Augustine and a Livy both printed by Vindelinus de Spira in 1470, is very large; the family group needs to be repeated in reverse in order to fill the lower margin with a pleasing composition. In a smaller book, a Cicero, *De officiis,* also printed by de Spira in 1470, only one group of centaur, nymph, and putto was employed to fill the *bas-de-page.* A pattern sheet in the workshop of the Master of the Putti must have been the model for the image in all three books.

A more experimental technique also suggests that the parties under consideration—printers, booksellers, and illuminators—were searching for ways in which larger numbers of books could be decorated more expeditiously. Woodblocks were cut with patterns that could be stamped by hand into the margins of incunables *after* they had been printed.[34] This process should not be confused with the use of woodcuts which are printed simultaneously with the type of a book; in that case the border or vignette appears in every copy of the edition, unlike these, which are added to selected copies. The patterns are units that can be repeated according to the dimensions of the folio, and many were based on the white vinestem borders of contemporary miniaturists. In most of the surviving copies, the woodcut patterns have subsequently been painted by illuminators who filled the areas between the vinestems with red, blue, purple, and green, as usual enlivened with triads of white dots. The woodcut lines thus

[33]Armstrong, *Renaissance Miniature Painters,* cat. nos. 4, ill. 17 (Oxford, Bodleian Library, Auct. L. I. 8, 9: Livy, V. de Spira, 1470) and 7, ill. 11 (Cambridge, Fitzwilliam Museum, McClean Inc. 111: Cicero, *De officiis,* V. de Spira, 1470); and BN, Vélins 296, on parchment: Augustinus, *De civitate Dei,* Venice, Vindelinus de Spira, 1470 (fig. 6.9). For the approximate size of the Livy and the Augustine, see note 15. The Cicero is about a third smaller, or 286 × 195 mm (*BMC* V, 155).

[34]Lamberto Donati catalogued more than seventy-five different woodcut motifs which were used in varying combinations, principally in Venetian books dating between 1469 and 1472 ("I fregi xilografici stampati a mano negl'incunabuli italiani," *La bibliofilia* 74 [1972]: 157–64, 303–27; and 75 [1973]: 125–74). Donati wished to locate the origin of the practice with miniaturists in Rome, but the author has argued that the phenomenon is principally a Venetian one (*Renaissance Miniature Painters,* 26–29). See also Susy Marcon, "Esempi di xilominiatura nella Biblioteca di San Marco," *Ateneo Veneto* 173 (1986): 173–93, figs. 50–63.

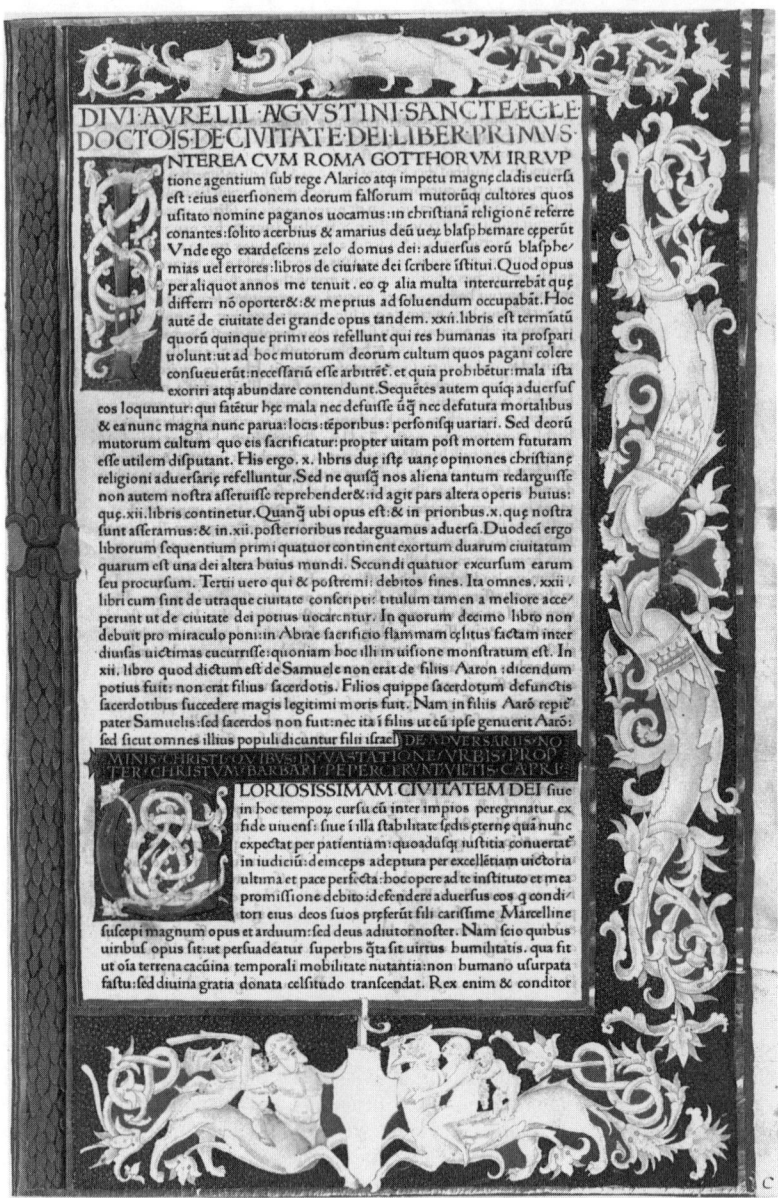

Figure 6.9. Master of the Putti, frontispiece with two centaur families flanking an empty shield, from Augustinus, *De civitate Dei,* Venice, Johannes and Vindelinus de Spira, 1470, BN, Vélins 296, fol. 1 (on parchment). Photo: Bibliothèque Nationale, Paris.

served to guide the illuminator in his painting, and were probably meant to speed him up.

The two examples illustrated here indicate the range of aesthetic possibilities of this process. The more typical example can be seen in a copy of the 1472 de Spira Boccaccio, *Genealogiae deorum,* in the Houghton Library (fig. 6.10).[35] In the right-hand margin two wood-cuts are repeated twice: the putto-Triton and the inverted bell-shaped object behind him are one block, and the interlace motif with a flower terminal is a second one. The same interlace pattern is repeated twice without the putto-Tritons in a Cicero, *Epistolares ad familiares* of 1471, in Paris, and again with the putti in a 1472 Jenson Pliny in Baltimore.[36] Other white vinestem units fill the remaining margins in the Houghton incunable. The upper-right corner reveals an awkward join between the two types of pattern, and shows that the miniaturist was often called upon to gloss over the areas where the woodcut designs overlapped or did not quite meet.

A second book into which woodcut patterns have been stamped, another copy of the 1470 de Spira Livy now in the Pierpont Morgan Library, is noteworthy in two respects (fig. 6.11).[37] First, the frontispiece is exceptionally rich for a volume in which the borders are based on woodcuts. The woodcut motifs have been applied with great care so as not to create any undesirable overlapping, and then have been painted in an intense green tempera with delicate highlights contrasting strongly with the background areas of gold leaf. The high quality of execution invites comparison with another copy of the same 1470 Livy in the Biblioteca Corsini to which the same blocks have been applied; two of the woodcut patterns in this copy awkwardly intersect in the upper-right corner, a detail that is not completely obliterated by subsequent painting.[38]

Second, the figural components of the Morgan Livy frontispiece permit attribution to a well-known miniaturist, Franco de' Russi. The two putti in the lower margin flanking the arms of the Donato of Venice closely resemble a pair in Franco's frontispiece in the *Gratulatio*

[35]Department of Printing and Graphic Arts, Houghton Library, Harvard University, Typ Inc 4045.2.

[36]Armstrong, *Renaissance Miniature Painters,* figs. 70–71.

[37]PML 266–67.

[38]Prince d'Essling, *Les livres à figures vénetiens* (Florence, 1907–1914), vol. I, pt. 1, color pl. opp. p. 48.

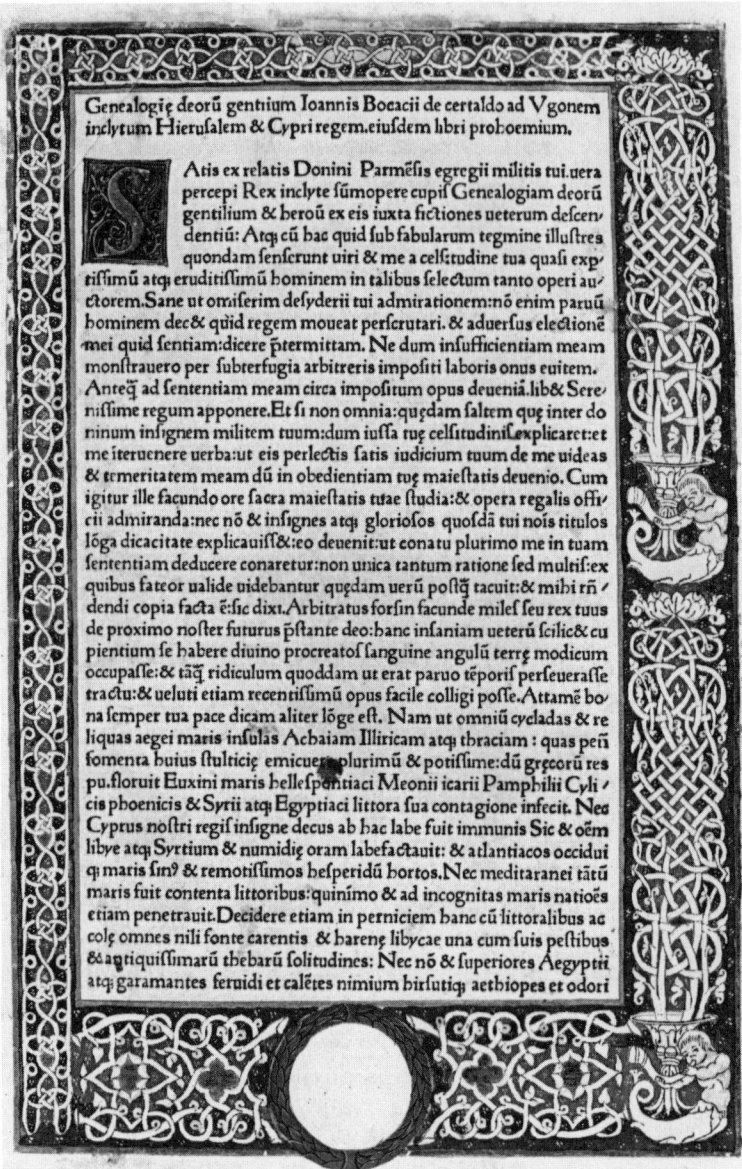

Figure 6.10. Master of the Putti, frontispiece with woodcuts designed by the artist, stamped into margins and colored subsequent to printing, arms never added, from Boccaccio, *Genealogiae deorum,* Venice, Vindelinus de Spira, 1472, Cambridge, Mass., Houghton Library Typ Inc 4045.2, fol. 1. Courtesy of the Department of Printing and Graphic Arts, The Houghton Library, Harvard University.

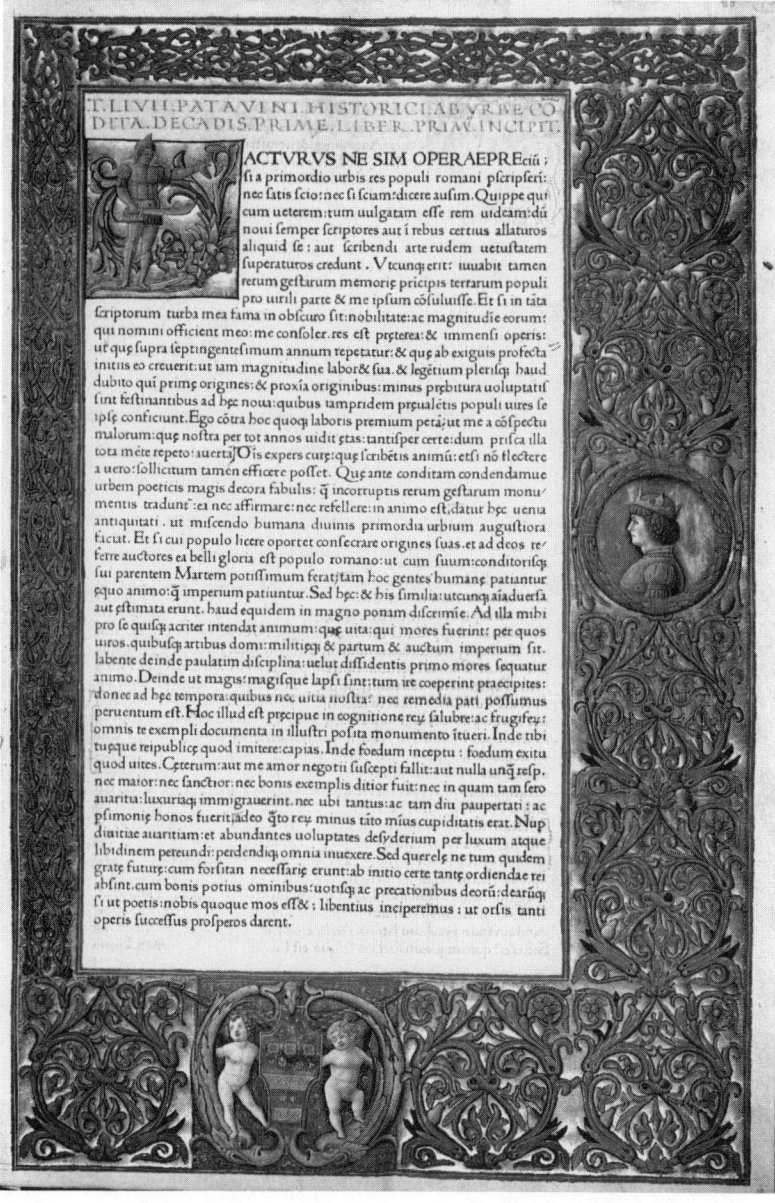

Figure 6.11. Franco de' Russi, frontispiece with woodcut designs stamped after printing and subsequently painted, portrait of a king, two putti flank Donato of Venice arms, historiated initial with a soldier *all'antica,* from Titus Livius, *Historiae romanae decades,* Venice, Vindelinus de Spira, 1470, PML 266, fol. 25 (on parchment). Courtesy of the Pierpont Morgan Library, New York.

di Bernardo Bembo a Cristoforo Moro of 1463–1465, mentioned earlier. Their swaying poses and curly hair are also reminiscent of another pair depicted in a signed de Spira *Biblia italica* of 1471, now in Wölfenbuttel; the blue soldier in the initial of the Morgan Livy may be compared to details of the figures in the *Judgment of Solomon* miniature of the Wölfenbuttel folio as well.[39] The exquisitely painted portrait of a youthful king bears comparison to the profile portrait of a scholar in a cutting signed by Franco in the British Library, and to the monochrome portraits of the Malatesta in a 1471 Jenson Tortellius in Paris attributed to Franco.[40]

That the Morgan Livy was illuminated by a miniaturist of the standing of Franco de' Russi shows that the process of adding woodcuts as a guide was not merely developed to assist amateurs. Nonetheless, the intriguing experiment seems to have been more trouble than it was worth. Even a miniaturist with limited experience could probably execute a white vinestem border almost as fast without a woodcut guide as he could with the extra step. The phenomenon is virtually never found in printed books bearing dates later than 1473, a mere three or four years after it first appears.

Increased Numbers of Miniaturists

A final observation that supports the idea that the situation for illuminators in Venice was greatly changed in the period immediately following the advent of printing is simply that there was a substantial increase in the number of these artists in Venice, attracted there, I believe, specifically to decorate printed books. In her fundamental study of Venetian miniaturists, published in 1969, Giordana Mariani Canova referred to at least twelve distinct masters who illuminated books printed in Venice in the 1470s, in contrast to Leonardo Bellini and an occasional visiting luminary active there in the 1460s. To this already significant number one could now add at least eight more.[41]

[39]Mariani Canova, *La miniatura veneta*, figs. 20, 22.

[40]Ibid., figs. 24, 25.

[41]Among these are the Master of the London Pliny (Armstrong, *Renaissance Miniature Painters*); Master of the Olschki Plutarch (Thorp, *Glory of the Page*, cat. no. 89; Susy Marcon, "Ornati di penna e di pennello: Appunti su scribi-illuminatori nella Venezia del maturo umanesimo," *La bibliofilia* 89 [1987]: 121–43, esp. pp. 125–28); Master of the Huntington Livy (fig. 6.6); the Pico Master (figs. 6.1, 6.3–5, 6.8, and

Thus there would have been at least twenty master miniaturists, in addition to their assistants, to whom printers and patrons alike could have turned for the decoration of the newly produced books.

Many additional works have also been identified by the artists already noted by Mariani Canova. The Pico Master is a particularly striking example of this phenomenon (figs. 6.1, 6.3–5, 6.8). The decoration of over sixty Venetian incunables dating from nearly every year between 1469 and 1487 may be attributed to him. Thus both the number of artists and the number of works argue for greatly increased opportunities.

Some of the miniaturists working in Venice in the 1470s had well-established reputations and would have taken individual commissions on the model of manuscript illuminators over the centuries. Others, however, were probably closely linked to the printer-booksellers by contracts or less formal agreements. Such an arrangement is suggested by a revealing document published by Antonio Sartori. In Padua on January 2, 1476, the miniaturist Master Antonio of Bergamo promised to work exclusively for Antonio d'Avignone, a seller of printed books. The miniaturist was to live with the bookseller during the three-year period of the contract, and in addition to illuminating books he was to do binding, selling, and perhaps rubrication.[42] Although we do not know who Antonio di Bergamo was, his contractual relationship to the bookseller fits a pattern suggested by the variety of decoration appearing in early Venetian incunables. Numerous artists such as Antonio would have found more than enough work executing initials and borders in the many hundreds of Venetian books decorated in the 1470s.

The *visual* evidence in early printed books that points to efforts to speed up decoration, and which suggests that books were decorated in anticipation of sale, may be summarized as follows: (1) many books received initials and borders in fairly standardized patterns

---

note 23); Petrus, or the Master of the Glasgow Breviary (Lilian Armstrong, "*Opus Petri*: Renaissance Miniatures from Venice and Rome," *Viator* 21 [1990]: 385–412; Thorp, *Glory of the Page*, cat. no. 101); and Master of the Rimini Ovid (see note 29).

[42]Antonio Sartori, "Documenti padovani sull'arte della stampa nel sec. XV," in *Libri e stampatori in Padova: Miscellanea di Studi Storici in onore di Mons. G. Bellini* (Padua, 1959), pp. 135–36. I am grateful to Jonathan Alexander for first having pointed out this important document to me.

which could be repeated with a minimum of effort; (2) books were sometimes rubricated and illuminated with initials in one style, while the frontispiece for the same volume was painted in another style or not painted at all; (3) areas for coats of arms were often left blank, awaiting a buyer's blazon, occasionally even in elaborately decorated books; (4) many miniaturists used two techniques: the more time-consuming process of painting in tempera and gold, and a pen and ink technique which permitted faster execution; (5) artists frequently used the historiated initial and coat of arms formula, personalizing a first page of text with a minimum of handwork; (6) miniaturists traced model drawings of figural motifs; (7) woodcuts were designed and stamped by hand onto margins of frontispieces to guide illuminators in painting borders; and finally (8) a significantly increased number of miniaturists were at work in Venice in the 1470s in contrast to the numbers there before the advent of printing.

The end of the story is of course the coming of the woodcut. The decoration by hand of thousands of printed books was eventually recognized as a physical and economic impossibility. The technology for printing woodcuts simultaneously with the type of a given edition had been worked out in Germany in the 1460s, and was in common use by the 1470s.[43] But aside from a few experiments, printers in Venice resisted making extensive use of woodcuts in their editions until about 1490. Thus the coming of printing to Venice in 1469 heralded twenty years of exceptional richness both for miniaturists of outstanding talent and for many lesser masters as well.

[43]Arthur M. Hind, *An Introduction to a History of Woodcut* (1935; reprinted, New York, 1963), pp. 273ff.

PART III

READERS

[7]

Importation of Books Printed
on the Continent into England
and Scotland before c. 1520

Lotte Hellinga

The evolution of the relationship between reader and book which took place in the fifteenth century after the invention of printing can be understood in terms of marketing and risks taken by publishers. The first books printed at Mainz were aimed at a clearly defined market, a clientele largely confined to monastic houses of particular orders (the Benedictine order dominant among them), with only occasionally an individual owner, who was usually prominent enough to equal an institution. Aeneas Silvius' letter to Cardinal Juan de Carvajal about the imminent publication of the Gutenberg Bible illuminates not only how difficult it was to secure a copy in advance, but also the stir caused by this event among the great of this world. It was as if the risk for such enterprises was practically subscribed in advance. Patronage was a variation on this theme.

As printing developed, we perceive a greater differentiation in printers' marketing tactics. Before venturing onto large enterprises, publishers would still attempt to define a market (as they may to the present day). But for smaller books more risks were taken: with lower

The present study is being used as a pilot project for a much larger research project undertaken by Margaret L. Ford in preparation for volume 2 of *The History of the Book in Britain,* of which J. B. Trapp and I are joint editors. Her research (funded by the Leverhulme Foundation) comprises readership in England and Scotland from 1400 to 1559.

prices publishers could be confident of being able to reach buyers, even if these were not known to them as individuals. Manuscript production "on spec" had been the exception; for printed books it became—with time—the norm. The most interesting development can be perceived with those publishers who decided that they could risk producing substantial books for clients who were quite unknown to them. Printers such as Koberger, Aldus Manutius, and the other great Venetian printers had found markets well beyond their own horizon, and they could be confident that their books would find their way to individual buyers all over the Latin-reading world. The still common occurrence of their books in collections all over the Western world, the fact that they are *not* rare, still bears eloquent testimony to their energetic sales drives.

Traditionally such matters have been studied from the point of view of production; the question of what books were produced when, where, and by whom can be answered for the fifteenth century with remarkable accuracy (if with considerable effort) owing to centuries of recording and identifying incunabula. It is much more difficult to determine what books were read, by whom, and when, but modern catalogues of incunabula have made important contributions which enable us to begin to face this question, and to speak of quantifiable proportions. If we therefore attempt to change sides, as it were, and view fifteenth-century book production as the contemporary readers did, it may be possible to arrive at an understanding of what was available, through which channels and from where, and who required the books. It appears profitable to select at first a limited geographic area for such an exercise, and within such an area we may arrive at defining more than one market, determined by social differentiation.

As a geographic area the British Isles seem particularly favorable. There was relatively little book production in England itself (and none in the other parts of the British Isles), and such as there was was highly biased toward English-language books, law, and other local needs. Almost all books in Latin were imported from abroad. The country, however, has been blessed with an exceptional number of bibliophiles and gifted bibliographers, and descriptions of collections have attained a very high standard. It is therefore possible to find materials on early owners in published form, and to assess whether they suffice to be rearranged in order to answer such new questions as: Where were the books imported into England and Scotland produced? Who were these readers? How did they perceive the world of books in the half-century since they were first introduced into these islands? Eventually the answers to such questions may lead us to a better-founded definition of the market certain publishers had in mind when they produced their books.

Not long after the invention of printing at least two copies of Gutenberg's 42-line Bible found their way to London, but it was not until the mid-1470s that the trade in printed books developed into a regular importation.

The importation of printed books from the Continent has been studied from various points of view: in the first place by E. Gordon Duff, who combined an interest in the history of printing with a focus on the history of the book trade. Duff had an unrivaled knowledge of early English books and of book collections in Great Britain, and he expressed the opinion that "at best the output of books in England was miserably scanty" and insignificant in comparison with the numbers of books available in England but printed abroad.[1] He then proceeded to produce a bibliography of the English books printed before 1501 (there are about 370), but in the same bibliography he gave as much attention to books produced abroad and intended exclusively for the English market, such as books in the English language printed in the Low Countries, in Bruges, Antwerp, and Deventer, or books with liturgies according to English rites, printed mainly in Paris, Rouen, and Venice. He listed seventy-two books in the category "printed abroad." Duff (and following him Henry Plomer)[2] linked the history of printing with the history of the book trade, and indeed saw no reason to consider these interests as separate. Plomer's contribution was a more extensive consultation of archival records to document the importation of books through the ports.

Scholars whose prime concern was the history of humanism in England had an entirely different angle from which to view the same phenomenon. Roberto Weiss pioneered this approach in his *Human-*

[1]Edward Gordon Duff, *A Century of the English Book Trade* (London, 1905), pp. xi, xiii.

[2]Henry Robert Plomer, "The Importation of Books into England in the Fifteenth and Sixteenth Centuries," *The Library,* 4th ser., no. 4 (1923): 146–50.

ism in England during the Fifteenth Century (1941), where he discussed Englishmen of learning, many of whom were educated at Italian universities. Later in their careers these men, by now bishops or other important dignitaries, would travel on diplomatic missions on the Continent and would bring home the books that were the tools of their trade, occasionally, from the late 1460s onward, including the modern form of books: printed codices. Weiss's approach was extended further by Elizabeth Armstrong, who provided in 1979 a synthesis of the subject.[3] In this context I should also mention some of the studies undertaken by Martin Lowry which highlight the individual enterprise of diplomats and their pursuit of books.[4]

A third approach may at first sight seem closely related to Gordon Duff's in that it focuses on the book trade, but it does not spring primarily from an interest in the history of printing. Graham Pollard contributed two important articles to the subject which allowed an insight into both the dissemination of books through the wholesale trade once they had reached England and the relationship between the wholesale trade, which dealt with books in large numbers, and the retail trade, which meant selling them one by one to customers.[5] The wholesale trade in books in Latin was entirely dominated by dealers who operated on an international scale. In 1484 they were favored by an act of Parliament which, while excluding foreign merchants from the right to carry out trade of any kind, excepted all foreign traders in books, both wholesale traders and the stationers and bookbinders who sold books through the retail trade.[6] This exception is thought to have been influenced by educated people who did not wish to lose

[3]Elizabeth Armstrong, "English Purchases of Printed Books from the Continent, 1465–1526," *English Historical Review* 94 (1979): 268–90. See also an elaboration in Nicolas John Barker, "The Importation of Books into England, 1460–1526," in *Beiträge zur Geschichte des Buchwesens im konfesionellen Zeitalter,* ed. Herbert G. Göpfert (Wolfenbüttel, 1985), pp. 251–66.

[4]Martin Lowry, "Diplomacy and the Spread of Printing," in *Bibliography and the Study of Fifteenth-Century Civilization: The Beginning of Printing and the ISTC Project,* ed. L. Hellinga and J. Goldfinch (London, 1987). See also idem., "The Arrival and Use of Continental Printed Books in Yorkist England," *Le livre dans l'Europe de la Renaissance,* Actes du XXVIIIe Colloque internationale d'Études humanistes de Tours, ed. Pierre Aquilon and Henri-Jean Martin (Paris, 1988), pp. 449–59.

[5]Graham Pollard, "The English Market for Printed Books: The Rise of the Wholesale Trade," *Publishing History* 4 (1978): 9–17. Idem., "The Names of Some English Fifteenth-Century Binders," *The Library,* 5th ser., no. 25 (1970): 193–218.

[6]1 Richard III, *Statutes of the Realm* II, p. 489.

the benefits brought by alien book dealers. It is not too fanciful, I think, to suspect that those same powerful diplomats and politicians who a few years earlier had bought their printed books on the Continent (because they were not available in England) may have had a hand in this. The dealers came mainly from Germany and the Low Countries, and there was also a Savoyard named Peter Actors. An act of 1534 which repealed the act of 1484 and forbade anyone to buy from foreigners books printed or bound abroad, except wholesale, did little to change the pattern of importation (what it did change, of course, was the trade of bookbinding), and it was the wholesale trade that was the crucial factor in the availability of books. Its importance lasted well into the seventeenth century, by which time it was known as the Latin trade.

Graham Pollard also contributed greatly to our insight into the retail trade by integrating into the emerging picture of the book trade the study of bindings which had been carried out by various experts in the preceding half-century. The resulting extensive documentation for English binding in the fifteenth and sixteenth centuries has brought the confidence that a binding can tell us whether a book was bound in England or not, where it was bound, and (roughly) at what date—invaluable information when interpreted by a historian of the book trade, especially one with the gifts of Graham Pollard, who always saw the history of the book trade as an element of intellectual history, whatever the period. Bindings bring us to a type of evidence that so far has been conspicuously missing in these approaches: the books themselves. By dissociating the availability of books from particular events such as records of importation or purchase, or the individual biography of the buyers, and instead concentrating on the mere fact that the books were there and available to buyers, we may gain an impression of how readers in England and Scotland availed themselves of the opportunities offered by the production of books on the Continent.

I have taken a sample of one thousand books with early English and Scottish ownership,[7] and I have divided my sample according to place

---

[7]The sample is based on John Claud Trewinard Oates, *A Catalogue of the Fifteenth-Century Printed Books in the University Library, Cambridge* (Cambridge, 1954); [A. G. Scott], *St. Andrews University Library, Catalogue of Incunabula,* (St. Andrews, 1956); Neil Ripley Ker, *Medieval Libraries of Great Britain: A List of Surviving Books,* 2d ed.

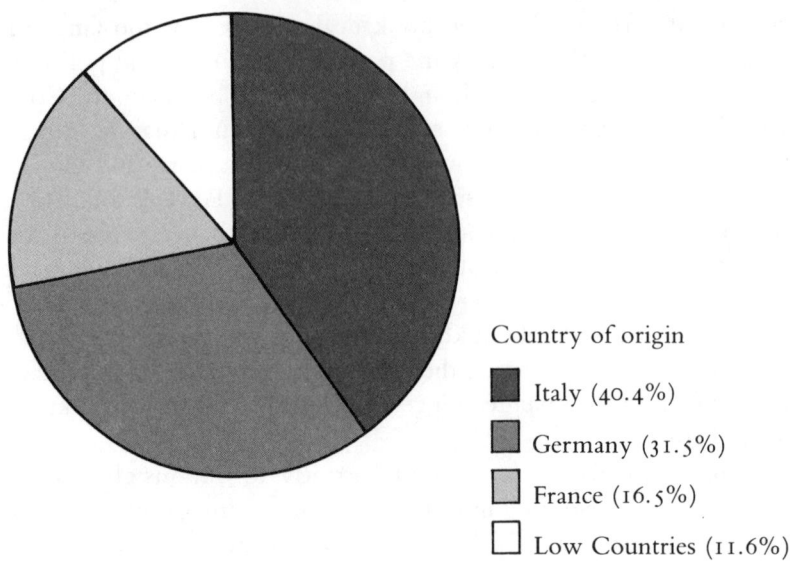

Country of origin

■ Italy (40.4%)

■ Germany (31.5%)

□ France (16.5%)

□ Low Countries (11.6%)

Figure 7.1. Chart showing countries of origin of books imported into England and Scotland before 1500 (distribution of 1,000-book sample).

of printing and country of origin. I have differentiated the figures by decades, according to the time of printing (see Appendix I). In this very simple division the figures show that books printed in Italy account for 40 percent of the total, followed by books in the German-speaking countries with over 31 percent, France with about half that proportion, or 16 percent, and finally the Low Countries with about 11 percent of the total (see fig. 7.1). Venice alone accounts for 28 percent of the whole sample. When these primary figures are divided into decades, we can see that there is a sharp rise in imports in the

(London, 1964), pp. 1–141 (alphabetical list of towns up to Oxford); Dennis Everard Rhodes, *John Argentine, Provost of King's (c. 1442–1508): His Life and His Library* (Amsterdam, 1967); William Smith Mitchell, *Catalogue of the Incunabula in Aberdeen University Library* (Edinburgh, 1968); Dennis Everard Rhodes, *A Catalogue of Incunabula in All the Libraries of Oxford University outside the Bodleian* (Oxford, 1982), subsequently cited as Rhodes; and part of Leslie Sheppard's catalogue (unpublished, on slips) of incunabula at the Bodleian Library. I also examined 120 books at the National Library of Scotland, Edinburgh. I included books in English bindings discussed passim in works by Mirjam Maria Foot, Strickland Gibson, Geoffrey Dudley Hobson, Howard Millar Nixon, James Basil Oldham, and Graham Pollard. Books from the Old Royal Library were included from a provisional list kindly provided by T. A. Birrell.

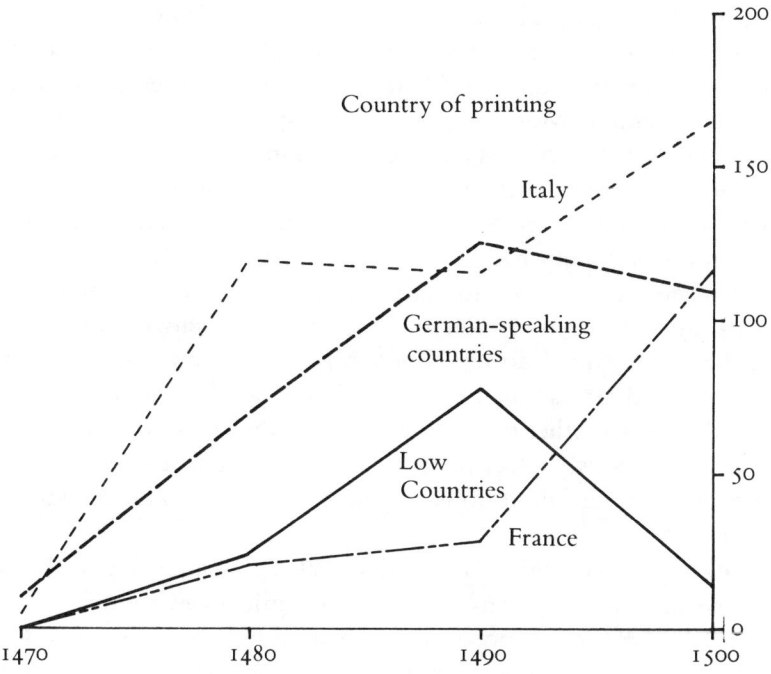

Figure 7.2. Chart showing changing patterns of countries of origin of sample 1,000 books imported into England and Scotland before 1500.

1480s, and that this upward trend continues into the 1490s, if not rising quite as steeply (see fig. 7.2). Furthermore, we can see that in the late 1480s the German-speaking countries led the field, this being also the period when the imports from the Low Countries were at their peak, but that in the 1490s Italy took the lead with a proportion of books (16.5 percent) higher than for any other country for any single decade. In the 1490s we also see that France shows a very steep rise, becoming by the end of the decade the second-largest contributor.

Further analysis (see Appendix II) shows that in the 1490s the Italian and French contribution was almost entirely produced by three centers, Venice, Paris, and Lyons. There is much material to suggest that at that time the Lyonnais printers started to compete with their colleagues in Venice to capture the academic and professional markets, notably in legal and classical texts.

In these statistics, if I may call them such, we must beware of

[211]

attaching too much value to absolute quantity. It is not the numbers relative to modern collections and their reflection of survival that matter but the quantities relative to one another that reveal the structure of the sample. Moreover, my percentage points ought not lead to the conclusion that there is any real precision in these figures. In fact, they are an exercise in balancing precision against imprecision. The precision lies in the work of the incunabulists on whose catalogues my sample is mainly based. The study of incunabula has reached a point where the identification of places of printing can be established with a high degree of certainty—or at least consensus among experts about a status quo. I do not think that for any book in my sample there is any doubt about the geographic area where it was printed. Exact dating is another matter, but the dates disputed by incunabulists would not seriously affect my sample either. There are several other causes for imprecision, however, some of which could be remedied in a more extensive study.

The first one concerns the question: What is being counted? I have counted titles, or "editions," the obvious units of publication issued by the printer. It needs no argument that, although the convention is widely practiced in studies such as this one, the title on its own cannot be a satisfactory statistical unit since it may equally cover a multi-volume Bible with commentary or a tract of only a few pages. Size has a fairly accurate ratio to price, and therefore some expression of size would be desirable. A conversion into masterformes, such as Miriam Usher Chrisman has carried out in her study of book production at Strasbourg,[8] would be a useful way to do this. In my statistics such a conversion would undoubtedly boost the figures for Nuremberg, Strasbourg, and Basel, producers of larger-than-average books, at the expense of Cologne and Paris, specialists in quartos and smaller formats.

Another defect in my pilot study lies in the conventions of incunable cataloguing. When describing copies, modern incunabulists will record their provenance, the earlier ownership which will often eluci-

---

[8]Miriam Usher Chrisman, *Lay Culture, Learned Culture: Books and Social Change in Strasbourg, 1480–1599* (New Haven, 1982). A discussion of how to estimate figures to reflect the realities of book production and their relative value is Carla Bozzolo, Dominique Coq, and Ezio Ornato, "La production du livre en quelques pays d'Europe occidentale aux XIVe et XVe siècles," *Scrittura e civiltà* (1984): 129–76, esp. p. 141.

date how the book in question found its way into the collection that is being catalogued. It is also standard practice to record any early names, whether or not they are identifiable as historically traceable persons; but where names are wanting, the question of where a book was first used—where it traveled after it was first printed—is not considered relevant to the purpose of cataloguing. Unlike manuscript experts, incunabulists will usually omit to record the presence of anonymous notes, although they often contain clues for locating the writer, either because they are in a vernacular language or—inevitably subject to dispute—on paleographic grounds. The catalogues I used are all works of exemplary scholarship: J. C. T. Oates's catalogue of the incunabula at the Cambridge University Library, the catalogues of the incunabula in the Scottish university libraries of Aberdeen and St. Andrews, my colleague D. E. Rhodes's catalogue of the incunabula in all the Oxford colleges, and the late L. A. Sheppard's unpublished catalogue of the incunabula at the Bodleian Library, available to me in photocopy. Yet in spite of the painstaking recording of all that is *known* or *knowable* about early owners, it remains rewarding to examine the books oneself for other evidence that may testify to the early presence of books in the British Isles.

To test this contention I went through a sample of incunabula at the National Library of Scotland in Edinburgh, where, through the kind help of my colleague Brian Hillyard, I examined in a short time 120 books; of those not fewer than fourteen, although not bearing names of owners or other such signs of identity, were beyond doubt scribbled over somewhere in the British Isles early in their existence. These books would not have been entered in an index of early owners or provenance. The figures I present could therefore be increased very significantly by the direct examination of copies in the relevant collections.

On the same lines illumination may provide evidence for the early migration of books unconnected with any individual names. Eberhard König has shown to spectacular effect how illumination can reveal the distribution of books by the printing house, and he has demonstrated that at least two copies of the Gutenberg Bible were decorated in London shortly after they were printed.[9] This is a new application of the early history of copies, and one cannot expect to

[9]Eberhard König, "A Leaf from a Bible Illuminated in England," *British Library Journal* 9 (1983): 32–50.

find this information in any but the most recent catalogues of incunabula; again, only examination of copies will bring this information to light.

Inevitably, the survival rate of books is reflected in my sample. Generally and crudely speaking, large books survive better than small books, Latin stands a better chance than vernacular, and so on. In England the Reformation, and following it the dissolution of the monasteries in 1539, diminished the chance of survival of books in ecclesiastical libraries. Academic libraries were much less disturbed, and in them one finds many of the most important collections of incunabula in England: the foundation collections of the Bodleian Library and the Cambridge University Library, and most of all the libraries of the colleges at Oxford and Cambridge. With the exception of the latter, these were all described in catalogues of incunabula that were the mainstay of my sample. The reason why I have not sampled several other major collections on a systematic basis, the British Library among them, is that as collections they are mainly the result of book collecting in the eighteenth and nineteenth centuries. I have, however, included the most ancient core of the British Library collection, the Old Royal Library (the collection of books of the successive English monarchs), which includes forty-two incunabula, most of them acquired in the last decade of the fifteenth century during the reign of King Henry VII. The Royal Library books show a strong French influence: fourteen are in French and three in Latin printed in France, giving a total of 40 percent printed in France, compared with 16 percent in the sample overall.

The academic bias in the sample can lead to a positive result. Among my sample the books in the Oxford colleges are at the highest academic level and are the most purely preserved. Unlike the great university libraries, with their convoluted histories and each with a function as guardian of the cultural heritage of the nation, the college libraries have had over the centuries only one function: to preserve the property of the college. Losses have been sustained, naturally, but in these collections we may still find a good reflection of the books owned during the fifteenth century by a well-defined layer of society. Of the 2,585 copies recorded by Rhodes with notes of early owners, I could decide on the basis of the ownership or of the binding, where recorded, that 391 were beyond doubt in England at an early date. I have made no attempt to enlarge this figure by examining copies. As it is, they form a substantial part of the overall sample. The statistics of their origin are significantly different from the total sample: in the Oxford colleges a much higher proportion of books came from Italy (58 percent against 40 percent overall), and a lower percentage than in the overall sample came from Germany, France, and the Low Countries.

It is therefore reasonable to split the sample and compare the Oxford colleges against the rest (see Appendix II). The difference in the representation of Italy now becomes quite dramatic: 58 percent in college libraries against 29 percent in the rest of the sample. The largest part of the Italian books in the Oxford section of the sample, 65 percent, consists of books printed in Venice, followed by Rome with only 13 percent. Of the enormously rich diversity of printing in Italy we find only a small representation: there are eight books printed in Pavia (mostly on canon law), seven printed in Florence, six in Milan, and only five printed in Padua. Nine other centers of printing in Italy are represented by a mere twenty books (see Appendix II). The books printed in Rome are almost all printed before 1480, and we are fortunate that many of them contain inscriptions recording their purchase. Most of these were bought in Rome by Bishop John Shirwood, who, before he became bishop of Durham, was apostolic protonotary in Rome, and did not miss the chance to bring together a collection of books, many of which were printed by Sweynheym and Pannartz. A similar collection was assembled by Bishop John Goldwell, who had traveled widely on diplomatic missions and was posted in Rome as king's orator from the late 1460s. These great men account for most of the books printed in Rome, and they give the impression that Roman printers, certainly at that time (and I think also later), did not depend on trade channels: they did not export books but catered to the international clientele that would gravitate sooner or later toward the center of the ecclesiastical world.

There are only few such notes of local purchase in the Venetian books, but in the Venetian sample we find convincing proof that books were bought in England. Buyers noted that books were bought in London, Oxford, or Bristol, and sometimes recorded the price they paid in shillings and pence.[10] How these books reached the

[10]John Claymond (1457–1537), whose books are in Corpus Christi College, sometimes noted prices of books bought in England: "Hoc volumen emptum est londini per Iohannem Studde ut existimo x^s xiiij^d" (Rhodes 714b); "Liber Claimondi emptus

English cities remains at this stage largely a matter for conjecture. We can expect a great deal of clarification here from Paul Needham's researches in the Public Record Office for the late fifteenth and early sixteenth centuries, which promise to improve considerably on the scarce customs records published so far. These record cargoes containing, among other goods, books that had arrived with the Venetian galleys on their annual call to the port of Southampton.[11] It is, however, reasonable to assume that many Venetian books came in via continental ports closer to England, via Bruges, Antwerp, and Rouen, through the alien wholesalers in London who had maintained their connections with their countries of origin. It is therefore the wholesalers in London more than traveling Englishmen who forged the link between Italian scholarship as found in books printed in Italy and the users of these books, who were scholars at the English and Scottish universities. The commercial aspect of this contact goes a long way toward explaining the very scant representation of other Italian centers of academic printing against the strong presence of Venetian books. Their influence on intellectual life in the English and Scottish universities can hardly be overvalued.

When we look specifically at the books in the Oxford college libraries, we must note, in the first place, that after the first decade, by 1480, we find printed books in the hands of men of not quite such exceptional eminence as Goldwell and Shirwood. Imports from Italy grew much faster than the others. New lines of communication had begun to develop, and scholars in Oxford had become increasingly aware of what was happening in Italy. It is striking to see how many of the Greek editions of Aldus Manutius, printed in the 1490s, can be found in those collections: no fewer than six editions are represented in the Oxford colleges with early notes of ownership—eleven copies altogether.[12] It is here that we find the beginning of the new direction

---

Londini iijs.viijd" (Rhodes 1598); "Liber Claimondi emptus oxonij ut existimo v s vj d" (Rhodes 1401b). Elizabeth Armstrong, "English Purchases of Printed Books," with reference to *Port Books of Southampton for the Reign of Edward IV*, ed. David Beers Quinn, Publications of the Southampton Record Society, vol. 38 (1938), pt. 2, 147; and Alwyn Amy Ruddock, *Italian Merchants and Shipping at Southampton, 1270–1600*, Southampton Record series, 1951, p. 75; cf. p. 194.

[11]I am grateful to Dr. Paul Needham for keeping me informed of his researches at the Public Record Office, London.

[12]Rhodes 129e (Aristophanes); 130f,g,i,j,l,m,n (Aristotle); 693c (Dioscorides); 812d (Gaza); 1685b (Theocritus); 1688d (Thesaurus Cornucopiae). This figure can in all likelihood be multiplied by examining the other copies for bindings and other features not recorded by Rhodes.

that Greek studies were to take in the sixteenth century when they became known as the New Learning.

On the basis of this sample it is, I think, correct to associate the Italian books in England with higher academic learning. The other part of the sample, excluding the Oxford colleges, also encompasses some academic libraries, but libraries whose collections represent books not so exclusively connected with academic scholarship. Larger libraries attract a greater variety of books. We can see there that lower education, the Latin textbooks used in schools, did not come from Italy at all but from Germany and the Low Countries, until toward the end of the century the London printers began to work for schools. It is more difficult to say what was the main source of textbooks for university students. In the early years they came from Cologne, Paris, and Louvain. It is likely that in the later years Lyons, rather than the Italian centers, began to play an important part. Paris books are found at the royal court, as we have seen, and many of these are editions by Antoine Vérard, but a substantial number of the very typical Paris quartos and octavos of the 1480s and 1490s were bought by a lay public.

It is fruitful to compare these findings with those presented in the recent study by Carla Bozzolo, Dominique Coq, and Ezio Ornato, in which the relative proportions of book production of Italy, the German-speaking countries, France and "others" are estimated, and also the market of books in these countries.[13] Since no separate estimates are given for England, the present study is complementary to theirs and does not appear to contradict it. Their graph 11, "La production et le marché des imprimés destinés aux lettrés," shows that the proportion of Italian and French books produced overall is consistently lower than the relative figures for their importation into England. Their figures of production in German-speaking countries and "others" are therefore higher. The "literati" in Oxford show an intensification of the now evident English bias for books produced in Italy and France.

In applying a social differentiation, the geographic structure begins to assume different contours. We could, therefore, try to reverse the course pursued so far and explore how, by the end of the fifteenth century, the world of books would have looked when viewed from

[13]See note 8.

England by different people. Let us begin by considering the early owners of some books that are *not* included in the sample: books printed in England. It is in the first place striking that there we encounter many names of women, whereas in the sample of one thousand books printed on the Continent I have not found one female early owner. But in English-language books one finds Elizabeth Englefield, Elizabeth Aske, Elizabeth Carew, Elizabeth Estey (the only readily identifiable Elizabeth is Elizabeth Woodville, queen consort of Edward IV, who owned a copy of Caxton's *Recuyell of the Histories of Troye*);[14] also Awdry Dely (who was a nun), Bridgett Edwardes, Anne Greasbrooke, Kateryn Hastyng, Susan Puresey. The fact that they were women is perhaps more significant in their classification as readers than any place one may assign them on the social scale. Many of the men's names in English-language incunabula are equally unidentifiable, with such notable exceptions as Richard Spensar, "letherseller of London," who owned a *Mirror of the World* now at Göttingen,[15] and a whole dynasty of drapers in Chester who wrote their names in a *Polycronicon* now in Aberystwyth at the National Library of Wales.[16] There is also the very splendid *Canterbury Tales* at Merton College, Oxford, illuminated for the London Company of Haberdashers.[17] And several merchants are known to have been connected with the patronage of some of Caxton's and Wynkyn de Worde's books.[18] It would not be right to generalize from these few instances and conclude that tradesmen and merchants made up Caxton's public; yet it seems logical that this printer who worked so much in the vernacular found his readers among those who could not read Latin. But we may say that merchants, who would not have attended university and thus would not have read languages other than English (although there are exceptions), became owners of English books. Books printed on the Continent did not touch their daily lives, as they did those of academics and the people who governed them.

[14]De Ricci 22.10; Goff C-431 (the copy at the H. E. Huntington Library, San Marino, Calif.).

[15]De Ricci 94.10.

[16]Julius Victor Scholderer, *Hand-List of Incunabula in the National Library of Wales* (Aberystwyth, 1940), no. 114 not listed in Ricci 49.

[17]Rhodes 537b.

[18]Such merchants were, for example, Hugh Bryce, London goldsmith and prime warden of the Goldsmiths' Company, alderman of the City of London (1475–1496), who sponsored Caxton's translation of the *Mirror of the World,* and the mercer Roger Thorney, a patron of Wynkyn de Worde and the owner of several important English manuscripts.

Among those who did read Latin, the rich world of Italian books in all their variety was known to some extent to the highest academic and professional classes. When they wished to purchase the tools of their trade, they knew they wanted books from Venice, which took the place of those treasures carried off from Rome in earlier days. Only occasionally did they profit from the riches produced by Italy's other centers of printing. For the academic, Italy in general, and Venice in particular, was the source of practically all up-to-date scholarship (which could mean, of course, modern editions of ancient texts). Still, they woke up to the fact that Lyons produced books that looked as good as Venetian as soon as these became available. The ecclesiastical clientele, the secular clergy, and the monastic houses were also very much aware of books produced in Venice, but in addition they drew heavily on the more traditional texts from the great German-speaking centers of Nuremberg, Basel, and Strasbourg. As with Italy, we can clearly see here the effect of trade at a long distance; there is very little perception of publishing other than in the principal centers of book production, and within them by certain printers: Anton Koberger, Aldus Manutius, and the less conspicuous but ubiquitous Bonetus Locatellus and some others in Venice.

Nearer home, as one can expect, there was more awareness of the variety of book production in the country nearest to Britain, the Netherlands. But in contrast, book production in France was perceived as having taken place in only two cities, Paris and Lyons. This reflects the nature of book production in most provincial towns in France, which was intended for only relatively small areas, but it is surprising that Rouen did not play a larger part. In addition to producing works printed at Rouen and destined exclusively for the English market, which I have excluded from my sample, the city was probably instrumental in channeling books to England that were printed elsewhere; this is where the London wholesale trade actually began. I think that in the last decade of the century this was also the role of the continental North Sea ports; the importation of books printed in that area had dropped sharply by that time.

After the scholars, including the lay scholars, as well as the clergy and the religious houses, English professional men were the greatest purchasers of books. They were the lawyers and doctors, dons and schoolmasters educated at university. Together with the merchant classes they represented at that time in England the layer of society that was rising on the social scale more than any other. The professionals, and also the merchant class, were more affected by the advent of printing than any other sector of society. Until that time there is, in England at least, not much sign that they were book owners on any large scale, but from that point on books became part of their daily life, and they began to count books among their usual possessions.

The professional man himself would use printed books as the tools of his trade, and his profession and interest would determine their origin. By the end of the century a doctor would professionally use books from Italy; a lawyer would also buy books from Lyons (as well as the English law books produced in the City of London); and, if he could afford to buy books at all, so would a schoolmaster. The professional man would expect to get for his household some schoolbooks for his son from Germany and the Low Countries, and when the lad grew up he would be further educated with books from Paris and Lyons and probably also from Germany. Wives and daughters read books in English produced in Westminster; it is not until the sixteenth century that we find those elegant little Paris books in their hands.

In the book trade a new element was to come in not long after the turn of the century. Some of the inscriptions in Oxford books suggest that the books were purchased secondhand in London or perhaps in Oxford.[19] When Ferdinand Columbus, the son of Christopher Columbus and founder of the Biblioteca Colombina in Seville, visited London in 1522 in his pursuit of books, he could buy secondhand incunabula printed in Italy and Lyons and take them home to Seville.[20] By then, owing to a lively importation of books by a whole

[19]An example of a book that changed hands in England is Rhodes 1021, a copy of Johannes de Imola, *Lectura super prima parte infortiati,* Venice, Johannes de Colonia and Johannes Manthen, September 13, 1475. This copy was bound, probably in London, by the Indulgence binder and bears the inscription "Petrus Potkyn habuit hunc librum ex venditione Mri Sterkey." Rhodes identified Peter Potkyn as a benefactor of New College (where the book now is) who died May 1, 1520.

[20]Dennis Everard Rhodes, "Don Fernando Colon and His London Book Purchases, June 1522," *Papers of the Bibliographical Society of America* 52 (1958): 231–58. Reprinted in idem., *Studies in Early European Printing and Book Collecting* (London, 1983), pp. 163–80. Ferdinand Columbus recorded the purchase of eighty books in London, exactly half of which were printed before 1501, and were therefore bought secondhand at least. He noted the price of each of them. His original records (in which he listed 4,231 items) are available in facsimile; see Archer Milton Huntington, *Catalogue of the Library of Ferdinand Columbus: Reproduced in Facsimile from the Unique Manuscript in the Columbia Library of Seville* (New York, 1905).

generation of readers, London had become one of those places that are distinguished as centers of culture because one goes there in the expectation of finding interesting secondhand books.

Appendix I: Sample of 1,000 Books Printed before 1500 with Early British Ownership

	Overall	Oxford colleges	Excluding colleges	Old Royal Library
Italy	40.4%	58%	29.2%	26%
Germany	31.5%	25%	35.5%	28%
France	16.5%	12%	19.5%	40%
Low Countries	11.6%	5%	15.8%	2%
Spain	–	–	–	–

OVERALL IN DECADES

	1461–1470	1471–1480	1481–1490	1491–1500	Total
	1.5%	23.5%	34.5%	40.5%	

Italy

	1461–1470	1471–1480	1481–1490	1491–1500	Total
Bologna		1	1	4	6
Brescia			5	3	8
Ferrara			1		1
Florence		1	6	4	11
Mantua		3			3
Milan		3	2	2	7
Naples		3			3
Padua		7	1		8
Pavia			4	4	8
Reggio d'Emilia			1	2	3
Rome	5	31	6	4	46
Treviso		2	7	3	12
Venice		67	79	137	285
Vicenza		1	1	2	4
Total	5	119	115	165	404

France and French-Speaking Countries

	1461–1470	1471–1480	1481–1490	1491–1500	Total
Geneva				1	1
Lyons		3	3	49	55
Paris		18	25	61	104
Rouen				5	5
Total		21	28	116	166

Appendix I (*Continued*)

	1461–1470	1471–1480	1481–1490	1491–1500	Total
Germany and German-Speaking Countries					
Augsburg		1	1	2	4
Basel		6	20	22	48
Cologne	5	29	45	12	91
Freiburg im Breisgau				1	1
Hagenau				3	3
Leipzig			4	1	5
Lübeck		2		1	3
Magdeburg				1	1
Mainz	3	3	1	1	8
Memmingen				1	1
Nuremberg		10	20	28	58
Reutlingen			1		1
Speier		2	6	2	10
Strasbourg	3	17	25	32	77
Tübingen				2	2
Ulm			2		2
Total	11	70	125	109	315
Low Countries					
Alost			2		2
Antwerp			17	6	23
Audenrade			1		1
Bruges		1	1		2
Brussels		3	4		7
Delft				1	1
Deventer		1	6	7	14
Ghent			1		1
Gouda			6		6
Louvain		12	40		52
Utrecht		7			7
Total		24	78	14	116

Appendix II: 391 Books in Oxford Colleges
with Early British Ownership

	1461–1470	1471–1480	1481–1490	1491–1500	Total
Italy					
Bologna		1		3	4
Brescia			4		4
Ferrara			1		1
Florence		1	5	1	7
Mantua		1			1
Milan		3	2	1	6
Naples		2			2
Padua			4	1	5
Pavia		2		6	8
Reggio d'Emilia			1	1	2
Rome	5	23	2		30
Treviso		1	5		6
Venice		31	42	73	146
Verona			1		1
Vicenza			1	2	3
Total	5	65	68	88	226
France					
Paris		7	3	10	20
Lyons		1	1	24	26
Total		8	4	34	46
Germany and German-Speaking Countries					
Augsburg			1		1
Basel		4	3	7	14
Cologne		4	7	2	13
Freiburg im Breisgau				1	1
Hagenau				1	1
Lübeck		1		1	2
Mainz	1	3			4
Nuremberg		5	12	9	26
Speier		2	1	1	4
Strasbourg	1	11	7	13	32
Ulm			1		1
Total	2	30	32	35	99

Appendix II (*Continued*)

	1461–1470	1471–1480	1481–1490	1491–1500	Total
Low Countries					
Antwerp				1	1
Brussels		1	2		3
Deventer			1	2	3
Louvain			10		10
Utrecht		3			3
Total		4	13	3	20

BOOKS PRINTED IN MAJOR CENTERS

	Rome	Venice	Paris	Lyons	Strasbourg	Nuremberg
before						
1470	5	–	–	–	1	–
1480	23	31	7	1	11	5
1490	2	42	3	1	7	12
1500	–	73	10	24	13	9
	30	146	20	26	32	26

[8]

Incunable Description and Its Implication for the Analysis of Fifteenth-Century Reading Habits

Paul Saenger and Michael Heinlen

In the past fifteen years the cataloguing of medieval and Renaissance manuscripts has flourished in America, England, and Germany, and with it the science of codicology. Such cataloguing has represented an international development of scholarship which has frequently laid as great or greater emphasis on the medium by which texts have been transmitted than on the texts themselves. Perhaps because in America the number of medieval manuscripts to be catalogued is relatively small, the zeal for exactness and comprehensive detail in describing manuscripts as artifacts has been particularly intense. The recently published and forthcoming catalogues of the Beinecke Library, the Huntington Library, the Walters Art Gallery, and the Newberry Library provide far more information concerning the physical aspects of individual books than do the ongoing cataloguing projects of the Bibliothèque Nationale or the British Library. As these American catalogues of medieval manuscripts appear, it is time to turn our attention from manuscript books to this nation's other great and largely ignored national treasure: codices containing pre-1500 printed texts.

Because of both their number and their quality, American collections of incunables deserve far more detailed cataloguing than now exists. In all, over 12,599 recorded titles and 47,188 copies are in

American libraries;[1] yet of our ten largest repositories, only two have published catalogues of their holdings, and these catalogues, like their contemporary European counterparts of the early twentieth century, were exclusively aimed at the incunable as printed book.[2] In contrast, three recent catalogues of West German collections offer a relatively more extensive body of copy-specific information; but even such catalogues, which show the influence of the excellent manuscript cataloguing now being done at the Bayerische Staatsbibliothek, give only modest attention to the manuscript texts contained in codices of which the principal significance is still assumed to be the printed works.[3] In these catalogues, description of annotations and alteration of punctuation is minimal or nonexistent.

The purpose of this essay is twofold. The first goal is to set forth a paradigm for viewing incunables based on the codicological principles developed in cataloguing medieval manuscripts. This paradigm is employable both as a worksheet and as a format for automated data retrieval.[4] The second is to suggest how the data thus obtained permit us to describe reading habits at the end of the Middle Ages. In the history of the book, evidence based on the perception of the individual artifact is inextricably related to the articulation of valid interpretations of general historical developments. For most American incunables the only catalogue remains Goff's *Incunabula in American Libraries,* a work of great value which, nevertheless, by its nature as a union list, omits almost all specific details that distinguish one copy from another. It is, however, very often the copy-specific attributes of the codices containing incunables that make them of potential interest to scholars, for, to a large degree, American incunables have been spared from the disbinding and rebinding that have eliminated from

---

[1]The number of incunables is based on Goff only and does not include those recorded in the Supplement or the H. P. Kraus reprint edition (Millwood, N.Y., 1973).

[2]The goals of this type of incunable cataloguing are clearly expressed by Henry Guppy, *Rules for the Cataloguing of Incunabula,* 2d rev. ed. (London, 1932). The sentiments expressed in these rules are clearly reflected in the incunable catalogues of the Huntington and Morgan libraries.

[3]Vera Sach, *Die Inkunabeln der Universitätsbibliothek und anderer öffentlicher Sammlungen in Freiburg im Breisgau und Umgebung* (Wiesbaden, 1985); Manfred von Arnim, *Katalog der Bibliothek Otto Schäfer Schweinfurt* (Stuttgart, 1984); Kurt Hans Staub with Christa Staub, *Die Inkunabeln der Nicolaus-Matz-Bibliothek (Kirchenbibliothek) in Michelstadt* (Michelstadt, 1984).

[4]See the appendix to this essay.

certain European collections much of what is most pertinent to the history of book manufacture, collections, and reading.[5]

The recent evolution of medieval manuscript cataloguing has placed considerable emphasis on description of support (paper or parchment), decoration, rubrication, reader marks, indices, marks of ownership, and bindings. It is immediately evident to those familiar with early printed books that precisely the same variable data, much of which is highly pertinent to the history of reading, can be gleaned from a scrupulous examination of incunables. Cataloguing incunables as codices allows us both to identify the unique aspects of each copy and to detect correlations between books of similar origin or provenance. By refining our conception of the variable aspects of incunables, we can also gain profound insight into as yet little-understood aspects of the production and the use of manuscript books in the later Middle Ages.[6]

Recent medieval manuscript catalogues have also redefined that which historically has been the primary function of all catalogues: the provision of access to the texts. For the eighteenth-century Benedictines of the Congregation de Saint-Maur, who prepared the excellent catalogue of medieval manuscripts in the Biliothèque Royale which today continues to serve as a principal finding tool for the manuscript holdings of the Bibliothèque Nationale, a manuscript's contents were the literary texts as copied by the scribe or scribes. The same Benedictines, in cataloguing printed books, recognized the equivalent textual unities to be the clearly denoted printed texts contained within each volume—that is, the titles that today usually correspond to those listed by Goff, the *Gesamtkatolog,* and other standard bibliographies of incunables. Such textual information formed a central concern for many nineteenth-century and early twentieth-century catalogues of incunables. Therefore for twentieth-century cataloguers to provide this kind of text identification as well as description of the printing

---

[5]The British Library and the Bibliothèque Nationale collections of incunables have been rebound in this manner, and their catalogues suppress all reference to copy-specific features.

[6]It is curious that cataloguers of medieval manuscripts, when they have described incunables in the context of composite volumes, have often treated them simply as printed texts without noting any copy-specific features; see, for example, Barbara Shailor, *Catalogue of Medieval and Renaissance Manuscripts in the Beinecke Rare Book and Manuscript Library, Yale University: Volume II MSS 251–500* (Binghamton, N.Y., 1987), MS 399.

itself again and again in each new catalogue of an incunable collection is of necessity a largely redundant task, which only provides data already admirably available in the *Gesamtkatalog,* the British Library's *Catalogue of Books Printed in the Fifteenth Century,* and other sources. Unfortunately, many American and European catalogues have engaged extensively in such repetitive description.[7] The new science of codicology, however, by broadening the definition of a manuscript's texts to include added glosses and commentaries, additions written on flyleaves and pastedowns, and especially fragments of earlier manuscript books and documents used as binding materials, has expanded the definition of an incunable's contents. All these newly defined texts, now regularly recorded in detailing the contents of a manuscript book, are present in many incunable codices.

The systematic examination of eighty-two incunable codices selected from the Newberry's collections to represent four of the principal geographic regions of incunable production (England, the Netherlands, south Germany, and northeast Italy) reveals examples of a variety of additional handwritten texts that do not form a part of the printed textual content. Such additions are recorded in three separate fields of our incunable paradigm.[8] Glosses and commentaries are recorded in field 4a. In our survey we encountered no book with a complete manuscript commentary added to a printed text. Examples of such texts have been recorded in other collections, however,[9] and a complete autograph marginal commentary of Pierre Froissart, forming a magistral university course on medicine, exists in a 1548 copy of Leonard Fuch's *De curandi ratione,* printed by J. de Tournes and Guillaume Gaseaux in Lyons in 1548.[10] We have retained this category in our description because we believe it likely that such texts may exist among the approximately two thousand volumes at the Newberry that contain incunables. Where continuous glosses or commentaries exist, their incipits and explicits ought to be recorded as in a catalogue of medieval manuscripts.

Additional texts written on separate quires, blank leaves, or flyleaves are recorded in field 4b. Examples of such additions include

[7]See, for example, Alfred W. Pollard, E. Gordon Duff, and Stephan Aldrich, *Catalogue of Manuscripts and Early Printed Books from the Libraries of William Morris, Richard Bennett, Bertram Fourth Earl of Ashburnham, and Other Sources Now Forming a Portion of the Library of J. Pierpont Morgan: Early Printed Books* (London, 1907).

[8]See our paradigm, included as the appendix to this essay.

[9]Von Arnim, *Katalog der Bibliothek Otto Schäfer,* no. 61.

[10]Aquired by the Newberry from Librairie Paul Jammes, Paris, in 1985.

Newberry incunable no. 5564, a Greek Psalter printed by Aldus Manutius c. 1496–1498.[11] This codex begins with a manuscript index table with reference to folios written by the same hand which added the foliation (fig. 8.1). Newberry incunable no. f1645, Pseudo Bonaventura, *Speculum beatae Mariae virginis,* printed by Anton Sorg of Augsburg in 1476, contains on its front flyleaf texts relating to the approbation at the Council of Basel of the doctrine of the Immaculate Conception added by a scribe who was intimately concerned with the overall confection of this book (fig. 8.2).[12] These textual additions are recorded in field 4b with cross-references to other fields so as to relate the added texts to a series of handwritten features for which the same scribe was responsible and which are discussed later in this essay.

Other handwritten texts which are unrecorded in Goff and either buried in or unrecorded by the Newberry's card catalogue are to be found in incunable no. 9056.5–9002.5.[13] This dual number represents a composite volume from the Carthusian monastery of Wesel containing two devotional texts printed in Deventer in 1492 and 1493, Theodoricus de Herxen, *Devota exercitia passionis* (Jacobus de Breda), and Johannes de Lapide, *Resolutorium dubiorum* (Richard Paffraet).[14] Between the two incunable elements, a contemporary monastic binder placed a quire of eight leaves of manuscript text, which includes a geographic table giving distances between the Charterhouse of Wesel and the Grande Chartreuse in Burgundy (fig. 8.3), excerpts of Bede and Ambrose on the Mass, a *Monotesseron* of the Passion, a *Speculum sacerdotum,* and a vernacular table of contents for the second incunable. Such information is recorded in our field 4b, and, just as it would be for a medieval manuscript, the heading, incipit, and, where appropriate and practical, the explicit ought to be transcribed.

The presence of table and indices among added texts is important because it shows ways in which incunables were used, affording interesting comparisons and contrasts with both prior and contemporary manuscript practice. The presence of more substantial manuscript texts is a potential indication of an appetite for texts that were not conveniently available in print, and which in at least some in-

[11]Goff P-1033.

[12]Goff B-959.

[13]Goff H-134 and J-360.

[14]The authors are indebted to Pieter Obbema, Keeper of Western Manuscripts at the University of Leiden, for his assistance in identifying the provenance and manuscript texts of this codex.

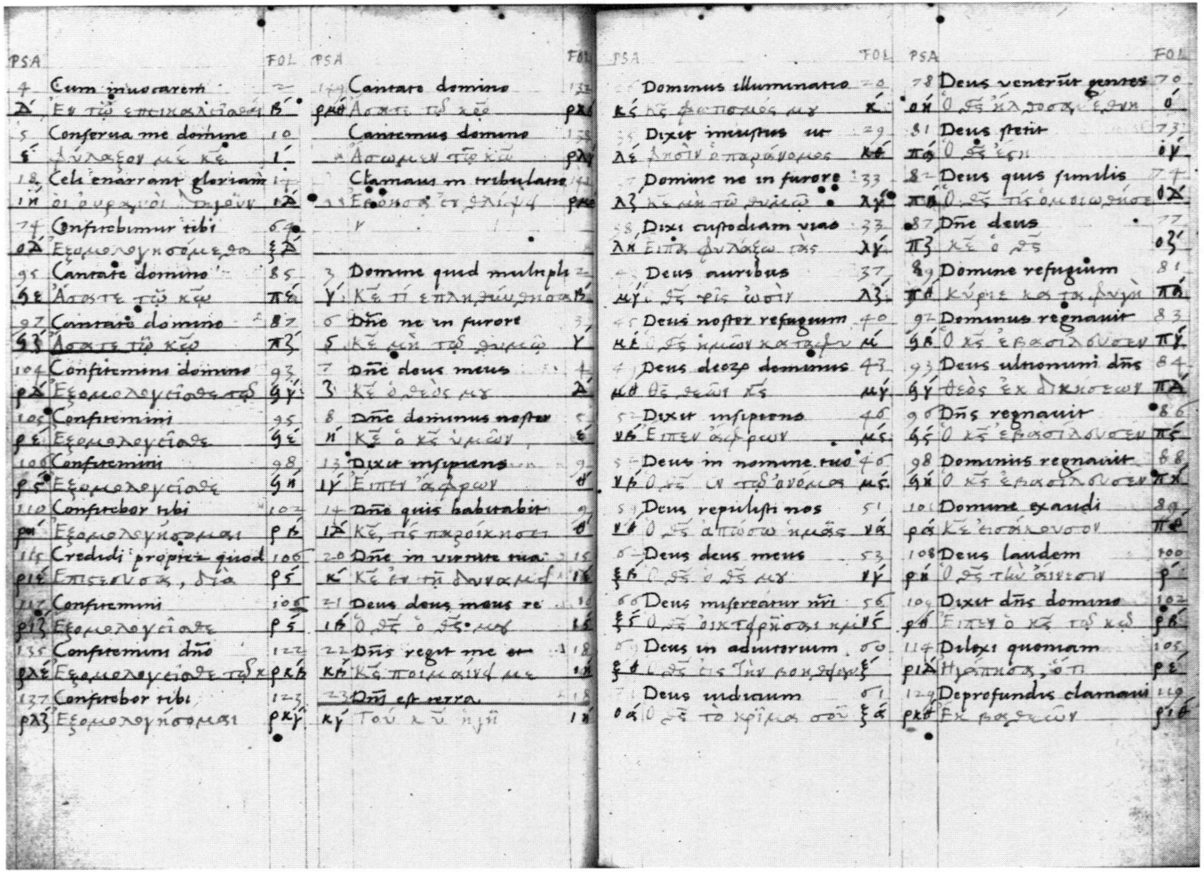

Figure 8.1. Manuscript index, from Psalter in Greek, Venice, Aldus Manutius, c.1496–1498, Chicago, Newberry Library, Inc. 1161, fols. 1v–2. Courtesy of the Newberry Library.

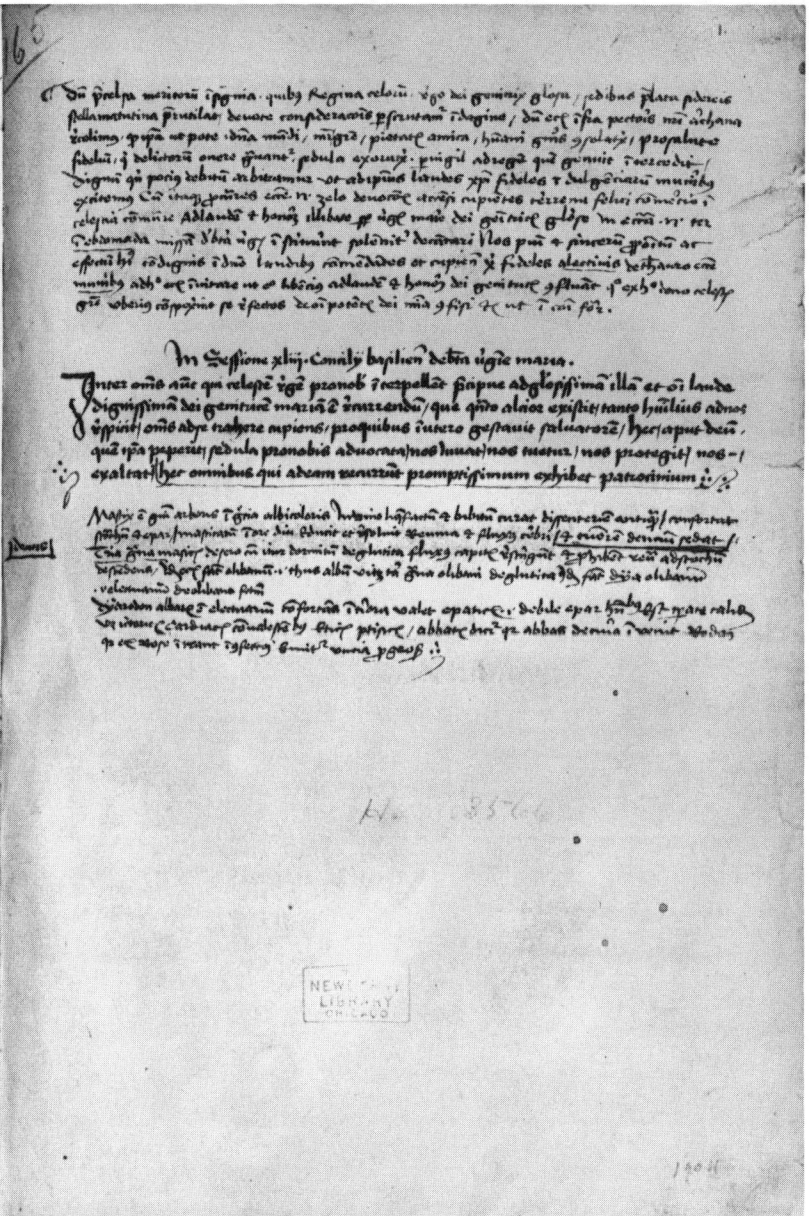

Figure 8.2. Manuscript texts, from Pseudo Bonaventura, *Speculum beatae Mariae virginis,* Augsburg, Anton Sorg, 1476, Chicago, Newberry Library, Inc. f1645, fol. 1. Courtesy of the Newberry Library.

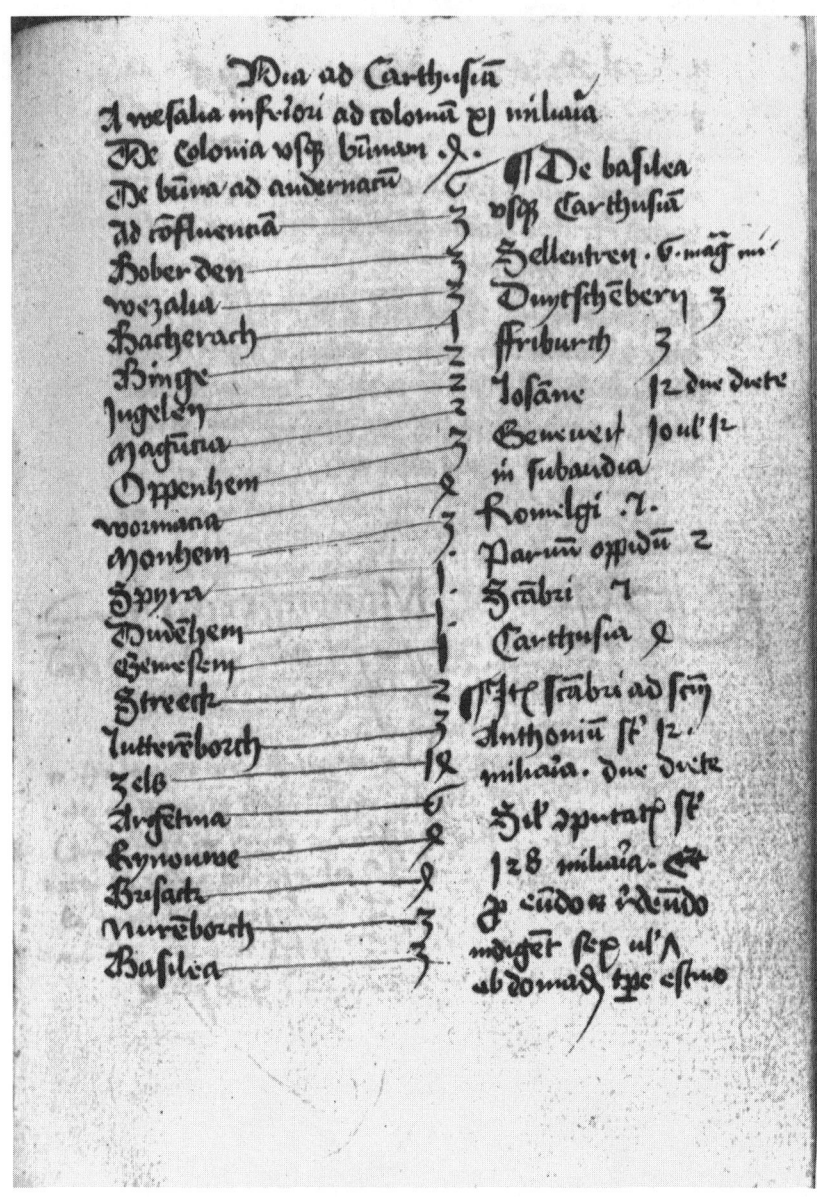

Figure 8.3. Manuscript table of the distance to the Grande Chartreuse, from Theodoricus de Herxen, *Devota exercitia passionis,* Deventer, Jacobus de Breda, 1492, and Johannes de Lapide, *Resolutorium dubiorum,* Deventer, Richard Paffraet, 1492, Chicago, Newberry Library, Inc. 9056.5–9002.5, fol. 101. Courtesy of the Newberry Library.

stances may have been uniquely intended for the use of a particular individual owner. Such added texts often represented personal excerpts of lengthy works and works in the vernacular which the owner sought to juxtapose with texts readily available in printed Latin.

The eighty-two incunable volumes examined for this survey included a number of fragments preserved as flyleaves or pastedowns which predate the printed elements. Such texts are also recorded in field 4c. The composite book described in the preceding paragraph contains as a pastedown and front flyleaf a folio of a still-unidentified thirteenth-century theological work, which was reused as a table of distinctions pertinent to the first printed text of the volume. The binder of incunable no. f1543(i), a volume containing one of Reinerius de Pisis' *Pantheologia,* used as pastedowns two substantial fragments of a late medieval Hebrew copy of the Book of Numbers (fig. 8.4).[15] The binder of incunable f9677, Christine de Pisan's *Fayt of Armes and of Chyvalarye,* printed in Westminster by Caxton in 1489, used three *bifolia* of a fifteenth-century liturgical book (possibly a breviary) as pastedowns,[16] and in incunable no. 3215.4/3215.5, containing editions of George of Brussels' *Cursus optimarum quaestionum super philosophiam Aristotelis cum interpretatione textus secundum viam modernorum*[17] and *Cursus optimarum quaestionum super totam logicam,*[18] both printed in Freiburg im Breisgau in 1496, the pastedowns were formed from a fragment of a fifteenth-century manuscript of an exposition of Aristotle's *De anima.*

Some binding fragments are significant in their own right for their content and textual variants, and all of them indisputably provide examples of books that people evidently were no longer interested in reading. In terms of textual content, format, and legibility, this corpus of reused debris generated by the apparently intentional destruction of old manuscript books and documents is potentially highly important as negative evidence for the history of reading habits. Only careful individual cataloguing and enumeration will allow us to detect patterns, confirmable by quantitative analysis, that may be significant for intellectual and social history.

[15]Goff R-6. The authors are indebted to Michael Terry, director of the Norman and Helen Asher Library of Spertus College of Judaica, for identifying this text.
[16]Goff C-472.
[17]Goff G-147; Proctor 7609.
[18]Goff G-148; Hain *3965.

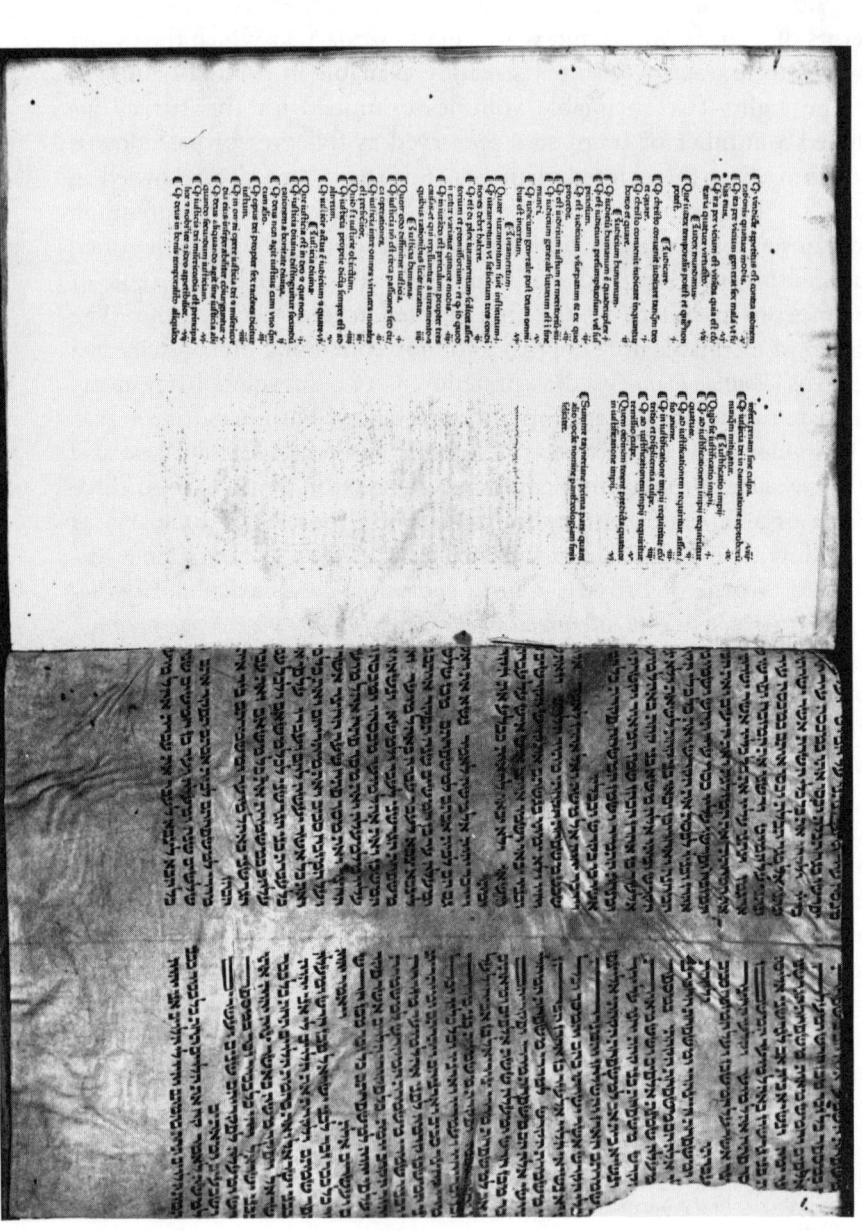

Figure 8.4. Manuscript fragment of Numbers 3:21–4, 30 from the binding, from Reinerius de Pisis, *Pantheologia*, Augsburg, Gunther Zainer, 1474, Chicago, Newberry Library, Inc. f1543. Courtesy of the Newberry

We may hope also that the codicological examination of incunable bindings may elucidate certain pervasive patterns in this textual destruction of old books for binding materials which may be directly related to the history of printing. The example, mentioned earlier, of Newberry incunable no. 3215.4/3215.5 is intriguing in this light. The first of the two printed titles contained in this volume, Aristotle's *Cursus quaestionum super philosophiam,* printed in Freiburg im Breisgau, contains a text in printed form closely related to that found in the very difficult-to-read fifteenth-century manuscript fragment used for the pastedowns (fig. 8.5). This appears to be a potential instance of a book bound at a scholastic center which was purposefully destroying manuscript books as superfluous and hard to read once more legible printed editions of the same works had been obtained. If the origin of this volume were to be established, and if the practice of the destruction of similar manuscript texts were to be confirmed from the other surviving books from the same library, it would permit us to document an important dimension of printing's impact on reading patterns—one that curiously parallels the effect of the introduction of word separation in the eleventh century.[19]

Modern descriptions of medieval manuscripts, prepared under the influence of codicology, carefully record all marks of ownership and notes pertaining to provenance. From this vantage point incunables contain as much significant data as late medieval manuscripts, for, as Dominique Coq has explained, librarians of the fifteenth century made no distinction between manuscripts and printed books in providing bindings, marks of ownership, summary tables of contents, and shelf marks.[20] Old press marks—which manuscript cataloguers such as, for example, Albinia de la Mare in her catalogue of the Lyell Collection at the Bodleian have painstakingly transcribed— are recorded in fields 7b and 7c.[21] Vera Sach's catalogue of incunables at the municipal library in Freiburg im Breisgau reflects important strides in recording such data.[22] Of the eighty-two incunables sur-

---

[19]The use of unseparated manuscripts in the bindings of eleventh-century codices is a topic considered by Paul Saenger in his forthcoming study on the evolution of word separation and its impact on medieval reading habits.

[20]Dominique Coq, "L'incunable, un bâtard du manuscrit?" *Gazette du livre médiéval* I (1981): 10–11.

[21]Albinia de la Mare, *Catalogue of the Collection of Medieval Manuscripts Bequeathed to the Bodleian Library, Oxford, by James P. R. Lyell* (Oxford, 1971).

[22]See note 3.

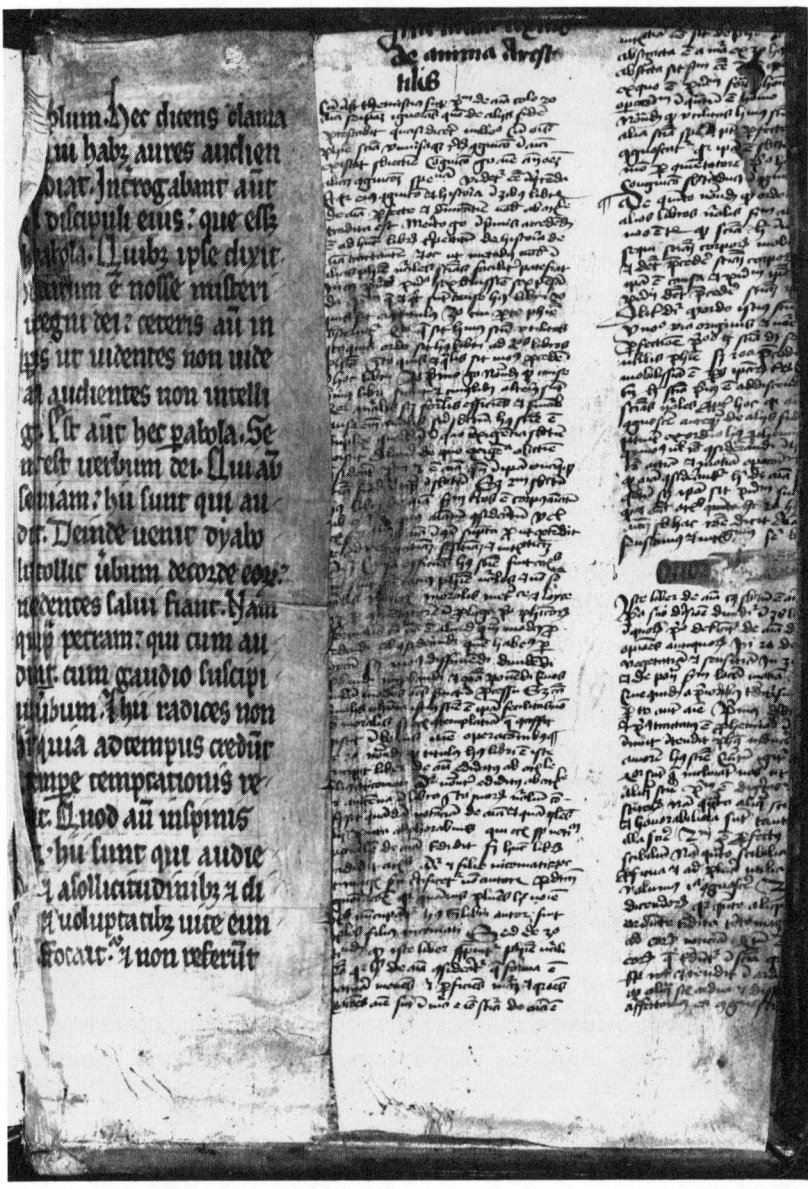

Figure 8.5. Manuscript text of Aristotle, *De anima,* from George of Brussels, *Cursus optimarum quaestionum super philosophiam Aristotelis cum interpretatione textus secundum viam modernorum,* and *Cursus optimarum quaestionum super totam logicam,* Freiburg im Breisgau, 1496, Chicago, Newberry Library, Inc. 3215.4/3215.5, rear pastedown. Courtesy of the Newberry Library.

veyed at the Newberry, twenty-two show early marks of ownership, and twelve of these indicate monastic ownership. These statistics are roughly comparable to those of the Newberry's pre-1500 manuscript holdings.[23] Twenty percent of the Newberry incunables sampled were still housed in original or fere contemporary bindings; in these instances full description of binding may yield additional identifications of ownership, and thereby the fragments of texts found within these bindings may yet be assigned specific provenances. Notes on the binding proper are recorded in field 8. These notes include identification or description of stamps and of watermarks found on original pastedowns or endleaves when they differ from that of the text. Incunables will undoubtedly provide missing links for the identification of certain binding stamps, and this in turn will permit the attribution of additional fragmentary texts to known libraries, particularly monastic and university collections. The presence of edge, cover, and spine titles may also reveal important patterns in shelving and information retrieval, particularly in regard to the highly significant transition from horizontal to vertical shelving which began to take place at the end of or shortly after the incunable period.[24] The fifteenth-century edge title of incunable no. +4019, Augustine, *De civitate Dei*, printed by Johannes and Vindelinus de Spira in Venice in 1470, is illustrative of this important genre of evidence (fig. 8.6).[25]

The systematic description and classification of American incunable bindings and identification of ex libris will also undoubtedly yield significant fruit for students interested in the global contents of late medieval manuscript libraries, where manuscript books and printed works were frequently bound by the same artisans and intershelved in the same process. For incunable no. 3215.4/3215.5, the sixteenth-century pressmark on the fore edge may indeed be the key for identifying the origin of both binding and manuscript fragments and may also cast light on evolving shelving practices. Even where we as cataloguers will not be able to identify the origin of a pressmark, a binding, or a manuscript fragment, careful description and selective reproduction in published catalogues will provide information for

---

[23]Paul Saenger, *A Catalogue of pre-1500 Western Manuscript Books at the Newberry Library* (Chicago, 1989).

[24]T. Kimball Brooker, Ph.D. candidate in the Department of Art History of the University of Chicago, is embarked on a study on this important topic.

[25]Goff A-1233.

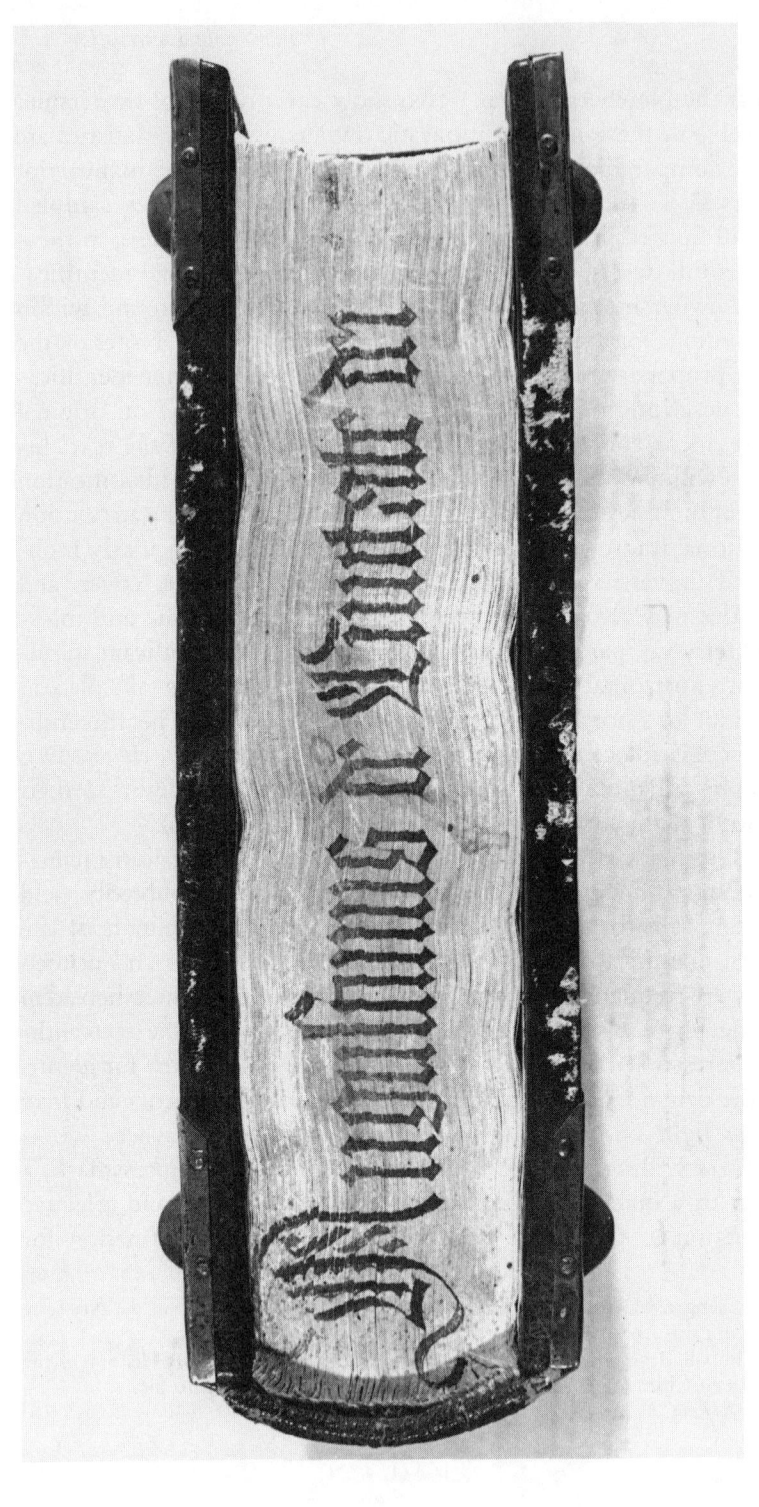

Figure 8.6. Edge title, from Augustine, *De civitate Dei*, Venice, Johannes and Vindelinus de Spira, 1470. Chicago, Newberry Library, Inc. +4019. Courtesy of the Newberry Library.

others to make connections between Newberry volumes and manuscripts and related incunables in other institutions. To some this claim
may seem overly bold, given the wide array of editions and presses
represented in American libraries. Viewed from a copy-specific vantage point, however, American collections may prove less diverse
than one might at first suppose. The Newberry, like most American
incunable collections, in general reflects the dissolution of German
and Austrian monastic libraries which began in the Napoleonic period and continued through the years preceeding the Second World
War. Thus the manuscript fragments contained in incunables in
America offer an especially rich resource for reconstituting the contents of south German and Austrian monastic and university collections and, thereby, for elucidating the specific reading habits of medieval central Europe.

Incunables also provide an invaluable source for the reading habits
of the late Middle Ages in more direct ways. Precisely because in
incunables the substratum of the principal text was printed, the division of labor between the copier of the text and the emendator or
emendators, who corrected the punctuation, added the foliation as
well as the rubrics, and provided annotations as finding notes for the
reader, was less problematic than in many late-medieval manuscript
books. In many fifteenth-century manuscript books it is frequently
difficult to distinguish with certainty the hand of the emendator from
that of the scribe. Moreover, the systematic examination of incunables
for handwritten added features reveals that the commonly supposed
distinction between these two different classes of manuscript additions to the principal text—those in colored ink and those in the ink
of the text—is often arbitrary. In our paradigm, handwritten additions to the principal texts are recorded in two fields: 5f (rubricating)
and 6 (non-red reader marks). In fact no firm distinction can be made
between that which is described as rubrication because it is in red ink
and annotations performing the same function made in black ink.
Contrary to what we had anticipated, emendations in red often followed the placement of emendations in black, including reader notes.
This observation has led us to understand these notes to constitute
provisions for the reader, and not necessarily, as is often thought,
evidence of reader use.

The interrelation of rubrication and reader notes can be vividly documented by a number of codices which we have examined on a preliminary basis. In incunable no. f1645, the Pseudo Bonaventura of Anton Sorg discussed earlier, reader notes in black ink including pointing hands, finding notes, and schematic diagrams were rubricated—that is, touched with and underlined in red by the same hand that underlined incipits, quotations, and authorities in the printed text (fig. 8.7). The rubricator also provided tie notes linking the printed text and marginal glosses. The reader notes were actually written by the same hand that added the supplementary flyleaf texts.[26] Thus, rather than being a standardized printed book, incunable no. f1645 represents a unique codex formed from an immutable printed substratum, clarified, annotated, and augmented by the scribe of the reader notes, whom we shall identify as the reader-emendator, and then further clarified by another scribe, the rubricator. In an extreme instance a scribe and rubricator might completely recopy a printed text, reproducing it verbatim, but substantially modifying both punctuation and decoration. Newberry manuscript no. +92 is an example of a codex copied directly from an incunable incorporating substantial revisions in punctuation from that of the incunable and decoration radically differ from that of the Newberry copy.[27]

In incunable no. f8843, Bernard of Clairvaux's *De consideratione,* printed by Nicolaus Ketelaer and Gearardus de Leempt in Utrecht c.1473, manuscript reader notes including symbols were stroked in red by the same rubricating hand that underlined the incipits and explicits, added red initials, and touched the printed capitals (fig. 8.8).[28] In incunable no. 1695, Johannes Nider's *Consolatorium timoratae conscientiae,* printed by Anton Sorg c.1484, initials, underlining, paragraph marks, and all reader notes were done in red by the hand of a single scribe.[29] This rubricator, acting as reader-emendator, foliated the codex with arabic numerals, highlighted existing punctuation, and added supplementary punctuation, including *traits d'union* at line endings. The correlation between arabic numbers and foliation is

---

[26]The flyleaf contains a discussion of the Immaculate Conception directly related to the printed contents of the volume.

[27]Hain 13955. For bibliography on the phenomenon of manuscript copies of incunables, see M. D. Reeve, "Manuscripts Copied from Printed Books," in *Manuscripts in the Fifty Years after the Invention of Printing: Some Papers Read at a Colloquium at the Warburg Institute on 12–13 March 1982,* ed. J. B. Trapp (London, 1983), pp. 12–20.

[28]Goff B-367.

[29]Goff N-167.

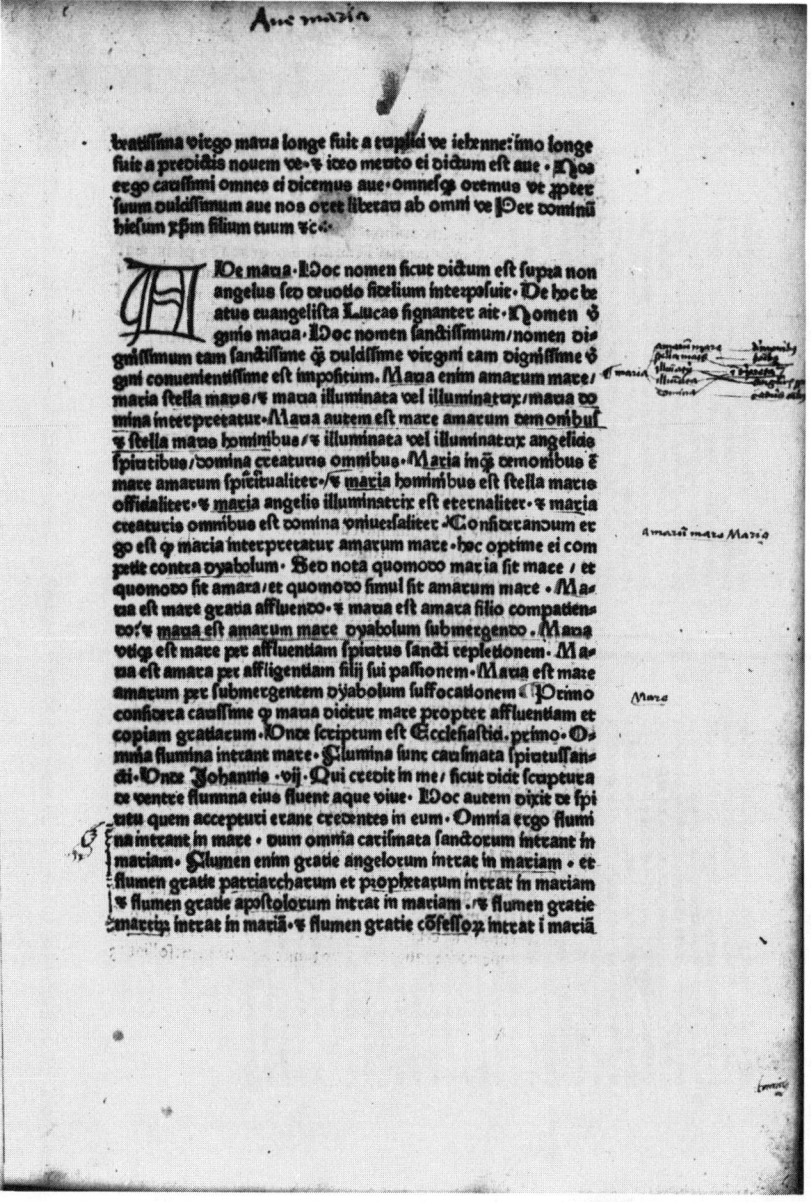

Figure 8.7. Reader's notes and finding notes, from Pseudo Bonaventura, *Speculum beatae Mariae virginis,* Augsburg, Anton Sorg, 1476, Chicago, Newberry Library, Inc. f1645, fol. 5. Courtesy of the Newberry Library.

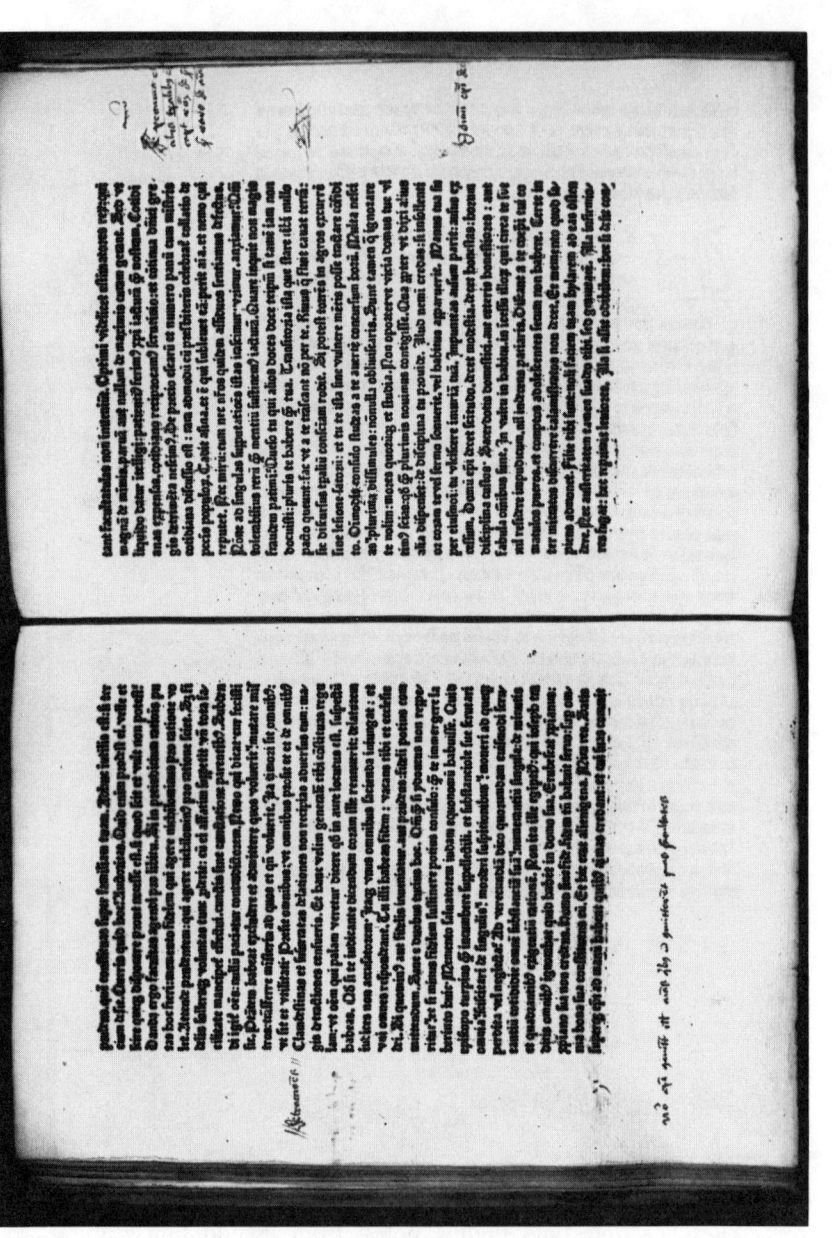

Figure 8.8. Reader's notes, from Bernard of Clairvaux, *De consideratione*, Utrecht, Nicolaus Ketelaer and Gerardus de Leempt, c.1473, Chicago, Newberry Library, Inc. f8843, fols. 27v–28. Courtesy of the Newberry Library

already a subject of interest to manuscript specialists, and the close cataloguing of incunabula should add important data.[30] The rubricator of incunable no. 1695 also transliterated verbal numbers in the texts as arabic numbers in the margin. We have designated this kind of reader notation, which also occurs in late medieval manuscripts, as redundant marginal numeration. Such redundant numeration was surprisingly common in our sample, and therefore it seems clearly to have been deemed highly useful for mnemonic purposes. We have reserved special fields within our description for it.[31] The rubricator also provided *nota* signs and finding notes, all entirely in red. For this codex it is clear that the rubricator-scribe envisioned his task to be a global confection of the book.

In incunable no. fi525, containing Rodrigo Sánchez de Arévalo's *Speculum vitae humanae,* printed by Gunther Zainer in Augsburg in 1471, the rubricator-scribe painted major initials, added paragraph markers and stroked capitals, and added finding notes and finding symbols in the margins.[32] Comparisons of these notes to other symbols and notes added in black ink by the reader-emendator reveal that he and the rubricator were in this instance one person using different inks.

Additions in both black and red ink were also intended to elucidate the text through the addition of supplemental punctuation to that already provided in print. Early incunables were typically far less punctuated than late-fifteenth-century manuscripts, and additional handwritten punctuation therefore provided the full complement of reader aids that would have been present in a comparable manuscript book.[33] In fulfilling this task of emendation, the scribe of incunable no. fi525 provided apparatus that in the context of a manuscript we might conventionally assign either to the scribe of the text or to a subsequent reader apparently unrelated to the book's preparation. In this manner detailed work on incunables inevitably leads to the reexamination of similar phenomena in contemporary manuscripts and may add to our understanding of a division of labor in late medieval

---

[30]A surprisingly high percentage of late medieval foliation is in arabic numbers rather than roman numerals; see Saenger, *Catalogue,* p. 257.

[31]Fields 5fi3 and 6g.

[32]Goff R-215.

[33]See Christiane Marchello-Nizia, "Ponctuation et unités de lecture dans les manuscrits médiévaux, ou: je ponctue, tu lis, il théorise," *Langue française* 40 (1978): 32–44.

scriptoria which appears to have been simply transferred to the printshops or monastic scriptoria that specialized in the confecting of incunables.[34]

The modification of printed texts by reader notes appears to be a frequent feature of the incunable. Over 75 percent of our sample evinces reader annotations in either red or black ink or both, and 12 percent evince handwritten reworking of punctuation. The simplest form of such modification was touching the printed punctuation with red ink so as to make it visible to the reader, and in this sense the highlighting of capitals in red or other colors served as a form of punctuation.[35] Indeed, the critical importance of capitalization as a form of punctuation is made abundantly clear by the examination of incunables. But the manuscript punctuating of printed texts went much further. In incunable no. f1566, Thomas à Kempis' *Imitatio Christi*, printed in Augsburg by Günther Zainer before June 5, 1473, a scribe added marks in black ink after terminal *puncti* so as to render these periods into signs of interrogation (fig. 8.9), and the same reader-emendator corrected transposed letters with a sign resembling a circumflex.[36] In a number of books the reader-emendator separated words with a simple vertical stroke where the printer's space seemed insufficient. This sign, which we call the vertical diastole, and which is frequently found in post-tenth-century manuscripts, was one of several medieval equivalents to the ancient diastole. The fusion of Gothic script increased the use of this form of diacritical note in manuscripts of the late Middle Ages, and the reader-emendator of f1566 used it repeatedly. In incunable no. 1713, Jacobus de Gruytrode's *Lavacrum conscientiae*, printed in Augsburg in 1489 by Anton Sorg, the reader-emendator, using black ink, employed the vertical diastole to separate words and phrases.[37] The same reader-emendator also accented the letter *i*, an important diacritical mark, first employed in the eleventh and twelfth centuries, for helping the reader recognize words containing adjacent letters composed of minimum strokes (fig. 8.10). In the same book the rubricator added numerous marks of punctuation in red. Since both the rubricator and

---

[34]See, for example, Newberry Library MSS -94 and f96.

[35]See Marchello-Nizia's interesting discussion of this often ignored subject in "Ponctuation."

[36]Goff I-4.

[37]Goff L-97.

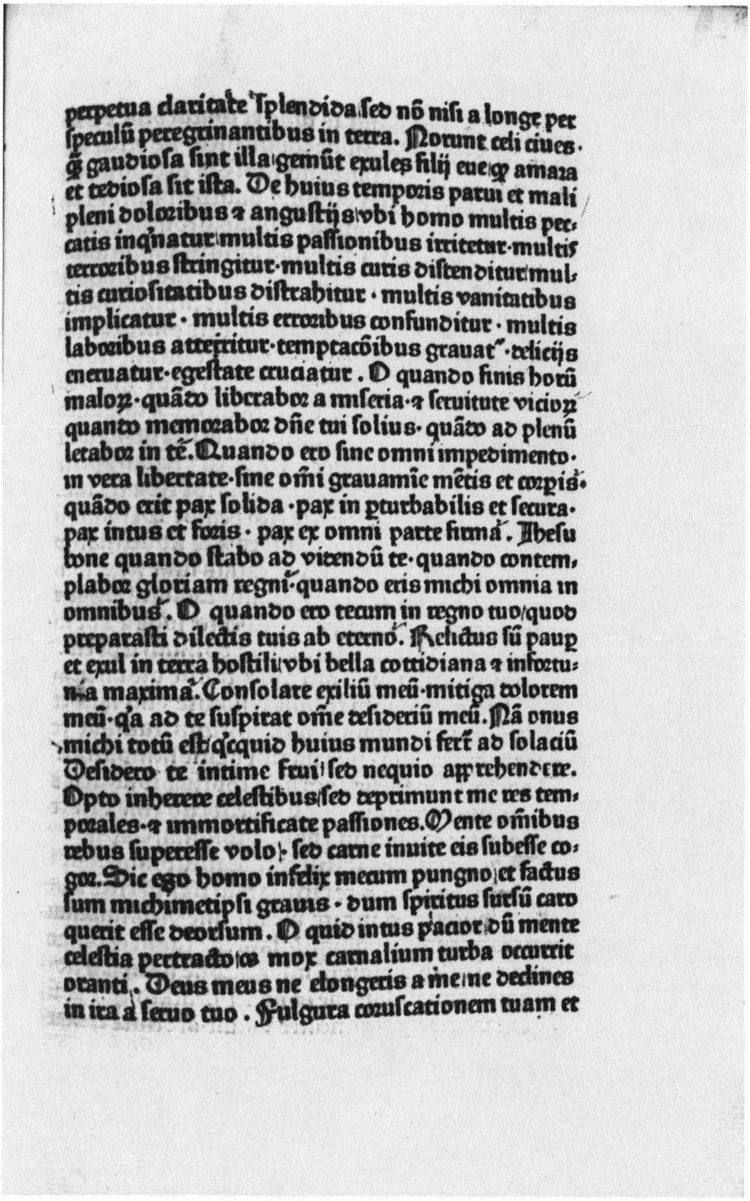

Figure 8.9. Punctuation and corrections added by hand, from Thomas à Kempis, *Imitatio Christi,* Augsburg, Günther Zainer, before June 5, 1473, Chicago, Newberry Library, Inc. fl566, fol. 50. Courtesy of the Newberry Library.

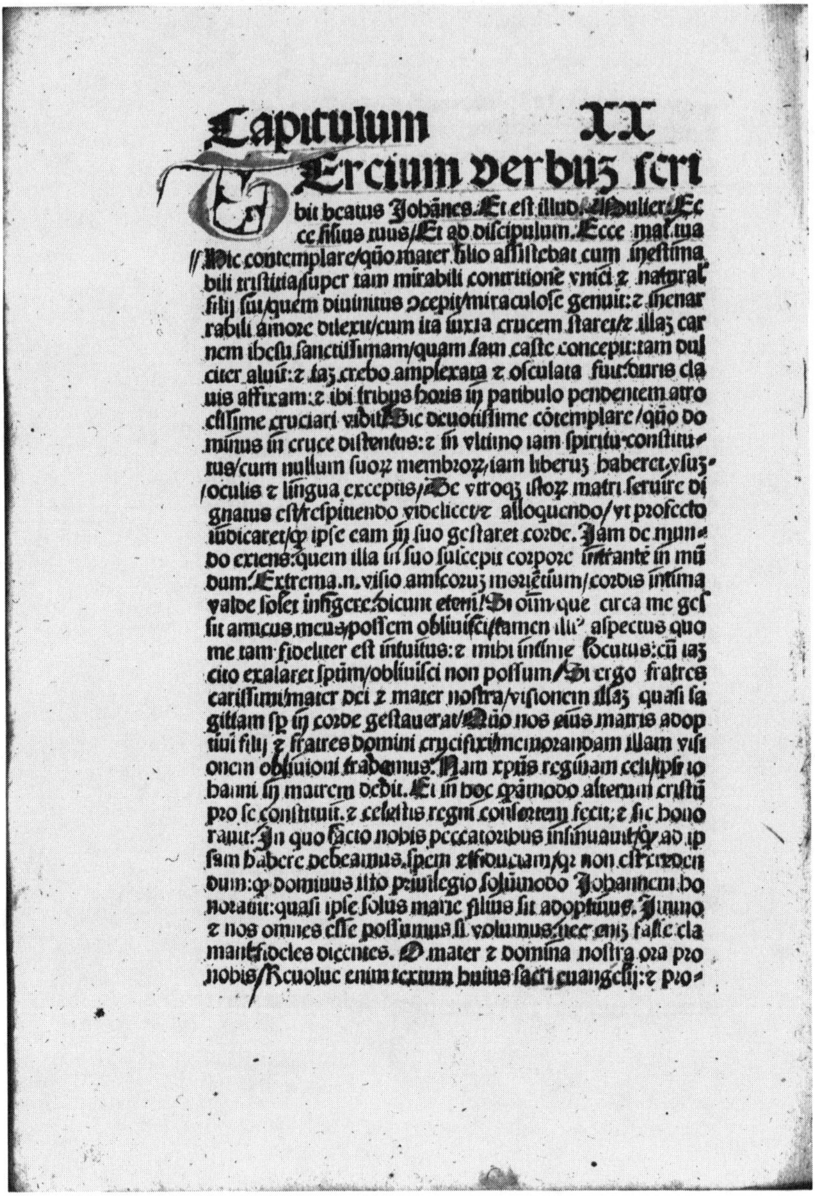

Figure 8.10. Reader emendations, from Jacobus de Gruytrode, *Lavacrum conscientiae*, Augsburg, Anton Sorg, 1489, Chicago, Newberry Library, Inc. 1713, fol. 76v. Courtesy of the Newberry Library.

the reader-emendator dated their handwritten additions 1491, we can be sure that they were collaborating in clarifying the printed text within two years of the printed book's impression. The dating of rubrication and reader annotation provide a time frame for the confection of printed books and therefore yields facts of crucial significance for which fields have been reserved within our paradigm description.[38] Dated rubrication and reader notation and codicological comparisons between different copies of the same work and of volumes from the same libraries are the key to determining whether printed books were confected by the printer, by monastic scriptoria, or, as many surely were, by private owners working independently, often well after the date of impression.[39]

One of the most frequent forms of emended punctuation was the adding of *traits d'union,* sometimes in red but, to judge from both our sample and common experience, more usually in black, as in incunable no. f8966, Leonardo de Utino's *Quadragesimale: Sertum fidei,* printed by Richard Paffraet in Deventer before 1480.[40] The most common form of *trait d'union* added to incunables was in two lines, but the one-line form is also known. In incunable no. f8966 the reader-emendator who added the *trait d'union* also added accenting to the letter *i,* finding notes, brackets, *notas,* and arabic foliation on the verso of each leaf (fig. 8.11). The rubricator in turn added punctuation points and some accenting, making this volume another example of collaborative elucidation. Another reader-added feature, historically and functionally related to punctuation, was the alteration of terminal letter forms, of which the most common was the lengthening of the letter *i* at the end of words to form a distinctive terminal *i* form. This type of emendation also constituted a continuity with eleventh- and twelfth-century practice. Correspondingly, certain printers reserved special forms of the letters *i, a,* and *r* for the initial and terminal positions.[41]

[38]Fields 5f11 and 6h.

[39]Close cataloguing is crucial for determining this fact. We cannot respond in regard to the Nicholaus Matz library, because this kind of detail was not recorded in the Michelstadt catalogue (see note 3). Newberry incunable no. +1418, containing Pliny, *Historia naturalis,* printed by Johannes de Spira before September 18, 1469, was still in the process of being confected in 1497.

[40]Goff L-141.

[41]Nicolas Jenson used the capital form of *R* at word endings falling at the end of lines. For the special forms of the letter *a, i,* and *r* used at the extremities of words, see Lotte Hellinga, *Caxton in Focus: The Beginning of Printing in England* (London, 1982), pp. 55–67.

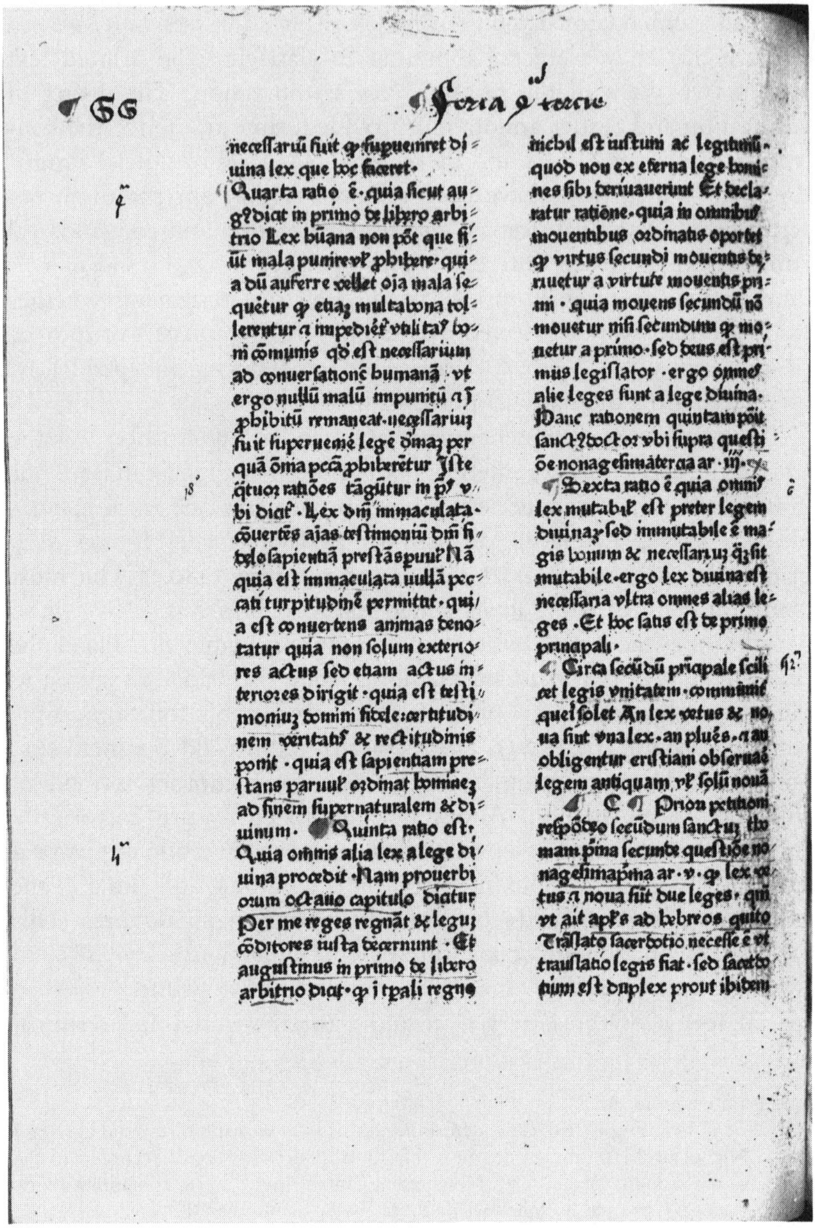

Figure 8.11. Reader emendations, from Leonardo de Utino, *Quadragesimale: Sertum fidei,* Deventer: Richard Paffraet, before 1480, Chicago, Newberry Library, Inc. f8966, fol. 66v. Courtesy of the Newberry Library.

The evidence we have seen suggests that reader-emendators and rubricators, who were sometimes a single individual, worked on several levels. First, they provided those marks the ancients termed *prosodiae* (accents, vertical diastoles, *traits d'union*) which helped readers recognize individual words. Second, they provided the punctuation marks the ancients termed *posturae* (including full stops, question marks, and signs of quotation) which clarified the meaning and delimited the boundaries of phrases and sentences. And third, they added major initials, paragraph marks, foliation, and running headings to break prose texts down into larger units of sense. The same hand that performed these three functions also frequently provided marginalia to elucidate the meaning of text and facilitate the retrieval of information. A copy of Diodorus Siculus, *Bibliothecae historiae libri VI,* printed in Venice by Andreas de Paltaszichis on January 31, 1477, formerly in the private library of a Tuscan priest and recently acquired by the Newberry, contains the following note: "I Louis, priest of Puperio presently at Pisa on 20 November 1484, according to the calendar of Florence, read and wrote the words and historical facts in alphabetically distributed series in the margins of this book to the extent that thus far I have located them in all my codices, because notes of this sort greatly aid our memory."[42] Generally marginal mnemonic notes included pointing hands, *nota* marks, redundant numbers, encoded signs, authority identification, biblical references, and schematic diagrams. The use of schematic diagrams in particular emulated a medieval practice which had continued in manuscript codices without interruption from the eleventh century onward.

For all these annotations, varying from clarification at the level of the word to the delimitation of complex units of abstract thought, the scribe as emendator was required to undertake careful reading of the text, and this careful reading must be recognized as an essential element in the final stage of the confection of the early printed book,

---

[42]Goff D-211. The note on the last leaf reads: "Ego Ludouicus presbiter de Puppio [Poppi, in the province of Arezzo] in presentiarum Pisis, die 20 nouembris 1484 more florentino hoc opus lectitaui et uerborum historiarumque seriem in alphabeti margine digessi quemadmodum in omnibus meis codicibus hactenus confeci, quoniam huiusmodi modus plurimum memoriae nostrae confert." We are indebted to Armando Petrucci for the transcription of this note. The meaning of "alphabeti digessi" in this context is not clear, but it may refer either to the medieval convention of alphabetical loci within the margins or to the fact that the words in the margin are spelled out in letters rather than noted emblematic encoded symbols.

whether done by professionals working close to the press, or by monks in an abbey scriptorium, or by laymen in their private libraries. In the final analysis, the ambiguous division of this task between manufacturer and owner implies a psychology of reading incunables distinctly different from that of modern books. The modern reader, if he or she adds marginalia, records personal reactions to the reading of the text. In contrast, the late medieval reading notes found in incunables reflect a preoccupation with clarifying the text on behalf of the community of the lettered through the removal of all visual ambiguity. This effort culminated in a desire to render each page into a memorable image, easily retainable and accessible to subsequent readers. Textual accuracy also represented a natural component of reader concern, and, to an astonishing degree, incunables were collated against other editions and manuscripts, and textual emmendations added.[43] (The presence of such textual correction is recorded in field 6e.) Comparison of handwriting reveals that such emmendations were often the work of the reader-emendator.

The early incunable page was, when fully confected, a colored page, like that of the post-tenth-century medieval manuscript.[44] The choice of color used in incunables is a matter of some importance and is recorded in three fields in our description.[45] A consistent nomenclature for the use of color is thus of crucial importance, and we have therefore employed as an authority the *Stanley Gibbons Stamp Colour Key*.[46] It is our impression, based on this initial survey, that the exclusive use of various shades of red was generally far more frequent in incunables than in fifteenth-century manuscripts. In manuscripts the exclusive use of red was characteristically German, and it is reasonable to suppose that its prevalence in incunables reflected the Teutonic origins of the printing craft.[47] Even in northern Italy, a region in which yellow washes and violet rubrics appear frequently in ordinary fifteenth-century manuscript codices, printed codices seem, from our survey, rarely to have been highlighted in colors other than various shades of red.

[43]Lotte Hellinga, "Manuscripts in the Hands of Printers," in Trapp, *Manuscripts in the Fifty Years after the Invention of Printing*, pp. 3–11.

[44]See incunable no. 9002.5 (note 13).

[45]Fields 5a, 5e3, and 5f2.

[46]For alternative color guides, see G. Thomas Tanselle, *Selected Studies in Bibliography* (Charlottesville, Va., 1979), pp. 139–70.

[47]See Newberry Library manuscript no. 90.1, in Saenger, *Catalogue*, pp. 166–69.

The colored page, so common to the late medieval book, had its beginning in the eleventh and twelfth centuries, when the written page of Western manuscripts had undergone so many rapid and enduring changes. In the twelfth century rubricators used red and other colored initials, frequently green and blue, to make each leaf a memorable and quasi-unique mnemonic locus. The technology of printing and the new humanistic conception of the page, based to a considerable degree on a desire to reject Gothic tradition and to emulate the oldest Caroline manuscripts, gradually effected a return to a blacker page characterized by an impression of relatively uninterrupted script. In an objective sense, one can wonder if this blackening of the page represented an advance for legibility, or if rather an important mnemonic quality was lost along with the loss of color. Whatever our final conclusion may be, and the use of felt-tipped markers by modern readers may give us pause for thought, the corpus of books printed before 1500 provides important data on the increasing prevalence of "black" books, many of the earliest of which were simply never fully confected by the reader-emendator or rubricator. The prevalence of such books helped to effect by the second decade of the sixteenth century the gradual triumph of the clean copy so cherished by nineteenth- and twentieth-century bibliophiles.[48]

One simple consequence of this evolution in book mentality pertains to punctuation. The modern configuration of the paragraph, formed by indentation, as opposed to the ancient and medieval paragraph, of which the first line extended into the margin, was born in incomplete books in which initials and rubricating were wanting. Such truncated books, virtually unknown from the eleventh to the fourteenth centuries, became increasingly common in fifteenth-century manuscripts. Printing increased their percentage of the whole beyond any precedent. The explanation for this prevalence of not fully confected books was the growing disequilibrium between the increased ability of scribes, using cursive and hybrid scripts, to produce texts and the inelastic ability of rubricators and reader-emendators to read, understand, and complete them. This disequilibrium, which was greatly exacerbated by printing, was initially most evident in regions of Europe, notably the Netherlands and Germany, where

---

[48]Only the careful application of a paradigm of analysis similar to that which we are proposing for incunables will reveal precisely when in the sixteenth century printers ceased to provide guide letters for rubricators.

the patrimony of books (as defined by Ezio Ornato and Carla Bozzolo) was limited, and the need of new books, both manuscript and printed, was consequently most intense.[49] Nonetheless, even in Italy, France, and England, where the corpus of books inherited from earlier generations was incomparably greater, each year a higher percentage of books seems to have been left unfinished. The convention of the indented paragraph represents the acceptance of the unfinished book as normative.

In order to document the unfinished quality of incunables, it is crucial to record those books for which spaces left by the printer for initials have been left unfilled. Such data is recorded in fields 5e1 and 5e2 of our paradigm. Yet, especially in Italy, the tendency to leave pages uncolored seems to have reflected not so much the strain of augmented production as a conscious emulation of the pre-twelfth-century Caroline codices which were used as models for the letter forms of humanistic script and type fonts. In particular, the humanistic shift from red underlining to quotation marks was indicative of a generally diminished role for rubrication in fifteenth-century Italian printed books.

After the late 1480s printers throughout Europe abbetted the blackening of the page through their greatly enhanced ability to provide the aids to the reader which formerly had been added by the reader-emendator. Increasingly, accenting and *traits d'union,* punctuation and capitals, paragraph marks, chapter headings, foliation, and running headings were all definitively provided by the printer. After 1500 the instances of *prosodiae* and *posturae* added by hand become rarer. Even in 1502, however, Aldus Manutius printed in Venice an edition of Ovid with instructions to the owner for the manuscript foliation of the volume and the insertion of the apposite numerals in the printed table, and in fact all sixteen volumes published by Aldus in 1502 were without printed foliation or pagination.[50] After 1503 most Aldine Press books were either foliated or paginated.[51]

The changes that printing ultimately wrought on the page and the ensuring consequences of these changes on the psychology of reading

[49]Ezio Ornato and Carla Bozzolo, *Pour une histoire du livre manuscrit au moyen age: Trois essais de codicologie quantitative* (Paris, 1983), pp. 15–121.

[50]Auguste Renouard, *Annales de l'imprimerie des Aldes,* 3d ed. (Paris, 1834), I, 32–39.

[51]Aldus printed his first paginated book in March 1503; Renouard, *Annales,* I, 45, no. 1.

fall to a considerable extent within the fifteenth century and therefore help justify the intense scrutiny of individual incunable copies which we propose to undertake. One of the most dramatic changes in the codex during this period was the triumph of foliation. Before 1400 foliation was extremely rare in manuscripts, and even after 1450 it was largely limited to a few scriptoria serving a rather restricted group of clients, such as the French-speaking aristocracy, particularly in Flanders and Brabant.[52] The prevalence of foliation and the general blackening of the page around the year 1500 coincide and are in our judgment closely related. As each opening of a book, through the absence of color, became less and less recognizable, the use of references to fixed loci established by the codex itself came to be indispensable. Manuscript books of hours, rich in illuminated and colored pages, were never foliated, while the all-black printed *horae* of the sixteenth century were invariably foliated. An examination of the four volumes of Aldus Manutius' first edition of Aristotle (Newberry incunable nos. f5547, f5555, f5553, and f5565) has revealed how foliation initially added by hand was later printed along with the text.[53]

The printer's provision of all the aids that previously had been added in both printed books and manuscripts, either by professional rubricators and readers or members of a religious community or by private owners, effected the final step in the transformation of reading. In antiquity reading had implied an active role in the reception of the text. Saint Augustine indicates clearly that the reader was expected to clarify ambiguous meaning through a process of cerebral parsing which was the Roman equivalent of punctuation.[54] For the medieval reader and emendator the arena of this mental activity was the written page. Throughout the Middle Ages readers, even long after a book had been confected, felt free to clarify its meaning through the addition and modification of *prosodiae*, punctuation, and marginalia.[55]

---

[52]Guillaume Fillastre's *Thoison d'or*, copied in numerous examples for the members of the chivalric order of the Golden Fleece, was foliated and prefaced by a table giving reference to folios.

[53]In the Aldus printing of January 1497 foliation was added by hand; in the February 1497 edition it was printed. See Renouard, *Annales*, I, 7–11.

[54]Augustine, *De doctrina Christiana*, III, 2–5; Migne, *Patrologia latina*, 34:66–69; H. I. Marrou, *Saint Augustin et la fin de la culture antique* (Paris, 1958), p. 21; idem., *Histoire de l'education dans l'antiquité* (Paris, 1965), pp. 241, 406, 567 n. 14, and 602 n. 30.

[55]Malcolm Parkes, "Punctuation, or Pause and Effect," in *Medieval Eloquence*, ed. J. J. Murphy (Berkeley, 1978), pp. 127–42.

Under the influence of printing, reading became increasingly an activity of the passive reception of a text that was inherently clear and unambiguous. The perfection of printing techniques divested the reader of the last vestiges of his ancient role as textual clarifier and planted the seeds for modern book etiquette, which views the printed page as sacrosanct and consequently all handwritten additions to the printed page as personal notes, detrimental to subsequent common use. The total prohibition of book annotation is a phenomenon of the epoch of printing and has only limited precedent in medieval library regulations.[56] By the end of the second decade of the sixteenth century, even the pointing hands, formerly provided by the reader-emendator, were placed in the text by the printer.[57]

The fact that printers increasingly thought of themselves as acting as their own reader-emendators explains in some measure the problematic distinctions in *prosodiae* and *posturae* characteristic of incunable and postincunable reprintings of the same texts, whether ancient, medieval, or contemporary. Classical texts, for example Cicero's *Opera,* printed by Robert Estienne in 1538–39, which appear to be verbatim replicas of earlier editions may differ greatly from their models in terms of punctuation and marginal apparatus.[58] To an ever-increasing degree, each printer's edition came to constitute his own individual reading of a text. The reader notations in incunables are therefore important as comparisons to later comprehensively punctuated printings. They illustrate examples of the intellectual process which resulted in the infusion of new forms of punctuation such as quotation marks and parentheses into classical texts.

The process of printing bestowed on fifteenth- and sixteenth-

[56]See, for example, the library regulations of the University of Angers, which distinguished between those who were and were not permitted to emendate the books; Célestin Port, "La bibliothèque de l'université d'Angers," in *Notes et notices angeviennes* (Angers, 1879), pp. 31n. and 33. See also Paul Saenger, "Silent Reading: Its Impact on Late Medieval Script and Society," *Viator* 13 (1982): 384 n. 95.

[57]See Clément Marot's recension of the *Roman de la Rose* (Paris, Galliot Du Pré for Jean Petit[?], privilege dated 1526), and the same text printed by the same printers in 1531. These are editions P and R in Francis William Bourdillon, *The Early Editions of the Romance of the Rose* (London, 1906).

[58]The Estienne edition of Cicero has been reported to be a reprint of the Giunta edition of 1534–1537; Elizabeth Armstrong, *Robert Estienne, Royal Printer: An Historical Study of the Elder Stephanus* (Cambridge, 1954), p. 103. I am grateful to Lucien Goldschmidt for this reference.

century authors a potential power of exercising a more explicit control over the presentation of the text. Erasmus exhibited a notable interest in the punctuation of his works, and there is every reason to suppose that he controlled the punctuation of texts he published in Venice with Aldus Manutius, with whom he worked in intimate association.[59] In many cases, however, the author did not exercise this authority, and it devolved upon the printer. The late incunable printer, by establishing a close and rigorous control over punctuation and the nuances of meaning that flow from punctuation, became, in effect, an editor in the modern sense of the word. The printer's total control over the presentation of text also permitted the development of numbered folios and alphabetical indexing systems, of which the exact equivalent rarely, if ever, existed in manuscript books.[60] Such printed codicological aspects of the book are recorded in field 4d of our paradigm, even though they do not change from copy to copy,

[59]See Johan Huizinga, *Erasmus and the Age of the Reformation,* trans. F. Hopman (New York, 1957), pp. 63–66. Of punctuation Erasmus wrote: "Ut autem obseuata symmetriae ratio non hic tantum plurimum confert ad decorem, ita recta distinctio credi vix potest quantum adferat lucis ad intelligendam sententiam, ut non inscite eruditus quidam aptam distinctionem commentarii genus esse. Expedit igitur et huic rei statim assuescere puerum; ita consuetudo vertetur in naturam, ut vel aliud cogitans seruet tamen in scribendo notulas huiusmodi non aliter quam litteras ipsas." ("Just as the principle of symmetry, when properly applied, makes great improvement in the appearance of script, so you would hardly credit how much good punctuation contributes to the understanding of a passage; so much so that a certain scholar said rather wittily that punctuation was a kind of commentary of the text. It is useful therefore that a boy should quickly familiarise himself with this feature also, and that the habit should become second nature so that, even when his mind is on something else, he should, as he writes, attend to the punctuation marks as much as to the letters themselves.") *De recta graeci et latini sermonis pronunciatione,* ed. M. Cytowska, in *Opera omnia Desiderii Erasmi Rotterdami recognita et adnotatione critica notisque illustrata,* ser. 1, vol. 4 (Amsterdam, 1973), p. 38. For the English translation, see A. S. Osley, *Scribes and Sources: Handbook of the Chancery Hand in the Sixteenth Century: Texts from the Writing Masters* (London, 1980), p. 34. In 1507 Erasmus wrote to Aldus concerning a revised edition of his translation of Euripides, *Hecuba et Iphigenia,* which Badius had previously published in Paris in September 1506. He offered to supply Aldus with a corrected copy, by which he probably meant an emendated copy of the printed text. The Aldus edition of December 1507 differs from the first edition in a number of respects, including its punctuation.

[60]Erhard Ratdolt's printing of Werner Rolewinck, *Fasciculus temporum* (Venice, 1480; Goff R-261), contains a table with references to folios in which a point following the folio number indicates the side of the leaf or page. Other incunables and postincunables use letters of the alphabet to indicate place within the page.

because they pertain directly to the incunable as codex and have never been recorded by students of printing. Finally, the printer, by controlling which marginalia survived in the transition from manuscript to printed book, established certain marginalia as a canonical part of the texts they accompanied.[61]

A final aspect of incunables that varies from copy to copy is their decoration. The presence of independent miniatures, colored woodcuts, painted initials, border margins, and line fillers must be recorded in a codicological catalogue. This information is recorded in fields 5a–5d. Line fillers in particular often played an important mnemonic function by conferring on the printed substratum a radically different appearance that in certain instances even served, like punctuation, to clarify the meaning of the text. We have already noted that the decoration of initials, borders, and line fillers was often the work of the rubricator and that such decoration was gradually reduced and eliminated by the printer as part of the phenomenon we have described as the blackening of the page. Although our sample includes no examples of manuscripts containing independent miniatures and only a few with colored woodcuts, both Sandra Hindman[62] and Martha Tedeschi[63] have demonstrated the importance of considering these aspects of early book production. Since differences in the illustration of the same text often reflect different interpretations of that text, this information too can provide insight into the ways in which early readers understood their books. Analysis of copy-specific decoration of incunables may also shed light on questions of production, such as determining whether the publisher or the eventual owner was responsible for providing the illustrations. Such analysis may also illuminate the nature of the relationship between either the publisher or the owner to the artists who did the decorating. It is significant too that the painted decoration in early incunable books can, in conjunction with other evidence, offer valuable clues to the provenance of certain books, and indeed such data may be of great value in identifying the use of certain printed liturgical texts as well as in identifying more precise origins for certain fifteenth-century manuscripts.

[61]See, for example, Ranulf Higden's *Polychronicon* and the *Roman de la Rose* (note 57).

[62]*Pen to Press*, pp. 157–211.

[63]See her contribution to this volume (Chapter 2).

Appendix: Incunable Paradigm

1. Shelf mark (Proctor no.)
   1a. *GW* (or Hain)
   1b. *BMC*
   1c. Goff
   1d. Other
2. Author and title (short form)
   2a. Printer
   2b. Place
   2c. Date
3. Support
   3a. Material
   3b. Watermarks
   3c. Dimensions
   3d. Printed space
4. Texts
   4a. Manuscript glosses or commentaries
      4a1. Incipits
      4a2. Explicits
   4b. Manuscript additions
      4b1. Incipits
      4b2. Explicits
   4c. Fragments
   4d. Printed tables
5. Decoration
   5a. Colors
   5b. Miniatures
   5c. Woodcuts (colored only)
   5d. Marginal
   5e. Initials
      5e1. Blank spaces
      5e2. Guide letters
      5e3. Colors and patterns
   5f. Rubricating
      5f1. Printed
      5f2. Color
      5f3. Titles and colophons
      5f4. Underlining
      5f5. Paragraph Markers
      5f6. Punctuation
      5f7. Strokes
      5f8. Corrections
      5f9. Marginalia
      5f10. Washes
      5f11. Date or name of rubricator
      5f12. Foliation or pagination
      5f13. Redundant numbers
6. Non-red reader marks
   6a. Foliation or pagination (including quire signatures)
   6b. Ruling
   6c. Titles and colophons
   6d. Finding notes
   6e. Textual emendation
   6f. Punctuation
   6g. Redundant numbers
   6h. Date or name of emendator
7. Marks of ownership
   7a. Coats of arms
   7b. Ex libris
   7c. Old shelf marks
   7d. Catalogue citations and clippings
   7e. Bookplates
8. Binding description
   8a. Material
      8a1. Interior
      8a2. Exterior
   8b. Metalwork
   8c. Color
   8d. Decoration
   8e. Signature
   8f. Endleaf watermarks
   8g. Finding tabs
   8h. Date
   8i. Title and position
   8j. Spine (numbers and type of bands, head caps, head bands)
   8k. Edge decoration
   8l. Doubleure (if any)

9. Copy-specific printing or assemblage errors
10. Reparation
11. Additional notes

12. Photographs needed
13. Rubbings needed
14. Acquisition data

[9]

Reading the Printed Image: Illuminations and Woodcuts of the *Pèlerinage de la vie humaine* in the Fifteenth Century

Michael Camille

I n a review of *The Early Illustrated Book: Essays in Honor of Lessing J. Rosenwald,* I asked several broad questions:

> Did the same audience enjoy the translucent painted surfaces of the *Hastings Hours* as an entirely separate reading experience from the hatched horizontal smears of a woodcut *Horae?* Were they just seen as different aspects on a scale of pictorial communication, just as we today separate the newer "cruder" medium of video from the "classic" detailed colour of film? As in these modern media, functions overlapped; many early printed books imitated manuscripts, as in the case of Antoine Vérard's lavish volumes. Why is it that during this very period when manuscript illuminations become "realistic" autonomous illusions, breaking the surface of the page, that printing seems to take over its old role in providing a quick and continuous visual equivalent for written narrative?[1]

In this essay I take the opportunity to answer some of these questions. I explore the transformations of pictorial narrative in the change from scribal to print culture through an examination of the illustration of one particular text—the *Pèlerinage de la vie humaine.* There are a

I thank Maryjane Dunn-Wood for her advice on the Spanish editions of Deguileville and Mary Beth Winn for her help in the preparation of this paper.
[1]Michael Camille, "Opening the Book," *Art History* 7 (1984): 513.

number of reasons for this choice. Written in 1330 by the Cistercian Guillaume de Deguileville as the first of a trilogy of entertaining doctrinal allegories, the second being the *Pèlerinage de l'ame* and the third the *Pèlerinage de Jesus Christ,* this work became one of the most popular vernacular texts of the late Middle Ages. There are eighty-six extant manuscripts of the original verse version (which exists in two recensions), more than half of them illustrated, as well as a number of illuminated manuscripts of the fifteenth-century adaptations, which translated the poem into French, German, and Dutch prose.[2] The 1464 French prose translation made for Jeanne de Laval, duchess of Angers, which exists in at least ten manuscripts, provided the text used for the first printed edition, published by Mathieu Husz at Lyons in 1485 as *Le pèlerin de la vie humaine.* The work was equally popular in the new medium, being reprinted in Lyons in 1486, 1489, and 1499.[3] The woodcuts of the Husz edition are the focus of this essay, but I also refer to other printed versions that depend for their pictorial cycles on the Lyons series, such as the Spanish translation printed at Toulouse in 1490 and Antoine Vérard's 1499 and Claude Nourry's 1504 editions, both produced in Paris.[4] Vérard also published an up-

[2]Michael Camille, "The Illustrated Manuscripts of Guillaume de Deguileville's 'Pèlerinages,' 1330–1426" (Ph.D diss., University of Cambridge, 1985), includes, in addition to the eighty-six manuscripts listed in Appendix I, a basic list of extant copies of fifteenth-century translations and printed versions in Appendix III, pp. 368–73. The best published introduction to the manuscripts and printed copies of Deguileville's works is still Rosamund Tuve, *Allegorical Imagery: Some Medieval Books and Their Posterity* (Princeton, 1966), pp. 145–215. On the *Vie* and its contents, see Edmond Faral, *Guillaume de Digulleville: Moine de Chaalis, Histoire littéraire de la France,* vol. 39 (Paris, 1952), and the facsimile of a fourteenth-century Heidelberg manuscript, Rosmarie Bergmann, *Die Pilgerfahrt zum himmlischen Jerusalem* (Wiesbaden, 1983).

[3]For the 1464 prose translation and its erroneous association with Jean Gallopes as well as a good guide to the complicated incunabula tradition of Deguileville's works, see Edmond Faral, "Guillaume de Digulleville, Jean Gallopes et Pierre Virgin," in *Études romanes dediées à Mario Roques* (Paris, 1946), pp. 89–102. For the career of Mathias Husz, see André Blum, *Les origines du livres gravures en France* (Paris, 1928), pp. 52, 90. Copies of the first Lyons edition are in the Department of Prints, Metropolitan Museum of Art, New York; Washington, D.C., Library of Congress, Rosenwald Collection, 1485:G8; and Paris, Bibliothèque de l'Arsenal, 4° B.4.2847. For changes in the 1499 edition "corrected" by Pierre Virgin, see Faral, "Guillaume de Digulleville," p. 95.

[4]The Spanish edition, *El pelegrino de la vida humana,* printed at Toulouse by Henricus Mayer in 1490, which adds a full-page prefatory woodcut showing Saint James of Compostella, has been studied by Maryjane Dunn-Wood, "El pelerinage de la vida humana: A Study and Edition" (Ph.D. diss., University of Pennsylvania, 1985). The images here are not produced from the same blocks as the Lyons edition but are recut

dated version of the second recension of the poem, for which he had a new and expanded set of woodcuts designed in 1511.[5] The pictures in the Dutch printing of 1486 by Jacques Bellaert, *Dat boek vanden Pelgherym,* are also quite independent of the Lyons cuts.[6] But rather than look at the differences between the various European incunabula editions, I want to ask what are the differences in the visual structure of the pictorial narratives in these woodcuts and in the miniatures of their manuscript forbears and contemporaries.

This leads to the second reason for focusing on the *Vie humaine.* Because of the consistency of the narrative cycle we are able to compare fifteenth-century manuscript copies of the work with the early incunabula and find that in the three hundred years of its illustration the most radical shift in this text's visualization occurs not when it is translated from one language or form to another—from French prose to French verse in 1464, from French to English prose c. 1430 and into verse in 1426, or the fifteenth-century translations into Dutch and German—but when it speaks a new presentational "language" in the medium of print.

A third factor that should not be overlooked is the nature of Deguileville's work itself, written in the form of a poetic dream-vision in which the reader is meant to identify with the "I" of the text, a pilgrim who travels through the world and encounters temptations

from the prints pasted on the new blocks, a process that necessitates the reversal of compositions. For Vérard's 1499 edition, see John MacFarlane, *Antoine Vérard* (London, 1900), p. 63, no. 122, and the introduction to the facsimile of the illuminated vellum copy made for Henry VII in Alfred W. Pollard, *Le pèlerinage de la vie humaine: Reproduced in Facsimile from the Printed Book in the Library of the Earl of Ellesmere* (Manchester, 1912), pp. 11–13. A copy of the 1504 Claude Nourry edition that follows the 1499 Virgin remodeling of the Husz edition (Bodleian Library, MS Douce P.339) raises the problem of woodcut reuse. The compositions are very close to those of the Lyons series but do not follow exactly the same lines as in the recut Spanish edition. It differs from the earlier Lyons editions in having a modernized text with more rubrication (including red titles); it is also larger and has more ornate script features.

[5] *Le pèlerinage de l'homme* is an edition of the second, longer verse recension of Deguileville's *Vie,* which is rarer and exists in only twelve manuscripts, five of which are illustrated; see Camille, "Illustrated Manuscripts of Deguileville," p. 212. It is different from the Lyons and earlier 1499 edition in many respects, being laid out in two columns with elaborate marginal glosses and a longer cycle of sixty-two newly designed woodcuts. The Vérard shop reuses some from the Terence of 1500; see MacFarlane, *Antoine Vérard,* no. 101, p. 51; Faral, "Guillaume de Digulleville," p. 100; and see fig. 9.3.

[6] *Pen to Press,* p. 117 and fig. 43.

on the way. In this allegorical journey the narrative trajectory and the discovery of knowledge through the act of reading the text and seeing the pictures are stressed by the poet himself. It is thus a crucial question to ask how this intimately involved reading of the vision-quest is affected by the shift from painted illuminations to printed woodcuts.

From Script to Print Layout

At first glance the difference between the manuscript illustration of the pilgrim's encounter with Envy and her daughters Treachery and Detraction in the well-known miniature from the famous Brussels manuscript of c.1400 (Bibliothèque Royale, MS 10176-8) and the woodcut in the Lyons edition nearly one hundred years later (fig. 9.1) seems small, apart from the rich colors of the earlier work and the obviously more linear handling of the woodcut.[7] But looking at these from the viewpoint of their prospective readers, we can see that the same basic design may perform quite a different function in these two places.

A red rubric announces the subject and the text that follows it in the Brussels manuscript—part of a constant interruption in the flow of the poem typical of its verse and its manuscript existence. The way in which the printed image is anchored to the page is quite different. First, the text is in prose and has been modernized from Deguileville's archaic verse forms. It is much larger on the page, and although the text below begins with the same words—"Ainsi comme flaterie parloit a moy"—it has an elaborate initial added by hand which signals an important break in the text. The forty-four woodcuts appear only at the head of chapter divisions. This was not the case in the much more densely illustrated manuscripts of the prose translation such as the fine late-fifteenth-century copy, likely painted in a Lyons atelier (Geneva MS 181), which has eighty-one miniatures.[8] The printed images function as introductory summaries of the succeeding se-

[7]This well-known scene by an unusual illuminator associated with Flemish "realisme pre-eyckien" (Brussels, Bibliothèque Royale, MS 10176/78, fol. 78) is reproduced in Erwin Panofsky, *Early Netherlandish Painting: Its Origins and Character,* vol. 2 (Cambridge, Mass., 1953), fig. 138.

[8]For the Lyons provenance and good reproductions of this manuscript, see Bernard Gagnebin, *L'enluminure de Charlemagne à François Ier: Les manuscrits à peintures de la Bibliothèque Publique et universitaire de Genève* (Geneva, 1976), pp. 133–34, no. 56.

Ce. vii. chapître comment apres ce que la vielle nõmee
õrgueil z flaterie qui fur elle cheuauchoit eurêt recite leur
meftier et ce quelles fauoient faire et deuifer õ leurs oftilz
et habillemens vne aultre moult hideufe et terrible vielle
arriua qui fur terre comme vng ferpent a quatre piez aloyt
et deffus fon dos cheuauchoient deux aultres vielles au
tant ou plus efpouantables quelle neftoyt. Et comment
icelles deux vielles par leur pere furent a lefcolle de malice
en doctrinees.

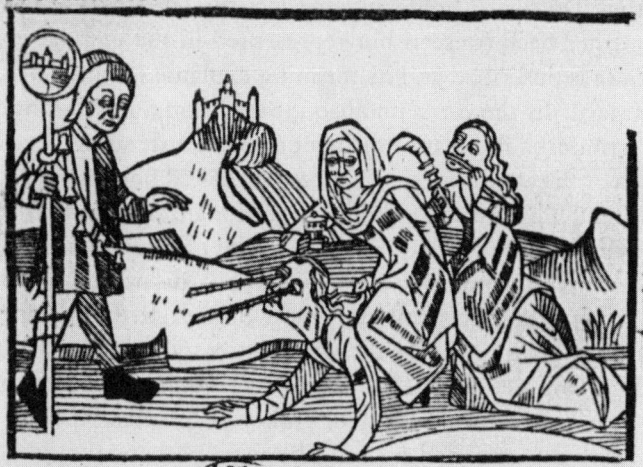

 ¶ Ze pelerin
Ainfi comme flaterie parloit a moy z me racõptoit
fon affaire et ce dont elle fe mefloit vne aultre viel
le vint a moy z me fift grant freeur Deur lances a
uoit procedans de fes deux ieulx et fur terre aloit a quatre
piez comme vng ferpent z fi maigre z fi mefchante eftoyt
que fes os la chair luy perfoient. Et deffus fon dos che
uauchoiêt deux aultres vielles aut.it ou pl° efpouêtables
horribles z redoubtables que celles qui la cheuauchoient

Figure 9.1. The Pilgrim Encounters Envy Carrying Her Daughters Treachery and Detraction, from *Le pèlerin de la vie humaine,* Lyons, Mathieu Husz,
1485, Paris, Bibliothèque de l'Arsenal, 4° 2847, liiii verso. Courtesy of the
Bibliothèque de l'Arsenal.

quence of action. A long introductory rubric at the head of the page tells us that this is the seventh chapter and recounts its contents, in effect describing the picture below—that the pilgrim encounters a "moult hideuse et terrible vielle" who goes on all fours like a serpent and who carries two other women on her back (fig. 9.1). It is crucial that the rubric does not give away the identity of these three hags, for it is important that the reader, like the pilgrim, encounter hideous and startling images which are only explained later. They are thus meant, on first reading, to appear like visual puzzles. As these vices explain themselves, the reader can turn back to look at the alluring ointment pot that Treachery holds and the fact that she carries the fatal knife behind her back (unseen but represented in the picture), and as each attribute is described and its meaning explained, link it with the original image. In the early manuscript tradition a much longer cycle of over a hundred illustrations often provided little subillustrations, miniatures of the attributes of the vices as isolated objects as they occurred in the text. This change is part of the rationalization and "paring down" that typify the printed as opposed to the painted narrative.

There is an interesting iconographic discrepancy between the manuscript and the print depiction of the attributes of Envy. The Brussels miniature shows the spears of envy in her hands rather than coming from her eyes. This is a direct response to a textual alteration that occurs in only two out of eighty-six manuscripts in which the text has been emended by a scribe who perhaps thought the image too ridiculous.[9] The same alteration in the traditional iconographic program also occurs in the illustration in another copy of the prose *Vie* in Geneva, (MS 182), illuminated by the Master of Anton Rolin c.1500 (fig. 9.2).[10] Such a transformation in the copying process and change in the poet's original iconographic intention is impossible in the printed book, which follows the standard text here. All the reprints of the Husz 1486, 1489, and 1499 as well as the two Paris editions and the Spanish translation of 1490 copy the first Lyons edition exactly. The woodcuts are either reused, recut on new blocks (which caused the reversal of the Lyons compositions in the Spanish

[9]The same emendation is found in Brussels (Bibliothèque Royale, MS 10197-8, the model for MS 10176-8) and Manchester (John Rylands Library, MS fr. 2) and is discussed in Camille, "Illustrated Manuscripts of Deguileville," p. 48.

[10]Gagnebin, *L'enluminure,* pp. 171–73, no. 75.

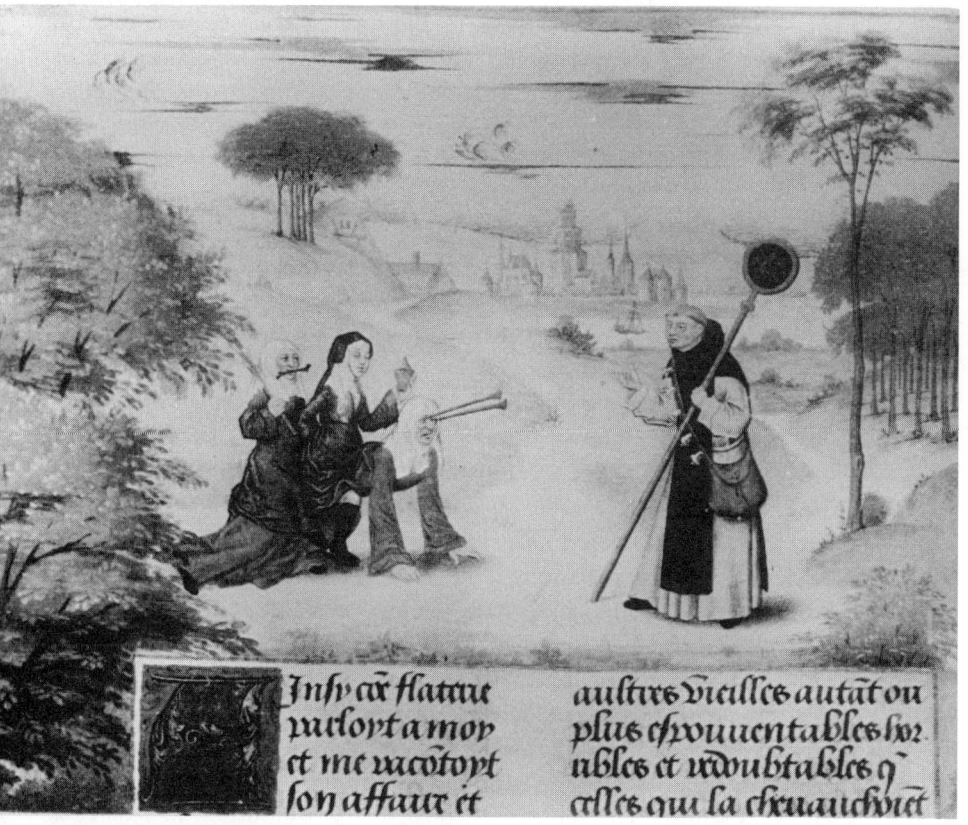

Figure 9.2. The Pilgrim Encounters Envy Carrying Her Daughters Treachery and Detraction, from *Le livre de pèlerinage de la vie humaine*, Geneva, Bibliothèque Publique et Universitaire, MS 182, fol. 109v (detail).

edition), or carefully repeated by an inferior craftsman, as in Vérard's 1499 edition. There is no emendation, except by erasure, and thus no change in the pictorial program in printed picture cycles such as can occur in the transmission of texts and images in the manuscript copies.

This uniformity and regularity affect how the reader sees the images. They fit into a system of defined textual control and a technology that can reverse and recut the block but not alter anything as radical as an iconographic attribute. What this creates is a standard series, which was not possible in the 150 years of copying in the manuscript tradition. The cuts of the 1485 Lyons edition had an influence all over Europe which far exceeded that of any single manuscript copy. Indeed, the fact that the Geneva illuminated copy also shows Envy's more rationalized spear eyes suggests that perhaps this illuminator was following the "established" printed version (fig. 9.1).

From Script to Print Perception

The differences between the reading of printed as opposed to painted images can be discussed in terms of cognitive psychology and reception aesthetics. The miniatures in the Geneva manuscript appear to us much more interesting and detailed (although this is tied up with questions of how taste and economic value are linked), and yet there is no appreciable difference in the amount of information conveyed in the illusionistic miniature and the woodcut of Treachery and her daughters (figs. 9.1 and 9.2). Using the concepts of figurality and discursivity, we might say that the Geneva miniature exhibits more of the former, moving outside and away from the text to describe the landscape and atmosphere of the setting, which is not mentioned by the author. The Lyons cut, while having the same crucial signs—the pilgrim's staff topped by a mirror that reflects the goal of the journey, the Heavenly Jerusalem, and the distant city itself—does not include such excess information as extraneous trees and clouds. The excess— in this case the landscape, which takes over the manuscript page, reducing the scale of the figures—fills the marginal space around the text, which is placed in the center of the page. There is no introductory rubric, so the first words about the previously encountered flattery create an ambiguity between what we read and what we see. Image and text are disjointed in this privileging of the visual over the verbal, whereas I would argue that in the Lyons page the balance between form and content conveyed is held steady within the black frame.

The more efficient communication of the woodcut series as opposed to the anecdotal realism of Franco-Flemish illusionism, like that in Geneva MS 182, can be seen in terms of an experiment on visual literacy undertaken in Africa: given five narrative sequences of different degrees of detail, subjects were most easily able to read the narrative not in the high-resolution photograph nor in the partly shaded and perspectival sequence in the series that consisted only of simple outlines.[11] Of course this begs the question of the "mental set" of the viewers and their perceptual skills. To some extent the audience of the late-fifteenth-century printed book was attuned to seeing highly naturalistic images, and the reduction of the print aesthetic would have seemed quite novel. Or would it? Are we not rather looking at experiences on a relative scale? It would be wrong to compare printed images with the "technicolor" flashiness of the Ghent-Bruges school miniatures of the same date rather than the outlines and washes of the run-of-the-mill book illustrators whose visual vocabularies are closer to what was attained in the simpler designs of woodcuts in many cases.[12] Surely the reader of a printed narrative brings a different set of expectations to bear upon the print narrative and reads it accordingly. Just because these cuts were sometimes colored does not mean that they were meant to appear like manuscripts; often the addition of color served a clarifying rather than an aesthetic function.[13]

The designer of the Lyons series reduces the visual complexity of the narrative. In a cut showing Aristotle discoursing with Divine Wisdom and then Wisdom baking the bread of the Eucharist with Charity, the components of the image do not make sense without a knowledge of the story. We would not know what the small round objects on the right were unless we had read the rubric, whereas in the Geneva manuscript the images can function quite independently of the text, adding elaborate details of the interior of the bakery.[14] Of course such details can be included by woodcutters such as the

[11]See Evelyn Goldsmith, *Research into Illustration: An Approach and a Review* (Cambridge, 1984), pp. 344–45. For the notion of pictures' functioning on the scale from "discursive" to "figural," see Norman Bryson, *Word and Image: French Painting of the Ancien Regime* (Cambridge, 1981), pp. 1–28.

[12]This is especially true in fifteenth-century Germany, where there was a vigorous tradition of line drawing in manuscripts. The notion of a "mental set" and the cognitive style of various cultures owes much to Michael Baxandall, *The Limewood Sculptors of Renaissance Germany* (New Haven, 1980), pp. 143–63.

[13]Initials are added in red and various other colors in copies of the Lyons editions, but the only examples I have seen of woodcuts colored by hand (as opposed to fully illuminated as in some of Vérard's books) occur in the Dutch edition of 1486 (PML checklist 1655, and Rosenwald Collection, Library of Congress); see *Pen to Press,* fig. 43. The Bellaert woodcutter's denser linear modeling is more amenable to the tonal and coloristic additions than the sparer French cuts.

[14]Compare the miniature reproduced in Gagnebin, *L'enluminure,* p. 172, from Geneva MS 182 with the "crude" cut of the scene from Vérard's 1499 edition, as described and reproduced in the introduction to Pollard, *Le pèlerinage,* p. 13.

Haarlem Master of the Dutch edition, with its spacious scene of divine domesticity.[15] But my point would again be that the printed image provides the basic information of the textual action quite adequately as an integrative part of the book.

This question of how the reader uses the images for information about the text is made clear in a fairly standard practice for early printers—the reuse of cuts in different places. This occurs only once in the forty-four woodcuts of the Lyons series in a "generalized" subject of the pilgrim listening on the left while Nature debates with Grace Dieu, or Grace of God (this appears in sequence as cuts nine and ten).[16] What function did this repetition serve? It is wrong to say that such duplication exists only after the invention of printing as a labor-saving and economical device. In a number of manuscripts of Deguileville's work the illuminator simply repeated the standard image of the pilgrim and Grace Dieu throughout the second half of the poem.[17] It is always easier to repeat than to invent. The difference here, of course, is that the exact duplication of the same composition is not possible in the manuscript copying process. But this sameness in the two woodcuts does not so much hold back as link the narrative. The duplications come at the beginning and the end of a long debate between Grace Dieu and Nature; the reader's perception of the second cut is quite different at the moment when he or she comes to this place in the book, since it now no longer stands for the beginning of the debate but the end, where Nature admits defeat and, unable to comprehend the miracle of the Eucharist, kneels before Grace Dieu. To create a whole new woodcut just to change the posture of one figure would have been a waste of labor, so the one design is made to represent two distinct stages in the story. One very important change in terms of text and image in all the fifteenth-century printed editions of Deguileville is the organization of the text around its dramatic personae. Rubricated headings throughout announce "le pelerin" or "grace Dieu," making the text a kind of dialogue drama with the

[15]This is fol. 21 of the fine hand-colored copy, PML checklist 1655.

[16]Paris, Bibliothèque de l'Arsenal, 4° B2847, fols. ciii and cvii verso.

[17]The most radical case of this occurs in Leningrad State Library, MS fr. v.XIV, no. 4, which is unpublished and can be dated c.1450 (with 385 miniatures), but stock miniature repetition is also visible in Paris, Bibliothèque Sainte-Geneviève, MS 1130, for which see A. Boinet, "Les manuscrits à peintures de la Bibliothèque Sainte-Geneviève de Paris," in *Bulletin de la Société française de reproductions de manuscrits à peintures,* vol. 5 (Paris, 1921), pp. 96–107.

pilgrim labeled "l'acteur." The woodcuts become part of this process by picturing the speakers at particular points rather than the action. In this sense the idea of having two identical woodcuts when the interlocutors are the same likewise serves to signal continuity in sameness—that we are still in the midst of this long debate on the nature of transubstantiation.

This is the case even in a very different woodcut series, designed for a different version of the *Vie* printed by Vérard in 1511. Here, there are more pictures interspersed in the verse and part of an elaborate modernization of the text and provision with marginal glosses (fig. 9.3). The speakers are often not only named before their speeches but are labeled within the scenes (fig. 9.4). This again, however, was not something invented in the printed image. In a Melbourne manuscript of the English translation Grace Dieu and Nature are so designated (fig. 9.5). Perhaps this is to separate them from the two trees, two useless fillers completely unthinkable in the highly charged spaces of the woodcuts. Interestingly, it used to be thought that these drawings were influenced by woodcuts; but this is impossible since the book was made for a pious member of the lower gentry in Yorkshire c. 1450. Its robust drawings do, however, reflect the "mental set" that would accommodate itself easily to the radical reduction of the print aesthetic.[18]

The Vérard edition of 1511 (fig. 9.4) is interesting because by contrast to and unlike the Lyons edition it apes the format and appearance of the luxury "illuminated" manuscript, even in the bare bones of the woodcut. This may be linked to its use of the older verse form rather than the 1464 prose translation. Copies were produced for various clients either illuminated on vellum, illuminated on paper, or just printed on paper. An especially interesting copy (ONB, CP1 D.2) interleaves vellum and paper and is probably made from scraps left over from various vellum and paper copies.[19] This is suggested because the illumination and text decoration of the vellum pages are by one artist (fig. 9.6) and those on the paper pages by a different and

[18]State Library of Victoria, MS *096/G94, published in Margaret M. Manion and Vera F. Vines, *Medieval and Illuminated Manuscripts in Australian Collections* (London, 1984), pp. 110–12, pl. 28 and figs. 96–103.

[19]Otto Pächt and Dagmar Thoss, *Die illuminierten Handschriften der Osterreichishen Nationalbibliothek: Französische Schule II* (Vienna, 1977), I, 179. For "double-edition" printing runs on vellum and paper, see *Pen to Press*, p. 133.

De la Vieille sa porteresse
Aser sa faisoit ou Vousoit
Et ung mirouer suy tenoit
Afin que dedans regardast
Et que sa face elle y mirast

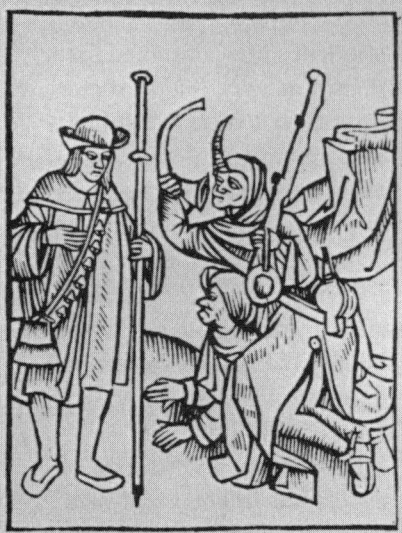

Sant ces deux Vieilles ainsi Vp
quest ce dis ie/doulp dieu merci
En ce pays que Vieilles na
Vieille de ca Vieille de sa
Ne scap se suis en femenpe

La tres plus Vieille et appellee
Auant que se monde fust fait
Et que se ciel fust tout parfait
Du nyd du ciel ie suz couuee
Op suz conceue et engendree
Et ung opsel quon appella
Jadis lucifer my couua
Et iamais si male couuee
Daucun opsel ne fut couuee
Car si tost que esclose ie fu
Et que congneu et aperceu
Mon pere/si fort se soufflap
De ce soufflet que Vois que iap
Que du hault nyd ius trebuchiet
Le fis et en enfer plungier
Blanc opsel par deuant estoit
Noble gentil et plus suisoit
Que le soleil en plain midp
Or est de present si noircp
Tant sale deuenu et oit
Que plus est lait que nest la mort
Et te dp quant ie seuz ainsi
Mis et boute hors de son np
Auecques luy trebuchap ius
Et ou ciel ne demouray plus
En terre Vins qui de nouuel
Estoit faicte dont pas moust bel
Ne me fut car Vng euure y Vp
Homme estoit fait pour hault ou np
Monter dont trebusche y estope

sunt specie
scis interic
intellcctus
affectu: et
terior i na...

Initium
peccati est
perbia. Ec-
siastes.ig.

Michaele
gellcus p
liabant
Diacone:t
co pugna
et angeli
et non val
runt neq
inuetus e
ru ampliu
celo. Apo
psis.gii.c...

Clidi de
diaconus
oit besie
exite spue
mundos.
Sunt eni
ritus der
no:ll. Ap
lipsis.g...

Figure 9.3. The Pilgrim Encounters Envy Carrying Her Daughters Treachery and Detraction, from *Le pèlerinage de l'homme,* Paris, Antoine Vérard, 1511, Oxford, Bodleian Library, Douce G.285. By permission of the Bodleian Library.

cruder hand (fig. 9.4). The vellum pages have mock ruling and fancier dentil initials. Significantly, a different audience seems to be aimed at, too. The vellum illuminator often omits the banderoles or paints over them in an effort to attain an illusionistic unity of effect, while his paper partner often leaves them in, retaining the discursive qualities of his print base. He sometimes even lets the black ink of the printer remain, as in the blackbird fleeing from the pilgrim at baptism (fig. 9.4). The discursive dominates the pure print aesthetic with its band-

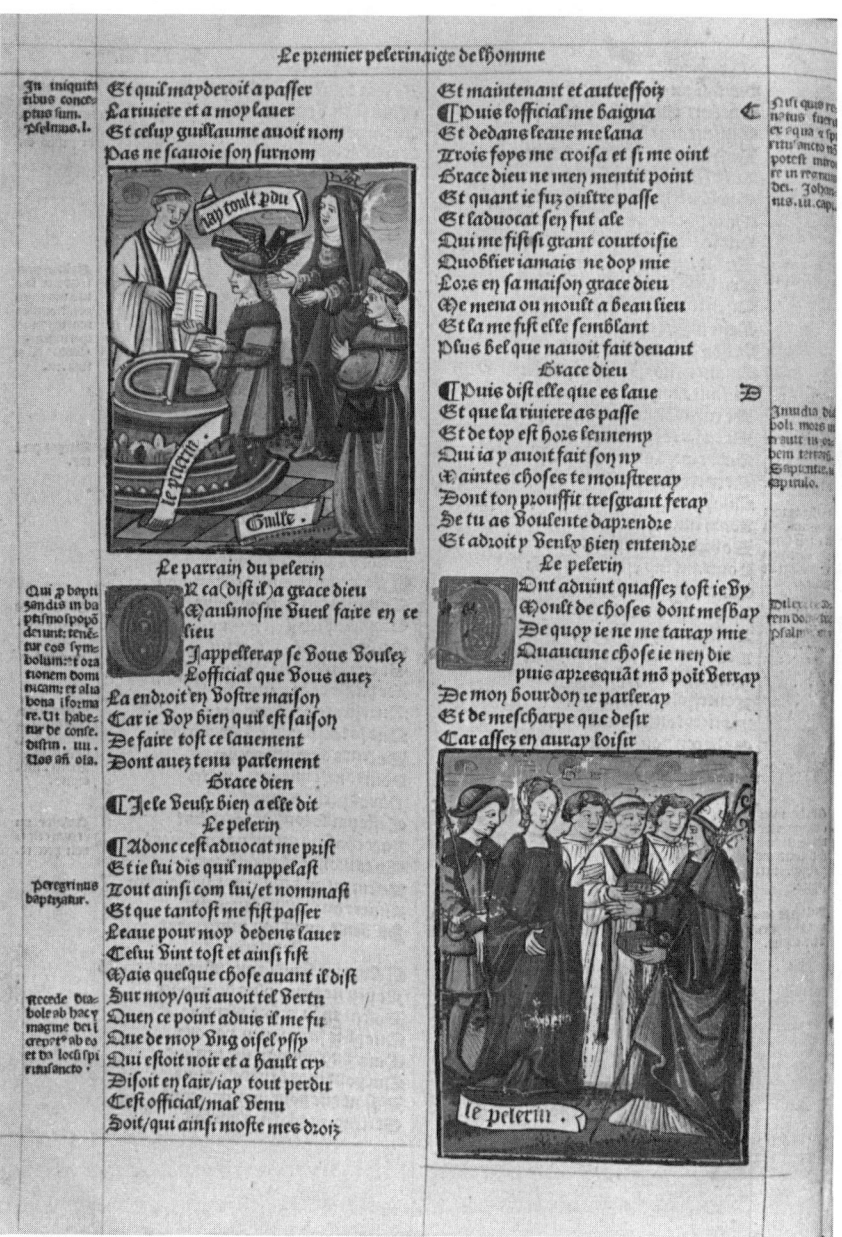

Figure 9.4. The Pilgrim Baptized and the Anointing of Officials by the Bishop, from *Le pèlerinage de l'homme,* Paris, Antoine Vérard, 1511, ONB, CP ID2, sig. VIv (on paper). Courtesy of the Österreichische Nationalbibliothek, Vienna.

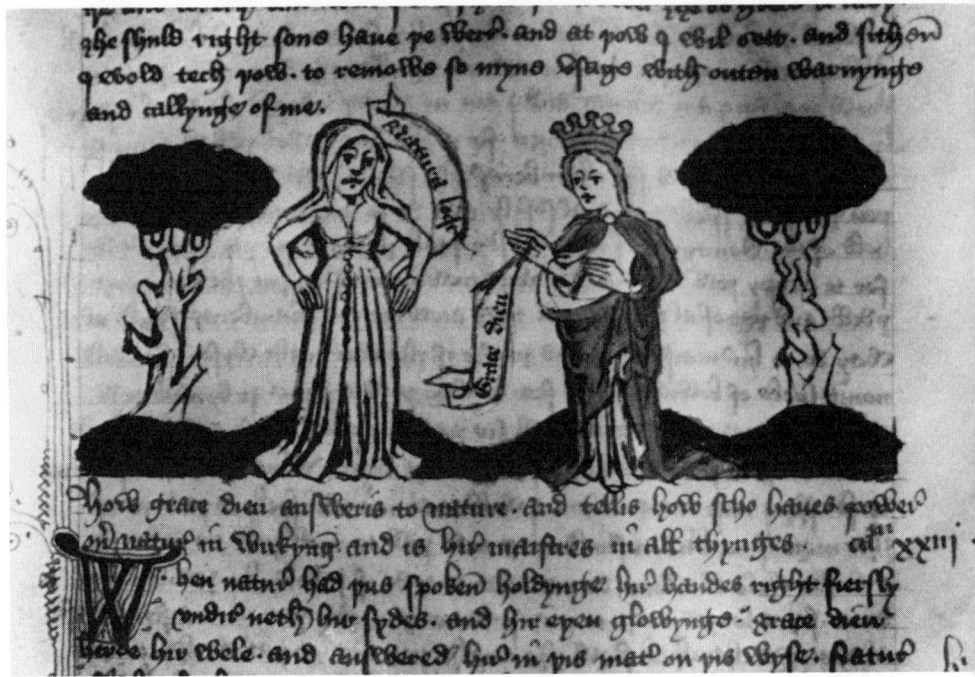

Figure 9.5. Nature and Grace Dieu Argue, from *Pilgrimage of the Life of Man*, Melbourne, State Library of Victoria, *096/G94 fol. 13r.

eroles and black and white symbols, while the "let's pretend" manuscript is an illusion on more than one level. On the one hand, it attempts to be what it is not; and an interesting question would be whether in reading such a book the readers duped themselves into believing that this was a handwritten as well as a hand-painted page. On the other hand, it is an illusion in the sense of its technical accomplishments. This hand-produced effort aims to erase the text from the picture (fig. 9.6). Those pictures that are full-blown illuminations by the finer artist, and which appear only on the vellum leaves, replicate manuscript modes of attention in one important way: they engage the viewer in the excess of landscape, the diversion of clouds, and the celebration of "art for art's sake." In the fifteenth century there were obviously some viewers who wanted to read and some who were more concerned with the "art" in the text. That these distinctions reflect the class and expectations of the reading audience is suggested by the fact that in copying the Lyons cuts in his much less elaborate

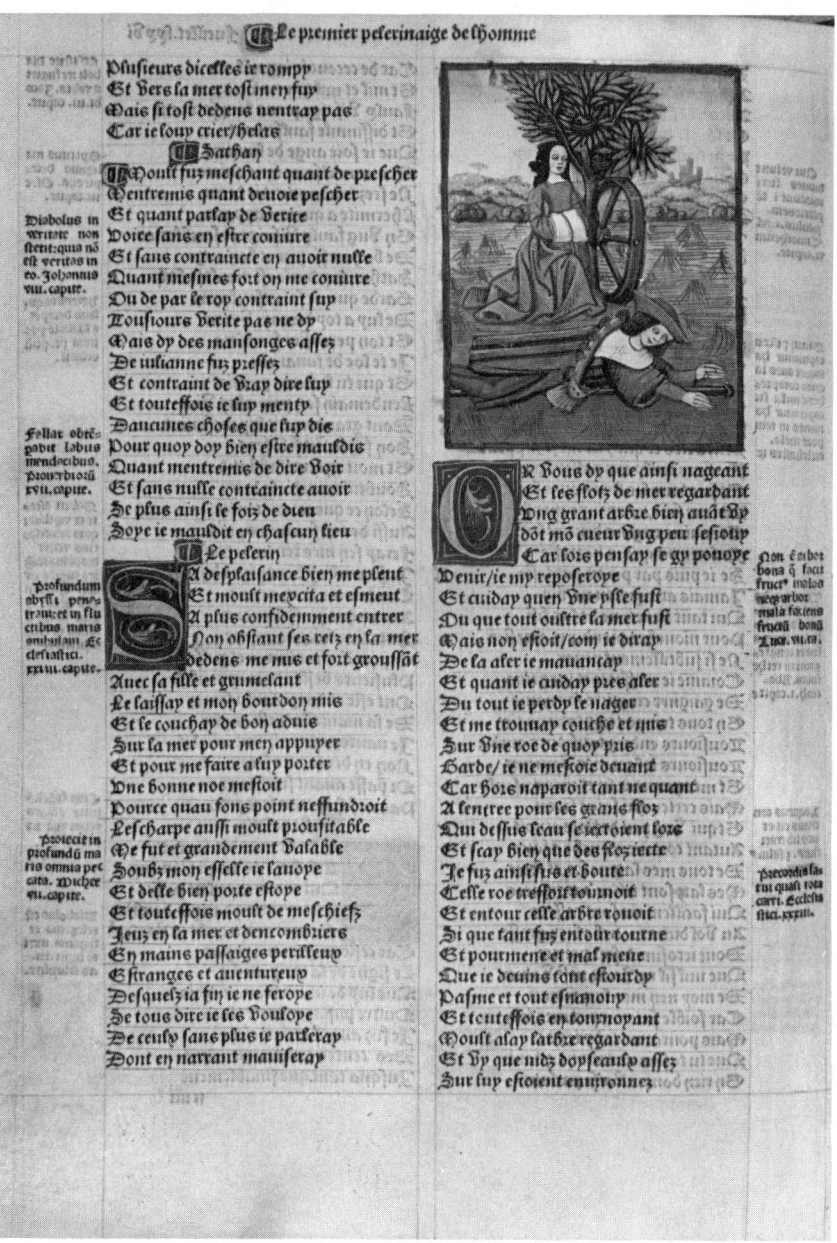

Figure 9.6. The Pilgrim and Fortune, from *Le pèlerinage de l'homme,* Paris, Antoine Vérard, 1511, ONB, CP ID2, sig. LXXVIv (on vellum). Courtesy of the Österreichische Nationalbibliothek, Vienna.

1499 edition of the prose *Vie*, Vérard still had "upscale" copies produced on vellum, such as that which bears the arms of Henry VII.[20]

From Script to Print in Space and Time

The woodcuts, especially those ever-popular designs for the Lyons edition, are a sophisticated rethinking of the pace and flow of the pictorial narrative and not just some cobbled-together sequence based on manuscript originals. The designer had available a full traditional cycle in his manuscript exemplar but had to compress and concentrate it radically in the new medium. The best way to show this is to examine the sequence at the end of the work where the pilgrim enters the monastery of the Ship of Religion. Here he encounters not vices but virtues in the form of a similar series of mysterious female personifications who are only later explained in the text.

From the very earliest illuminated cycles of the poem we see these virtues isolated in separate miniatures. There are five on one folio of the earliest dated manuscript (PML, MS M. 772, dated by a colophon 1348). The first miniature shows Charity and Voluntary Poverty entering the monastery; the next shows Discipline and Obedience. Study, who bears her food on a parchment and is hounded by the dove of the Holy Spirit, follows, and then Abstinence wearing her gorget of Sobriety. Prayer, who feeds the dead with one hand and pierces the heavens with other, is last on the page.[21] Seven ladies appear in five separate miniatures, whereas the designer of the Lyons series had to fit all of these as well as two others who follow into one picture (fig. 9.7). The first four figures entering the door of the monastery are still included, but here they are placed in the middle distance. Prayer is separated off at the far right, but the final lady to appear in this sequence, Latria, who blows her horn of praise, is pushed right into the foreground along with the pilgrim. Architectural spaces within the monastery itself serve to divide up what had

[20]See Pollard, *Le pèlerinage*, and, in addition to MacFarlane, *Antoine Vérard*, two essays on Vérard in *Manuscripts in the Fifty Years after the Invention of Printing*, ed. J. B. Trapp (London, 1983): Eleanor P. Spencer, "Antoine Vérard's Illuminated Vellum Incunables," pp. 62–66, and Mary Beth Winn, "Antoine Vérard's Presentation Manuscripts and Printed Books," pp. 66–75.

[21]Reproduced in *An Exhibition of Illuminated Manuscripts Held at the New York Public Library* (New York, 1934), pl. 64, no. 71. For this manuscript, see Camille, "Illustrated Manuscripts of Deguileville," pp. 20–40.

dames lefquelles feruoient de plufieurs et diuers offices
Et comment grace de dieu luy declaira la fignificacõ des
dames deffufdictes et de leurs offices. Et apres lune pi-
celles dames laquelle portoit liés z cordes luy lya les piés
les mains et la langue tres eftroictement.

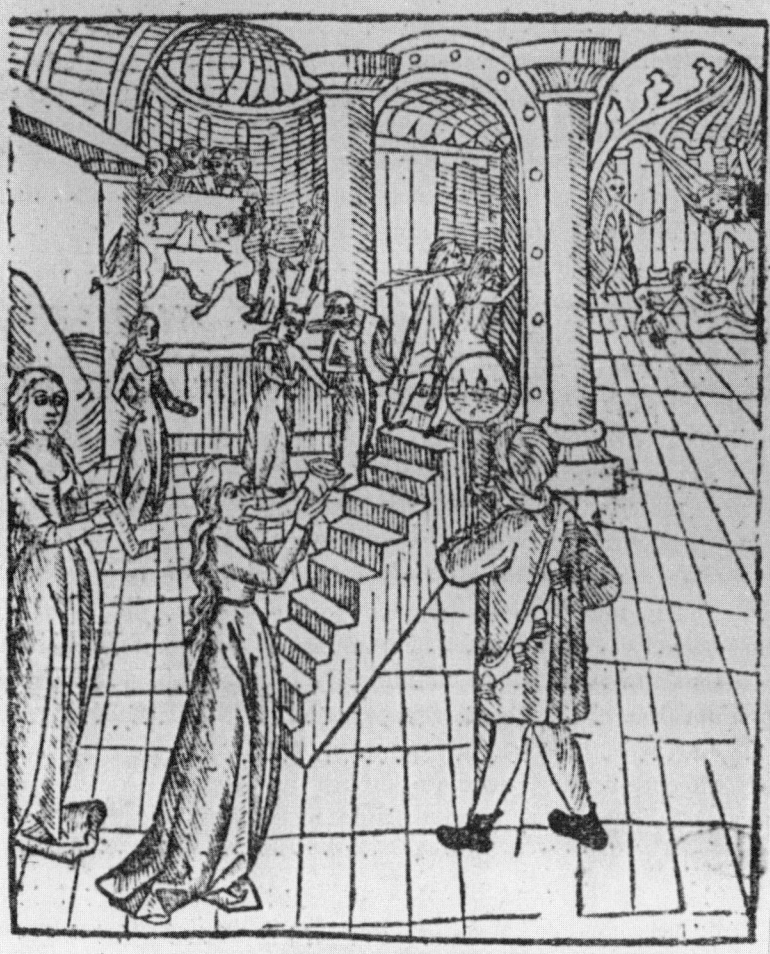

Figure 9.7. The Pilgrim Meets the Virtues inside the Monastery, from *Le pèlerin de la vie humaine,* Lyons, Mathieu Husz, 1485, Paris, Bibliothèque de l'Arsenal, 4° 2847, sig. viii verso. Courtesy of the Bibliothèque de l'Arsenal.

been the separate scenes in the manuscript cycle, and space provides the means through which we read the various personifications and their attributes. Also, the fact that all these virtues inhabit the monastery is something that cannot be conveyed in the isolated emblematic scenes in manuscripts.

The Lyons designer might have had such a set of models at hand which he had to compress into one scene. His solution is followed in subsequent incunabula versions, including a little-known and perhaps unique copy of an edition of the work printed by Michel le Noir in 1520, now in the Bibliothèque de l'Arsenal (fig. 9.8).[22] This is a much smaller book, and although the woodcuts are reduced in size, they too are based on the Lyons designs (fig. 9.7). Here, however, the Virtues seem squashed into the monastery, and beside them Le Noir has reused a half-length figure from the border decoration of another book to fill out the already overcrowded space.

Following a different set of Dutch manuscript models for the sequence of the Virtues in the Ship of Religion, the Haarlem woodcutter spread out this part of the narrative over a number of scenes, although his space was limited by the meaningful repetition of the "dreamer" cut as the visionary experiencer of each scene to its right (fig. 9.9). In contrast to Le Noir's decorate reuse of woodcuts as space fillers (fig. 9.8), here was yet another device of repetition, special to the print medium, which enhances the reading of the work by underlining throughout its visionary source.[23]

Not that the manuscript illuminator had total freedom of space compared to the woodcut designer, who might be limited by the standardized size of his cuts. The illuminator could work only in the spaces left him by the scribe, and this often led to problems, as in the two miniatures of the pilgrim's encounter with Avarice (figs. 9.10 and 9.11). She is the most visually complex of the vices; the artist of an early-fifteenth-century northern French manuscript (Bodleian Library, MS Douce 300) even tried to include the allegory of the chessboard which she displays to the pilgrim (fig. 9.10). Squeezing

[22]Paris, Bibliothèque de l'Arsenal, 4° B2848. See Robert Brun, *Le livre français illustré de la Renaissance: Catalogue des principaux livres à figures du XVIe siècle* (Paris, 1969), p. 207.

[23]*Pen to Press*, p. 117. See also James Snyder's evocative piece in *The Early Illustrated Book: Essays in Honor of Lessing J. Rosenwald,* ed. Sandra Hindman (Washington, D.C., 1982), pp. 41–62.

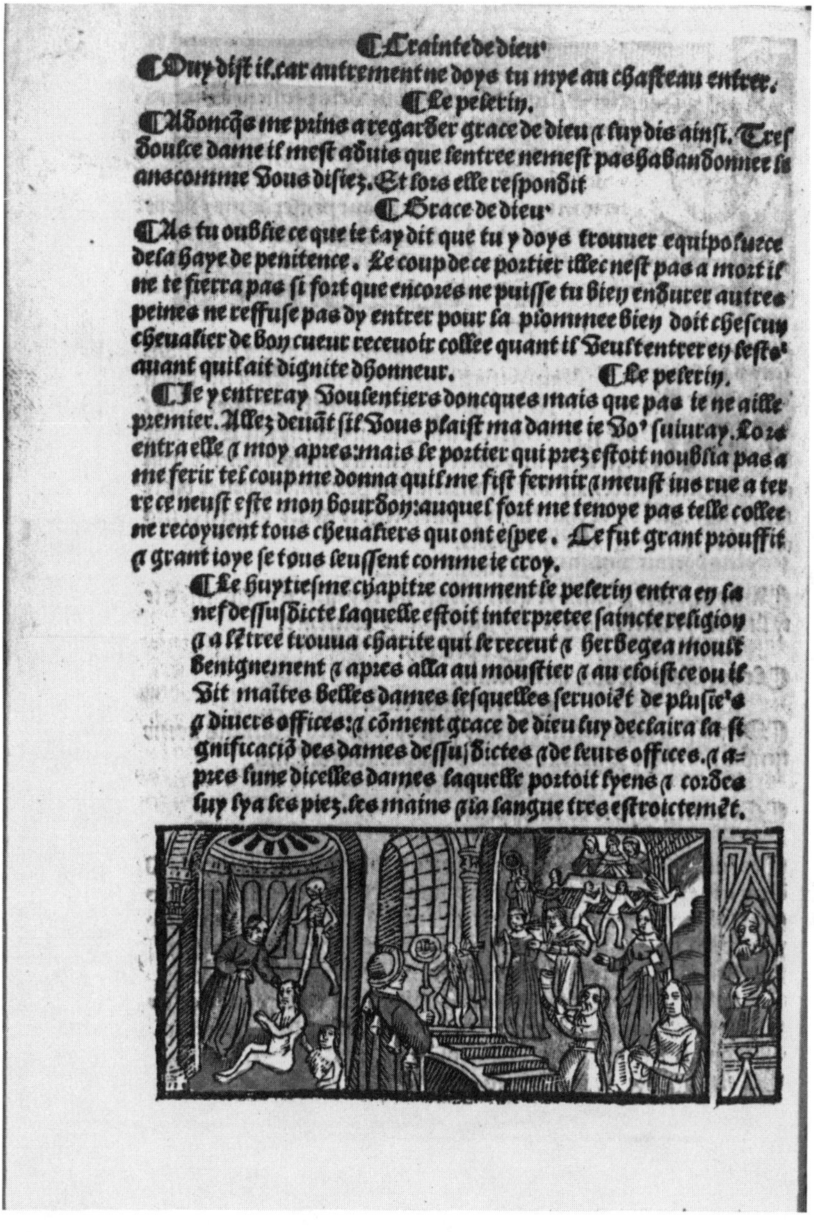

Craintede dieu.
Ouy dist il.car autrement ne doys tu mye au chasteau entrer.
Le pelerin.
Adoncques me prins a regarder grace de dieu q luy dis ainsi. Tres
doulce dame il mest aduis que lentree nemest pas habandonnee si
 anscomme vous disiez. Et lors elle respondit
Grace de dieu.
As tu oublie ce que ie tay dit que tu y doys trouuer equipolence
dela haye de penitence. Le coup de ce portier illec nest pas a mort il
ne te sierra pas si fort que encores ne puisse tu bien endurer autres
peines ne reffuse pas dy entrer pour sa piommee bien doit chescun
cheualier de bon cueur receuoir collee quant il veult entrer en sest
auant quil ait dignite dhonneur. Le pelerin.
Ie y entreray voulentiers doncques mais que pas le ne aille
premier. Allez deuant sil vous plaist ma dame ie vous suiuray. Lors
entra elle q moy apres: mais le portier qui pres estoit noublia pas a
me ferir tel coup me donna quil me fist fermir a meust ius rue a ter
re ce neust este mon bourdon: auquel fort me tenoye pas telle collee
ne recoyuent tous cheualiers qui ont espee. Ce fut grant prouffit
q grant ioye se tous seussent comme ie croy.
Le huytiesme chapitre comment le pelerin entra en sa
nef dessusdicte laquelle estoit interpretee saincte religion
q la sestree trouua charite qui le receut q herbegea moult
benignement q apres alla au moustier q au cloistre ce ou il
vit maintes belles dames lesquelles seruoient de plusie[u]rs
q diuers offices: q comment grace de dieu luy declaira la si
gnificacio des dames dessusdictes q de leurs offices. q a-
pres lune dicelles dames laquelle portoit lyens q cordes
luy lya ses piez. les mains q la langue tres estroictement.

Figure 9.8. The Pilgrim Meets the Virtues inside the Monastery, from *Le pèlerin de la vie humaine,* Paris, Michel le Noir, 1520, Paris, Bibliothèque de l'Arsenal, 4° B2848, sig. TVv. Courtesy of the Bibliothèque de l'Arsenal.

[277]

Michael Camille

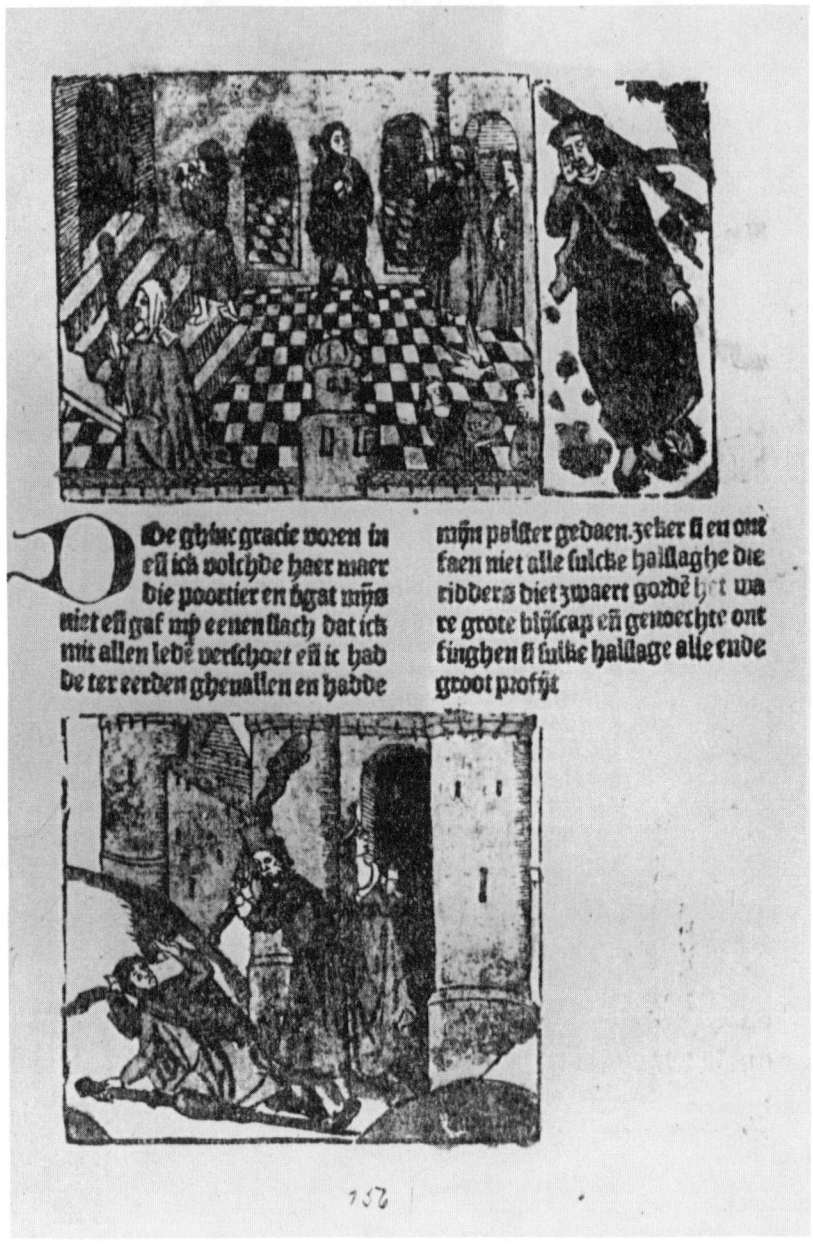

Figure 9.9. The Pilgrim Meets the Virtues inside the Monastery, from *Boeck van den pelgherym,* Haarlem, Jacob Bellaert, 1486, PML, Ch. L. F. 1665 79v (modern numeration). Courtesy of the Pierpont Morgan Library, New York.

[278]

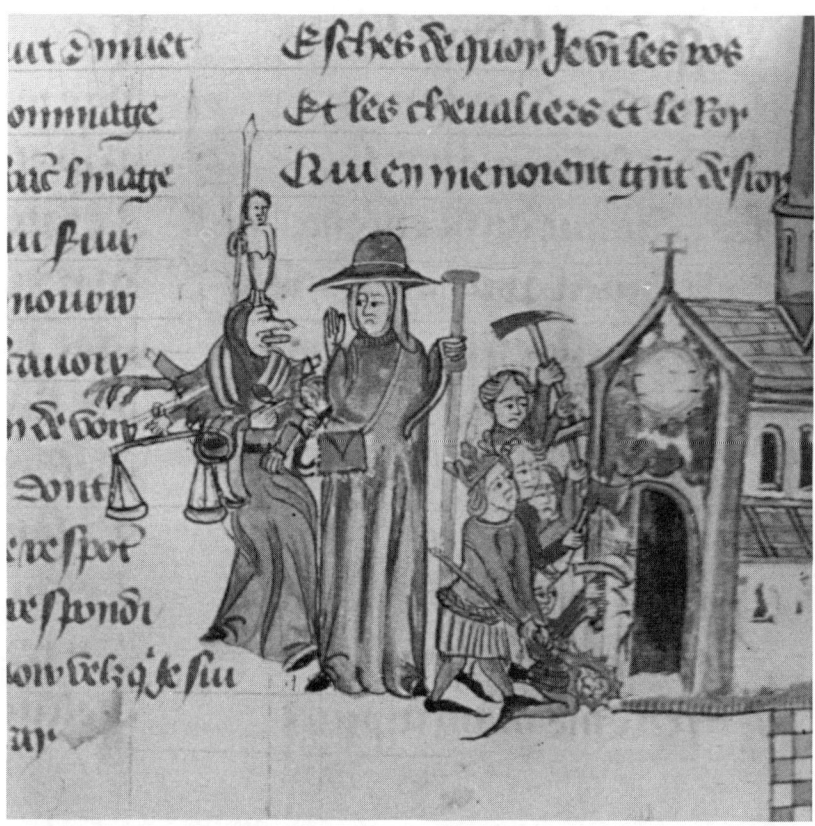

Figure 9.10. The Pilgrim Meets Avarice, from *Le pèlerinage de la vie humaine,* Oxford, Bodleian Library, MS Douce 300, fol. 82v. By permission of the Bodleian Library.

everything into the small, unframed space left by the scribe causes some difficulty, and some of the hideous hag's attributes encroach upon the text to the left. She has far more space and is more logical in her appearance in the Lyons edition (fig. 9.11), where at the left foreground she confronts the pilgrim and then on a distant hill shows him the kings and bishops battling on a chessboard for control of the taxes in this complicated allegory on the word *exchequer.* The illustration of the latter is rare in the manuscript tradition, and this is a case where in the new medium a radical rereading of the work is promulgated, emphasizing this secular satire. The Spanish translation and edition of 1490 copied the Lyons designs direct from the prints pasted on a block and then recut, resulting in a reversal and simplification of

gue traicte/et si auoit six mains et deux mougnons. Et sur
sa teste portoit vne ydolle/laqlle vieille apres soy me me‑
na sur vne grant roue. Et puis me monstra en vne moult
belle plaine vng moustier. Et au pres vng eschacquier ou
quel auoit eschas gros et menus dont le roy diceluy escha
quier a layde de ses eschas et pions mynoit le fondement
diceluy moustier. et de la croce dung euesque il faisoit bes
che et houete comme cy apres vous orrez.

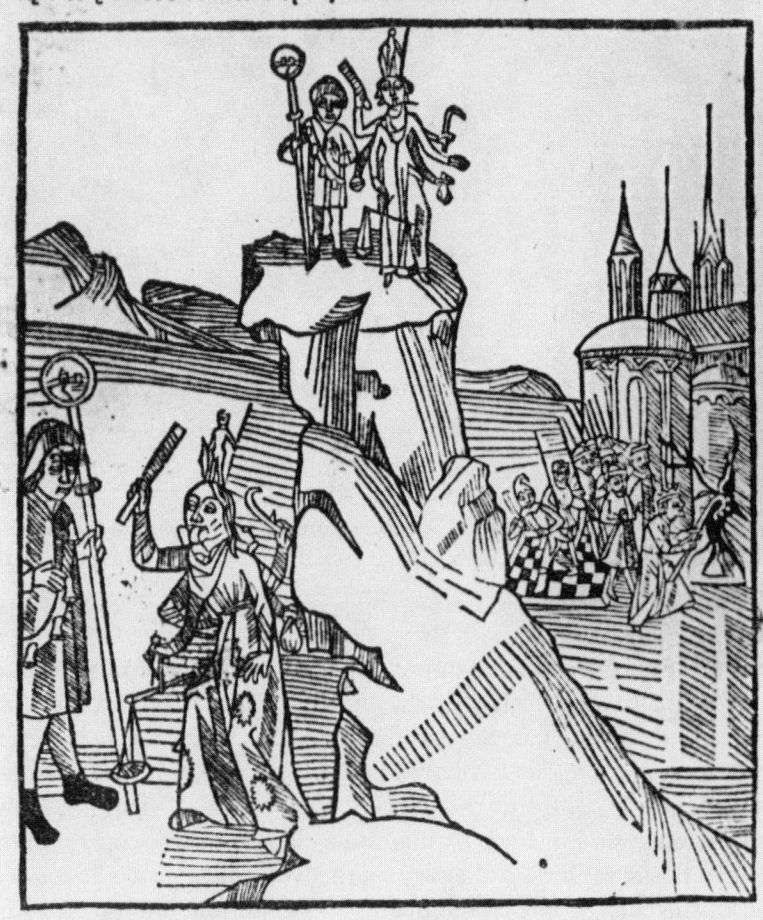

Figure 9.11. The Pilgrim Meets Avarice, from *Le pèlerin de la vie humaine*,
Lyons, Mathias Husz, 1485, Paris, Bibliothèque de l'Arsenal, 4° B 2847,
sig. mvii verso. Courtesy of the Bibliothèque de l'Arsenal.

the designs. In this case the natural way of reading the Avarice scene, starting at the left, is not possible.

But the odd thing is that sometimes the Spanish cuts, with their reversed direction, seem easier for us to read in their "wrong" left-to-right trajectory. The pilgrim's being given his armor and then appearing fully dressed in it is an example (fig. 9.12). The five parts of this narrative are: (1, far left) the pilgrim stands dressed in his armor (of Virtue), given to him by Grace Dieu; (2, far right) the pilgrim throws off the armor, which is too heavy; (3, center right) the armor is given to Memory, who has eyes in the back of her head; (4, center back) the pilgrim takes communion from the bishop before (5, right back) setting off on his journey. This is read not only from right to left but also from foreground to background. The fact that the cut from the reversed Spanish edition flows from left to right as we would expect suggests that even at this date narratives did not have to flow in any standard way—that the position of the figures in space is more crucial to continuity and narrative temporal suggestion than their arrangement on two sides of the plane. The reader, as in a diagram, looks for what is significant and what has been described as such in rubric or text. Such visual compression and continuity of narrative action makes reading these images quite different from anything one encounters in the manuscript cycles of the poem. There, every encounter was an isolated and discrete miniature without a unifying spatial or temporal principle. It is this incursion of space and time into the design, and therefore necessarily the reading of these woodcut images, which makes them so powerful.

Of course, between 1330 and 1500 the pictorial language of and the reception of manuscript painting changed too. But from the schematic miniatures with their abstract fields to the late-fifteenth-century illusionistic Eyckian landscapes, miniatures interrupt the text in the sense described by Kenneth Goodman in his analysis of the psycholinguistics of the reading process: "Some cues are external to the reading process but they may be used by the reader. Pictures are cues which may be decoded as a substitute or supplement to language. . . . These external cues get between reader and written language. In a sense they interfere with the vital recoding process."[24]

The print medium creates less of a rift between image and text than

[24]Kenneth S. Goodman, ed., *The Psycholinguistic Nature of the Reading Process* (Detroit, 1968), p. 25.

[281]

Ðraçia de dios.

Efpera me pues yo creo te traera la que bie n te ayudaa z foſ.en dra tus armas que no quieres contigo poztar.

El pelegrino.

l Ðego partio de mi graçia de dios z fue yo no fe donde z que de todo folo z me acaue de defarmar ffeteniendo fin mas de mandar mi çnſſon z borzdon. E defpues de defarmado me vino vn grand defconfozte.z començo de dezir/que hare mezquino que tanta pena dy a graçia de dios mi guiadoza que tan ffica mente me a via armado/z fueffe yo ffey o de muy gran eftado no las avria meiozes:z ptra fus ta buenas amoneftaçiones yo las he detadas.Ð trifte coño he yo mi fuerça perdida:poz que no fo yo fuerte alleuar eftas armas. Ca yo feria muy mas temido z nombrado:mas fin duda me parefçe el endurarlas feria ympofible. E poz efto yo encomendare a graçia ð dios efte cafo.ca yo creo no me faltara.ca fiempze me touo de fu mano z bien me lo ha moftrado.ca avn agoza es yoa o bufcar quien eftas armas me pueda lleuar.

Capitulo.xviij. z vltimo del libro del pelegrino de vida humana do fe trata coño defpues de defarmado el pelegrino de lus armas todas graçia de dios le truzo vna muy linda feruidoza que las lleuaua do el queria.

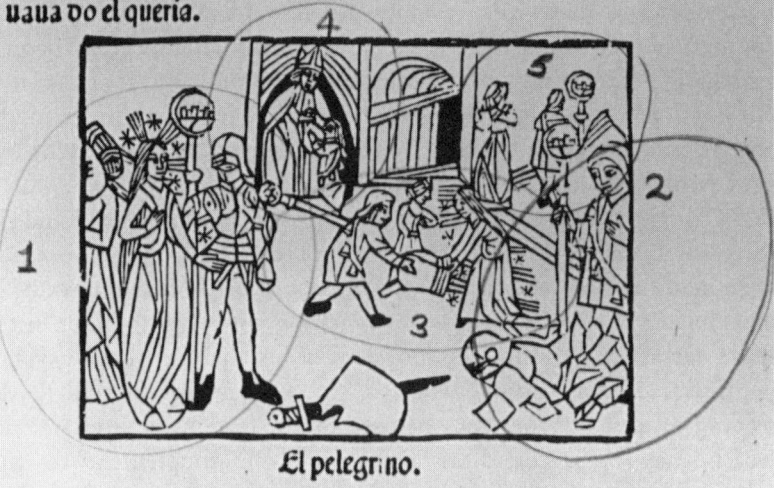

El pelegrino.

Figure 9.12. The Pilgrim Throws off His Armor and Gives It to Memory to Carry for Him, from *El pelerinage de la vida humana,* Toulouse, Henricus Aleman (Mayer), 1490, Madrid, Biblioteca Nacional, I 1300, sig. e Vv. Courtesy of the Biblioteca Nacional.

occurs in manuscript illustration. This is partly because of production—the different agendas of the scribe and the illuminator, who often operate apart from each other. More work needs to be done in this respect, comparing the "hiring-out" methods of the illuminators' shop with what seems to be the more uniform organization of the print shop.[25] From the viewpoint of reception, the woodcut image would have less "interference" in Goodman's sense, precisely because the image has the same black and white structure as the word, and although it is read in space, is also read in time, following a linear pattern just as in the flow of language. In the illusionistic manuscript painting, or the painted printed image for that matter, the eye is led outside the text and into an alternative and ever-visible world of atemporal contemplation. This can be seen even within the work of one printer such as Vérard in his division between print and painted miniatures. The relay or place of transit through which the eye must pass to reach its goal is much shorter in the print medium, where individual units are compressed and individual stylistic features are erased.

The use of the print medium to address vast and hitherto unreached audiences in the fifteenth and sixteenth centuries and to transmit ideas has been stressed by Elizabeth Eisenstein and William Ivins.[26] Deguileville's stated purpose in writing his *Pèlerinage* was to teach, and the new medium stresses this dogmatic nature of his plan. Twice in the text he mentions images, carefully isolated as "Figura" by rubrics, which are to be pictured on the page—memory images or diagrams that sum up a complex doctrine—like the PAX or carpenter's square and the heart holding the world as Aristotle explains it.[27] Significantly, it is in the manuscript tradition that these two crucial diagrams are most often fumbled or left out. Illuminators were not sure what to make of such abstract depictions, and so the scribe often made these

[25]On the organization of the printing shop, one can start with Curt F. Bühler, *The Fifteenth-Century Book: The Scribes, the Printers, the Decorators* (Philadelphia, 1960), and the excellent bibliography in Sandra Hindman, "Cross-Fertilization: Experiments in Mixing the Media," in *Pen to Press*, pp. 101–57.

[26]Elizabeth Eisenstein, *The Printing Press as an Agent of Change: Communications and Cultural Transformations* (Cambridge, 1979), and William Ivins, *Prints and Visual Communication* (New York, 1969).

[27]The importance of visual mnemonics in Deguileville's enterprise has been studied by Susan K. Hagen, *"Allegorical Remembrance": A Study of the Pilgrimage of the Life of Man as a Medieval Treatise on Seeing and Remembering* (Athens, Ga., 1990).

particular images. Oudin de Cavarnet, the Parisian scribe of a 1393 manuscript, wrote to the artist Remiet, "Do not put anything in this space I will do it," and the space is still blank in the manuscript.[28] In the more cohesive structure of the print shop, the relationship between pictorial and verbal contents can be much more efficiently fused. The Heart of the World is never illustrated in the manuscript versions, but its diagrammatic mnemonic formula is ideally suited to the fast medium of print (fig. 9.13).

The logic of reading as a systematic, continuous process fostered by the arrival of printing can be seen in these narrative cycles. Medieval manuscript images were read like their texts, slowly, in fits and starts, with constant stops to reread and pore over complexities and difficulties. The image, like the marginal glosses in Vérard's edition (fig. 9.3), serves the individually read text rather than the communally recited poem, helping the reader locate his place in the narrative and understand its significance. Print, in Walter J. Ong's description, is a much less performative, much more mental experience. This is the greatest difference between script and print—the transition from slow oral communication to fast written signs.[29] Deguileville opens his poem by encouraging all those who "listen to" it to pay attention. He structured the original poem in four books to be read on four successive days at an open gathering, another important image of the poem's oral delivery which was standard in the manuscripts but is not included in the printed picture cycles. The modernized version, with its internal "speakers" and its chapter construction outlined in a new table of contents at the beginning, removes the work from its roots in oral presentation and sets it securely within the single gaze of the reading "I"-eye. Here a much more personal and dynamic mode of reading is going on, something verging on Paul Saenger's notion of silent reading,[30] which, I prefer to argue, is a late medieval development.

The prefatory picture to Book Four, where the pilgrim comes to

[28]BN, MS fr. 823, fol. 14r. For this and further discussion of the PAX diagram in various manuscripts, see Camille, "Illustrated Manuscripts of Deguileville," pp. 10–13. The Lyons edition (on fol. diiii) depicts the $\mathfrak{L}$-shaped carpenter's square upright with the corner A at the top rather than, as the text states, on the ground. It also sits in a landscape setting rather than appearing as a diagram proper, as in the more "learned" layout of Vérard's 1511 edition (fol. xvii verso).

[29]See Walter J. Ong, *Orality and Literacy: The Technologizing of the Word* (New York, 1982), pp. 117–38.

[30]Paul Saenger, "Silent Reading: Its Impact on Late Medieval Script and Society," *Viator* 13 (1982): 367–414.

der como el querer. Poz ende te afyno en aver hecho lo que me ffe-
prehendes fer la caufa mas grande mi buen querer/ z no deues du-
dar li crees que no falto en hazer lo mi grand poder. Tu queftion
toma fuerça enel exemplo que difte que es mayoz la cafa que no la
parcd/o que alguna delas partes que fon dentro/z que poz yo hazer el contrano en efte fanto facramento eftaua mal lo as mirado.
As tu vifto en tu vida el cozaçon de vn hombre quanto es grande
o pequeño/di me lo fi te acuerdas.

Ariftotiles.

Acuerdo me aver le vifto z avn muchas vezes/z fe bien que es
tan pequeño que vna ave poz pequeña fuelle no feria del arta: tanto me parefçe pequeño.

Sapiençia.

Pues yo te demando tan pequeña cofa de quanto feria arta fe-
gun tu capaçidad/o que cofa baftaria allenchirle.

Ariftotiles.

p Or experiençia conozco que no todo el mundo avn q̃ le fuelle dado afu
abandon: mi diçiplo alexanore del fue fe
ñoz z dezia q̃ avn li.x.oviera dios hecho
los oviera el conquiftado/z avn no fuera
contento fu cozaçon. vna figura ffedóda
es ympofible lincha vna triangular que fi-
empre no quede el vn angulo vazio. El co
raçon es de figura triangular: z el mundo
ffedondo como es pofible que le conten-
te lo que no le puede lenchir. Conclujo q̃
todo el mundo no hartaria el cozaçon del hombre. E ves lo ma-
nifiefto en efta figura.

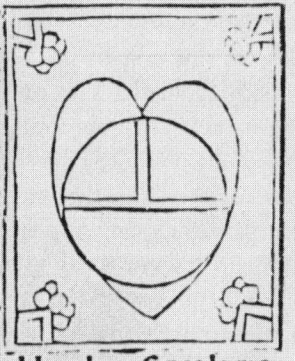

Sapiençia.

Cumple pues que aya alguna cofa que lo pueda henchir. ca fe
gun tu autozidad verdadera no ay cofa vazia enel mundo.

Ariftotiles.

yo confidere que es vn bien foverano el qual folo lo deue llenchir
z hafta aver lo no fera contento.

Figure 9.13. The Figure of the Heart Holding the World, from *El pel-
erinage de la vida humana*, Toulouse, Henricus Aleman (Mayer), 1490,
Madrid, Biblioteca Nacional, I 1300, sig. D IIv. Courtesy of the Biblioteca
Nacional.

the Sea of the World, in a lavish manuscript made for René de Laval is typical of the tendency of the early printed cycles to synthesize scenes into a single unified image.[31] But it really shows only one narrative moment—the Sea of the World with the people floating or sinking in it. It is an enlargement of a tiny miniature into full-page size rather than a compression of diverse narrative moments. Much of it shows excessive figurality, as in the landscape and the trees. Vérard's 1499 imprint illuminated for Henry VII has more dynamic interaction between the pilgrim and Satan, who fishes for souls in the Sea, and includes the dreamer in bed at the left.[32] But much more conceptually precise is the Lyons cut showing Satan and his daughter Heresy (fig. 9.14). The Net of Sin is brilliantly poised above the whole composition along the orthogonals, a device impossible to imagine outside the woodcut medium. On the right in the Lyons series (left in the Spanish version) Grace Dieu leads the pilgrim out of the picture. The continuity of the narrative experience in the Lyons compositions is greater than that in the 120 or so of the manuscript tradition since the reader's eye follows the same figure, the pilgrim, in and out of pictures as in this case or in the earlier baptism scene, where the pilgrim after bathing in the Tub of Tears is led away out of the picture.

The meaningful manipulation of linear space is at work in Vérard's 1499 sequence where relationships between divine and human experience is registered in thrilling oblique designs. But one does not need the illuminator's dressing up the woodcut to have the most powerful illusionism, as in the table falling obliquely into our space in one the best woodcuts of the *Ars moriendi*.[33] In the same way, though on the level of narrative devices, the early woodcuts of the *Vie* use the reader's experience of space and time not to evoke but to enact the dynamic process of allegorical understanding in the reading process itself.

The woodcuts I have examined here are normally termed "crude." The modern sensibility is less concerned with function than with form, and thus gives priority to the inconsequential—the bloom on the grapes, the distant landscape—and, taken in by pictorial tricks,

[31]Fol. 128 of this manuscript, once in the library of Lord Eldenham, is reproduced under lot 23 in the Gibbs sale, Sotheby's, March 23, 1937.

[32]See this scene in Vérard's illuminated copy made for Henry VII in the facsimile, Pollard, *Le pèlerinage.*

[33]Reproduced in Arthur M. Hind, *An Introduction to a History of Woodcut,* vol. 1 (New York: 1963), fig. 94.

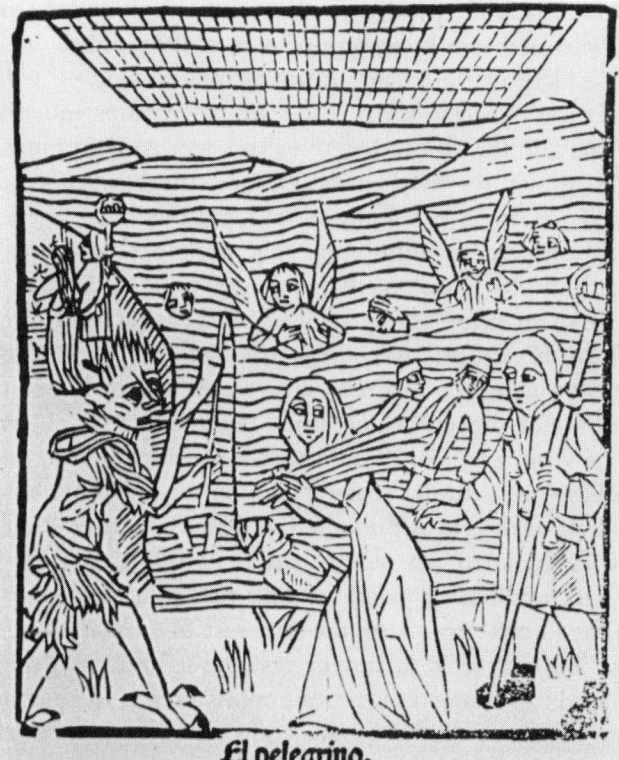

El pelegrino.

Ason es pues aves/oydo los paſſados peligros de mi co-
mençado camino que osdiga al preſente los que deſpues
ſe ſiguieron. E deſto vos dire los q̃ mas tocaron a mi aſi en
montañas como en valles profundos yo vy coſas diuerſas las qua
les todas contar ſeria muy luengo. çerca del camino por do yo yva
halle vn grand mar ꝛ a mi pareſçer en demaſia muy profundo enel
qual coſſian vientos diuerſos ꝛ avian ꝛ ſe moſtrauan grandes tēpe
ſtas/dentro eran hombꝛes ꝛ dueñas de eſtados diuerſos avn q̃ no
ygual mente enel agua profundos/ ca los vnos avian las cabeças
alos pies delos otros/ꝛ otros avia que erā todos derechos ꝛ aviā
alas como ſi deuieſſen volar ſi el mar no les hiziera empacho. otros
eran atadas los pies alas yervas dela ſſua del agua/ ꝛ otros que
avian atados los ojos/ꝛ de otras guyſas diuerſas eran ende dete-

Figure 9.14. The Pilgrim Meets Satan and Heresy at the Shore of the Sea
of the World, from *El pelerinage de la vida humana,* Toulouse, Henricus
Aleman (Mayer), 1490, Madrid, Biblioteca Nacional, I 1300, sig. L VIIv.
Courtesy of the Biblioteca Nacional.

we forget that these elements are not essential to an understanding of the text. We forget that books are read as well as looked at. Perhaps locating the place of the image in the history of reading will tell us more about the expectations of the kinds of patrons (notably royal and aristocratic in the case of Deguileville's works) who sought fancy naturalistic miniatures in their books and those who were better served by the cheaper, terser, and more rapid medium. These images are neither simple nor simplifying. The prefatory cut in the Lyons series, for example, is one of the most powerful visual statements I know about the nature of Deguileville's work, in its separation of the dreamer from his dream (as in fig. 9.16). Traditionally in the manuscript illustrations two miniatures showed the author in bed beside a mirror and then a separate scene of the Heavenly City. The woodcut presents the visionary goal of the work both on the left in the round mirror and as a whole other spatial reality in the "woodblock" image. The right half of the cut is presented as a block, a three-dimensional picture at an angle to the picture plane. Is this some play on the materials and methods of printing? This tells us a lot about the sensibility of the Lyons designer to the structure of the poem and its new reading audience. Printed picture cycles tend to underplay the origins and production of the text. Elaborate miniatures at the beginning of manuscript copies of the 1464 translation picture the presentation of the book to Jeanne de Laval, who commissioned the translation (fig. 9.15).[34] But such an image of production which enhances the prestige of the text is not really of much use to someone who wants to understand the meaning of the work. While the Laval dedication is retained as a textual prologue, in the Lyons edition it is not given a picture.

The cycle begins rather with the powerful image of the dreamer-

[34]At least ten illuminated copies of the 1464 translation are extant. One lavish copy sold at Sotheby's on July 8, 1970 (lot 106), was made for Charlotte of Savoy, consort of Louis XI, and was illuminated by a follower of the "Master of King René of Anjou." It appears in the inventory of Charlotte's library made in 1483. Others can be related to the Angers court in the late fifteenth century either through patronage or style. Geneva MS 181 (Gagnebin, *L'enluminure*, p. 134) bears the arms of Aymar de Poitiers, count of Saint-Vallier. This might suggest that illuminated manuscripts of the *Vie* were enjoyed as signs of rich *retardetaire* or conservative nostalgia by a higher social group than enjoyed the printed editions. But the finely illuminated manuscript (Paris, Bibliothèque de l'Arsenal, MS 2319) which has only five large miniatures (fig. 9.15) belonged in 1553 to a "Pierre Demarestz," a "bourgeois de Paris," according to a colophon on fol. 152v. Much more research is needed on this question of the audience for and attitudes toward printed as opposed to manuscript books.

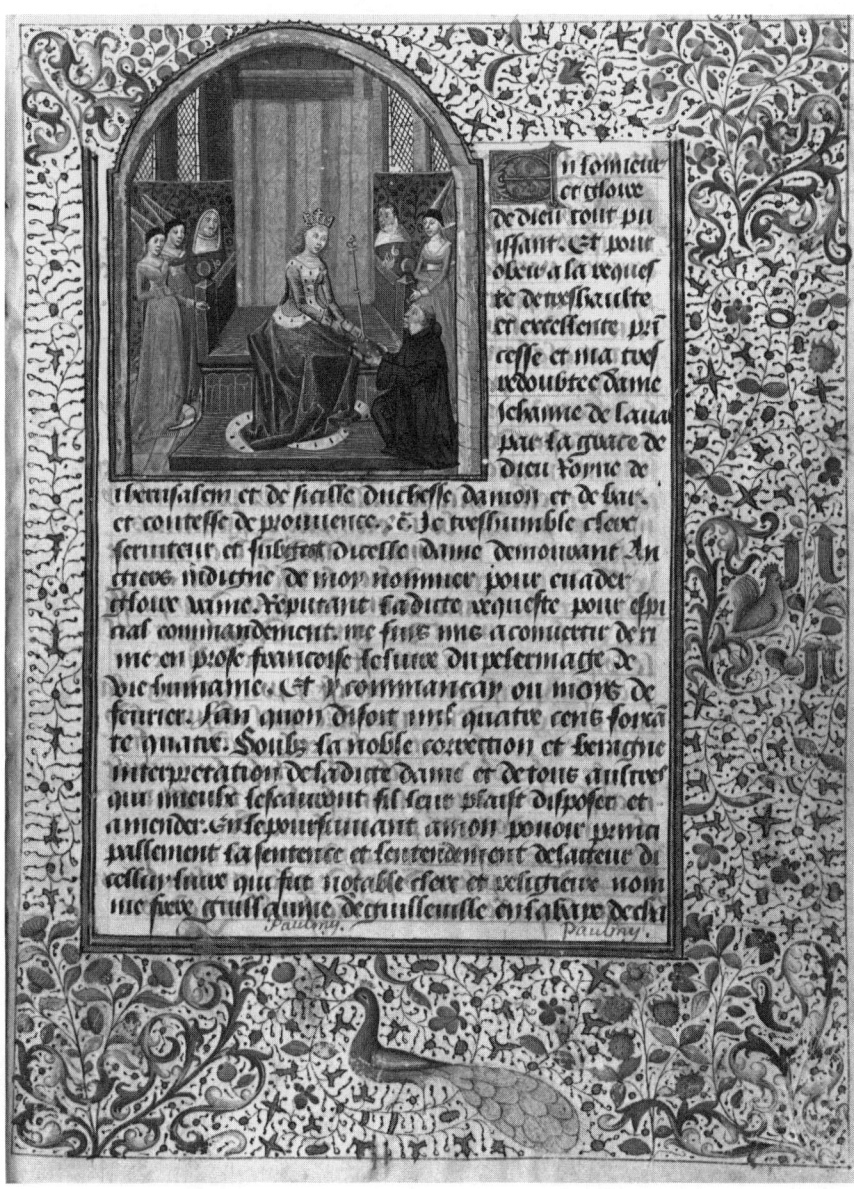

Figure 9.15. Presentation Miniature Showing Jeanne de Laval Accepting the Prose Version from an Anonymous Translator, from *Le livre de pèlerinage de la vie humaine,* Paris, Bibliothèque de l'Arsenal, MS 2319, fol. 1. Courtesy of the Bibliothèque de l'Arsenal.

poet having his vision of the Heavenly Jerusalem and the four orders climbing its walls (fig. 9.16). This is a compression of four separate narrative scenes commonly seen in the manuscript tradition. The dual image in the print provides a literary framework for the whole narrative as a dream poem and vision. This is not to suggest that this move toward unified spatial frontispieces is missing from late-fifteenth-century manuscript illumination.[35] But when these occur they merely elaborate the fantastic architecture of the Heavenly City; they do not introduce the interesting bifurcation of the dreamer and his dream which is so crucial to the allegory. The fifteenth-century reader was not interested in the work as a description of a place or events or even of fantastic creatures encountered. What mattered was the clear articulation of the surface of the allegory so that its depth and multiple registers of meaning are accessible.

In this sense the woodcut approaches much more closely the original schema of illustrations I believe the austere Cistercian Deguileville had devised for the poem long before. This advice on how to read the work written by John Lydgate in his 1426 translation also stresses the importance of understanding the allegory through its lucid images:

> And that folkk may in the Ryhte weye se
> Best assuryd to-warde ther passage
> lat hem beholden in the Pylgrymage,
> Which called ys pylgrymage de mounde,
> In the wych fful notably ys founde,
> Lernyd and taught, who can well construe
> What folk shal take and what they shall eschue
> In this book, yf that they rede yerne,
> Pylgrymes schall the veray trouthe lerne,
> Yff they sette ter trewe dyllygence
> To understand clerly the sentence
> What yt menyth and the moralyte;
> Ther they may, as in a merour se
> holsom thynges, & thynges full notable.[36]

It is not in the illusionistic mirror of paint that Deguileville's elaborate allegory best served its fifteenth-century audience but in the more "holsom" and "notable" medium of print.

[35]These large frontispiece compositions appear in the manuscript made for Charlotte of Savoy and in Geneva, Bibliothèque Publique et Universitaire, MS 182, fol. 3v.

[36]John Lydgate, *The Pilgrimage of the Life of Man*, ed. F. J. Furnivall (London, 1889), p. 3, 11.74–87.

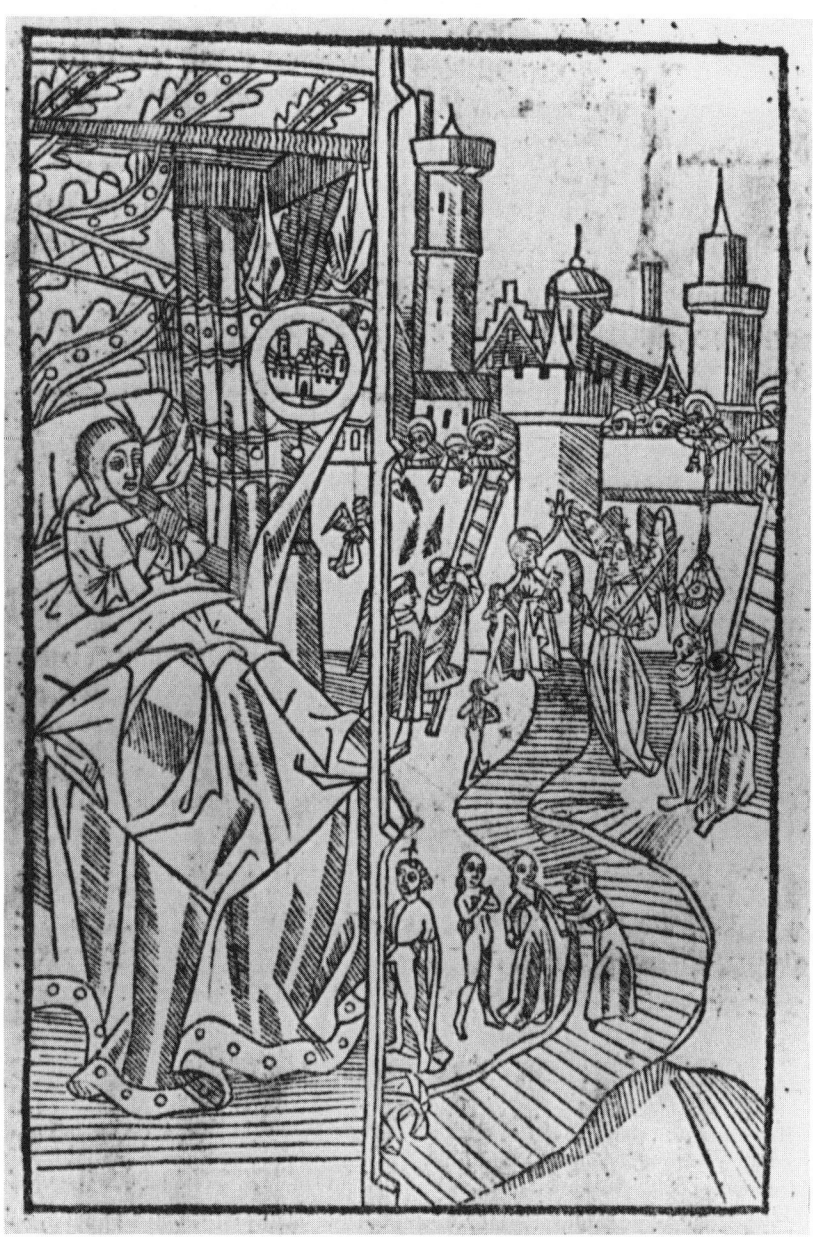

Figure 9.16. The Author Dreams He Sees the Heavenly Jerusalem in a Mirror, from *Le pèlerinage de la vie humaine,* Lyons, Mathias Husz, 1485, Paris, Bibliothèque de l'Arsenal, 4° 2847, sig. a iv recto, frontispiece. Courtesy of the Bibliothèque de l'Arsenal.

[10]

Mementos of Things to Come:
Orality, Literacy, and Typology
in the *Biblia pauperum*

Tobin Nellhaus

I t is well established that the *Biblia pauperum,* the mid-fifteenth-century blockbook compendium of typology, was both popular and widely influential. The blockbook derives from manuscript versions of the *Biblia pauperum,* which were also very popular in the Middle Ages, starting from at least the late thirteenth century, and possibly even the late twelfth century. The blockbook was probably printed in the Utrecht or Haarlem area sometime around 1460. Later, versions printed with movable type also appeared.

The remainder of our knowledge about the *Biblia pauperum* is limited. Some scholarship focuses on the *Biblia pauperum*'s evolution and character as a manuscript.[1] Another area of discussion concerns the chain of influences between the *Biblia pauperum* and other texts and artworks that use typology.[2] The place and date of the blockbook's production, the identification of different imprints, and their se-

[1] For example, Henrik Cornell, *Biblia pauperum* (Stockholm, 1925); and Gerhard Schmidt, *Die Armenbibeln des XIV. Jahrhunderts* (Graz, 1959). See also the summaries in Avril Henry, *Biblia pauperum: A Facsimile and Edition* (Ithaca, 1987), pp. 4, 22–24; and in Elizabeth Soltész, *Biblia pauperum: Facsimile Edition of the Forty-Leaf Blockbook in the Library of the Esztergom Cathedral,* trans. Lily Halápy, rev. Elizabeth West (Budapest, 1967), pp. iv–xiii.

[2] Such as Schmidt, *Die Armenbibeln;* and Theodor Musper, "Die Urausgabe der Biblia pauperum und der Apokalypse," *Gutenberg Jahrbuch* (1938): 53–58. See also Henry, *Biblia pauperum,* pp. 9–16; and Soltész, *Biblia pauperum,* pp. xiii–xvi.

quence are also subject to continuing research.[3] So is the book's name, which some scholars feel is problematic, inaccurate, or misleading because (they argue) the book was not in any modern sense a "Bible of the Poor."[4] Despite extensive investigation, we know little about who produced the *Biblia pauperum,* who used it, what its purpose was, or the way it was used. For example, Elizabeth Soltész believes that it was produced both for poor clerics and for the moderately wealthy laity.[5] In her facsimile Avril Henry, considering several suggestions about the purpose of the book, discards notions that it was an instructional tool for children or nonliterates, propaganda against the Cathar heresy, a memory aid for preachers, or a Bible for the lesser clergy. Her own proposal is that the *Biblia pauperum* served in personal meditation.[6]

All of these questions, though important, are essentially bibliographical; and all answers are hampered by the fact that the only certain evidence we have is in the book itself. But in crucial ways that evidence has been taken as a given and not investigated, particularly as it presents itself to the reader. The *Biblia pauperum* presents a striking organization of texts and images demanding particular strategies of thought in order to make sense of the book—strategies that were common enough in the Middle Ages (if less customary today) but nevertheless had to come from somewhere. The purpose of this essay is thus twofold. First, I intend to examine the structure of the *Biblia pauperum,* especially as it encourages the reader's use of typology. Second, I aim to connect typology to the dynamics of oral and written communication, and to explore the place of the *Biblia pauperum* within the social contexts of orality and literacy. I will then show how the analysis of oral-literate dynamics contributes to our understanding of the composition and reading of a single page of the *Biblia pauperum.* In the end I argue that, as Henry suggested, the *Biblia pauperum* was used as an aid to personal meditation, but I am able to

---

[3]E.g. Wilhelm L. Schreiber, *Manuel de l'amateur de la gravure sur bois et sur metal au XVe siècle,* vol. 4 (Leipzig, 1902); Musper, "Die Urausgabe"; Allan Stevenson, "The Quincentennial of Netherlandish Blockbooks," *British Museum Quarterly* 31 (1967): 83–87; Robert A. Koch, "New Criteria for Dating the Netherlandish *Biblia pauperum* Blockbook," in *Studies in Late Medieval and Renaissance Painting in Honor of Millard Meiss,* ed. Irving Lavin and John Plummer, 2 vols. (New York, 1977), I, 283–89.

[4]Henry, *Biblia pauperum,* p. 3; Soltész, *Biblia pauperum,* pp. vi–viii.

[5]Soltész, *Biblia pauperum,* pp. vi–viii.

[6]Henry, *Biblia pauperum,* pp. 17–18.

articulate more fully than has been previously possible the particular conceptual strategies involved in such meditation.

The Structure of the *Biblia pauperum* and the Use of Typology

The blockbook *Biblia pauperum* consists of forty full-page illustrations combining various kinds of biblical images and Latin texts, visually united by an architectonic frame. Many copies are hand-colored. The pages are printed on one side only but are paired to form openings. At the center of each page is a scene portraying a moment from the life of Christ or the Second Coming (see fig. 10.1). This central scene is flanked on either side by an incident from the Old Testament, except on the last page, where a scene from the Book of Revelation appears. Old Testament authors are portrayed in pairs above and below the central image. Various texts surround the illustrations. These include internally rhymed captions (*tituli*) for the three pictures, quotations ("prophecies") from the four Old Testament authors, and exegeses (*lectiones*) of the two scenes flanking the central image. Thus, for the reader of the *Biblia pauperum* the primary question is how the nine texts and three images work together, what role or effect they have on one another and on the reader.

The manuscript version of the *Biblia pauperum* is the earliest illustrated book of the typological system, and in both its manuscript and blockbook forms the book had a profound and enduring effect on the typological tradition.[7] Typology is in fact absolutely fundamental to the *Biblia pauperum:* it is virtually the book's sole principle of composition. Henry devotes considerable space in her edition to commentaries interpreting the typological significance of each page. Nonetheless, although we can readily recognize the enormous role of typology in the *Biblia pauperum* (and in the theology, literature, and art of the Middle Ages generally) and use this recognition to interpret the blockbook's content, it is less clear why typology proliferated, and why it has such importance in the *Biblia pauperum* specifically.

More than a "technique" to be applied or abandoned at will, typology is a habitual strategy of thought or conceptual composition, which shows how people or events in the Old Testament (the *types*)

---

[7]See, for example, the observations in Henry, *Biblia pauperum*, pp. 9–17, 35–38.

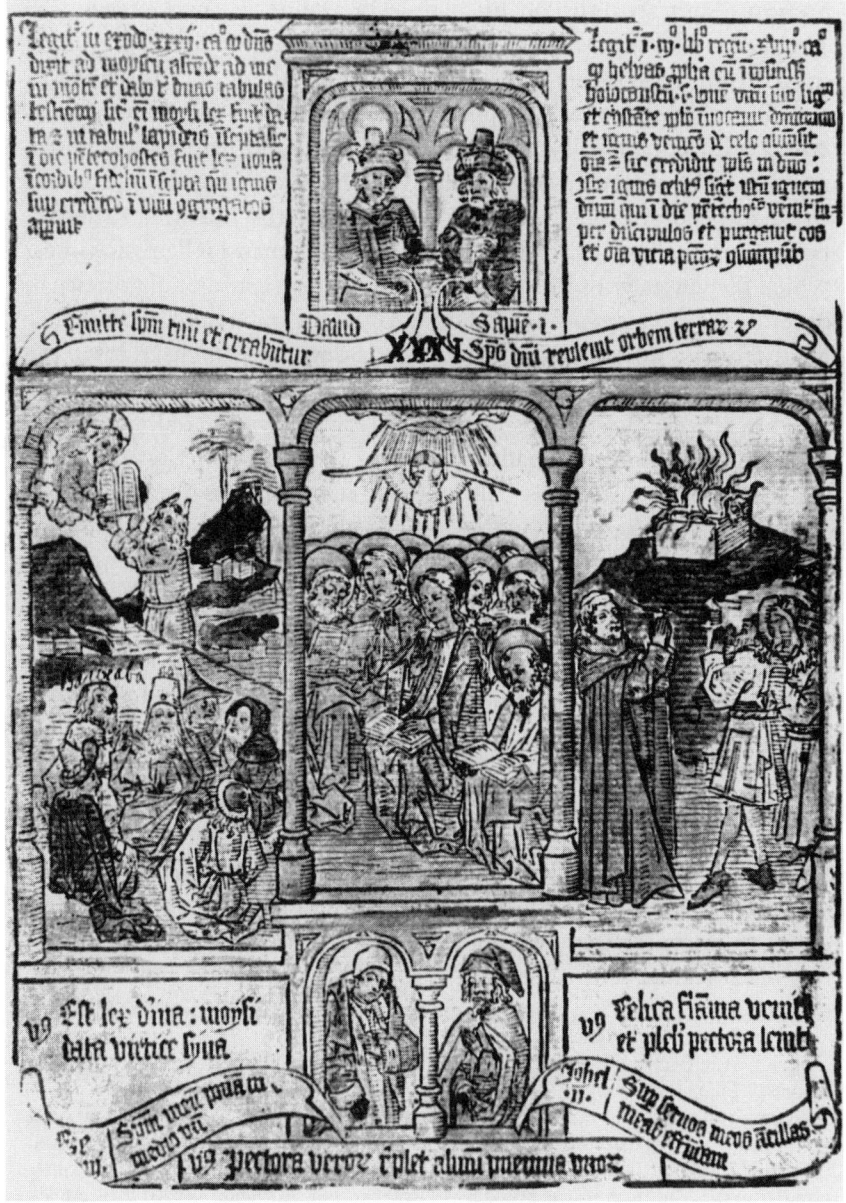

Figure 10.1. *The Pentecost,* sheet •**p**•, from the *Biblia pauperum* at the Esztergom Cathedral Library, as reproduced in Elizabeth Soltész, *Biblia pauperum: Facsimile Edition of the Forty-Leaf Blockbook in the Library of the Esztergom Cathedral* (Budapest, 1967), p. 35. Courtesy of the Esztergom Cathedral Library.

prefigure and are fulfilled by people or events in the Gospels (the *antitypes*). (The term *typology* is also used more broadly to mean any similar figuration of the future in the past, whether or not these events are biblical.) Historically, typological prefiguration was closely associated with Christianity from its beginnings, and it greatly proliferated in the twelfth century. It had rivals from interpretive approaches that had been dominant previously. Erich Auerbach distinguishes typology on the one hand from allegory, popular in Hellenistic times, which dispenses with the literal meaning and its sense of historicity in order to plumb a deeper ethical or spiritual meaning; and on the other hand from symbolism, an even older approach which endows the symbol not with historical force but with magical power.[8] Despite the differences, these three approaches are closely related and sometimes inseparable, principally because of their construction of meaning through resemblances. All kinds of resemblances are brought to bear in the *Biblia pauperum*. Along with typology, the types and antitypes are frequently portrayed with visual analogies; some individual images have allegorical content; the power of symbolic objects appears in several scenes. All of these strategies belong to the family of similitudes, which dominated Western thought into the seventeenth century. For convenience I will sometimes call the general strategy *allegorical thinking*.[9]

It is generally recognized that typology is rooted in textuality and the literal meaning of Scripture. For example, Leonhard Goppelt maintains that the literal meaning of the text is foundational to typology.[10] Auerbach similarly argues that figural interpretation must preserve both figure and fulfillment as literal historical occurrences in order to interpret these events as revelations, and he points out that this historical basis ties together three of the four meanings of Scripture.[11] F. P. Pickering emphasizes the "philological" development of

[8]Erich Auerbach, "'Figura'" (1944), trans. Ralph Manheim, in *Scenes from the Drama of European Literature* (Minneapolis, 1984), pp. 36, 54–57.

[9]For another account and taxonomy of the similitudes, see Michel Foucault, *The Order of Things: An Archaeology of the Human Sciences* (New York, 1970), pp. 17–45. One might also be justified in including puns as a similitude. Puns were enormously popular in the Middle Ages, as noted by F. P. Pickering, *Literature and Art in the Middle Ages* (London, 1970), p. 91. Henry, *Biblia pauperum*, p. 8, points out that many of the *Biblia pauperum*'s *tituli* make puns.

[10]Leonhard Goppelt, *Typos: The Typological Interpretation of the Old Testament in the New*, trans. Donald H. Madvig (Grand Rapids, Mich., 1982), p. 18.

[11]Auerbach, "'Figura,'" pp. 42, 68.

a vast array of medieval imagery from the biblical texts, which had first of all a literal and historical meaning.[12] But while it is clear that typological compositions were the products of the literati, it is less clear who the readers were. We tend to expect picture books to be aimed at the uneducated. But Henry builds on the connection between typology and the literary to contend that typology in general, and the *Biblia pauperum* in particular, cannot have been intended (as some have claimed) for an unlettered audience.[13] The grounding of typology in textuality and the questions concerning the *Biblia pauperum*'s audience are thus linked to the fact that the majority of people in the Middle Ages could not read or write, yet writing was crucial for both religion and governance.[14] I believe that this fact is crucial to the development of the *Biblia pauperum,* and that the social relations grounding the use of writing and speech strongly affect signifying and interpretational practices—in other words, that typology as an artistic and intellectual strategy is linked to the dynamics of literacy within a culture that was predominantly oral.

The historical course of typology, spanning 1,500 years or more from its rise, through its expansions and contractions, to its decline, suggests that it was part of some enduring social structure. One candidate of course might be the class relations of feudal times, but typology long preceded feudalism. Developments in allegorical thinking, however, roughly coincide with the vicissitudes of manuscript culture. Typology in particular depends on the existence of holy and thus socially privileged texts. Moreover, resemblance was a strategy for constructing thought, and modes of communication pertain precisely to the dissemination, organization, and preservation of thought. So the mode of communication seems a likely ground for understanding the development of the similitudes. This vantage point

[12]Pickering, *Literature and Art in the Middle Ages,* pp. 117, 165, 227, 245, 298.

[13]Henry, *Biblia pauperum,* pp. 10, 17–18. Michael Camille has argued that despite the common medieval claim that pictures functioned as the books of the illiterate, the pictures could not actually have worked that way because of their reference to and dependence on written texts; see his "Seeing and Reading: Some Visual Implications of Medieval Literacy and Illiteracy," *Art History* 8 (March 1985): 32–37. In contrast, Pickering states that the *Biblia pauperum* was "an illustrated primer for the use of clergy in the instruction of layfolk"; *Literature and Art in the Middle Ages,* p. 266.

[14]See also the surveys by Franz H. Bäuml, "Varieties and Consequences of Medieval Literacy and Illiteracy," *Speculum* 55 (1980): 237–65; and Malcolm Parkes, "The Literacy of the Laity," in *Literature and Western Civilization,* vol. 2, *The Medieval World,* ed. David Daiches and A. K. Thorlby (London, 1973), pp. 555–77.

can help clarify the questions of the blockbook's use, function, and audience, for the *Biblia pauperum* would represent a particular and highly potent crystallization of the historical relationship between literacy and orality.

The Historical Contexts of
Orality, Literacy, and Typology

In locating the explanation for typology and the functioning of the *Biblia pauperum* in manuscript culture, I am placing it in a context of a social organization of communication practices. The first concern for my analysis must therefore be the social context of orality and literacy. With this in mind it is possible to investigate the dynamics and interaction of oral and written communication. Such an exploration will establish the basis from which we can then consider how the *Biblia pauperum,* as an expression of manuscript culture and eventually of early print culture, articulates the social relationships between orality and literacy.

For our purposes, the crucial turning point in the social development of communication occurred during the twelfth century. For many centuries literacy had been subordinated to oral communication in all but a few groups and communities. Pragmatically, writing was read aloud and often served as a mnemonic aid to oral performance; politically, it was treated as an untrustworthy supplement to oral transactions.[15] But by the twelfth century monastics usually read silently, as did most of the laity two hundred years later. Still more significant, documents and scribes became increasingly crucial to the administration of power, property, and education.[16] Texts slowly supplanted oral testimony as the source of evidence, guidance, and factual knowledge. They became an externalized, physical form of memory.[17] The church, of course, largely dominated literacy and literate people; the twelfth century, however, saw the beginnings of a

[15]Paul Saenger, "Silent Reading: Its Impact on Late Medieval Script and Society," *Viator* 13 (1982): 370–71; Brian Stock, *The Implications of Literacy: Written Language and Models of Interpretation in the Eleventh and Twelfth Centuries* (Princeton, 1983), pp. 59–62.

[16]Saenger, "Silent Reading," pp. 379, 405, 410; Stock, *Implications of Literacy,* pp. 16–18.

[17]Stock, *Implications of Literacy,* pp. 7, 49, 62.

slow increase in literate education for the laity.[18] But what makes the church significant is not just its institutions and the concomitant sociology of literacy but also its theology, which (unlike classical Greek or Roman religion) was centered on sacred texts that only the church had authority to interpret. At the same time, it should not be forgotten that virtually everyone took part in oral culture.

With these basic points in mind, we can approach the internal dynamics of literacy. Silent reading and writing disengage the reader from social interaction, an isolation that is conducive to abstract contemplation. Writing is much slower than speaking and can be revised, and reading can become rereading. In compositions of even modest length, these activities permit detailed planning and organization, syntactic complexity, and subordinative construction. Much weight goes to the procession of words through graphic space: thought, to be written at all, must be organized in a linear manner. This in turn suggests a linear concept of time. In cultures in which writing is the privileged form of communication, texts are the storehouses of memory, and references to them are critical for the elaboration of knowledge.[19]

Orality, in contrast, requires direct interaction between a speaker and an audience, and so it generally gives priority to the immediate, concrete, and particular. The compositional style is usually additive and often redundant, since speakers think while speaking, and emphasize along the way. In a wholly oral culture the only way to store knowledge is through memory. Thought is fixed through the use of patterns, such as verse, verbal formulas, maxims, and rituals. Physical objects are also employed to memorialize events or agreements, and so they become symbolic. Through memory, the past of the ancestors stays ever alive. It coexists with the present, and time becomes nonlinear and often circular.[20]

Under the conditions of manuscript culture, orality and literacy

[18]Bäuml, "Medieval Literacy and Illiteracy," p. 244; Parkes, "Literacy of the Laity," pp. 556–58.

[19]Walter J. Ong, *Orality and Literacy: The Technologization of the Word* (London, 1982), pp. 40, 72–74, 99–105; Stock, *Implications of Literacy,* pp. 77–78, 82–83; Saenger, "Silent Reading," pp. 374–76, 382, 390.

[20]Ong, *Orality and Literacy,* pp. 33–50, 96–98; Stock, *Implications of Literacy,* pp. 14–16. It is interesting to note, in this regard, that many of the verbs for bringing a thought up from memory use the prefix of repetition, *re-*: remember, recall, remind, recollect, reminisce, recognize.

interacted in a way that encouraged thought based on similitudes. Four facets or processes were involved, all tied to memory. Whether preserved in the mind or on the page, memory is always at stake in communication, all the more so in an age when the loss of one book or the loss of a single life could mean a permanent loss of knowledge. So the four points that I will raise here concern the problem of preserving knowledge and confirming its validity.

The semiotic chain. As I mentioned earlier, writing often served as a mnemonic device, helping to recall words or ideas to the reader (who would often deliver the text orally, as in a sermon or lecture). In this function writing serves as a supplement to speech, helping to restore it to life. Semiotically, where the spoken word is a sign for a thing, phonetic writing becomes a sign of a sign. For the literate few this seems to have had profound ontological and epistemological implications. Speech could also be a system of signs of signs—that is, the referent could be a sign as well.[21] The written word *tree* recalls the spoken word "tree," which recalls an image of a tree, which recalls the crucifix. Everything becomes a sign of a sign in a chain of meanings that, for the devout, must ultimately end in one transcendental signified: God and the divine purpose. But of course this is known only through yet another text, the Bible, the embodiment of God's Word. This argument helps to clarify why the medieval scholar saw a world full of signs needing to be interpreted. The concept of signs of signs is the foundation for the distinction between literal and figurative senses; but of course it does not really explain why resemblance arose as a conceptual strategy.

Textual memory. Just as texts could remind the reader of images, images could recall texts. The continuing importance of orality meant that living memory was still prized; but when writing increased, so did the knowledge to be remembered. Classical authorities had described an Art of Memory, which had been geared toward oratorical

---

[21]See Foucault, *Order of Things,* esp. pp. 25–30, for a discussion of the sense in the sixteenth century that the referent of speech was itself a sign. Although the idea that in the Middle Ages speech was a sign of signs may sound similar to Derrida's critique of the sign, I believe it would be a mistake simply to equate the two views. The chain of signifiers for us is different, in part because writing now plays a more encompassing role. See Jacques Derrida, *Of Grammatology,* trans. Gayatri Chakravorty Spivak (Baltimore, 1976), pp. 27–73, 141–64.

needs.[22] This art was revived during the twelfth century (when writing again became pivotal) and remained popular until the seventeenth (when allegorical thinking faded into the background). In fact, medieval learning turned the development of memory into a part of Prudence, one of the virtues, and many treatises on the Art of Memory were written and circulated (see fig. 10.2). The treatises guided their readers through a somewhat arcane process, leading the reader to construct mental images that condensed the basic issues of an argument. Traditionally it was felt that human (or at least anthropomorphic) figures made the strongest images. Often the figures were then imagined to be located at points inside a building, so that one could recall them in a specific sequence. But memory is best restored by something similar or connected to the thing that needs to be recalled. Hence the imagery included visual parallels, metonymies, and sometimes puns. In this way texts were embodied in mental images full of similitudes; interpretation of the image led to recovery of the text. From these mental personifications it was a short step to actual pictures that served as reminders, and from there another short step to pictures that functioned as allegorical figures.[23]

The Art of Memory helps elucidate the importance of similitude for medieval thinking. Its influence is somewhat contingent on the historical accident that preserved certain classical writings, but once the Art was preserved, it is not surprising that ecclesiastic education (and the new preaching monastic orders) reinforced it. So far, however, my arguments have been from the perspective of literacy interjected into an oral environment; other aspects can be seen by examining how oral culture was restructured by the privileges of literacy.

Validation. This aspect concerns the status of images and physical symbols. Brian Stock, who has written on the effects of burgeoning literacy during the eleventh and twelfth centuries, points out how in oral culture physical objects were invested with symbolic meaning, often through gesture and ritual. There was no particular need to prove the symbols' validity or interpret their meaning because both emerged from the performance of actions. If a question arose, the participants (or their descendants) could provide information. But

[22]Frances Amelia Yates, *The Art of Memory* (Chicago, 1966), pp. 1–26.
[23]Ibid., pp. 50–104.

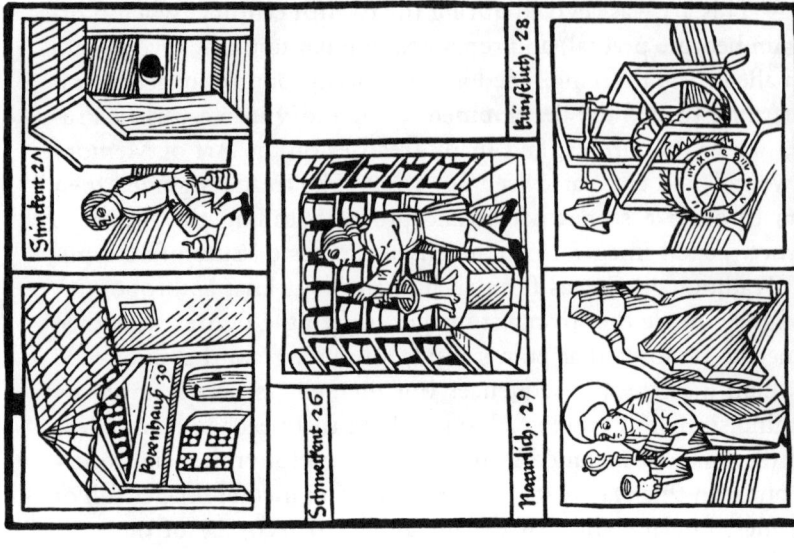

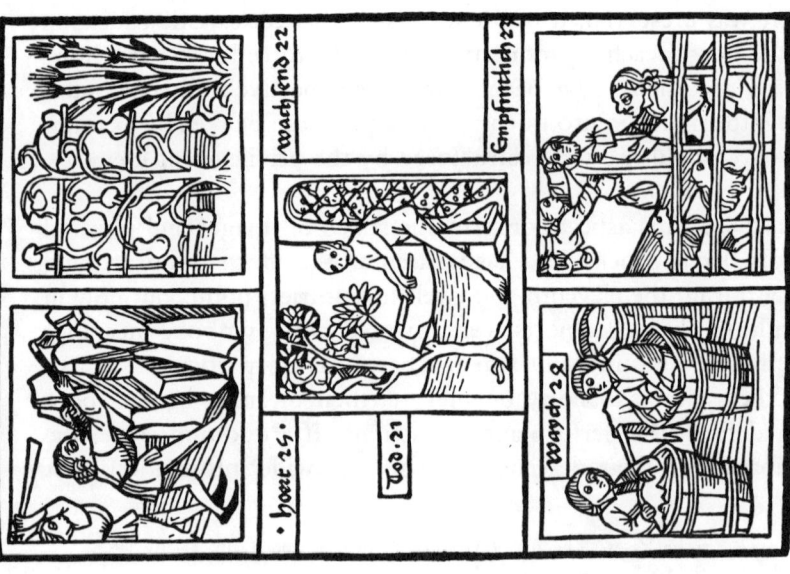

Figure 10.2. Squares 21–30 from the *Ars memorativa* of Johann Bämler, c.1480, as reproduced in facsimile (Augsburg, 1922). Courtesy of the Newberry Library, Chicago.

when writing became privileged, it became necessary to authenticate or validate symbols of agreements, miracles, and other signs through textual evidence. Human memory was no longer satisfactory; the truth of the past was better guaranteed by writing. From a literate viewpoint, images were deeply ambiguous, polyvalent, in need of interpretation. They were figures endowed with an inner meaning that one must seek. So now images were incorporated into a textual realm, a "con-text," and for the literates this made interpretation obligatory and memory more stable. One or two symbols even obtained their primary motivation through writing: for example, the fish is a symbol of Christ chiefly because the first two letters in the Greek word for fish, *ichthus,* form the initials for Jesus Christ in Greek. The world now was not simply one of signs but one of writing. Only through texts could meaning be secured or even established.[24] Thus validation through writing, like the semiotic chain, grounds the hermeneutic orientation of medieval thinking.

The persistence of orality. While the symbols and rituals of oral culture now had to be validated by texts, the way in which they were validated was essentially in oral terms. As I described earlier, orality fixes thought in memory by the use of patterns, whether of speech or of action. Words and movement were repeated, identically or with small variations, so that knowledge could be preserved. Thus imitation, mimesis, and similitude underlie the structure of oral thinking. In the new literate environment this strategy continued to affect the organization of thought. The texts that validated oral material themselves took up many of the analogical and symbolic motifs of oral culture.[25] In other words, medieval manuscript culture involved not only the alteration of oral culture to suit literate needs, but also the accommodation of literate resources to fit around an oral mentality. (The need for oral performance, for example, made writing a mnemonic aid and brought about the Art of Memory.)

There is a sense, then, in which text and image depended on and supported each other in medieval manuscripts. Texts recalled, invoked, or were condensed in images; the images were considered a higher truth, yet possessed validity only because of their textual au-

---

[24]Stock, *Implications of Literacy,* pp. 64, 71, 90–91, 243–52; see also Camille, "Seeing and Reading," p. 33.
[25]See also Stock, *Implications of Literacy,* p. 91.

thority. If images supplemented the text, they also needed texts to supplement themselves, to be their evidence. Likewise, the ambiguity of visual images demanded stabilization through adjoining texts; but as Pickering emphasizes, word-oriented speculation was anchored or restrained by religious art in order to control interpretation.[26]

In discussing the basis of allegorical thinking in the relationships between orality and literacy in medieval manuscript culture, I have treated the similitudes as all alike. What made typology as a specific kind of similitude possible and prominent was the existence of the holy texts and a church with sole rights over interpretation. Nonscriptural texts could serve essentially as a spur to memory and speculation, leading to allegory; but the two testaments had to be taken at their word, and the church (as the bride of Christ) deemed what that word was. The literal, historical truth of the Bible was consubstantial with its sanctity: lose the one and you risked losing the other. Thus the Church defended the Old Testament as God's word but interpreted it as full of figures fulfilled in the New.[27]

In this section I have shown how the dynamics of communication in the Middle Ages, especially the connection to memory, encouraged allegorical thinking. Let us now consider how those dynamics are manifested in the *Biblia pauperum*.

The *Biblia pauperum* in the Context of Orality and Literacy

If my explanation for typology is correct, then it is no accident that the manuscript *Biblia pauperum* first appeared in the thirteenth century, shortly after writing gained its privileged place in medieval society as a whole, and that versions of it continued to be popular through the sixteenth century, by which time printing had restructured the production of religious books and their interpretive context. It should be possible, then, to bring evidence from the *Biblia pauperum* itself to support my theory, and to use the theory to help understand the *Biblia pauperum*. I will frame my discussion under the same four headings that I used to analyze the role of orality and literacy in the

---

[26]Pickering, *Literature and Art in the Middle Ages*, p. 264.

[27]See also Auerbach, "'Figura,'" pp. 51–52. Thus Judaism, which has a holy text, sees God as working through history, but since it does not have a second testament, it has little need for typology.

construction of allegorical thinking: writing as a mnemonic and a sign of signs; the Art of Memory, in which images condense and recall texts; the use of writing for validation; and the continuing influence of the oral mentality.

The semiotic chain. There are several instances in the *Biblia pauperum* in which a text serves to spur memory of other texts. The sheet containing the scene *The Egyptian Idols Fall (f)*[28] uses a quote from Zechariah which, in its original context, follows a line that had become a prophecy of the Crucifixion. Similarly, the sheet *Christ Is Pierced* (•f•) includes a verse from a psalm which Jesus spoke on the cross. The *Conspiracy* and *Christ Opens Limbo* sheets (q and •h•) present fragmentary lines that are very obscure unless the reader can complete the text; full interpretation of the page requires the reader to remember (or even refer to) the Scriptures. The line from Genesis on the *Christ Opens Limbo* page (•h•) is actually completed in the following sheet, *The Resurrection* (•i•), which, however, is in the next opening (see figs. 10.3 and 10.4). A similar relationship occurs when the sheet with *The Flight into Egypt* (e) includes a prophecy which is illustrated on the next page, *The Egyptian Idols Fall* (sheet f, which is in the same opening) (see figs. 10.5 and 10.6): the prophecy is behaving prophetically, foretelling an image to come.

The use of writing to suggest or "foretell" more texts recalls the implications of writing as a system of signs of signs. When I discussed the semiotic chain in the previous section, I described how each sign was the notation of another sign, moving backwards from text to speech to thing, leading to an ultimate, original, transcendental signified. But if we follow the semiotic and mnemonic chain forward, allowing the sign to be the basis of deeds, the system of signs of signs bears the promise of restoration and redemption, with messianic overtones. The written word stands as an emissary for its author (and

[28]I generally refer to each sheet of the *Biblia pauperum* by the title of the New Testament scene at its center, followed in parentheses by the "page" number or signature on that sheet. The *Biblia pauperum* employs an unusual pagination convention: the pages are in a double alphabetical sequence, running **a–v**, followed by •a•–•v• (with a dot on either side of the letter), both sequences skipping the letters *j* and *u*. This pagination is also adopted by Henry, *Biblia pauperum*. I use Henry's titles for the illustrations and her translations of the Latin texts. I am indebted throughout this and the following section to Henry's edition for background and guideposts in interpretation.

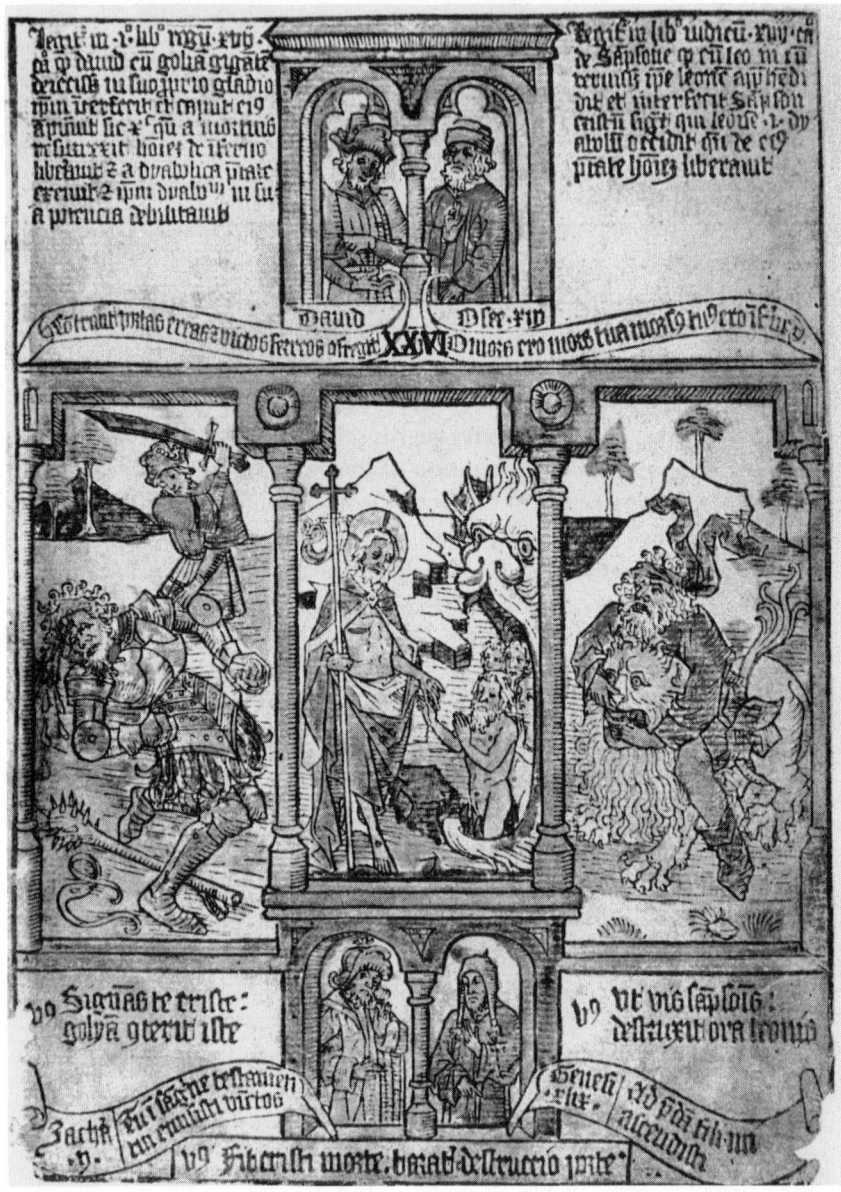

Figure 10.3. *Christ Opens Limbo*, sheet •h•, from the *Biblia pauperum* at the Esztergom Cathedral Library, as reproduced in Elizabeth Soltész, *Biblia pauperum: Facsimile Edition of the Forty-Leaf Blockbook in the Library of the Esztergom Cathedral* (Budapest, 1967), p. 28. Courtesy of the Esztergom Cathedral Library.

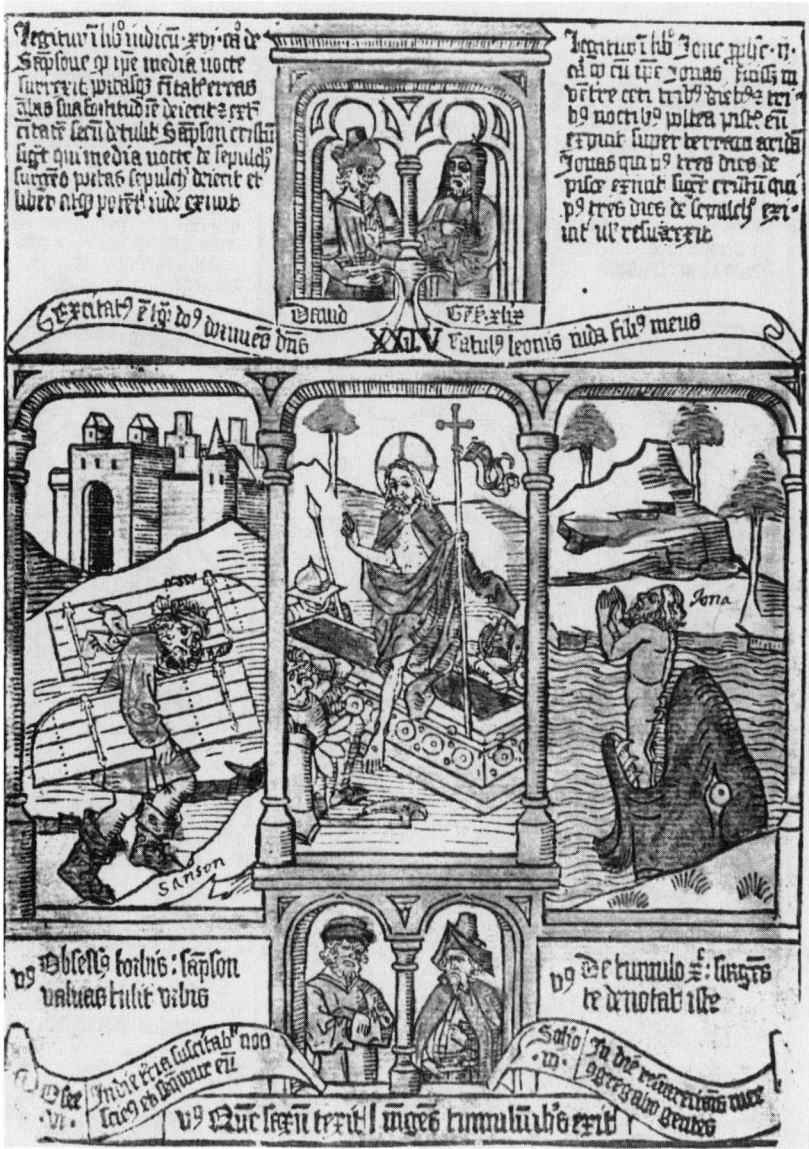

Figure 10.4. *The Resurrection,* sheet •i•, from the *Biblia pauperum* at the Esztergom Cathedral Library, as reproduced in Elizabeth Soltész, *Biblia pauperum: Facsimile Edition of the Forty-Leaf Blockbook in the Library of the Esztergom Cathedral* (Budapest, 1967), p. 29. *Jonah Is Released* is at the right; note the annotation by Jonah's head. Courtesy of the Esztergom Cathedral Library.

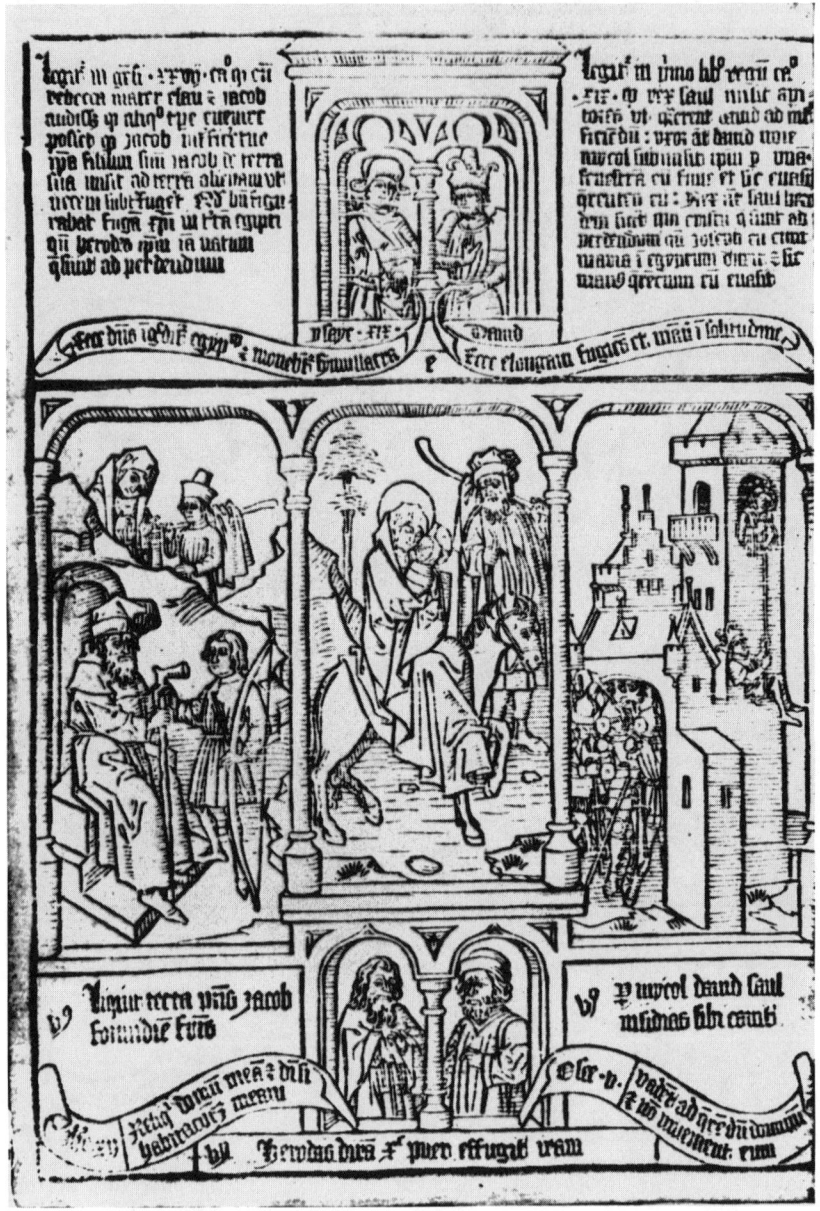

Figure 10.5. *The Flight into Egypt,* sheet **e**, from the *Biblia pauperum* at the Dresden Sächsische Landesbibliothek, as reproduced in Avril Henry, *Biblia pauperum: A Facsimile and Edition* (Ithaca, 1987), p. 56. Reprinted by permission.

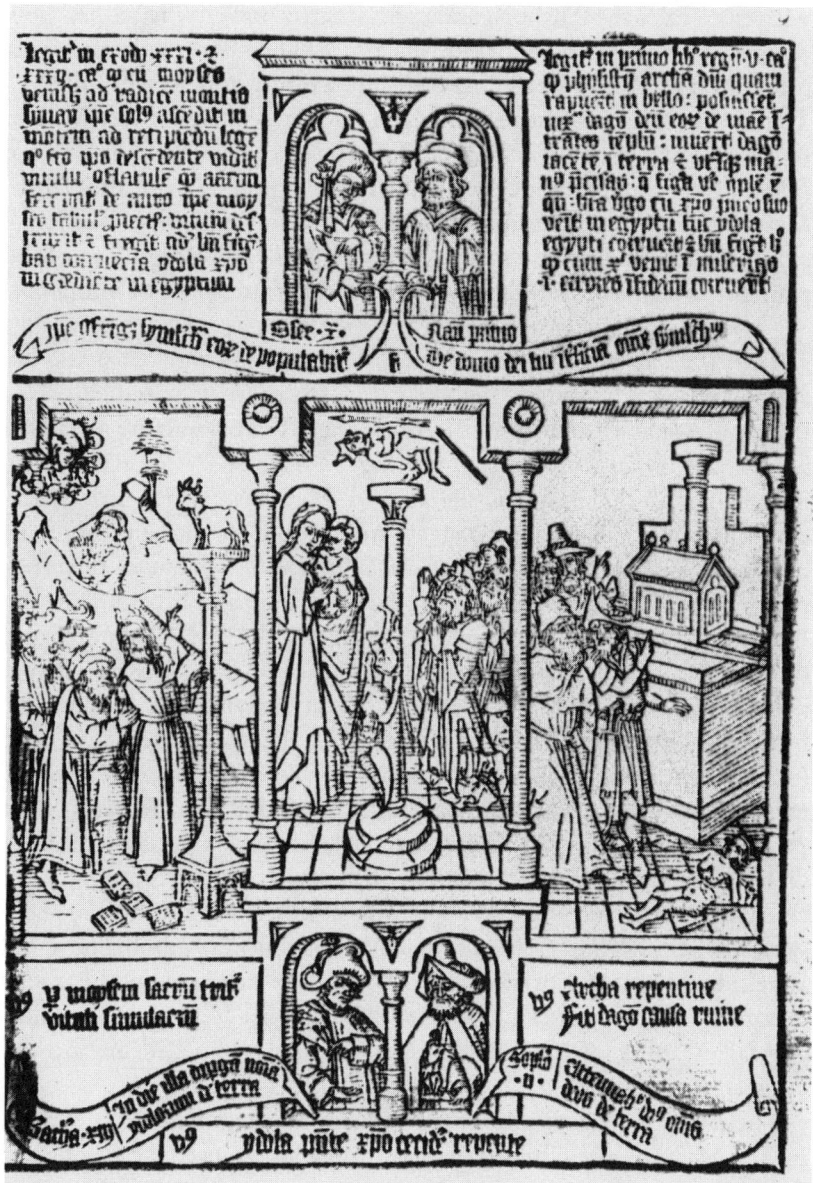

Figure 10.6. *The Egyptian Idols Fall,* sheet **f**, from the *Biblia pauperum* at the Dresden Sächsische Landesbibliothek, as reproduced in Avril Henry, *Biblia pauperum: A Facsimile and Edition* (Ithaca, 1987), p. 57. Reprinted by permission.

[309]

with the Bible, the Author), and gains its true power when it prompts speech. According to 2 Corinthians 3:6, "The letter killeth, the spirit bringeth life." Writing itself has become a figure awaiting fulfillment. The use of texts to restore the full, living presence of speech is, in a sense, a model of resurrection. And this is, of course, the theme of the *Biblia pauperum*. The sequence of images, beginning with the Virgin Mary reading, culminating at the Resurrection of Christ, and concluding with the Last Judgment sequence (with its resurrection of the penitent souls), is a parable for the individual and for all of humanity.

Textual memory. Regarding writing as a system of signs of signs, the abbot Gilbert Crispin of the early twelfth century noted: "Just as letters are shapes and symbols of spoken words, pictures exist as representations and symbols of writing."[29] This observation brings us to writing as the basis of the Art of Memory, which led to the construction of allegorical imagery. An example of such an image can be found on sheet **f**, *The Egyptian Idols Fall,* in which one of the types presents the Philistine idol Dagon, having fallen and broken after the Ark of the Covenant was placed before it (fig. 10.6). Henry notes that this scene is frequently allegorized: "The holy Ark . . . is the Gospel taken to gentiles. Dagon's fall itself is idolatry giving way to faith, his broken hands are the curtailed deeds of idolaters, his detached head (not shown) is the broken pride of the Devil or of idolatry's rule, his torso flight."[30] Similar examples may be found on the right-hand panel of the *Raising of Lazurus* sheet (**l**), in which the Shunammite woman (mother of the child that Elisha resurrected) represents the church, and the furniture has spiritual significance; and on the sheet with *Christ Is Mocked* (•**c**•), in which Noah's vines (symbolizing wine, Israel, the Cup of Sorrow, and so on), are depicted in the background.[31] In the *Christ Opens Limbo* sheet (•**h**•) (fig. 10.3), the allegorical meaning of David's killing of Goliath is spelled out by the exegetical text itself.

The *Biblia pauperum* often uses space in an allegorical way as well. In *The Magi* (**c**), the Child is in a position analogous to the scepters in the two types, thus following Numbers 24:17—"There shall come a star out of Jacob, and a scepter shall rise out of Israel" (the star appears

[29]Quoted in Camille, "Seeing and Reading," p. 32.
[30]Henry, *Biblia pauperum*, p. 59.
[31]Ibid., pp. 70, 94.

too)—which mixes with some of Isaiah to form one of the four prophecies. The three images each present similar movement from the authoritative realm on the left half to the subordinated realm on the right. Self-abasing figures occupy the bottom halves of the three pictures in the *Mary Magdalene Repents* sheet (**n**). A comparative symmetry among the pictures on the *Christ Appears to the Disciples* page (**•m•**) puts Joseph, Jesus, and the Prodigal Son on the right of each illustration. The *Biblia pauperum* frequently uses such spatial analogies to suggest the distinction and movement between the spiritual and the temporal worlds.

Validation. Validation of images is another function of writing in the *Biblia pauperum*. The most obvious example is its use of captions under the three pictures. Most of the *tituli* tell the story of the type. But the exegetical texts also do this, and in addition they describe how the type relates to the antitype. Yet despite the apparent redundancy, the captions appear, confirming that the illustration is indeed what the exegesis claims it is. Thus, for example, the *lectio* for *Judas Machabeus Purifies the Temple,* the type to the right of *Christ Purifies the Temple* (sheet **p**), tells how Judah Maccabee ordered the Jews to cleanse the Temple because it had been defiled, and goes on to state how this episode prefigures Jesus' clearing of the Temple (the antitype on this page); the *titulus* reads: "Machabeus is eager to purify your holy places, O God." The *titulus* employs the present tense to confirm the (eternal) verity of the image and the historical prefiguration of the *lectio.*[32]

An exception to this pattern occurs on the sheet of *The Resurrection* (**•i•**), which on the right shows Jonah being released by the sea creature (fig. 10.4). The caption says: "This man denotes you rising out of the tomb O Christ." Instead of locating the image in the type's historical narrative, the *titulus* links the figure directly with its fulfillment. Curiously, on the Esztergom copy of the *Biblia pauperum,* one of the previous owners has written the name "Jona" next to the figure's head—as though it were still necessary to confirm the image's identity through writing. Several other annotations by this owner in the Esztergom copy also verify identities.[33] One wonders what kind of

---

[32]See my discussion later in this essay, especially note 39 and the text it amplifies.
[33]See Soltész, *Biblia pauperum,* pp. 3, 35, 38 (**c**, **•p•**, **•s•**). Henry records that other extant copies of the *Biblia pauperum* also have annotations (*Biblia pauperum,* p. 175). I

reader would make such annotations. A scholar or preacher might be
expected to make more extensive commentaries and feel little need to
note such rudimentary information. Yet the readers could hardly have
been extremely uneducated, not of course because the texts are in
Latin (since most education in literacy would be in Latin), but because
writing required more schooling and skill than reading. My own
guess, based on this evidence, is that the *Biblia pauperum*'s audience
consisted primarily of at least moderately wealthy laity, accustomed
to books but not professional users of them.[34]

Another form of validation appears through the use of prophecies.
Text as validation in this sense has become the obverse of text as
mnemonic aid (discussed earlier). The Old Testament serves as a
reference book to confirm the miracle of Jesus; in effect, the text is
reconstructed to foretell a particular future.[35] Such reconstruction
also turns up in some of the pictures: to the right of *Christ Opens
Limbo* (•h•; see fig. 10.3), Goliath opens the lion's mouth instead of
tearing the lion to pieces, as in the Bible; he can thereby prefigure
Christ opening Hellmouth. Likewise, on the *Ascension* sheet (•o•)
Elisha is placed into the same pose as Peter. The past now points to a
future. This is emphasized by the use of a pyramidal pattern on many
of the pages, in which the two type pictures lead the eye to a crown-
ing image in the antitype scene.[36]

Validation embeds images in text. Larger and larger textual frames
encompass the images, starting with the captions, then moving to the
prophecies, and ending with the typological exegeses—or perhaps

---

have not been able to examine any of these to see what the notes concern. There is,
however, a photographic reproduction of two pages (**h** and **p**) of the *Biblia pauperum* in
Wolfenbüttel, both of which contain some annotations that appear to be the names of
the figures portrayed (see Musper, "Die Urausgabe," pp. 55, 56). Camille comes to
similar conclusions about the use of texts to validate illustrations ("Seeing and Reading," pp. 33–34).

[34]Parkes discusses professional, cultivated, and pragmatic readership in "The Literacy of the Laity."

[35]This is akin to Jesus' and the evangelists' own use of Old Testament prophecy in
the Gospels, although the rhetorical impact is different. Of course, Jesus' declaration
that all things about him were to be found in the Old Testament (Luke 24:44) helped
encourage and justify typological explanations.

[36]See, for example, the sheets with *The Entry into Jerusalem* (o), *The Jews Fall Back
from Christ* (v), *Judas Betrays Christ with a Kiss* (•a•), *The Resurrection* (•i•; fig. 10.4); and
The Ascension (•o•).

not ending there, for they refer outward to the Bible. Everything receives its biblical con-text in order to establish its meaning.[37]

The persistence of orality. Typology, like the quotation of prophecy, reorients the Old Testament toward the New. What turns persons, events, or objects into types is their participation in certain *actions,* which are in some way repeated or imitated in the New Testament. Most of the exegetical passages in the *Biblia pauperum* suggest this interpretation. For example, on page **c** Abner comes to David, Sheba comes to Solomon, and in the center the Magi come to the Christ Child: showing reverence is an important act, and these actions are analogous to spiritual pilgrimages.[38] Repeated action is essential to ritual, in which gestures and activities aim to preserve memory. Hence it is arguable that typology, based on the repetition of action, is a representation of ritual that helps to sustain the memory of special deeds and consecrate their meaning. Thus, for instance, the rituals of eating and fasting both become allegories of spiritual development, as illustrated in **k**, in which Adam and Eve eat the apple, Esau sells his birthright for some lentil soup, but Jesus refuses the devil's temptation to turn a stone into bread.

In recalling the past and ensuring that the knowledge of the ancestors remains alive, typology introduces a nonlinear concept of time akin to that of ritual. History is filled with analogous moments which reappear with each spiritual cycle. The Old Testament past is fulfilled in the New Testament past; but this in turn proffers the hope and signs of a present-day fulfillment, its presence felt in everyday reality; and the promise awaits final fulfillment in the Second Coming. The *Biblia pauperum* encompasses these moments by portraying the types, the antitype, contemporary costumes and settings, and the entire cycle of episodes, and it stabilizes them through the architectural frame. The figure remains real and historical, yet it is only a shadow of the authentic, ultimate reality to come. The chain of similitude links the earthly event to the divine order, and so in that sense the

[37]The blockbook *Apocalypse* shows the embeddedness of all things in texts another way—by often littering the illustration with one or another form of verbal material (see fig. 10.7). At times texts become the set, props, perhaps even actors and forces in this mystic drama.

[38]Henry, *Biblia pauperum,* p. 54.

event partakes of eternity. The ultimate reality, then, is not only in the future but to God it is also in the present, and so it imbues all pasts with its presence.[39] In short, the typological portrayal of two historical moments includes linear chronology but also transcends it.

Nonlinear time appears in the *Biblia pauperum* not only in its use of typology, combining the Old and New Testaments, but also in some of the individual illustrations, which portray simultaneous scenes. In the left panel of the *Egyptian Idols Fall* sheet (**f**) we see Moses both at the top and at the foot of Mount Sinai (fig. 10.6); three stages in the scene of the *Massacre of the Innocents* appear at the same time in sheet **g**. In the *Transfiguration* sheet (**m**) the types present Nebuchadnezzar on the right catching a glimmer of the Trinity, and Abraham on the left seeing it in a concealed form; the antitype in the center displays the Trinity as the figures of Moses, Christ, and Elijah. Thus all three scenes conjoin the two testaments, breaking across the boundaries of time to fulfill history in a transcendent eternity.[40]

Finally, it is likely that typology is not only the *Biblia pauperum*'s strategy of artistic composition but also its rhetorical goal. Its use of contemporary dress and scenery, although a commonplace strategy, nonetheless helps drive home the message that the story of salvation, foretold in the Old Testament and fulfilled in the New, is and must be reenacted in the reader's everyday life. In this manner the *Biblia pauperum* encourages devotion and meditation.

A Sample Reading and the Reading Process

At this point it would be useful to analyze a single page more fully. I will focus on **f**, with *The Egyptian Idols Fall,* a sheet that poses some interesting questions (see fig. 10.6). I have already discussed some of its features: the quotation from Zechariah that subtly recalls a prophecy of the Crucifixion, the allegory behind Dagon's fall, the simultaneous scenes of Moses in the *Golden Calf* picture, and the presentation of an antitype that illustrates a prophecy given on the previous page. The antitype shows how "in the presence of Christ, the idols

---

[39]Auerbach, "'Figura,'" p. 72. In this regard the difference in tense between the *lectio* and the *titulus* addresses the ties between the historical past, the living present, and the prefigured future.

[40]Henry, *Biblia pauperum,* p. 71.

suddenly fell" (as the caption puts it). The incident does not occur in the New Testament: it is from a popular legend. This raises questions about the construction of types and antitypes. I have already mentioned how writing could "invent" symbols, like that of the fish for Christ. I believe that sheet **f** demonstrates a related process. The Old Testament's vivid episode of the Golden Calf, its parallel in the story of Dagon's fall, and its many prophecies of the destruction of idols (four of which are quoted in **f**) were simply too memorable to be ignored. All of the antitypes in the *Biblia pauperum* obtained their authority from prophecies and types in the Old Testament; if the Gospels failed to provide an antitype for this group of types, then it was proper to provide one—in this case from oral culture.[41] Moreover, Henry found that in sheet **e**, *The Flight into Egypt* (which faces **f**; see fig. 10.5), only the prophecy from Isaiah had a previous association with the Flight; the other three quotations were innovations by the *Biblia pauperum*. The quote from Isaiah is: "See, the Lord will enter Egypt and the idols shall be dislodged." This is the prophecy that behaves prophetically, being illustrated in **f**.[42] The designers of the *Biblia pauperum* appear to have exploited this quotation's double association with the scriptural Flight into Egypt and the legendary fall of the Egyptian idols in order to authorize their completion of a "gap" in the Gospels, and at the same time to authorize something that oral culture had contributed. They fulfilled the types with an interpolated antitype; and they strengthened this action by constructing the prophetic prophecy, and by placing the *Flight into Egypt* and *The Egyptian Idols Fall* face to face.

As the text stands, then, sheets **e** and **f** (in a sense, figure and fulfillment) appear on facing pages. The two sheets are further linked through their left panels, *Jacob Flees Esau* and *The Golden Calf*, which are organized similarly. Both present a double scene, one above the

---

[41]Pickering describes an even more complex instance of an invented antitype (*Literature and Art in the Middle Ages*, pp. 271–73). He believes that one of the purposes behind the efflorescence of typology in the twelfth century was to give the church control over narrative elaborations and interpolations on evangelical and apocryphal writings—all the stories that used "fulfillment of prophecy" as their legitimation (if not provocation). He adds that if typology did help stabilize Christian narrative, it held the line only temporarily (pp. 256–57). Literate culture could exert but limited control.

[42]Henry's commentary (to further complicate matters) indicates that the Isaiah prophecy was apparently tied to the Flight because it was already connected to the Fall of the Idols (*Biblia pauperum*, p. 58).

other. In **e** (fig. 10.5) Jacob is taking leave from his mother (above), while Esau is confronting his father (below). In the upper part of **f** (fig. 10.6) Moses is at the top of Mount Sinai speaking with God; he reappears on the bottom having smashed the tablets and berating Aaron and the idolizers of the Golden Calf. In both, an earlier and a later moment appear simultaneously.[43] But the pictures also contrast: Jacob escapes in order to avoid being destroyed at the hands of someone defending his own authority, whereas Moses returns to destroy the idol and impose a new authority. Both scenes, then, construct a conflict between the Old Law and the New through the use of simultaneous scenes, but the conflict leads to escape in the one and confrontation in the other. Yet the victory presented in **f** is depicted as a process, through a series moving from left to right. In *The Golden Calf* it is the tablets that are broken and the Calf that is whole; but we know that the tablets will be renewed and the Calf will be destroyed. At center the Egyptian idols have broken up and are falling before Christ. The contrast between idolatry and Christianity is emphasized through the division of space by the vertical pedestal. Then, at right, the idol Dagon is on the ground, vanquished by the Ark and its scriptural contents, which dominate the right half of the picture. Thus the Old Law–New Law struggle continues throughout the three images of **f**.[44] Sheet **e**, as Henry has found, is principally about escape; so anagogically, the pictures show how spiritual retreat leads to spiritual victory. But it is a slow, difficult process, requiring the destruction of false idols, faith in Christ, and protection of the sacred texts.

Underlying the relationships between **e** and **f** and their internal organization is a complex interweaving of oral and literate strategies. The overall page organization is basically nonlinear: three images and nine texts reflect on one another in the mind. They follow no necessary sequence, although there is a likely one. When one initially looks at the page, the eye is caught first by the antitype at center; then one's vision opens out to the two types at the sides, then to the *tituli*, to the prophecies, and finally to the exegetical texts. The page is loosely organized into concentric circles. The centerpiece has the closest

---

[43]In fact, one can argue that *three* moments appear simultaneously in *The Golden Calf*, since Moses actually received his "horns" (i.e. radiance) on his next trip up the mountain (see also Henry, *Biblia pauperum*, p. 134 n.9 for **f**).

[44]See also Henry, *Biblia pauperum*, p. 59.

bonds to the sacramental (ritualized) imagery of oral culture. Movement away from the center corresponds to movement away from oral modes and toward literate styles of composition: the titles are in verse, the prophecies are quotations from often lyrical biblical discourse in its Latin translation, and the typological exegeses are in prose. But if the reader's visual encounter with the pages of the *Biblia pauperum* moves outward from the Christological center, interpretation builds from the periphery in. The *lectiones* explicate the basic ideas behind the choice of pictures. While the images dominate the page, they are selected and controlled by the writing at the periphery. Thus one's eye is drawn inward and outward as one experiences and reexperiences, interprets and reinterprets, collects and recollects the signs and symbols on the page. Likewise, if the *Biblia pauperum* conformed to the demands of linear narrative, one might expect *The Massacre of the Innocents* (**g**) to precede or at least immediately follow the *Flight into Egypt* (**e**) in order to display the motivation for the latter. Instead these impulses are subordinated to nonlinear, meditational priorities; yet meditation in the Christian tradition is normally based on reading. The centrality of reading to Christian faith is represented in the *Biblia pauperum* itself, first of all (as we have seen) by pairing **e** and **f**, which show how spiritual withdrawal from the world leads to spiritual victory and how the Ark (whose secret is the holy tablets) vanquishes the idols, and also by presenting the beatified reading books, such as Mary in *The Annunciation* (**a**) and *The Nativity* (**b**), Elijah in *The Woman of Sareptha* (•**d**•), and Mary and the Apostles in *The Pentecost* (•**p**•; fig. 10.1). Silent reading itself involves withdrawal from the world and so models the spiritual quest. Thus, underneath the "oral" aggregation of words and images on the page there is a deeply text-oriented thought process that draws together a range of materials and approaches in order to capture the memory.

I have argued that the relationship between orality and literacy in medieval manuscript culture, especially from the twelfth century onward, fostered the development of the similitudes in general and typology in particular as conceptual strategies. Oral and literate cultures interacted (and often struggled), especially around the issue of how to organize thought and preserve it for the future. In the process, writing became both a mnemonic device and a guarantor of the authenticity of objects, people, and events; thus through writing the world consisted of signs. But even within the new literate milieu oral culture persisted. Hence it was not enough for an individual to check the meaning of the signs by referring to a book or by asking a scholar. Education, administration, and jurisprudence each put a premium on recall, in order to permit oral engagement and debate. Moreover, for salvation itself each person needed to know, believe, and at all times remember the meaning of the Gospels. Memory had to be encouraged, and this was achieved through association and repetition—in short, through the similitudes. As Aquinas observed: "We remember less easily those things which are of subtle and spiritual import; and we remember more easily those things that are gross and sensible. And if we wish to remember intelligible notions more easily, we should link them with some kind of phantasm" (that is, a mental image).[45] The *Biblia pauperum* offers a great many such "phantasms" to be entertained and ruminated upon in the reader's imagination.

In the later Middle Ages reading in silence and privacy became the preferred devotional exercise. Spiritual and even mystical experience began with the act of reading the Scriptures, during which the thoughts of the devout were meant to associate and wander while they reflected on the text's meaning. In the fourteenth century, friars began to encourage the laity to use the Art of Memory as a devotional discipline. Thomas à Kempis' *Imitation of Christ,* for example, was built on the mutual devotional processes of reflection and memory. The *Biblia pauperum* also fits this purpose well. It thus appears very likely that the purpose of the *Biblia pauperum* was personal meditation.[46]

In fact, the ties between memory and devotion that appear in the *Biblia pauperum* may be a characteristic uniting the majority of blockbooks. The *Speculum humanae salvationis* is similar to the *Biblia pauperum* in its reliance on typology and similitudes. The *Apocalypse*'s intermeshing of strange images and sometimes lengthy texts may have been born from the Art of Memory as much as from mystical lore as it seeks to validate the final fulfillment of the Old Testament

[45]Quoted in Yates, *Art of Memory,* p. 71.

[46]Saenger, "Silent Reading," p. 401 (on mystical reading); Yates, *Art of Memory,* p. 91; and see Henry, *Biblia pauperum,* p. 18. I cannot entirely rule out the possibility that the *Biblia pauperum* was used as a memory aid for preachers, as proposed by Schreiber (*Manuel,* p. 1). The force of book illustrations for sermonizing, however, is hardly comparable to the power of a church window.

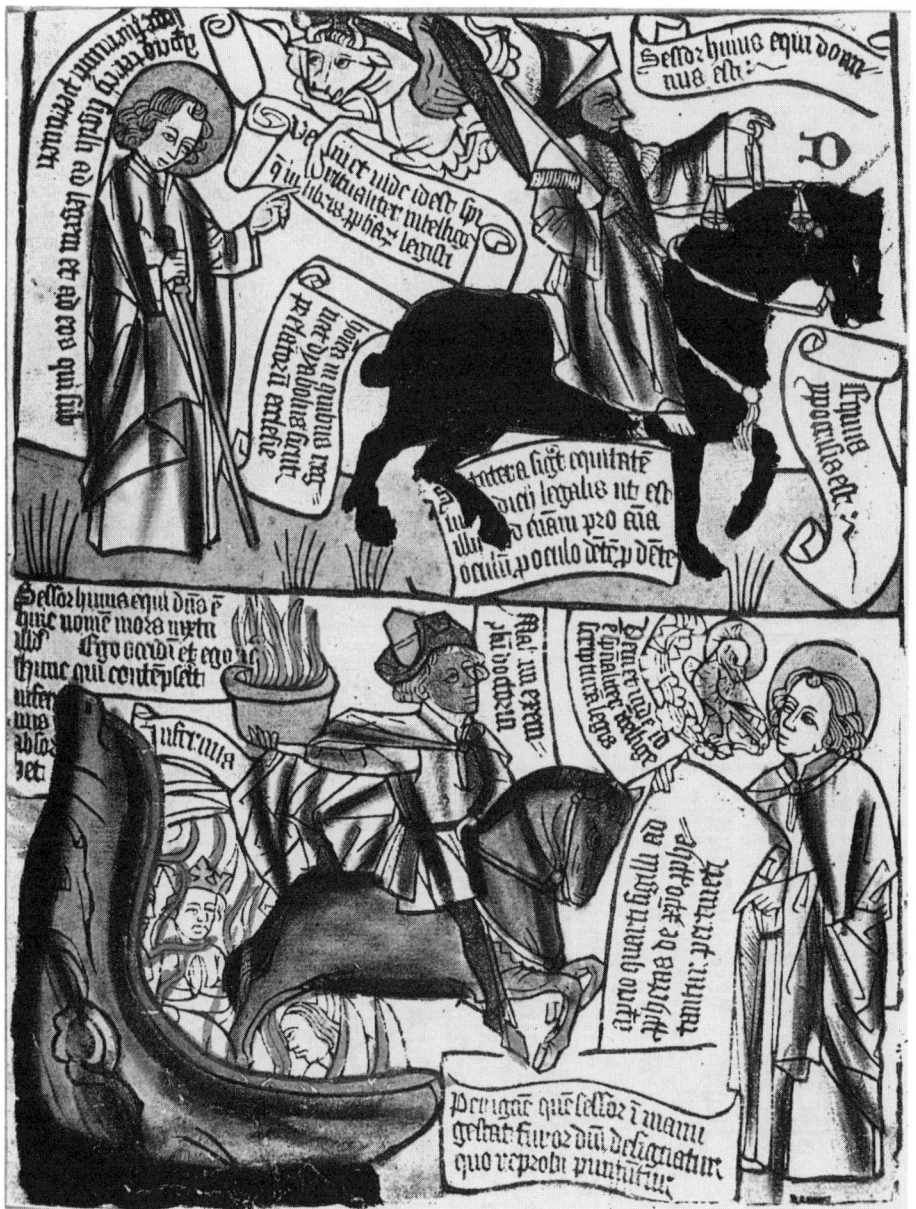

Figure 10.7. Two Horsemen, from an *Apocalypse,* c.1470, Modena, Biblioteca Estense, AD.5.22, as reproduced in *Apocalisse xilographica estense* (Parma, 1969). Courtesy of the Newberry Library, Chicago.

[319]

Figure 10.8. Bull from an *Ars memorandi*, c.1470, as reproduced in facsimile (Paris, 1883). Courtesy of the Newberry Library, Chicago.

past in the future of the Second Coming (see fig. 10.7). The *Ars moriendi*, like the *Apocalypse* concerned with final things, impresses on its readers the adage "memento mori." And many blockbooks even presented the *Ars memorandi*, the Art of Memory itself, rendered in textual and pictorial form (see fig. 10.8). The *Biblia pauperum* and many of the other blockbooks, then, functioned as aids to the spiritual memory.

It is probably not coincidental that the blockbook versions of the *Biblia pauperum* appeared around the same time that numerous treatises on the Art of Memory were also published, whether with woodcuts or movable type.[47] New technologies of communication are often used at first to amplify old patterns of thought.[48] Understood in this way, early print culture and especially blockbook culture initially reinforced the interaction of oral and literate strategies that characterized the later Middle Ages. Thus the blockbook, which, like the printing press, was an innovation in the production of writing, was also a final, complex elaboration of medieval conceptual strategies. But the use of the printing press would eventually undercut the need for memory arts and similitudes, as it irreversibly transformed the relationships between orality and literacy.

[47]Yates, *Art of Memory*, p. 105.
[48]See Ong, *Orality and Literacy*, pp. 135–36.

Notes on the Contributors

LILIAN ARMSTRONG is the Mildred Lane Kemper Professor of Art at Wellesley College. Her field of specialization is fourteenth- and fifteenth-century Italian painting and sculpture, with particular emphasis on Venetian painting and book decoration. Her books include *The Paintings and Drawings of Marco Zoppo* (New York, 1976), and *Renaissance Miniature Painters and Classical Imagery: The Master of the Putti and His Venetian Workshop* (London, 1981). She has also published numerous articles in the *Journal of the Warburg and Courtauld Institutes, Yale University Library Gazette,* and *Viator: Medieval and Renaissance Studies.*

CYNTHIA J. BROWN is Associate Professor of French and Italian at the University of California, Santa Barbara. Her publications include *The Shaping of History and Poetry in Late Medieval France: Propaganda and Artistic Expression in the Works of the Rhetoriquers* (Birmingham, 1985), and a critical edition of André de la Vigne's *Ressource de la Chrestienté* (Montreal, 1989). She is completing a monograph on the interactions between poets, patrons, and printers in late medieval France.

MICHAEL CAMILLE is Associate Professor of the History of Art at the University of Chicago. His work focuses on the functions of Romanesque and Gothic manuscript illumination and the relationship between medieval literature and the visual arts. His publications include the book *The Gothic Idol: Ideology and Image-Making in Medieval Art* (Cambridge, 1989), and "Seeing and Reading: Some Visual Implications of Medieval Literacy and Illiteracy," *Art History* 8 (1985), as well as other articles. He is completing a book on marginalia.

SHEILA EDMUNDS is Curator of the Wells College Art Collection in Aurora, New York. She has published numerous articles and reviews on various aspects of fifteenth-century Savoyard and Hebrew manuscripts, the engravings of the Master of the Playing Cards, and illustrated incunabula in *Art Bulletin,* the *Journal of Jewish Art, Romania,* and elsewhere. She is completing a monograph on the Augsburg printer, rubricator, and illuminator Johannes Bämler.

MICHAEL HEINLEN is Assistant Professor of Art at Lake Forest College in Lake Forest, Illinois. He wrote his dissertation on the ideology of reform in the French moralized Bible. He is a specialist in later medieval manuscript illumination and has written articles and catalogue entries for *Museum Studies,* the *Dictionary of Art* (forthcoming), and the exhibition in Leningrad of medieval art from American museums (1990).

LOTTE HELLINGA is Deputy Keeper in Collection Development and Deputy Director of Preservation at the British Library. Her interests in incunabula include the study of the transition from manuscript to print and the application of textual bibliography. Her publications include *The Fifteenth-Century Printing Types of the Low Countries* (Amsterdam, 1966); *Henry Bradshaw's Correspondence on Incunabula with J. W. Holthrop and M. F. A. G. Campbell* (Amsterdam, 1968–1978), both with her husband, Wytze Hellinga; and *Caxton in Focus: the Beginning of Printing in England* (London, 1982); as well as numerous articles. She is editor of the ISTC automated database of incunabula at the British Library, of the *Catalogue of Books Printed in the XVth Century Now in the British Museum,* vol. 11, and joint editor (with J. B. Trapp) of *History of the Book in Britain, 1400–1557* (Cambridge University Press, forthcoming).

SANDRA HINDMAN is Professor of Art History at Northwestern University. Her field of research is later medieval and Renaissance book illustration, including manuscripts and printed books. She is the author of *Text and Image in Fifteenth-Century Illustrated Dutch Bibles* (Leiden, 1977); *Christine de Pizan's 'Epistre Othéa': Painting and Politics at the Court of Charles VI* (Toronto, 1986); coauthor (with J. D. Farquhar) of *Pen to Press: Illustrated Manuscripts and Printed Books in the First Century of Printing* (Baltimore, 1977); and editor of *The Early*

Illustrated Book: Essays in Honor of Lessing J. Rosenwald (Washington, D.C., 1982); as well as various articles. She is completing a book on the illuminated manuscripts of Chrétien de Troyes.

EBERHARD KÖNIG is Professor of Art History at the Freie Universität, Berlin. He is author of a monograph on fifteenth-century French manuscripts entitled *Französische Buchmalerei um 1450: Der Jouvenel-Maler, Der Maler des Genfer Boccaccio und die Anfänge Jean Fouquets* (Berlin, 1982), and editor of a number of facsimiles of French liturgical and secular manuscripts. He has also published extensively on German incunabula, including an essay in *Johannes Gutenbergs 42-zeilige Bibel: Kommentarband zur Faksimile-Ausgabe,* ed. Wieland Schmidt and Friedrich-Adolf Schmidt-Künsemüller (Munich, 1979).

TOBIN NELLHAUS holds a doctorate from the Interdisciplinary Program in Theatre and Drama at Northwestern University and wrote his disseration on "Changing the Script: Orality and Literacy in the Performance Strategies of the York Cycle, Ben Jonson, and Richard Steele." He has published on literacy and Greek tragedy, as well as Jonson, in the *Journal of Dramatic Theory and Criticism.*

PAUL SAENGER is George A. Poole III Curator of Rare Books at the Newberry Library. His field of interest is the history of medieval reading. His publications include "Silent Reading: Its Impact on Late Medieval Script and Society," *Viator: Medieval and Renaissance Studies* 13 (1982); with R. Chartier, A. Boureau, M.-E. Ducreux, C. Jouhaud, and C. Velay-Vallantin, *The Culture of Print* (Paris, 1987; Princeton, 1990); and *A Catalogue of the pre-1500 Western Manuscript Books at the Newberry Library* (Chicago, 1989), as well as various articles.

MARTHA TEDESCHI is Associate Curator of Prints and Drawings at the Art Institute of Chicago. Her publications include *Great Drawings from the Art Institute* (Chicago, 1985), and contributions to the catalogue raisonné of James McNeill Whistler's lithographs (Chicago, 1990). She is also a doctoral candidate in the Department of Art History, Northwestern University, where she is writing a dissertation on Whistler and the English print market in the second half of the nineteenth century.

Index

Library of Congress Cataloging-in-Publiation Data

Printing the written word : the social history of books, circa
  1450–1520 / Sandra Hindman, editor.
    p.   m.
  Includes index.
  ISBN 0-8014-2578-6 (cloth : alkaline). — ISBN 0-8014-9902-X (paper : alkaline)
    1. Printing—History—Origin and antecedents.   2. Book industries and trade—
Social aspects.   3. Books and reading—Social aspects.   4. Printing—History—16th
century.   5. Books—History—1400–1600.   6 Incunabula—History.   I. Hindman,
Sandra, 1944–   .
  Z126.P73   1991
  002—dc20

                                                           91-55236